Gone With the Wind

as Book and Film

Gone With the Wind

as Book and Film

Compiled and edited by
Richard Harwell

Paragon House Publishers

New York

First paperback edition 1987.

Published by

Paragon House Publishers
2 Hammarskjöld Plaza
New York, NY 10017

Library of Congress Cataloging-in-Publication Data

Gone with the wind as book and film.

   Reprint. Originally published: Columbia, S.C.:
University of South Carolina Press, © 1983.
   Bibliography: p.
   Includes index.
   1. Mitchell, Margaret, 1900-1949. Gone with
the wind.   2. Gone with the wind (Motion picture)
3. Novelists, American—20th century—Biography.
I. Harwell, Richard Barksdale.
[PS3525.I9729G683   1987]   813'.52   86-30633
ISBN 0-913729-66-3 (pbk.)

To

J. B. B.,

An overdue book

Contents

Illustrations

Preface

"It is no exaggeration to say that if all the stories and articles on Margaret Mitchell and the book (factual, fantastic and false) were published," wrote Ralph McGill in 1962, "they would make a half a dozen or more volumes as thick as the novel itself." When that was written scholars had scarcely begun serious consideration of *Gone With the Wind*. A score of years later the book is the object of continuing popular enthusiasm and widening scholarly interest. The bibliography of books and articles about *Gone With the Wind* as book and film and about its author still grows and confirms for the 1980s what Mr. McGill wrote more than a score of years ago: "That the deluge of interest and curiosity in her and it has never halted is eloquent evidence of the book's healthy longevity."

Gone With the Wind as Book and Film is not an attempt to collect "all the stories and articles on Margaret Mitchell and the book." They would indeed fill several volumes. It is instead a sampler of the many kinds of things that have been written about the novelist and her book—avoiding, however, the fantastic and the false and giving its readers as full a quota as practicable of the factual.

The factual is not always limited strictly to the facts. It includes the responses of different people at different times and in different ways to the facts. The compiler of this anthology does not, therefore, vouch for every fact as given in the recollections and interpretations that fill this volume. That the various authors believed what they said is truth enough in matters of opinion. Articles "fantastic" or patently "false" have not been included. In a few cases, falsities have crept into pieces accurate in general. Where necessary, such deviations from fact have been corrected in editorial notes.

The first section of *Gone With the Wind as Book and Film* is primarily a record of the background of the class of novels into which *GWTW* strode as a giant in 1936 and of its publication and its reception into the book world. Its second section is about Margaret Mitchell and how her novel changed her life. Section III describes the social background against which *Gone With the Wind* made its appearance—the South as a historical and pyschological region in the 1930s—and some specialized aspects of the novel and novelist—theological, political, and psychiatric.

In its fourth section this collection details how *GWTW* moved from book to film and samples its reception as a cinematic production. It concludes with E. D. C. Campbell, Jr.'s fine summary article, "Gone With the Wind: The Old South as National Epic." The final section is critical in nature. Its seven scholarly essays range in date of composition from Robert Y. Drake, Jr.'s pioneering "Tara Twenty Years After" (1958) to Harold Schefski's 1980 essay comparing *GWTW* with *War and Peace.*

Malcoml Cowley stated the touchstone of *GWTW* criticism when he wrote in *The New Republic* for September 16, 1936, that the novel was an encyclopedia of the plantation legend, "false in part and silly in part and vicious in its general effect on Southern life today." Not all the critical essays in this anthology are favorable; Floyd Watkins' and James Boatwright's are particularly unfavorable. But all can be interestingly judged in relation to McGill's triad—"Factual, fantastic and false"—and to Cowley's—"false . . . , silly . . . , and vicious." The reader is, after all, the final critic.

* * * * *

The pieces in this volume have been chosen to represent as widely as possible the scope of writings about *Gone With the Wind.* They have been selected to give the reader as accurate and as interesting information as possible. Unfortunately it has not been possible to obtain permission to include one selection originally picked for *Gone With the Wind as Book and Film.* Other items, such as Philip Jenkinson's "Gone With the Wind" (*Radio Times*, 19 December 1981); Robert E. May's "Gone With the Wind as Southern History" (*Southern Quarterly*, fall 1978); and Jerome Stern's "Gone With the Wind: The South as America" (*Southern Humanities Review*, winter 1972) were especially enticing candidates for inclusion but had to be ruled out because they are too like other articles that appear here.

I am indebted to a great many others in bringing this book about. My gratitude goes first to each contributor. In addition I record my debt to my former colleagues at the University of Georgia Libraries: Robert M. Willingham, Larry Gulley, Tom Dietz, Mrs. Dorothy Shackelford, Marvin Sexton, Mrs. Faye Dean, Mrs. Geneva Rice, Mrs. Mary Ellen Brooks, and James A. Taylor, Jr. Others who have helped include Mrs. Margaret L. Branson, Herbert Ross Brown, Kay Brown, Beverly M. DuBose, Jr., Anne Edwards, David E. Estes, Tom Fletcher, Mrs. Marion B. Harwell, Mrs. Annie Pye Kurtz, Mrs. Patty Leard, Susan Lindsley, Jed Mattes, Mrs. Linda Matthews, Joseph R. Mitchell, Stephens Mitchell, Richard Mohr, Diane Windham, and Mrs. Ann E. Woodall. I thank them all.

Richard Harwell

Washington, Georgia

Sources and Credits

"Gone With Miss Ravenel's Courage; or Bugles Blow So Red: A Note on the Civil War Novel," by Richard B. Harwell; *The New England Quarterly*, XXXV (1962), 253–61. Reprinted by permission of *The New England Quarterly*.

"Non Sum Qualis Eram Bonae Sub Regno Cynarae," by Ernest Dowson; *Cynara: A Little Book of Verse by Ernest Dowson* (Portland, Me.: 1907), pp. 3–4.

Announcement of *Gone With the Wind*; The Macmillan Company, Inc., *Catalog for 1936* (New York: 1936), p. 4.

The Book of the Month: Reviews—Sam Tupper in *The Atlanta Journal*, June 28, 1936; Isabel Paterson in *The New York Herald-Tribune*, June 30, 1936; Stephen Vincent Benét in *The Saturday Review of Literature*, July 4, 1936; Julia Peterkin in *The Washington Post*, July 12, 1936.

"The Best Friend GWTW Ever Had," Herschel Brickell in *The New York Post*, June 30, August 27, and October 19, 1937.

"The Title 'Gone With the Wind,' " by William Lyon Phelps [syndicated column for October 13, 1936]. (New York: 1936), [1] p.

"Margaret Mitchell," *The Wilson Bulletin*, XI, no. 10 (September 1936), 12.

"When Margaret Mitchell Was a Girl Reporter," by Medora Field Perkerson; *The Atlanta Journal Magazine*, January 7, 1945, pp. 5–7.

"The Private Life of Margaret Mitchell," by Edwin Granberry; *Collier's* XCIX, no. 11 (March 13, 1937), pp. 22, 24, 26. Reprinted by permission of Edwin Granberry.

"The Story Begins at a Luncheon Bridge in Atlanta," by Lois Dwight Cole; *The New York Times Book Review*, June 25, 1961, pp. 7, 22. © 1981 by The New York Times Company. Reprinted by permission.

"People on the Home Front: Margaret Mitchell," by Sgt. H.N. Oliphant; *Yank, The Army Weekly*, October 19, 1945.

"Little Woman, Big Book: The Mysterious Margaret Mitchell," by Ralph McGill; *Show*, no. 10 (October 1962), 68–73. © 1962 by Hartford Publications. Reprinted by permission of Mrs. Bernard Smith.

"Mr. Mitchell Remembers Margaret," by Keith Runyon; *Louisville Courier-Journal*, December 17, 1972. Reprinted by permission of *The Courier Journal*.

"Are We Still Fighting the Civil War?" by Clifford Dowdey; *The Southern Literary Messenger*, n.s., I (1939), 12–15.

"Introduction" to *Kiss the Boys Good-bye*, by Clare Boothe; *Kiss the Boys Good-bye* (New York: Random House, 1939), pp. vii–xvii. © 1939 by Random House. Reprinted by permission of Mrs. Clare Boothe Luce.

"Reflections of Theology from *Gone With the Wind*,," by the Rev. Howard Tillman Kuist [Richmond, Va.: 1936], 15 p. Reprint from *The Union Seminary Review*, October 1939.

"Our Second Reconstruction," by Westbrook Pegler; *American Opinion*, XI, no. 4 (April 1963), pp. 21–28. © 1963 by *American Opinion*. Reprinted by permission of the General Birch Services Corporation.

"The Hysterical Personality and the Feminine Character: A Study of Scarlett O'Hara," by Charles E. Wells; *Comprehensive Psychiatry*, XVII (1976), 353–59. Reprinted by permission of Dr. Charles Wells.

"News from Selznick International Pictures," Selznick International Pictures, News release, July 23, 1936 (New York: 1936), [1] p.

"For the Defense," by David O. Selznick; New York *Daily News*, October 1, 1938.

"Studies in Scarlett," by Gavin Lambert; *The* [London] *Sunday Times Magazine*, December 30, 1973, pp. 14–17, 19, 21, 22, 25. Reprinted by permission of Gavin Lambert.

"How Hollywood Built Atlanta," by Wilbur G. Kurtz; *The Atlanta Journal Sunday Magazine*, December 3, 1939, pp. [1]–2.

"Three Years of Hullabaloo;" *Newsweek*, XIV, no. 26 (December 25, 1939), 26–29. © 1939 by Newsweek, Inc. All Rights Reserved. Reprinted by permission.

"Atlanta's Most Brilliant Event," by Harold Martin; *The Atlanta Georgian*, December 16, 1939. Reprinted by permission of Harold Martin.

David Selznick's Film Is World's Greatest; *Hollywood Spectator*, December 23, 1939.

"An Open Letter to Mr. Selznick," by Carlton Moss; *The Daily Worker*, New York, January 9, 1940.

Max Steiner Establishes Another Film Music Record . . . by David Bruno Ussher. [Los Angeles: Fox West Coast Theaters, 1940], [8] p. (Cinemusic and Its Meaning)

"Scarlett Materializes," by Nell Battle Lewis; *The Raleigh News and Observer*, February 18, 1940.

"*Gone With the Wind:* The Old South as National Epic," by E. D. C. Campbell, Jr. Revision of "Gone With the Wind: Film as Myth and Message" in *From the Old to the New: Essays on the Transitional South*, edited by Walter J. Fraser, Jr. and Winfred B. Moore, Jr. (Westport, Conn: Greenwood Press, 1981.) © 1981 by Greenwood Press. Reprinted by permission of the Greenwood Press.

"Tara Twenty Years After," by Robert Y. Drake, Jr.: *The Georgia Review*, XII (1958), 142–50. © 1958 by the University of Georgia. Reprinted by permission of the *The Georgia Review* and Robert Y. Drake, Jr.

"The Last of Its Genre," by Henry Steele Commager; introduction to Margaret Mitchell, *Gone With the Wind* (New York: The Limited Editions Club, 1968, I, [v–ix]. ® 1968 by the George Macy Companies, Inc. Reprinted by permission of Henry Steele Commager.

"*Gone With the Wind* as Vulgar Literature," by Floyd C. Watkins; *The Southern Literary Journal*, II (1970), 86–103. © 1970 by the Department of English, University of North Carolina. Reprinted by permission of *The Southern Literary Journal*.

"Totin' de Weery Load," by James Boatwright; *The New Republic*, CLXXIX, no. 9 (September 1, 1973), 29–32. Reprinted by permission of THE NEW REPUBLIC, © 1973 The New Republic, Inc.

"*Gone With the Wind* and *The Grapes of Wrath* as Hollywood Histories of the Depression," by Thomas H. Pauly; *Journal of Popular Film*, III (1974), 202–18. Reprinted by permission of the *Journal of Popular Film & Television*.

"Margaret Mitchell: *Gone With the Wind* and *War and Peace*," by Harold K. Schefski; *Southern Studies*, XIX (1980), [243]–260. Reprinted by permission of Harold K. Schefski.

"The Anti-Tom Novel and the Great Depression: Margaret Mitchell's *Gone With the Wind*," by Leslie A. Fiedler; *The Inadvertent Epic; from Uncle Tom's Cabin to Roots* (New York: Simon and Schuster) [© 1979], pp. 59–70.

Introduction

Book and film, *Gone With the Wind* has been running nearly half a century, piling up records and building its own history and legends. The book has sold more than 25 million copies—in 27 languages and in at least 185 editions. The film has been seen by more individuals than the total population of the United States and revenues from its sales for television showings in the United States, Japan and England approximate $45,000,000.

James A. Michener wrote of the novel as its fortieth anniversary approached that the essential fact about *Gone With the Wind* "is its extraordinary readability." Margaret Mitchell, he says, "is best considered, I think, a unique young woman who before the age of ten loved to tell stories and who at twenty-six began a long and powerful recollection of her home town. That it was destined to become a titanic tale of human passions, loved around the world, was a mystery then and remains one now."[1]

Three years later (in the year before the film reached its fortieth birthday) Rex Reed selected it as his choice for the all-time best motion picture. "Although there have been more artistic triumphs," he declared, "it is the film I've seen most and I have never been even slightly bored or disappointed. Forty years later it is still fresh minted."[2]

Gone With the Wind burst upon the world a bestseller by its publication date, June 30, 1936. Macmillan printed a first edition of 10,000 copies for release April 21. Publication was deferred to May 5 and then to May 31 when the publishers realized the book was a potential moneymaker of unusual extent. The author was asked to sign a large number of copies (she signed endpapers to be bound into 750 copies and then autographed an additional 500 books) for distribution as promotion copies amongst bookshops and to reviewers. When it was made the Book-of-the-Month Club selection for July, its release was set for June 30. Despite the author's public surprise at its reception, she and her publisher knew the day it was put on sale that they had a hit. No one guessed the extent of that hit.

---

1. James A. Michener, "Introduction" to Margaret Mitchell, *Gone With the Wind* (New York: 1975; anniversary edition), pp. x, xii.
2. "Academy Awards of All Time," *The Saturday Evening Post*, CCL, no. 5 (Jy/Aug 1978), 40.

Three weeks into July 176,000 copies had been sold. Sale of the screen rights was reported July 16 and announced July 23 and the contract with Selznick International Pictures was signed July 30. By mid-November there were 750,000 copies in print and in early December the publishers produced the millionth *Gone With the Wind.* It was eagerly gobbled up by a depression audience equally hungry for success and for entertainment. For along with its other merits, *GWTW* was a bargain; 1,037 pages for $3.00.

Critical reception of *Gone With the Wind* was almost as enthusiastic as the public's. Scoffers denigrated the success of such a plain, straightforward yarn. But sober judges of good books acclaimed it. Richmond's Ellen Glasgow, herself the author of a fine Civil War novel, *The Battle-Ground,* wrote: *"Gone With the Wind* is a fearless portrayal, romantic yet not sentimental, of a lost tradition and a way of life." Another author of a distinguished novel about the Confederacy, Charleston's DuBose Heyward, judged it "as fine a novel as has come out of our generation." In Chicago Sterling North called it "one of the great novels of our time." Paul Jordan Smith described *GWTW* for Los Angeles as "the most satisfactory, the most convincing, the most powerful presentation of that tragic period that has ever been put into fiction." And Henry Steele Commager, then an up-and-coming young historian at New York University, rhapsodized in the New York *Herald Tribune Books:* "The story told with such sincerity and passion, illuminated by such understanding, woven of the stuff of history and of disciplined imagination is endlessly interesting. It is a dramatic recreation of life itself."[3]

The years have seen Miss Mitchell's work discounted but never torn down, nor yet bettered. Scholarly papers have been undertaken to attack it—and completed to praise it. Amateur and professional historians have combed it for flaws of fact—and have found none of consequence. One honors paper at Amherst College went to great length to explain how Scarlett could not have known to leave Atlanta when she did because she could not have heard by then of the Confederate defeat at Jonesboro. Miss Mitchell proudly produced the record of a Confederate telegrapher showing at what time the news reached Atlanta. So with item after item.

There is surprisingly little of textbook history in *Gone With the Wind.* The reader fills in the background of military history from the author's deft references to the facts of the Civil War. But an illusion of exact and detailed history is produced by her exact and detailed descriptions of day-to-day life in the period of the Civil War and Reconstruction. As Michener declares: "The abiding merit of this novel is not that it has given us the portrait of a headstrong young woman, but that it has depicted with remarkable felicity the spiritual history of a region."[4]

---

3. These reviews are quoted in The Macmillan Company, *Margaret Mitchell and Her Novel* Gone With the Wind (New York: 1936), pp. 9, 10, 22.

4. Michener, p. xi.

Concerning her use of history, Miss Mitchell told Lamar Q. Ball of the Atlanta *Constitution* in a long interview in 1936:

> After I had sold the book, I knew I would have hundreds of well-informed persons ready to leap at any inaccuracy. As a matter of fact, I had done no actual studying for the writing of the book. Of course, in years past, I had read a lot of history and, of course, I had listened to lots of stories told me by the old folks who had lived through this period. But, when I was reading history or listening to stories, I never thought I would use them in a book. When I sat down to write the book, I wrote out memories of long ago. I never thought I'd sell the book, so I didn't see any reason why I should bother with looking up the incidents in history books. After I really had sold the book, I realized I'd have to check every detail and I did. It took about eight months and the job was awful.[5]

Attesting the qualities that Michener says mark it as "the spiritual history of a region" Mildred Seydell, a veteran Atlanta newspaperwoman even in 1936, wrote of the younger woman's book the week it was published: "I don't know whether *Gone With the Wind* is a true picture of the South of those days. But I do know that it is a true picture of the picture of those days that I had gotten when a child from listening to ageing, graying relations and friends of their youth."[6] If it does not fit the history of the Civil War as revisionists since her time have seen it, Margaret Mitchell's view does fit the view that was the Southern view for many years and itself has a validity as history. To put it another way, it is that great desideratum of the United Daughters of the Confederacy, an unbiased history of the war from the Southern point of view.

It is a commonplace in the history of *Gone With the Wind* that Miss Mitchell wrote her last chapter first and then wrote portions of her narrative leading up to that climactic chapter in no particular order. In Ball's interview with her, she discussed her methods of writing at considerable length. She told him how difficult writing the story of Scarlett's flight from Atlanta to Tara had been:

> This part of the story worried me. I struggled with it in my mind. I prowled around it mentally for a long time, looking at it from all angles and not getting anywhere. I could never write a line of it and never made a try at it, on paper.
>
> I didn't seem able to capture the smell of the cedars; the smell of the swamp; the barnyard odors, and pack them into those chapters. I was in the Ritz Hotel at Atlantic City when it all came to me. I can't explain why. The Ritz is nothing like Tara.
>
> I can only tell you this. I was not even thinking about the story when all this came to me very simply and very clearly. It was a cold, wet winter when we were at Atlantic City and yet I could see clearly how dusty and stifling a red clay road in Georgia looks and feels in September, how the leaves on the trees are dry and there isn't any wind to move them, and how utterly still the deep country woods are. And there is the queerest smell in the swampy bottom lands at twilight. And I suddenly saw how very haunted such a section

---

5. Atlanta *Constitution*, November 9, 1936.
6. Atlanta *Georgian*, June 19, 1936.

would look the day after a big battle, after two armies had moved on. So I came home and wrote it. . . .

Writing is a hard job for me. I don't have that facility for just dashing along. . . . Those three chapters that I wrote as soon as I returned home from Atlantic City are about the only ones in the book that I did not rewrite at least twenty times. As they appear in the book, they are substantially as they were first written. . . .

Persons who have read the book have told me it must be marvelous to be able to sit down and dash off sentences that read so smoothly. I have a hard time convincing them that the sentences I consider the easiest to read in the book are the ones that I labored over and rewrote and rewrote before I was satisfied I had made my meaning clear.[7]

Margaret Mitchell has been repeatedly upbraided for *Gone With the Wind's* lack of a distinguished style. She told Herschel Brickell of the New York *Post* that she had "deliberately chosen to write as clearly and as simply and as unobtrusively as possible, and that she had also studiedly given the style as much of a colloquial flavor as she could."[8] In talking to Ball, she expanded on this point:

I tried to make my story more or less colloquial and easy to read. I determined when I first sat down to the writing of this book that I would try to write as a native north Georgian speaks. I would rewrite sentences that sounded a trifle purist and try to get down to earth by rewriting and rewriting until I felt I had captured the conversation of the north Georgian in my descriptive paragraphs.[9]

Gone With the Wind was apprenticed in Margaret Mitchell's years on the Atlanta *Journal's Sunday Magazine.* It was begun in 1926 and virtually completed in 1929. She did a little work on it in 1930 and in 1931. It was then laid aside till Macmillan's H.S. Latham came to Atlanta on a manuscript hunt in the spring of 1935. She hastily recast the beginning of the book and wrote a new first chapter before letting Latham have the manuscript. After Macmillan accepted it very nearly the rest of her life was in one way or another spent working on *GWTW.*

She wrote an old acquaintance in the late summer of 1936:

I started "Gone With the Wind" when I had a broken ankle and couldn't walk. I finished it several years ago and never even tried to sell it. Therefore you can imagine my complete consternation when an editor came along, dug it up, published it and made a bestseller of it.[10]

It was not the publisher who made a bestseller of *Gone With the Wind.* It was the story and the characters and the hard work that Margaret Mitchell put

7. Atlanta *Constitution,* November 9, 1936.

8. New York *Post,* August 27, 1936.

9. Atlanta *Constitution,* November 9, 1936.

10. Margaret Mitchell to Morris H. Williams, Atlanta, Ga., 3 September 1936; quoted in Richard Barksdale Harwell, " 'A Striking Resemblance to a Masterpiece'—Gone With the Wind in 1936," *Atlanta Historical Journal,* XXV, no. 2 (summer 1981), 25.

into writing it. It became a part of the America of the 1930's, and—book and film—*GWTW* continues to be a very large slice of Americana.

The sale of *GWTW's* screen rights in July 1936 should have solved some problems for its author. Instead it created new ones. Miss Mitchell was adamant in her decision to have as little to do with the making of the film as possible. She was, however, inevitably drawn into the hullabaloo that surrounded Selznick's public search for a "new girl" to play Scarlett and was called upon by the producer's staff for advice on more than one occasion.

The book spawned legends. *GWTW* the film had even less chance to escape the kinds of stories—gossip, myth, whatever—that are part of the ambience of Hollywood. The most persistent myth about the filming of *Gone With the Wind* is that Vivien Leigh walked into the part of Scarlett O'Hara when she accompanied Myron Selznick, the agent brother of producer David O. Selznick, to the studio lot where the burning of Atlanta was being filmed December 10, 1938. Legend has it that Myron introduced her to D. O. S. saying: "Here is your Scarlett."[11]

The truth is that Miss Leigh had coveted the role for more than a year. She had been Selznick's ace-in-the-hole during much of the long talent search, and her arrival in Hollywood had been carefully timed. David Selznick, it is true, had not previously met her, possibly so she would qualify as new when he did eventually meet her. But they had been in touch through intermediaries and Selznick had kept for months in his private screening room a print of her performance in *A Yank at Oxford*.

Atlantan Wilbur G. Kurtz was on the lot for the fire scene. He was a friend of Margaret Mitchell who had been hired by Selznick as historian for the film. In his diary he wrote of the "charming young lady" who appeared just before the filming of the fire sequences began. "I watched her a while," he recorded, "suspecting she might be a personage. After the shooting ceased, I accosted Marcella [Marcella Rabwin, Selznick's principal secretary] with the question as to who she might be. Marcella whispered—'Vivien Leigh. Mr. Selznick is seriously considering her. I think she is the most ravishing thing I ever saw and she fulfills my idea of what Scarlett looked like!' Later, when Selznick walked off the set, going toward his car, he had Miss Leigh by the arm."[12]

Leigh was still no cinch for the part. The producer wrote his wife December

---

11. This persistent legend is based on Howard Dietz's paragraph in the souvenir program prepared for the initial run of *Gone With the Wind*. Dietz wrote: "The burning of the military supplies of Atlanta, one of the major spectacular scenes in the picture, was filmed on the night of December 15 [i.e., 10], 1938, at which time David O. Selznick met Vivien Leigh, a spectator, who had accompanied his brother Myron, the well-known talent representative, to the studio. Struck by her physical resemblance to the Scarlett described by Miss Mitchell, in that she has the green eyes, narrow waist and pert features, he suggested a test. It was made and on January 16 [i.e., 13], 1939, he signed her for the role." Howard Dietz, ed., *Gone With the Wind* [souvenir program] ([New York: 1939]), p. 8.

12. Wilbur G. Kurtz, "Technical Adviser: The Making of 'Gone With the Wind,' the Hollywood Journals of Wilbur G. Kurtz," edited by Richard Barksdale Harwell, *Atlanta Historical Journal*, XXII, no. 2 (summer 1978), 99.

12: "She's the Scarlett dark horse, and looks damn good. (Not for anybody's ears but your own: it's narrowed down to Paulette, Jean Arthur, Joan Bennett, and Vivien Leigh . . .)."[13] By Christmas the finalists were Paulette Goddard and Leigh. By the first week of January, studio gossip had shifted from Goddard as the favorite and had Leigh in the part. She signed her contract on January 13, 1939.

Shooting on *Gone With the Wind* began January 26. It continued with the full company to the end of June and was not actually completed till November 11. By then 449,512 feet of film had been shot. From this, 160,000 feet were printed. Editing reduced the film used in the picture to 20,300 feet.

Shortly after Selznick purchased the film rights for $50,000, a record price for a first novel, he engaged Sidney Howard to write *GWTW's* screenplay. Howard wrote a fine screenplay, but its presumed running time far exceeded the two hours then regarded as the maximum for a film. (As shown *GWTW* runs three hours and forty minutes. Publicist Howard Dietz estimated that to film the whole book would produce a picture taking a week to show with the projector running twenty-four hours a day.)

To help convert Howard's screenplay into a shooting script Selznick called in O. H. P. Garrett. It was with a Howard-Garrett script that production began. Selznick had to get the picture under way, but he was far from satisfied with the shot-by-shot script. As late as March 12 Susan Myrick, another close friend of Margaret Mitchell who was working on the film, wrote her: "We have 60 pages marked 'completed script,' but every few days we get some pink pages marked 'substitute script' and we tear out some yellow pages and set in the new pink ones. We expect blue or orange pages any day now."[14]

Blue pages were not long in coming and the shooting script became a rainbow script. Seventeen writers and tinkerers worked on it before the film was done: John Balderston, F. Scott Fitzgerald, Michael Foster, Garrett, Ben Hecht, Howard, Barbara Keon, Kurtz, Val Lewton, Charles MacArthur, John Lee Mahin, Edwin Justus Mayer, Winston Miller, Selznick, Donald Ogden Stewart, Jo Swerling, and John Van Druten.

It is impossible to identify in the screenplay the work of each writer. Selznick credited a few scenes to Hecht, a little of the work to Garrett, and a little to Van Druten. Fitzgerald wrote a scene or so that never made it to the screen and condensed and tightened several that did. Foster was largely responsible for the scenes at Tara in 1864 and 1865. Howard deserves credit for about 85 percent of the screenplay, but no one should forget that Selznick's mark is on every frame of the picture. The film is as indelibly his creation as the novel is Margaret Mitchell's. Since its premier at Atlanta's Loew's Grand Theatre December 15, 1939, it has belonged to the world.

---

13. David O. Selznick, *Memo from David O. Selznick,* selected and edited by Rudy Behlmer (New York: 1972), p. 180.

14. Sidney Howard, *GWTW: The Screenplay,* edited by Richard Harwell ([New York: 1980]), p. 30.

Would Margaret Mitchell have written another novel? As long as the pace into which book and film thrust her life lasted she had no time for writing, but I am convinced that ink was in her blood and that she would eventually have produced another book except for her untimely death August 16, 1949.

I knew her from before the publication of *Gone With the Wind* and had the pleasure of a long dinner conversation with her only a little while before her death. She talked of a possible book about Thomas Holley Chivers, an eccentric Georgia poet of the mid-nineteenth century who was, successively, friend and rival of Edgar Allan Poe; or one about the Confederate medical service during General Johnston's attempts to defeat Sherman in the Dalton area of north Georgia before he reached Atlanta; or a play about her own experiences as the author of a planetary bestseller; or a novel of Atlanta in the 1920's. She was full of ideas. Perhaps she would never have time to make any of them into books, but time was at last beginning to open for her.

She had made notes for work on a book about the Confederates who migrated to Brazil after the Civil War but had put them aside. Before *Gone With the Wind* was published she had begun and then destroyed a novel about Atlanta in the Jazz Age. And she had written a novella, "'Ropa Carmagin," which had been inadvertently sent to Macmillan along with the manuscript of *GWTW*. Macmillan's editors found it awkwardly brief, and they did not want to contract for two books from the same unknown author at one time. By the time they and other publishers were clamoring for it, it was too late. Its author declined to permit its publication and it too was eventually destroyed.

My best guess is that her fertile mind would sooner or later have settled on one of her ideas and produced another book. And this much can be certain: She had no intention of publishing any new book until she was satisfied that it was as well done as *Gone With the Wind*. Neither had she any intention of writing a sequel to *GWTW*. For her the story ended when Rhett left Scarlett. For what happened after that she, like Rhett, did not give a damn.

One

Gone With Miss Ravenel's Courage: or Bugles Blow So Red; A Note on the Civil War Novel

By Richard Harwell

Edwin Granberry began his rave review of Gone With the Wind *in the New York* Sun *June 30, 1936, with a caveat on Civil War novels. "It is perverse and strange," he wrote, "that the richest material America has to offer her novelists should also be the most treacherous. Sooner or later, every novelist below the Mason-Dixon line, and a deal of those above it, are beckoned to that fatal whirlpool where the sirens sound their perpetual song of moonlight and honeysuckle, cabins and crooning slaves, and the beautiful, beautiful Old South in her agonies of the Civil War. Despite the mawkishness which has come to be associated with all of this, the fact remains that no time or scene in history has offered the novelist a more magnificent gathering of forces. Yet even the best of our writers run afoul of the purple cataracts which lead to the cotton fields and the colonels beyond."*

This (and a good bit more) was preface to saying that at last "a profoundly stirring and what looks now like a great novel has appeared from the South— 'Gone With the Wind.' . . . The history of criticism is strewn with the wrecks of commentators who have spoken out too largely, but we are ready to stand or fall by the assertion that this novel has the strongest claim of any novel on the American scene to be bracketed with the work of the great from abroad— Tolstoy, Hardy, Dickens, and the modern Undset."

As a tyro reviewer in 1936 I was not quite so sweeping in The Emory Alumnus *in my claims for* GWTW *as Granberry, but I pulled out all the stops I dared for a book I thought "a true expression of the most dramatic era of Southern history." As the novel approaches the fiftieth anniversary of its publication I wish I had been as assertive of my enthusiasm as Granberry. The essay reprinted here is one I wrote as an "essay-review" for* The New England Quarterly *the year after* Gone With the Wind *had passed its twenty-fifth anniversary. The tyro is now the gaffer, happy to speak out largely and ready to stand with Granberry in asserting that* Gone With the Wind *fully deserves a place among the great novels.*

For a quarter of a century we have watched the building of a literary bombast that we now characterize as Civil War literature. In less years than the ante-bellum South took to move from the Nullification Controversy of the 1830's to secession and Civil War, we have moved from *Gone With the Wind* to a full-scale refighting of the war of 1861–1865 in books. In 1962 we can say hopefully that in our current cold war a shooting war is not inevitable, but the Civil War Centennial is already upon us, and readers are on its front lines—in the line of fire of both authors and publishers.

The accelerating interest of the last quarter of a century is warning enough of the popularity that will come to Civil War books in the next few years. As a rhymester noted earlier this year:

> We face a Pickett's Charge of books
> Which limn the grim tableau—
> And the Civil War Centennial
> Still has three years to go.[1]

The total of Civil War books to date is variously estimated at from thirty thousand to fifty thousand titles, the variance being relative to differing definitions of what constitutes a Civil War item. From a flood of books during the war itself and new waves of volumes about it as veterans poured out their reminiscences and historians assessed and reassessed it, the flow of titles about the war reached a low about thirty years ago. Then something in our national psychology during the Depression released a new wave of interest. Such novels as *Gone With the Wind, Bugles Blow No More,* and *So Red the Rose,* and such biographies as Douglas S. Freeman's *R. E. Lee,* Lloyd Lewis's *Sherman, Fighting Prophet,* and John Thomason's *J. E. B. Stuart* gave new stature to Civil War writing. Since the mid-thirties there has been no slackening in interest in the war.

Why this interest? Perhaps because the story of the Civil War is the common heritage of all Americans—the defeated Rebel and, sometimes, still defiant Southerner, the Yankee yeoman of New England, the Midwesterner whose region has known ony one war on American soil, and Americans of later immigration now established in a new world and seeking American roots. More, our Civil War is a convenient war for reading. It had a beginning and an end. Though its causes reached back to the beginnings of our national existence and its effects are still with us, 1861–1865 is a tangible period. Its people, simply because they wore clothes which do not necessarily look like costumes, seem

---

1. "Civil War Battle Cry," by Barbara Toohey, *Wilson Library Bulletin,* XXXVI, 374 (1961–1962).

real in 1962. It was a one-language war in its actions and in its records. Compared to later wars, it was a small war. It was a well-reported war. Most of all, it was a gallant, heroic, exciting war.

The literary shadow that represents the Civil War even more closely than history to many of its legion of devotees is the recreation of the war in fiction. Novels are strong meat with which to introduce new readers to an historical era, and a delightful leaven to the heavier reading of even the most confirmed armedchair tacticians and strategists. And—along with the constant stream of memoirs, personal narratives, battle accounts, and general histories of the last century—there has been a steady stream of Civil War novels, a few fine ones and a multitude of bad or trivial ones. The total to date reaches a figure somewhere between fifteen hundred and two thousand.

The beginning was long ago, long before the war itself. The first Civil War novel was published in Boston in 1808. It was *Memoir of the Northern Kingdom,* by William Jenks, a minister in Bath, Maine, and an Overseer of Bowdoin College, and told of a nation divided between North and South. In this early prophecy, however, the secessionists were Northerners who moved to the Old Northwest Territory and established a Republic of Illinois.

A more pretentious and more accurate prophetic novel came nearly thirty years later when Judge Beverley Tucker of Virginia published in Washington in 1836 his *The Partisan Leader. The Partisan Leader* foretells with uncanny accuracy the secession of the Southern states and war in Virginia. Its prophecies extend to such relatively minor points as the effects of a salt shortage and, coincidentally, to the author's quoting to end his book, just as John Wilkes Booth quoted to end—in a sense—the war, Virginia's motto *"Sic semper tyrannis."* Two other prophetic novels were published in the late 1850's: John Beauchamp Jones's *Wild Western Scenes* and Edmund Ruffin's *Anticipations of the Future.* If the war began with material considerations against the South, the Confederacy was nevertheless in fiction, where it did not count, well ahead, for in these books it was the Southern Confederacy that won. Such was not to happen again in fact or fiction until 1952 brought Ward Moore's *Bring the Jubilee,* a mélange of history and science-fiction that tells the story of the Southern Confederacy and its poor neighbor to the north after the South had won the battle of Gettysburg.

The war itself is better represented in contemporaneous poetry than in fiction. Topical poetry thrived on events that were too big and too close in time for the novelist to handle effectively. But in the North, war pieces formed a considerable part of Beadle's dime-novel series, and these meretricious paperbacks found their Southern counterparts in fragile publications that were bought by Confederate soldiers, read to pieces, and thereby made forever rare. Two Southern women seized upon the exploits of the glamorous Kentucky partisan, General John Hunt Morgan, as a basis for novels. Mrs. Jane T. H. Cross with *Duncan Adair: or, Captured in Escaping* and Mrs. Sally Rochester Ford with *Raids and Romance of Morgan and His Men.* Mrs. Ford's was the first full-length novel based on actual events of the war and, though it does justice neither to its genre nor to its subject, deserves a line in American literary history. Most ambitious and most successful of the contemporaneous novels of the war was Augusta Jane Evans' *Macaria*. This fiction was the literary sensation of the Confederacy, much as the author's later *St. Elmo* (she was Augusta Evans Wilson by the time that was published in 1867) was a continuing triumph that has stayed in print more than ninety years and ranks as an all-time best-seller. *Macaria* was printed in two Confederate editions of ten thousand copies each that were sold out by its publishers. A New York publisher issued a pirated edition (and paid its royalties to Miss Evans in the poverty-ridden days of Reconstruction), and it was published in London as a typical Victorian three-decker. *Macaria* has the distinction of having had a leading Confederate general, G. T. Beauregard, take time from his military duties to read its chapter on the first battle of Manassas and advise on its accuracy. And both *Macaria* and *Raids and Romance of Morgan and His Men* have the distinction of having had their sale within Union army lines forbidden by an official army order.[2]

But John Esten Cooke, himself an ante-bellum novelist of distinction, a wartime member of J. E. B. Stuart's staff, a postwar chronicler in fiction of the exploits of the Army of Northern Virginia, and, always, an incurable romantic (he buried his silver spurs on the surrender ground at Appomattox), wrote truly for both sides when he commented in 1867: "Ah! those 'romances of the War!' The trifling species will come first, in which the Southern leaders will be made to talk an incredible gibberish, and figure in the most tremendous adventures. . . .But then will come the better order of things, when writers like Walter Scott will conscientiously collect the real facts, and make some new 'Waverley' or 'Legend of Montrose.' "[3]

Of the first Northern novels about the war, Henry Morford's *The Days of Shoddy* (1863), John Townsend Trowbridge's *Cudjo's Cave* (1864), and Epes Sargent's *Peculiar* (1864) retain some interest and value, but the best of the early Civil War novels is John W. DeForest's *Miss Ravenel's Conversion from*

---

2. A Federal Army order issued at Lexington, Kentucky, in 1864 cited particularly John Esten Cooke's *The Life of Stonewall Jackson* (Richmond, 1863: reprinted in New York in the same year) but was intended to apply to all books glorifying the Confederates. It reads in part:

The object of such books is not to afford the people correct information regarding the history of the rebellion and its leaders, but are put forth by the traitors themselves, and republished in the loyal states for the purpose of stirring up discontent: and sedition, and encouraging treasonable practices and treasonable conversation by representing the crime of treason in false and alluring colors, and should no more be tolerated than an emissary sent direct by the revolted States to advocate the justice of the rebellion publicly before the enemy. Any one found with copies of such books in his possession, offering or intending to offer them for sale, is either a traitor or one who loves money better than his country, and his right to the book is declared forfeited and the same is ordered to be seized and destroyed.

U. S. War Department, *The War of the Rebellion: A Compilation of the Official Records of the Union and Confederate Armies,* Ser. I, XXXIX, pt. 2 (Washington, 1892), 7.

3. John Esten Cooke, *Wearing of the Gray* (New York, 1867), 204–5.

Secession to Loyalty. Realistic in 1867 (before realism became fashionable) it did not receive in its own day the popularity it deserved. Fortunately it was never, however, completely forgot and is even now available in a superior paperback edition.

The first really great Civil War novel was not a production by one of the war's participants but by one of the first postwar generation. Stephen Crane was not born till after the end of the war, but his *The Red Badge of Courage* (1895) caught the brutal actuality of war and the feelings of an individual soldier as few novels ever have. Albion Tourgée followed DeForest in realistic treatment of it with *Toinette* in 1874 and *John Eax and Mamelon* in 1882. Harold Frederic's *The Copperhead*, Silas W. Mitchell's *In War Time*, George W. Cable's *Dr. Sevier* and his *Kincaid's Battery*, and Francis Baylor's *Beyond the Blue Ridge* are novels of distinction. Joel Chandler Harris' *On the Plantation*, T. C. DeLeon's *John Holden*, and Thomas Nelson Page's *Meh Lady* are of more than regional interest. And who among Southerners has not read John Fox's *The Little Shepherd of Kingdom Come*, great book or not?

The flow of bad novels more than kept pace with the flow of good ones. If the books are no longer worth reading, the titles of some are themselves amusing: Mrs. Sallie F. Chapin's *Fitz-Hugh St. Clair; or, It Is No Crime To Be Born a Gentleman* and J. V. Ryal's *Yankee Doodle Dixie* are two of my favorites. Does it surprise you that *The Grapes of Wrath* is a war novel by Mary H. Norris, published in 1901? The war appealed to amateur and to professional, to Northerner and to Southerner. Everybody got into the act. The roster of authors of Civil War novels includes some old friends from other areas of literature and not a few real surprises: Louisa May Alcott, Bess Streeter Aldrich, Horatio Alger, Jr., James Lane Allen, Henry Ward Beecher, James M. Cain, Irvin S. Cobb, Sheila Kaye-Smith, Upton Sinclair, Edward Stratemeyer, and Jules Verne.

The first years of the twentieth century brought distinguished novels in Winston Churchill's *The Crisis* and John Uri Lloyd's *Warwick of the Knobs*, Ellen Glasgow's *The Battle-Ground*, and Mary Noailles Murfree's *The Storm Center*. A few years later Mary Johnston wrote two fine books in *The Long Roll* and *Cease Firing*. Then, for some time, there was a hiatus in the writing of good Civil War novels.

A remarkable resurgence began in the 1920's. In the traditions of realism, research, and good writing is James Boyd's *Marching On*, published in 1927. The next year saw the first publication of a truly great book about the war which is also a great book in modern American literature. Not a novel, Stephen Vincent Benét's *John Brown's Body* is more than a novel. It is a poem breathing a kind of national nostalgia. It is the nearest thing America has to an epic. Free in concept and poetic in every line, it tells a story of the war that might well qualify as the story of the war. As no one else ever has, Benét caught the spirit of the war—the spirit of the North and the spirit of the South—and conveyed it to the printed page. *John Brown's Body* is a book to read and to savor and to turn to again and again.

Perhaps it was a national nostalgia—by then far enough removed for writers to look at the war with new eyes—that brought fresh popularity to Civil War novels in the 1930's. Certain it is that with the thirties came a new era. Mrs. Evelyn Scott's *The Wave* belongs with the books of those years. Published in 1929, it appeared too soon to rise to fame with some that followed during the next decade, but it is a remarkably good novel and set a new standard for fictional treatment of the war. Mrs. Scott gave the Civil War novel a depth that, with few exceptions, it had previously lacked in the hands of writers content merely to arrange and decorate the facts of history.

The thirties brought a pride of distinguished novels: in 1931 Joseph Hergesheimer's *The Limestone Tree* and T. S. Stribling's *The Forge*, in the next year DuBose Heyward's *Peter Ashley*, in 1933 Roark Bradford's *Kingdom Coming*, in 1934 MacKinlay Kantor's *Long Remember* and Stark Young's *So Red the Rose*. Then in 1936, Andrew Lytle's *The Long Night* and the big one—Margaret Mitchell's *Gone With the Wind*. 1937 brought Clifford Dowdey's *Bugles Blow No More*, Caroline Gordon's *None Shall Look Back*, and Edgar Lee Masters' *The Tide of Time*. Hervey Allen's *Action at Aquila*, William Faulkner's *The Unvanquished*, and Allen Tate's *The Fathers* all appeared in 1938, and Francis Griswold's *A Sea Island Lady* followed in the penultimate year of the decade.

My own favorites among these are *Action at Aquila, Bugles Blow No More, Gone With the Wind,* and *Peter Ashley*. These, like all truly successful Civil War novels, are good novels as well as good war stories. Their authors' feeling for their work is strong and so well grounded in their country's past that they convey the spirit of the war with no exhibition of learned knowledge but with a competent ease which allows the reader to participate with them and with their characters in an exciting and meaningful experience.

My choice of Civil War novels remains *Gone With the Wind.* Its continuing fame attests to its enduring appeal and scoffs at the critics who confused Miss Mitchell's mastery of straightforward storytelling with a lack of style. A quarter of a century after its publication it is still a great yarn and one of the most widely read books in the world. If there is a special secret that brought success to *Gone With the Wind,* no one has been able to discover it—or, if to discover it, no one has been able to duplicate it. It was the right novel at the right time—a novel of comeback from war published when America was searching for a boost out of a depression. Miss Mitchell wove the background of Civil War and Reconstruction into her story with infinite skill and imagination—and with amazing accuracy. Her characters seem to walk the streets of Atlanta. Their actions are as consistent and as unpredictable as the actions of your next-door neighbor. The rapscallion Rhett Butler becomes almost a real person. (And a generation later he is irrevocably combined in the public mind with Clark Gable.) The willful opportunism of Scarlett O'Hara becomes a part of American tradition. Ashley and Melanie Wilkes are symbols of a portion of America's past literally gone with the wind. Even *GWTW*'s minor characters (Belle Watling, Aunt Pittypat, Gerald O'Hara, Mammy, Prissy) take their places in American folklore, become the people everyone knew—back home and in another day.

Will these centennial years of the Civil War bring another such novel? I doubt it. Though there has been a remarkable acceleration in the total number of Civil War books and a concomitant increase in the number of novels, there is nothing since to compare with the remarkable spate of good Civil War novels of the thirties. Outstanding among the few Civil War books published during World War II is Joseph Pennell's *The History of Rome Hanks,* but, for me at least, it leaves much to be desired. Clifford Dowdey's *Where My Love Sleeps* and *The Proud Retreat* do not fulfill the promise of *Bugles Blow No More.* The Baroness Eleanor Pérenyi's *The Bright Sword,* Jack Schaefer's *Company of Cowards,* and Don Robertson's *The Three Days* rise above average but fall far short of achieving greatness. More nearly memorable are two short novels, Scott Hart's *Eight April Days* and Jere Wheelwright's *The Gray Captain.* Viña Delmar's *Beloved* is a remarkable fictional treatment of the life of Confederate Secretary of State Judah P. Benjamin. Miss Delmar "arranged and decorated" masterfully, and she produced a wonderful feeling of validity in portraying a man's consciousness of racial minority, but *Beloved* lacks the creativity which makes a novel endure.

Andersonville? It is a great hulking novel that overpowers more than it impresses. Long and lusty, it packs a terrific, pulverizing wallop. It bulldozed itself to popularity and to a Pulitzer Prize (which might as appropriately have gone to its publishers for their promotion of the book), but it is without discipline and, despite some great episodes, without total greatness. MacKinlay Kantor bowls his readers over. One admires him for his depth of knowledge, his diversity of style, and his ability with a narrative; but his steam-roller technique is too much. He could have spared some details, some vulgarity, and produced a better book. But, admitting my personal distaste for the book, *Andersonville* is the best of recent Civil War novels. It is full of life and pulsates with a feeling of war. It is head and shoulders above most recent fiction about the war.

A measure of credit beyond that due his book must go to Kantor for tackling the great epic fact of American history in the grand manner. Most of the real novelists (as opposed to fictionists) of our time have shied away from it. There is something of the Civil War as a heritage in all that William Faulkner writes, and one can suspect that he wages a sort of Civil War within himself from the manner in which his intellectuality and his integrity seem to oppose one another in his public statements; but his most direct use of the war in his fiction is in his Sartoris stories, and these—good though they are—are relatively minor Faulkner.

The most recent try at a Civil War novel by a major novelist is Robert Penn Warren's *Wilderness.* Warren has written fine poetry, one excellent novel, several good ones, and distinguished essays and other commentary about the South. His *Legacy of the Civil War* is one of the distinguished books of 1961 and a stunningly succinct, sensible, and perceptive statement of what the war means to modern Americans. But he has let himself down in *Wilderness.* The novel is an extended parable of what "men and in their error" endure in war. His "Adam" (in this case Adam Rosenzweig, a German immigrant who comes to

America to fight "Für die Freiheit!") does not become a figure of reality, and the author's intent of giving universality to his story fails to such an extent that instead of a reader's having the impression that it could happen anywhere, he is content to believe it could happen nowhere. The novel is too polemic, too intense, too eager. Perhaps we have gone full circle and are in these centennial years once again too close to the war to write enduringly of it. *Wilderness* cannot be dismissed as a completely bad novel. Warren writes too well and thinks too well for that to be possible, but it is not the "new 'Waverley' or 'Legend of Montrose' " of Cooke's prediction.

It is too early to assess accurately the Civil War novels of the past decade or even of the last generation, but these books already are serving a useful purpose. When Dr. Freeman published his *The South to Posterity* in 1939 he commented: "After the publication of Margaret Mitchell's *Gone With the Wind* and Clifford Dowdey's *Bugles Blow No More* . . . those of us who work in that field received many inquiries that could be summarized in five words: 'What shall I read next?' "[4] Novels have always been an invitation to further reading. Those novels, and others of the same type, provided the impetus which has produced a whole new generation of readers about the Civil War. Perhaps such novels have helped to lead the thousands of Civil War buffs across the country into serious study of history, to the great books of nonfiction such as Dr. Freeman's *R. E. Lee* and *Lee's Lieutenants,* to Mary Boykin Chesnut's marvelously revealing *A Diary from Dixie,* or to the absorbing military analyses of T. Harry Williams or of Colonel K. P. Williams. But whether or not an acquaintance with the novels has led to wider reading about the war, it has certainly led to a fuller understanding of it. A single novel sometimes conveys the truth of an era more fully than whole libraries of fact. No man can know all the details of life in a day gone by, but the spirit of that life he may know through fiction which uses the essential facts, the crucial details, to convey the past to the present.

4. Douglas Southall Freeman, *The South to Posterity* (New York, 1939), ix.

Non Sum Qualis Eram Bonae Sub Regno Cynarae

By Ernest Dowson

Margaret Mitchell wrote Arthur Krock of the New York Times *December 7, 1937, correcting a statement concerning the title of* Gone With the Wind:

> *I know it is a matter of no earth-shaking importance, but I do want to tell you that my Publishers, The Macmillan Company, did not bestow the title of "Gone With the Wind" on my book, as you said. Would to Heaven they had, for it would have saved them and me much tearing of hair. The truth of the matter is that, as I never expected to get the book published, I never gave any thought to a title for my manuscript. When The Macmillan Company bought it they very naturally, after the manner of publishers, demanded a title, and I was out on a limb. I suggested many which they did not care for, and they were right about my suggestions being no good. For a while I did think of calling it "Tomorrow Is Another Day," but two things deterred me. The first was that the word "tomorrow" had appeared in the titles of dozens of books published in the last few years. The second and most important reason was that I blocked out the title on cardboard and saw that it was too long. As we were preparing to go to press The Macmillan Company shook the limb on which they had me with increasing violence. In sheer desperation I thought of "Gone With the Wind." I had been reading Ernest Dowson's poem to Cynara in which that phrase occurs. There is, of course, no relation in thought and idea between my book and the poem. The phrase appears in the text on page 397. The Macmillan Company found it acceptable.*

It was far more than acceptable. It had the magic which Ernest Hemingway wrote that a good title must have—the magic of For Whom the Bell Tolls, Breakfast at Tiffany's, The Hard-Boiled Virgin, A Streetcar Named Desire, *or* Bury My Heart at Wounded Knee. *And* Gone With the Wind. *In replying to Miss Mitchell on December 9, Krock said: "Your selection of the title was probably as great a master-stoke as the book itself."**

---

*Editor's Note: This exchange of letters is preserved in the Margaret Mitchell Marsh Papers, University of Georgia Libraries.

Last night, ah, yesternight, betwixt her lips and mine
There fell thy shadow, Cynara! thy breath was shed
Upon my soul between the kisses and the wine;
And I was desolate and sick of an old passion,
Yea, I was desolate and bowed my head:
I have been faithful to thee, Cynara! in my fashion.

All night upon mine heart I felt her warm heart beat,
Night-long within mine arms in love and sleep she lay;
Surely the kisses of her bought red mouth were sweet;
But I was desolate and sick of an old passion,
When I awoke and found the dawn was gray:
I have been faithful to thee, Cynara! in my fashion.

I have forgot much, Cynara! gone with the wind,
Flung roses, roses riotously with the throng,
Dancing, to put thy pale, lost lilies out of mind;
But I was desolate and sick of an old passion,
Yea, all the time, because the dance was long:
I have been faithful to thee, Cynara! in my fashion.

I cried for madder music and for stronger wine,
But when the feast is finished and the lamps expire,
Then falls thy shadow, Cynara! the night is thine;
And I am desolate and sick of an old passion,
Yea hungry for the lips of my desire:
I have been faithful to thee, Cynara! in my fashion.

Announcement of
Gone With the Wind

In Macmillan's "Spring Announcement" preliminary list of New
Macmillan Books, 1936, *Margaret Mitchell's novel was listed fourth among "five
great novels." Its title was noted as* Come With the Wind, *and the copy sent the
author by her friend and editor Lois Dwight Cole was marked in manuscript:
"This will be corrected in final list." The publication date was given as April 21
and the price as* $2.50. *The four other novels of the "five great" were (in the order
listed) Charles Morgan's* Sparkenbroke, *Phyllis Bentley's* Freedom Farewell,
Winifred Holtby's Take What You Want, *and Agnes S. Turnbull's* The Rolling
Years.

The following item is page 4 of Macmillan's Catalog for 1936. *The publication date is still given as April 21, and the price as* $2.50. *Publication was
postponed till May 5 and then to May 31 to take advantage of an unusually
widespread distribution of review copies and postponed still another time—till
June 30—when* Gone With the Wind *was selected for July distribution by the
Book-of-the-Month Club. By publication date nearly a hundred thousand copies
were in print and the retail price had been raised to* $3.00, *with* $2.75 *as a
pre-publication and book club price.*

Gone With the Wind
By Margaret Mitchell

The stirring drama of the Civil War and Reconstruction is brought vividly to
life in this really magnificent novel.

Scarlett O'Hara, born of a gently bred mother from the feudal aristocracy of
the Georgia coast and an Irish peasant father, inherited charm from the one, and
from the other determination and drive.

As the belle of the county, spoiled, selfish, Scarlett arrives at young womanhood just in time to see the Civil War sweep away the life for which her
upbringing has prepared her. After the fall of Atlanta she returns to the planta-

tion and by stubborn shrewdness saves her home. But in the process she hardens. She has neared starvation and she vows never to be hungry again. In the turmoil of Reconstruction she battles her way to affluence.

Scarlett's friend, Melanie Wilkes, of finer fiber, meets the same hardships with equal courage and better grace. Scarlett uses any available weapon; Melanie refuses to break with her ideals. Side by side with Scarlett and Melanie are the two men who love them: Ashley Wilkes, for whom the world died when Appomattox 'fell;' and Rhett Butler, blockade runner and charming scoundrel.

The story epitomizes the whole drama of the South under the impact of the War and its aftermath. The ruggedness and strength of north Georgia's red hills are in the characters—bluff, blustering Gerald O'Hara; Ellen, his wife; Mammy, who both loved and chastened Ellen's daughters; the rollicking Tarleton twins; the quick-tempered and murderous Fontaines; stately John Wilkes, and a host of others, white and black, forming a rich picture of Southern life.

The author is descended from people who have loved and fought for Georgia since the Revolutionary War. She was born and raised in Atlanta and was for several years feature writer on the Atlanta *Journal*.

Cloth, 12mo. $2.50. To be published April 21.

The Book of the Month: Reviews

Reviewers gave Gone With the Wind *a reception that would be surpassed only by the welcome readers bestowed on it. Most newspaper reviews were ecstatic. Margaret Mitchell found herself a celebrity overnight. She "pranced" with delight at rave reviews and shied away from the fame that soon virtually imprisoned her.*

Authors and publishers place as much stock in the prominence and length of reviews as in their content. GWTW made the front pages of the New York Times Book Review *and the* Herald-Tribune Books. *In the first of these J. Donald Adams, in a review of 1350 words, wrote: " 'Gone With the Wind' seems to me the best Civil War novel that has yet been written." Historian Henry Steele Commager gave it two thousand words of praise in* Books, *saying: "It is dramatic, even melodramatic; it is romantic and occasionally sentimental; it brazenly employs all of the trappings of the old-fashioned Southern romance, but it rises triumphantly over this material and becomes, if not a work of art, a dramatic re-creation of life itself."*

There were dissenters. Isabel Paterson wrote quite favorably in the June 30 Herald-Tribune *but in* Books *for October 25 qualified her opinion: "The writing is redundant and devoid of distinction; Miss Mitchell is likely to make two words grow where even one would be superfluous." Novelist Evelyn Scott low-rated it in* The Nation *for July 4, and John Peale Bishop was less than enthusiastic in* The New Republic *of July 15. Writing to Stark Young on September 29, 1936 concerning unfavorable remarks by Malcolm Cowley in the September 16* New Republic *Miss Mitchell said:*

I suppose I must lack the exquisite sensitivity an author should have. Otherwise, I should be upset by such criticism. But the truth of the matter is that I would be upset and mortified if the Left Wingers liked the book. I'd have to do so much explaining to family and friends if the aesthetes and radicals of literature liked it. Why should they like it or like the type of mind behind the writing of it? Everything about the book and the mind are abhorrent to all they believe in. One and all they have savaged me and given me great pleasure. However, I wish some of them would actually read the book and review the book I wrote—not the book they imagine I've written or the book they think I should have written. From Mr. [Heywood] Broun, who calls it "sweetly Southern," to (I can't remember the reviewer's name [Evelyn Scott] who announced that I had missed all the sociologic-

al implications and mass movements, they have reviewed ideas in their own heads—not ideas I wrote.*

The reviews which follow are Samuel Tupper, Jr.'s in the Atlanta Journal *for June 28, 1936, Isabel Paterson's for the New York* Herald-Tribune *for June 30, Stephen Vincent Benét's in* The Saturday Review of Literature *for July 4, and Julia Peterkin's for the Washington* Post *for July 12.*

By Samuel Tupper, Jr.

Margaret Mitchell (Mrs. John Marsh) has enough friends in Atlanta to assure a large audience for any book of hers; but her first novel is so arresting that it demands appraisal on its merits alone. Her friends will forget everything but to admire and enjoy; they will forget even that she has won an enviable accolade in having this work selected by the Book of the Month Club for July. Miss Mitchell has told a story of Atlanta immeasurably above the usual story of local interest, a kind of southern "Vanity Fair" with lovely high-bred Melanie and unscrupulous, fascinating Scarlett instead of Amelia and Becky; and so wide is its scope, so acute its social discernment and so vigorous its characters, that it may well become a book for all time.

Here is the Civil War and Reconstruction seen from a new angle, that of the southern lady turned adventuress. Scarlett O'Hara, daughter of a robust Irish immigrant, could see in the future no occasion that would demand from her the terrific energy which was her birthright. Reared to be as lovely and ornamental as her mother, the satiny Ellen, she spent herself thoughtlessly, first on casual flirtations, then on an acquisitive passion for her neighbor, Ashley Wilkes. Her world was scarcely larger than her father's plantation.

But she had reckoned without the war. Widowed and with an unwanted child to support, she returned to her north Georgia plantation after a hideous experience in the shelling of Atlanta, to witness the destruction of her life's foundations. She saw her father's mind fail under the strain, she went hungry, she picked cotton with her own hands—and Federal troops burned it a second time.

With not only illusions but the very bread of life snatched away in a moment, Scarlett hardens. All her sturdy will to survive springs up, and she tells herself that if she can help it—by whatever means—she will never be hungry again. In this determination she is helped by Rhett Butler, a profiteer and outcast as brutally realistic as herself. Assisted by his cash and his half-cynical, half-admiring encouragement, she fights for financial security, only dimly

---

*Editor's Note: Margaret Mitchell, *Margaret Mitchell's Gone With the Wind Letters, 1936–1949,* edited by Richard Harwell (New York [and] London: [1976]), p. 66. Further quotations from Miss Mitchell's correspondence are from this publication unless otherwise noted.

aware of the high price she must pay in the esteem of her neighbors. The conquered South, with its inexorable rules had no place for a woman who had made a living by traffic with scallawags and carpetbaggers.

Miss Mitchell presents this milieu with remarkable understanding. By anecdote, by glowing scenes, by pleasantly ironic comments, she shows the Old South hating, loving, making interminable visits, dying, living again, scrambling back to power and integrity. She sees its beauty, its weakness, the doomed strength of its young manhood, its slaves who also are despots and as the war drums beat with a deeper note, neither the weak nor the strong escape her scrutiny. Scarlett, who struggles to live by bread alone; Ashley, who escapes the harsh dawn of reconstruction by escaping into the radiant past; Cathleen, who falls into cheapness; Mammy and Melanie and Dr. Meade, who doggedly hold to old loyalties—the reader knows them all. He sees them idling on their porches, talking politics, riding, flirting, dreaming of a future that will never come. Later he sees them transformed, boys grown men overnight, gentle women mad with destroying hate. But not all their heroism can save this life that has gone with the wind.

This is not poetry or philosophy or fine writing—it is life. Reflection is not absent, but is subordinated to the powerful story, which is startling in the casual skill with which interest is maintained through so many pages. Not many modern books leave the reader so breathless to know what is coming next. Even the minor characters are so sharply differentiated that Miss Mitchell can be bold and introduce a score at once, as she does many times without confusion. Scarlett, Melanie, Aunt Pitty, Ashley, and the Tarleton twins all stand clearly apart. Rhett Butler, adventurer and blockade runner, the most subtle and audacious characterization, is perhaps not always accounted for convincingly. But he is so bold and brilliant a figure that most readers will take the author's word for his actions.

It is not too much to say that "Gone With the Wind" is among the most powerful and original novels in American literature. With its scope, its high emotion, and shrewd picturization, it is a book to own and re-read and remember forever.

By Isabel Paterson

The demoralization of character during the ironically named Reconstruction period in the South after the Civil War is the real theme of Margaret Mitchell's long novel "Gone With the Wind" (Macmillan, $3). The main thread of the story follows the fortunes of one woman, Scarlett O'Hara; and it is something of an achievement to have made her so broadly representative of the worst aspects of her time and yet not abnormal or even unlikable. She is a satiric figure of civic virtue in the carpetbag regime. Her special quality was vitality, the will to survive. Integrity might have spelled material defeat. She couldn't afford scruples, so it was fortunate for her that she had none to begin with. But it was an evil omen for society that she should be the triumphant type. She is, unhappily, the inevitable answer to "reform" by force, however good the intention which dictates the forcible measures.

Scarlett got her training in the school of sheer femininity. She was only sixteen when the Civil War began. By no means a beauty, she had made herself a belle by external observation of the rules and grim determination under cover. In her limited sphere she was already a success. And yet she had failed in her heart's desire. She was in love with Ashley Wilkes. Furthermore, she knew that he loved her. But, for all that, he was going to marry Melanie Hamilton.

He tried to tell Scarlett his reasons. They were true as far as they went; he was obeying the aristocratic tradition of marrying, so to speak, for marriage, not for love. Melanie was his own kind, refined, sensitive, cultured, capable of exquisite fidelity not only to a husband but to an ideal. But Scarlett slapped him in the face with the other half of the truth that he ignored. There was an element of cowardice in his choice. He was afraid of the "passion for life" that Scarlett embodied. He didn't really want to live; he wanted to exist in a gentle dream drawn from the past.

And he might just as well have taken his chances, for while he and Scarlett were exchanging the bitter words of rejection the guns at Sumter shattered the past to irrevocable ruin.

Scarlett tried to save her pride by marrying Charles Hamilton, Melanie's brother, out of hand. Ashley married Melanie; and for a time the tide of war submerged their private and personal concerns. Scarlett hated the war, as sheer waste of the good years when she should have had gayety and love; but when she was called upon for physical courage and quick wits she was not wanting. She bore her first child resentfully. Charles was killed, and she felt no grief but an impatient weariness of widowhood. As a refugee from Atlanta, she saved the life of Melanie and Melanie's newborn child, Ashley's child, taking them out of the city, through the lines of fighting men and stragglers of war, to the O'Hara plantation. She found desolation; her mother was dead, her father doddering, the slaves freed, the cotton burned, the stock driven off. She almost hoped that Ashley was dead. But he wasn't. When the war ended Scarlett's struggles had just begun.

For some years she tried to bring the plantation back to productiveness. Without capital it was impossible. Ashley and Melanie were no help; they could only endure with a certain dignity.

To pay the taxes she offered to become the mistress of the man she hated most, Rhett Butler, who had made money out of the war and, incidentally, was very near to being hanged for it. Rhett was in love with Scarlett, and this was his revenge—to refuse her. She was driven back upon respectability and married another man, Frank Kennedy, because he at least had a small lumber business that was earning him a living. But he had no enterprise, and Scarlett masterfully took over the business. She was determined to have money—money—money.

She got it, at what it cost, in Atlanta's boom years of rebuilding. She dealt with the carpetbagger regime; she ground down her workmen; she hired convict labor. And when she was widowed again she married Rhett Butler.

They were two of a kind, but even Rhett's conscious cynicism did not make him a match for Scarlett's natural, self-justifying expediency. She broke him, not financially but morally, as she had broken every one who came in contact with her. And when it was too late she found she had spent her life in pursuit of a shadow—she, the materialist, in the midst of her material success. And by a final irony, she is shown beginning all over again, in the same spirit.

Miss Mitchell has inexhaustible invention, and her people are always credible, even in their melodramatic moments. A Southerner might judge best of the authenticity of background and details; but they carry conviction to the uninitiated, and if there are any errors they'll never be seen from a galloping horse, as our grandmothers used to say. The narrative pace is unflagging. And if depth and literary distinction are wanting—well, it is the lesson of Scarlett's career that one can't have everything. The style is commonplace.

One should add, also, that the secondary characters are consistent and significant; Melanie especially is admirable as a portrait of a lady, with the qualities of her defects. The curious twists of feminine loyalty imposed upon the wife of a weak man would afford sufficient subject for a review in itself.

By Stephen Vincent Benét

This is war, and the wreck and rebuilding that follows it, told entirely from the woman's angle. We have had other novels about the Civil War by women, including Mary Johnston's excellent ones and Evelyn Scott's remarkable "The Wave." But I don't know of any other in which the interest is so consistently centered, not upon the armies and the battles, the flags and the famous names, but upon that other world of women who heard the storm, waited it out, succumbed to it or rebuilt after it, according to their natures. It is in the diaries and the memoirs—in Letitia Macdonald and Mrs. Roger A. Pryor and a dozen more. But it has never been put so completely in fiction before. And it is that which gives "Gone With the Wind" its originality and its individual impact.

It is a long book and a copious one, crowded with character and incident, and bound together with one consistent thread, the strong greediness of Scarlett O'Hara who was bound to get her way, in spite of the hampering ideal of the Perfect Southern Gentlewoman and the ruin that follows men's wars. She didn't, quite, in the end, though she got a great many other things, including money and power—but the tale of her adventures and her struggles makes as readable, full-bodied, and consistent a historical novel as we have had in some time—a novel which, in certain passages, as in the flight from burning Atlanta, rises to genuine heights. Miss Mitchell knows her period, her people, and the red hill country of North Georgia—she knows the clothes and the codes and the little distinctions that make for authenticity. Tara is a working plantation, not a white-porched movie-set—and Atlanta is itself and an individual city, not a fabulous combination of all the first-family features of Richmond, Charleston, and New Orleans. The civilization of the antebellum South was something a little more than a picturesque gesture in gentility—and to a public a little surfeited with wistful reminiscence of the cape-jessamine side of it, Miss Mitchell's rather more realistic treatment should come as a decided relief.

For they are here, the duelists and the belles that we are accustomed to—but there is also Gerald O'Hara, the adventuring Irishman whose quick, restless vitality was able to build Tara into the pattern of a gentleman's plantation and whose charm, together with his finely-bred wife, got him accepted at last as one of the County. And there is his daughter Scarlett, who learned all the outward signs and symbols of the Perfect Gentlewoman, without ever, in the heart, subscribing to the code. We see her first in the raw blooming pride and ruthlessness of youth, with a most unladylike determination to marry the sensitive, appealing, rather dawdling Ashley Wilkes whether he happens to like it or not. We see her last, after three marriages, none of them to Ashley; bruised and hardened by life but still defiant, still with the strong, blind confidence of the dominant that tomorrow or the next day she will yet bend life completely to her will. It is a consistent portrait and a vivid one. And as consistent is the portrait of her opposite, Melanie Wilkes, who never had to think about being a lady because she was one, and who kept to the end the slight steel courage of the fine. The two women, their innate difference, and the curious bond between them are admirably characterized. And it is they, with Rhett Butler, the other nonconformist to the genteel code, who make the book—for Ashley, though ably sketched, is bound to be something of a walking gentleman and a romantic dream.

As background and accompaniment, there is the breakdown of a civilization and the first tentative steps at its rebuilding. Miss Mitchell, as I have said, attempts no battle-pieces, but the grind of the war is there, the patriotic fairs and the slow killing of friend and acquaintance, the false news and the true, the hope deferred and the end and the strangeness after the end. When Scarlett and Melanie, fleeing from Atlanta before the approach of Sherman's army, return to the O'Hara plantation, they return, quite literally, to a ruined world. That was the way it was, and Miss Mitchell's description of Scarlett's frenzied, tireless attempt to rebuild some semblance of life and vigor into Tara is one of the most fascinating sections of her novel. The young men were dead in the war, the land wasted, the field-hands gone. And a plantation, under those conditions, was about as easy a place to live in as a battleship in mid-ocean without its crew. But Scarlett bullied for it, slaved for it, and starved for it—and resolved, with bleak determination, that, come what might to the old code of gentility, she, Scarlett O'Hara, would never be hungry again.

How she made her determination good and what paths her determination led her through form the theme of the last sections of the book. I shall not spoil Miss Mitchell's plot by recounting it in detail, for it is a good one. But her picture of the early days of Reconstruction and the tainted society of scalawags and carpetbaggers through which Scarlett moved with Rhett Butler is quite as vivid as her picture of the war years. Throughout, she draws her distinctions with a sure hand. The extraordinary episode of the rescue of the ex-Confederates by the testimony of Belle Watling and her girls may not please Miss Mitchell's Atlanta audience but it has the convincing ring of folk-lore. And the post-war attitude of a dozen different types of human being, from Rhett Butler's to Ashley Wilkes's, is surely and deftly done—as is the amazing incident of Archie the ex-convict, who acted as chaperone and bodyguard to the ladies of Atlanta during Reconstruction days.

It is only one of a score of such incidents, for Miss Mitchell paints a broad canvas, and an exciting one. And, in spite of its length, the book moves swiftly and smoothly—a three-decker with all sails set. Miss Mitchell has lost neither her characters in her background nor her background in her characters, and her full-blooded story is in the best traditions of the historical novel. It is a good novel rather than a great one, by the impalpables that divide good work from great. And there is, to this reviewer, perhaps unjustly, the shadow of another green-eyed girl over Scarlett O'Hara—as Rhett Butler occasionally shows traces both of St. Elmo and Lord Steyne and Melanie's extreme nobility tends to drift into Ameliaishness here and there. Nevertheless, in "Gone With the Wind," Miss Mitchell has written a solid and vividly interesting story of war and reconstruction, realistic in detail and told from an original point of view—and, as the Book-of-the-Month selection for July, it should reach the wide audience it very genuinely deserves.

By Julia Peterkin

It seems to me that "Gone With the Wind," by Margaret Mitchell, is the best novel that has ever come out of the South. In fact, I believe it is unsurpassed in the whole of American writing. Perhaps this sounds like extravagant praise, as if I too were afflicted with that old and well-known Southern blindness which causes all those who suffer from it to declare that anything coming out of the South is necessarily better than what comes from any other section. But I am inclined to think that able critics who are not Southern at all will join me in urging all lovers of good books to read it.

Not only is it a stirring drama of individual lives and an authentic account of the fortunes of a community of Southern plantation owners during the Civil War and the dark days of reconstruction that followed, but it makes clear as no history ever did or could those racial and social prejudices that resulted in differences of opinion among Southerners which finally caused the destruction of the people who held so proudly to them. Those who lived in this region were solidly united in a firm belief in "States Rights" and in a determination to hold fast to the economic security which had resulted from the valuable crops of cotton produced by slave labor on the rich plantation lands. But then, the same as now, cultivated and civilized people were in a comparatively small minority; then, the same as now, the inferior, even those who were known to have lately sprung from the peasant class in Europe, professed to believe and proclaimed in loud voices, that any Southern-born soul, regardless of quality or attainments, was superior to every other citizen of the United States, merely because he was "Southern Born."

Miss Mitchell is clear-eyed and well informed. She knows the South and its history as well as she knows the red hills of northern Georgia. She also knows how many types of Southern people there are. She understands them all and she does not flinch as she reveals their shortcomings and vices, their illusions and pretentions. She does this simply and without harshness, showing no sign of sentimentality when she tells of the superior civilization of the older coast country, where living had really become a fine art. She gives a clear picture of the successful way in which this art was imitated by newcomers, who recognized its advantages and its charm, and were bent on enjoying them.

The people of the coast country had a deep conviction that no gentleman could be raised above tidewater. They always regarded the people who lived inland as crude, no matter how prosperous or how civilized they became. Most of the people in the north Georgia country, where the first scene of the book is laid, were crude in spite of their wealth. The requirements for social standing among them was abundance of money and land, of horses and slaves. Lack of education, ignorance of books, use of bad grammar, made no difference at all. If a man raised good cotton and could shoot straight, dance lightly, squire the ladies elegantly and carry his liquor well, his standing as a gentleman was secure.

It is not easy for Southerners of the present generation to accept all these facts as the stark simple truth. Nor is it easy for them to understand the scorn in which honest manual labor and laborers were held. This scorn forbade the building of cotton and woolen mills, machine shops and arsenals which might have made the result of the Civil War very different. These pleasure-loving people took pride in their lack of industries and held that all such low businesses were better suited for Yankees and white trash than for Southern gentlemen, who preferred to be statesmen and lawyers, planters and poets.

"Gone With the Wind," with its more than a thousand pages, even if it had no historical value, would be important merely as entertainment for there is not a dull page, not even a dull paragraph in it. The characters are drawn so vividly they stir our interest at once. When the book ends, they are like intimate friends whose hearts and minds we understand.

The chief character, a girl, Scarlett O'Hara, was the oldest daughter of a capable, cultivated mother of French descent who was born and reared in Savannah. Scarlett's father was a wild Irish peasant who had been forced to flee from the old country because he killed a man in cold blood for whistling the tune of a song whose words reflected upon Irish courage. From her mother, she inherited delicate features; she had the smallest waist, the tiniest feet, the whitest bosom in three counties and more beaux than any other girl in five. Her real nature, however, was willful, selfish and scheming, almost identical with that of her father, and it was only thinly concealed under the veneer of gentle manners which had been developed by the counsel and training of her mother and the sterner discipline of her old black nurse. At 16 she had no education and wanted none since lack of it was no cause for shame. But she was courageous. She knew what she wanted, and never did she hesitate to sacrifice anybody or anything to get it.

Scarlett's problems and the problems of those associated with her make exciting reading, but the experiences and the opinions of this whole group are a faithful record of the mistaken ideas and ideals that brought about the destruction of a prosperous land. This destruction was complete. Scarcely a vestige of what had been was left. As we read, we can see plainly why that old life of ease and plenty could never have been continued by those who survived the war even if the Confederate Army had been victorious.

When peace was declared, however, the defeated South was made to suffer such bitter humiliation and punishment that the Northern armies would have been far more merciful if they had killed every man, woman and child outright than to have left them to endure what they had to face after the last battle was fought. Poverty, physical suffering, sorrow of every kind [had] broken stout hearts during the war, but the years that followed it were worse.

Scavengers swarmed in. Scalawags, carpet-baggers, fortune hunters from the four corners of the earth crowded together as they preyed on the remnant of an exhausted people who had only a few years before been proud and able. Too proud alas, too arrogant, too confident. Their devout faith in Southern superiority had resulted not only in a wreckage of lives but in hurts too deep ever to heal. The South had wanted ease and prosperity. It achieved them and then through them it lost everything but bitter memories and defeated hopes.

"Gone With the Wind" is a great book! Every lover of good books should read it and so should everyone who has the least interest in the history of these United States.

The Best Friend GWTW Ever Had

By Herschel Brickell

Herschel Brickell was the best friend Gone With the Wind *ever had. Margaret Mitchell wrote him May 9, 1937, just after she learned her book had won a Pulitzer Prize: "You did a lot for me in this matter. You pulled for that book from the day it was published and I can't ever thank you enough."*

In 1936 Brickell was a veteran reviewer for the New York Post. *He wrote a long and enthusiastic review for the* Post *of GWTW's publication date. Miss Mitchell wrote him an effusive, but sincere, thank-you July 7. Later that month she met him at Blowing Rock, North Carolina, where she had gone (at the invitation of Edwin Granberry, who had reviewed GWTW just as enthusiastically for the New York* Sun) *to escape the fame that was threatening to imprison her in her Atlanta apartment. She and Brickell became good friends, the friendship soon becoming a firm and lasting one between Peggy and John Marsh and Norma and Herschel Brickell.*

Brickell followed his review with a long report on August 27 of a talk with Margaret Mitchell and devoted the major portion of his column to Gone With the Wind *October 19. She wrote him October 22: "The column was grand and as I told you before, if I don't win the Pulitzer prize it certainly won't be your fault. No one has ever done as much for me as you have and when I think how you started your kindness long before you knew me, I am doubly grateful." To this letter she added a long postscript October 26. In that she said: "Today there arrived the dummy of the pamphlet the MacM. Company is getting out about* GWTW [Margaret Mitchell and Her Novel *Gone With the Wind* (New York: 1936)]. *I was so happy to see that they had included your interview. I keep telling you it's the best thing that's been written about me—not only the kindest, Heaven knows, but the most accurate."*

[June 30, 1936]

I can recall a few books out of the thousands I have read since I began to write a daily column that left me feeling I'd much rather just go on thinking about them, savoring their truth and treasuring the emotional experience that reading them was, than to try to set down my impressions of them.

This is the case with a novel you will hear much about in the months that are coming, and which you will read, in all probability. I am speaking of Margaret Mitchell's magnificent story of the Civil War and the Reconstruction Period, "Gone With the Wind," which is the July choice, and a good one, of the Book-of-the-Month Club.

A first novel by a young Atlanta woman who has worked steadily on it for seven years, and just how steadily intelligent readers will at once appreciate, this striking piece of fiction, which is much too sound and too important not to pass into the permanent body of American literature, comes closer to telling the whole story of the most dramatic episode in our history, the War Between the States and the dark and bloody days that followed the breaking-up of a culture, than anything that has ever been written or printed.

I have no more hesitation in making these assertions than I have in saying that Miss Mitchell's book has its faults. If, for example, you pause to analyze the writing, you will find it, as writing, often undistinguished. I ought to add that you are quite unlikely to pause, so swift and so breathlessly interesting is the flow of the narrative.

The hypercritical may say, too, that at times the story borders on melodrama, and that its principal character, Captain Rhett Butler, is too much of a combination of Jack Dalton and Byron. To these charges, which will almost certainly be made, I should have to answer that the times about which Miss Mitchell writes were in themselves essentially melodramatic, just as much as the ante-bellum civilization of the South was essentially romantic. And as for Captain Butler, my reply would be that to a Southerner he is perfectly recognizable, perfectly credible, therefore not at all a manufactured character.

The remarkable thing is not that Miss Mitchell has failed, perhaps, to write a masterpiece but that she has succeeded with her first book in writing the best novel available on her chosen subject. The faults dwindle into nothingness when they are considered against the merits of the book, and the most profound merit of all is the simple and elemental truthfulness of the picture.

This accuracy, of which I feel wholly competent to judge, since I grew up in the midst of the Civil War and Reconstruction, the greater part of my knowledge of it coming directly from a grandmother and great-grandmother, so that I got the woman's point of view from which Miss Mitchell has written, is a matter of both detail and of the whole.

It is quite possible for a novelist to be right in his details and wrong in the totality of his impression, but Miss Mitchell, whose keenly realistic, very feminine and completely honest intelligence is always in evidence, has succeeded in both places. There are hundreds of observations in the novel that are so penetratingly true as to bring the reader to a halt with an exclamation of surprise—this was my own experience—and still the author's sense of balance and proportion keeps everything in its proper place.

If I tried to single out one overwhelming point of merit in "Gone With the Wind"—the title, of course, refers to the pre-Civil War South and its civilization and is painfully apt—it would be the way this young novelist has given life to her characters. These are people, not dummies moving through a historical setting like puppets, people you come to know inside out, from Scarlett O'Hara, the center of the story, down to the most minor and momentary figure.

If I have not known every one at first or second hand, certainly most of them are as familiar to me as the people I am with every day in my present life. Their prototypes were in my own family, or they lived next door, and if you are willing to accept them as both skillfully created individuals and as human symbols of a certain period in history, you will gain from Miss Mitchell's book a clearer idea of the South and Southerners than from all the histories that have ever been written.

"Gone With the Wind" has a deftly handled double theme, the life of Scarlett O'Hara, daughter of Gerald O'Hara, an Irishman who had to flee his native land because of a murder, and a Savannah aristocrat, and the life of Atlanta as a city.

Miss Mitchell does not labor the relationship, nor does it matter materially, except that it is so well done. Scarlett did not belong to the gentle tradition of the Old South any more than the young Georgia metropolis, which first became a city during the Civil War and was regarded as an upstart by Charleston, Savannah, Montgomery and the other older towns.

The fortunes of the girl and the city were linked; Scarlett, for all the love she bore Tara, the O'Hara plantation, liked the newness and the brashness and the young vigor of Atlanta because it answered some need in her, and she liked it, too, because when she decided that she would have money because she had once been hungry, it gave her the opportunity to get what she wanted.

It was infinitely wise of Miss Mitchell to take Scarlett for her heroine because the hard, realistic, predatory O'Hara girl fits so perfectly into the whole realistic scheme of the book, and because, too, she offers so perfect a contrast to her sister-in-law, Melanie, so purely of the older tradition.

The book opens just before the war, with a quick and effective picture of what life was like then in the plantation country of Central Georgia. It follows the hard struggles of Scarlett when she flees Atlanta during the siege to feed the family at Tara, struggles complicated as much by raids for the Confederate commissary as by the visits of the invading Yankees.

The war has ended before a third of the novel is finished, so that by far the larger portion is devoted to the Reconstruction period. Scarlett is one of the people who will not be beaten and there are others, just as there are many about her who cannot stand their losses. She uses every resource and always without the slightest scruple to gain her ends, marrying the fiance of one of her sisters because he has money she needs to save Tara, and when he is killed, as a member of the Ku Klux, becoming the wife of the enormously wealthy Captain Rhett Butler, whose fortune has been made in blockade running and other somewhat nefarious schemes.

For this, and for many other things, this son of Charleston aristocrats, who is a bitter realist, is despised by the loyal Southerners. His own struggle, however, is with Scarlett's idealistic passion for the husband of Melanie, whose brother she had married at the outset of the war. He adores Scarlett—they are very much alike inside—and Miss Mitchell's account of this strange triangle is by all odds one of the most amazing parts of her book.

It is, in fact, an answer to the question that may arise in the minds of some readers about her purely imaginative and creative ability as opposed to her undoubted soundness as a research worker and her quite astonishing memory for what older people have told her. This is genuine psychological drama, the conflict between Scarlett and the handsome Captain Butler, and as exciting in its own way as the siege of Atlanta itself, which Miss Mitchell has done beautifully.

The book ends with the conflict unresolved; you may make your own guesses as to its outcome.

Miss Mitchell's novel is 1,037 pages long, closely printed, and took me the better part of three days and nights to read it, so that it will provide a summer's reading for most people, I suspect, and they ought to be grateful to have something as good and as absorbing to read.

Perhaps it ought to be explained, since I suspect this Southern, although wholly honest and realistic, story may offend some Northern readers, that artistically Miss Mitchell is in a safe position, because what she has set out to do is to present the whole situation from the point of view of a Southern woman alive in the period, and from this she never deviates.

I have marked a dozen passages in the book for quotation and have said only a few of the things about it that I wanted to say. It is, however, impossible to summarize, a novel with all the human elements richly worked into its splendidly handled narrative. I cannot see how any one could fail to find it tremendously exciting.

A good Southern novelist who is also an excellent critic wrote me the other day that he thought it was probably the greatest novel ever written in the United States. I am not willing to go this far, but, as I said before, it is far and away the best novel that has even been written about the Civil War and the days that followed.

I can only compare it for its definitiveness, its truthfulness and its completeness with Douglas Southall Freeman's splendid "R. E. Lee," and I know of no higher praise that can reasonably be bestowed upon it than this.

[August 27, 1936]

Having watched the course of many popular novels from the first burst of critical praise to the end of their careers, I have been especially interested in observing that Margaret Mitchell's record-breaking book, "Gone With the Wind," has followed an unusual, not to say unique, course from the time of its publication.

To begin with, I can recall no recent first novel by an author wholly unknown to literary fame that has swept the country as has Miss Mitchell's. On the basis of its present sales figures, it will in all probability top the final totals of "Anthony Adverse," its only rival of our period.

It should be recalled, however, that Hervey Allen was a writer of established reputation when his long romantic novel was published and praised, I think, considerably beyond its real merits. One result of this excessive critical enthusiasm was a reaction, which, while it did not stop the rapid progress of the book, was powerful enough to persuade at least a few strong-minded people that they did not have to read it unless they wanted to.

Ordinarily, I should have expected some such back-kick on "Gone With the Wind," although I am sure it was not overpraised, but the reports that reach me from all quarters are strangely unanimous. I have heard it said again and again that not even the enthusiastic reviews of the novel have succeeded in conveying its unusual appeal, and the general tenor of the comment is not only highly favorable but abounds in superlatives.

This sort of thing does not happen to books that are merely good. There are usually differences of opinion, and quite frequently the novels that we reviewers praise do not arouse popular enthusiasm. They lack the qualities that made the famous fiction of the Victorian period, for example, welcome to everybody and spread its appeal over far wider areas of population than can ever be touched by writing notable for its purely literary merit.

Such a phenomenon will stand some investigation, I believe. What makes a book so popular that everybody wishes to read it and, having read it, to tell everybody else about it in a desire to share the excitement?

I have talked at length with Margaret Mitchell herself on the subject, particularly when I saw her in Blowing Rock, North Carolina, just after the book had appeared and when she was still in a daze at the suddenness of its success. I repeat here some of the things she told me in the hope that they may go part way, at least, toward explaining why a historical novel of the Civil War should in this year of a national election and a threatened European conflict occupy the leisure of thousands of Americans in every part of the country.

The fact that Miss Mitchell wrote the novel to please herself without any thought of its eventual publication is, I think, both striking and significant. It bears upon my own unshakable theory that at bottom "Gone With the Wind" is popular because it is a book that *had to be written,* a book, in other words, that proceeded from an irresistible inner compulsion.

In other words, that it was written for no other reason than that the youthful author, who was in her twenties—the book was in the making from 1926 to 1929, and many days, so Miss Mitchell told me, she wrote on it from early morning until midnight without a pause—had to write it. This drive remains in the quality of sheer excitement that characterizes the novel and which is apparently inescapable, no matter what sort of person reads it.

But the fact that the novel was written without any idea that it would be published, and certainly with none at all that it would be read by hundreds of thousands of people, did not mean that its author failed at any point to recognize and to understand the technical problems involved.

Many of these we discussed, because there are many in the book, and without exception I could raise no point that Miss Mitchell had not carefully considered and, wherever she was faced with alternative choices, had not chosen her own way quite deliberately and consciously.

There is the matter of the style of the novel, for example, which brought down a good deal of unfavorable criticism. I myself said the book had everything except style, and that the writing, as such, often struck me as commonplace. Miss Mitchell's reply to this criticism was that she had deliberately chosen to write as clearly and as simply and as unobtrusively as possible, and that she had also studiedly given the style itself as much of a colloquial flavor as she could.

I took less seriously, because of my familiarity with the variations of dialect among Southern Negroes, some of the mild attacks that were made upon her use of dialect. But here again she knew what she was doing and why. She simplified the phonetic reproduction of the dialect as much as she could, always with the intention of making it read correctly, and she was careful, she told me, to have her Negroes speak the dialect of the part of the Georgia where the scenes of the book are laid.

In the larger and more important problems of architecture, Miss Mitchell, for all her inexperience in fiction—her writing career up to the time she started "Gone With the Wind" had consisted entirely of newspaper work on the Atlanta *Journal*—showed by her very method of writing the book that she had a complete grasp of the whole tremendous panorama of the novel before she sat down to put any of it on paper.

She wrote, so she told me, the last chapter first, and during the four years she was engaged upon the book she took up whatever chapter she wished to and worked on that a while, turning from one part to another from day to day without ever losing her way. The first chapter, which she insists is not very good, although I think she is wholly mistaken in her opinion, was not written until after the novel had been accepted by the Macmillan Company, and was the final result of some seventy-odd trial flights.

The title was also missing when the manuscript was turned over to H. S. Latham, its discoverer. A number of titles were offered, but none of them pleased the publishers, and none of them, I might add, was even an approach to the present one. Miss Mitchell found it, she reports, in Ernest Dowson's famous poem which she was reading to get her mind off the difficulties of christening the child!

Those who have been struck by the extraordinary aptness of the names of the characters will be interested to know that Scarlett O'Hara did not receive her name, either, until long after the book had been started, although other characters almost chose their own names, as Miss Mitchell puts it.

I asked her if she had any explanation of her own of the novel's widespread appeal, and she said at first she hadn't any to offer—except some humorous ones—but she supposed it was because the book dealt in primitive emotions which moved in straight lines, instead of the fantastic zigzags of human and sexual relationships that clutter up so much of modern fiction.

She knows, and so do I, that as good as the book is in its historical background and as essentially dramatic as is the material these things alone would not make people who have barely heard of the Civil War insist upon reading it and talking about it. The double appeal of the conflict between Scarlett and Rhett Butler and the stirring background contain at least a part of the secret of the popularity of the novel, I think, although the perfection of the characterization is also inescapable.

Speaking of this matter of historical accuracy and accuracy in every other detail, costumes, customs, crops, and so on, Miss Mitchell told me the miraculous story that she had written the whole book which was, incidentally, much longer in its original version than it is at present, without the use of a single reference book.

Since, she said, nobody else was to see the book except herself and her husband—her husband had been telling her for years that she had written a fine novel but she couldn't be persuaded—there seemed to be no point in checking over the thousands of things that go into the pattern of so long a narrative.

But after the book was accepted Miss Mitchell, who was especially keen for her home-folks to like her book and to think it correct, went to any length to have everything right. There were, she told me, exactly two minor errors, neither of which would ever have been found outside of Georgia.

Among Southern novels her book is also unique in that up to this time it has had nothing except praise in the South. The Georgia newspapers, large and small, have rung with its praises for weeks, which has pleased its author, she says, more than anything any of the rest of us have thought or said. It is also being bought in the South, which is even more remarkable.

Miss Mitchell is small, has red hair, or dark brown hair with red highlights, blue-gray eyes and a fair skin. She looks, in other words, as Celtic as anybody could, which is not surprising considering that there is a good deal of Irish blood in the family.

She is as amusing as she is goodlooking, a first-rate story-teller and mimic, speaks with a perfect Georgia accent in spite of her years at Smith College, and is married to John R. Marsh, a former newspaper man who is now advertising manager for the Georgia Power Company in Atlanta.

The truly amazing amount of background material in her book came to her not only from widespread reading but from her numerous family, many of whom were deeply interested in the historical phases of the Civil War as well as being active participants in its battles and in the Reconstruction Period.

Just now Miss Mitchell says she is through with writing, but I, like many others, hope she isn't. "Gone With the Wind" is a sufficient accomplishment for anybody, perhaps, but is reveals too striking a talent to be allowed to go unused.

One of the heartening things about the book to me is that it tosses out of the window all the thousands of technical tricks our novelists have been playing with for the past twenty years and goes straight back to honest story-telling and to writing that anybody can understand.

I suspect it may have an important effect on the future course of American fiction in this regard, and I sincerely hope it does. I can see no competitors to "Gone With the Wind" for this year's Pulitzer Prize in fiction.

[October 19,1936]

Before the annual autumn flood completely overwhelms me it seems that a backward look over the year, and more especially over the season, might not be out of place.

As for general impressions, I do not think the level of excellence in this year's books quite so high as it was last year. Certainly it strikes me that the fiction output continues to be mediocre, as it was in the first half of the year, with a few outstanding exceptions to keep us from feeling altogether hopeless.

When the publishing history of the year comes to be written, the tremendous, perhaps unprecedented, success of Margaret Mitchell's "Gone With the Wind" will quite obviously be the most important event to be recorded. In the time left to us nothing can possibly touch it from the point of view of sales volume, nor from the point of view of genuine popularity.

A week after this novel appeared I made the prophecy that it would sell 400,000 copies by January 1, 1937, and 600,000 by June 30 of the same year, a twelvemonth after its appearance. There is every chance that it will have touched the 600,000 mark by November 1, 1936, with the big rush of the Christmas season still to come.

I should not be at all surprised now to see it sell a million copies in this country alone, since it is rapidly approaching the mathematical point where almost anything may happen. And, as I just got through saying, it will go on and on, because there is nothing factitious about its success; people are reading it and recommending it because they enjoy it.

It seems to me the most likely candidate for the Pulitzer Prize, and if it is selected it will receive another natural impetus in sales late next spring, when it might be expected to begin dropping off. It remains my own nomination for the honor.

I have tried once before to explain here, with some help from Miss Mitchell, the reasons for the popularity of the novel. Reason No. 1 remains the simplest answer: It has a grand story. Some have called it melodramatic, ignoring its fidelity to history, but the authentic excitement is in it page after page. For all its length, you don't want to stop reading it, and anything any easier than stopping the reading of most modern novels I cannot think of. They may have many excellent qualities, but narrative power such as is to be found in "Gone With the Wind" is not one of them.

I observe a tendency on the part of some people, now that the book has reached the wide American public, to think somewhat less well of its other merits than they appeared to when it first appeared, an inevitable reaction. For me, it still has Plot, Characters and Background and, as I look back over the sweeping successes of the last ten or fifteen years in fiction, I cannot recall a single book in the lot that touched this one in literary merit. In other words, it is both popular and good, as you may have heard, and there are an infinite number of its technical accomplishments that would reward study on the part of critics given to such matters.

What I am getting at is that if I were forced to pick a single novel from this year's list to read for both entertainment and edification, my choice would unhesitatingly be Miss Mitchell's book, wherein I apparently string along with most literate Americans. My opinion is not influenced either one way or the other by the popularity of the book; I thought it an amazing achievement when I read it and I think more of it rather than less now that three months or more have elapsed since I finished it.

The Title "Gone With the Wind"

By William Lyon Phelps

In 1936 William Lyon Phelps of Yale was, in the popular mind, the great panjandrum of American literature. Each year he gave a lecture at Pointe Aux Barques, Michigan, in which his selection of the best novel of the year was held in only a little less esteem than the Pulitzer Prize. Margaret Mitchell wrote Phelps on September 23, 1936: "Some days ago when I was lying in a dark room with a black bandage over my eyes, regretting very much that I had ever written that book and strained my eyes, I turned on the radio . . . and to my intense excitement heard a newspaper commentator call my name. Of course, I practically laid my ear on the radio and was never so thrilled as to hear him say that you had judged 'Gone With the Wind' the best novel of the year. In that minute I recovered from my regret at having written it, even if it did put my eyes out of commission for several months."

Phelps turned his attention to the title of Gone With the Wind *in his syndicated column written for publication October 13, 1936.*

Titles of novels are interesting; and I dare say novelists spend more time and care on choosing names for their literary off-spring than they do for those of flesh and blood. Mr. Howells was very fond of taking titles from Shakespeare: "A Modern Instance," "The Undiscovered Country," "The Quality of Mercy," "A Counterfeit Presentment," etc.

Two new books that reached me last week have titles from Browning: "No Hero," and "Wake and Remember."

Where did Margaret Mitchell get that title, "Gone with the Wind"? In all probability, from Ernest Dowson's poem "Cynara," which lent its name to a poor but popular play a few years ago. There is a line in this poem,

"I have forgot much, Cynara! gone with the wind,"

But it is quite possible that Ernest Dowson (1867–1900) got the phrase from a similar passage in a poem by the famous Irish poet James Clarence Mangan (1803–1849). Here is Mangan's poem, and note that both poets pronounce wind to rhyme with bind, which does not make it necessary for us to call the novel in that fashion:

GONE IN THE WIND

Solomon! where is thy throne? It is gone in the wind.
Babylon! where is thy might? It is gone in the wind.
Like the swift shadows of Noon, like the dreams of the Blind,
Vanish the glories and pomps of the earth in the wind.

Man! canst thou build upon aught in the pride of thy mind?
Widsom will teach thee that nothing can tarry behind:
Though there be thousand bright actions embalmed and enshrined,
Myriads and millions of brighter are snow in the wind.

Solomon! where is thy throne? It is gone in the wind,
Babylon! where is thy might? It is gone in the wind.
All that the genius of Man hath achieved and designed,
Waits but its hour to be dealt with as dust by the wind.

Pity thou, reader! the madness of poor Humankind,
Raving of Knowledge,—and Satan so busy to blind!
Raving of Glory,—like me,—for the garlands I bind
(Garlands of song) are but gathered, and–strewn in the wind!

This striking poem is in "The Catholic Anthology," by Thomas Walsh, published by the Macmillan Co., New York.

Margaret Mitchell in 1922, a photograph by John Marsh.

Snapshot of Margaret Mitchell on the ice of Paradise Pond, Smith College, winter 1918–19.

Margaret Mitchell (between the two men) and colleagues on the *Atlanta Journal Sunday Magazine*.

Rudolph Valentino and Miss Mitchell, interview at the Georgian Terrace Hotel, 1923.

Margaret Mitchell in her New York apartment shortly before publication of *Gone With the Wind*. Kenneth Rogers of the *Atlanta Constitution* photographed her with manuscript pages on the table.

A widely distributed 1936 photograph by Asasno used by Macmillan to illustrate *Margaret Mitchell and Her Novel* Gone With the Wind.

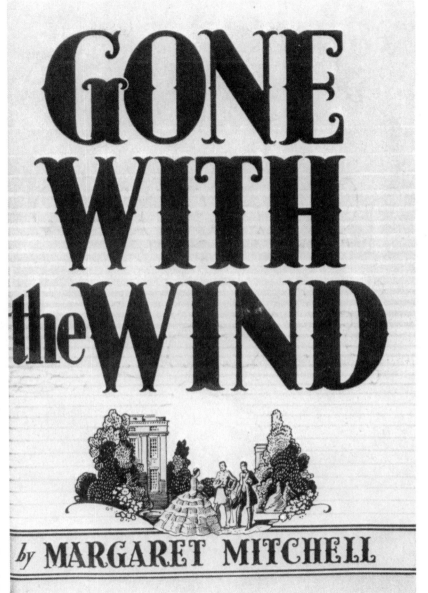

A familiar sight in the late 1930s, the jacket vignette was drawn by George Carlson. For book collectors, the "correct" first edition jacket has a back panel headed "Macmillan Spring Novels."

Herschel Brickell, Margaret Mitchell, and Edwin Granberry in Blowing Rock, N.C., July 1936.

TWO

Margaret Mitchell

By Margaret Mitchell

Margaret Mitchell wrote an autobiographical sketch for the Wilson Bulletin *that was published in September 1936. Such sketches (usually of newly prominent authors) were a monthly feature of that magazine for many years. Though Miss Mitchell gave a good many interviews over the years this brief sketch is the only piece she ever wrote about herself and the only article by her ever to appear in a national magazine.*

I was born in Atlanta and have lived here all my life. My parents were born in Atlanta. My grandparents had cotton plantations in the vicinity of Atlanta before the town was built. As far as I can trace, my people have always lived in the South, most of them in Georgia, since the Revolution. I can find no record of any of my people living further north than Brittan's Neck, North Carolina. My people have been cotton planters, lawyers, and Methodist ministers.

My father is Eugene M. Mitchell, a lawyer of considerable prominence here in Georgia. He is an authority on Georgia and Southern history and president of the Atlanta Historical Society. My mother, now dead, was Maybelle Stephens, also an authority on Southern history, particularly that pertaining to the Civil War. I have one brother, older than I am, Stephens Mitchell. He is a lawyer, president of the Atlanta Lawyers Club and editor of the *Atlanta Historical Bulletin*.

My ancestors have been getting into wars ever since 1680. They've fought in Colonial Indian campaigns, the Revolution, the War of 1812, Mexican War, Seminole Wars, Civil War, and the younger fry fought in the last war.

I was educated in the Atlanta Public Schools and at Washington Seminary, an Atlanta preparatory school. I hoped to study medicine but while I was at Smith College my mother died and I had to come home to keep house. A year or so later I got a job on the *Atlanta Journal* and wrote run-of-the-mine reporting stuff as well as signed feature stories, for about six years.

After giving up active newspaper work I began on *Gone With the Wind*. I think I started it in 1926 but can't be sure of that. Practically all of it was written between 1926 and 1929. It was high tide of the Jazz Age and the Boom Era was on us but I would write a Victorian type novel and one about hard times. The reason it took so long in the writing was that my own health was not so good and also every member of my family and all my friends were seriously ill during that period. I spent months and years in hospital corridors and outside of operating rooms. Finally it seemed that I would never finish it, due to the many outside calls on my time, so I put it away and forgot about it. I never submitted it to any publisher or any agent as I thought it pretty terrible.

When Mr. H. S. Latham was in Atlanta, a little over a year ago, he heard about the manuscript and took it away with him and bought it. He was the first person beside myself who had ever laid eyes on it. Except my husband—and he had not seen all of it nor could he make heads or tails of it due to my unfortunate habit of writing from the back of the book toward the front.

My husband is John R. Marsh, a Kentuckian. We were married in 1925. He is manager of the advertising department of the Georgia Power Company. He is a former newspaper man. We have no children.

I chose the Civil War period to write about because I was raised on it. As a child I listened for hours on Sunday afternoons to stories of fighting in Virginia and Georgia, to the horror of Sherman's approach, his final arrival and the burning and looting, and the way the refugees crowded the trains and the roads to Macon. And I heard about Reconstruction. In fact I heard everything except that the Confederates lost the war. When I was ten years old, it was a violent shock to learn that General Lee had been licked. And I thought it had all happened just a few years before I was born.

If the novel has a theme, the theme is that of survival. What makes some people able to come through catastrophes and others, apparently just as able, strong, and brave, go under? We've seen it in the present depression. It happens in every upheaval. Some people survive; others don't. What qualities are in those who fight their way through triumphantly that are lacking in those who go under? What was it that made some of our Southern people able to come through a War, a Reconstruction, and a complete wrecking of the social and economic system? I don't know. I only know that the survivors used to call that quality 'gumption'. So I wrote about the people who had gumption and the people who didn't.

When Margaret Mitchell Was a Girl Reporter

By Medora Field Perkerson

Medora Field went to work for the Atlanta Journal's *Sunday Magazine in 1919. By the time Margaret Mitchell joined its staff in December 1922 Medora had become its Assistant Editor and the wife of its editor, Angus Perkerson. On the hiring of the younger writer, Bill Howland quoted Angus Perkerson in May 1950 in* The Atlanta Historical Bulletin:

I was a little worried about putting her on the staff, because she was a society girl, and I said . . . "Medora, I reckon we'll always be waiting for her to get to work." But I was wrong there—she was always waiting for us when we got there in the morning, because she came to town and had to leave home before the cook got there. So she ate her breakfast in the little cafe in the building—the Journal folks called it "The Roachery"—and then she sort of opened up the office. One thing I liked about her was that she was always ready to take any story—she never looked down on any story. And she wrote like a man.

The friendship between Margaret Mitchell and Medora Perkerson was life long. No one was better qualified than Mrs. Perkerson to write about Margaret Mitchell. She wrote this story for The Atlanta Journal Magazine *for January 7, 1945.*

When Margaret Mitchell wrote the first chapter last for *Gone With the Wind* she had her own historic precedent. That is the way she wrote her first story for The Journal Magazine back in December, 1922. She says this was purely inadvertent the first time, because it was the editor who turned her story hindside before, but afterward she nearly always wrote the lead—or opening paragraph—of her Magazine stories last. It got to be a habit.

She wrote hundreds of stories during her four years as a member of the Magazine staff. She signed them Peggy Mitchell, and went on signing them that way even after she married John R. Marsh, advertising manager of the Georgia Power Company, in 1925. The Marshes now live at 1268 Piedmont Avenue.

Peggy wrote about everything. The Junior League Follies, Georgia camp meetings, Confederate generals, Bell House bachelors, bobbed haired bandits, bootleggers, inventors, explorers. She dealt with all the burning issues in which an earlier postwar generation felt a passionate interest. She interviewed her share of celebrities—Mrs. W. H. Felton, of Cartersville, first United States woman senator—Gilda Gray, the shimmy queen—Rudolph Valentino, the sheik of movie fame—Tiger Flowers, Atlanta's Negro middleweight champion of the world and a steward in the Butler Street Methodist Episcopal Church. She did perhaps more than her share of stunt stories, in one of which she was lowered over the side of an Atlanta skyscraper in the swing which the sculptor, Gutzon Borglum, used for his early carving on the still unfinished Confederate memorial on Stone Mountain.

"Those were the days when I had no better sense than to risk my neck to keep people from thinking I was scared," she admits now with a smile. "The photographers who went along on these assignments were always hoping I would scream or faint or back down or something and I was just as determined not to. Some of these stunts I thought up myself, but one that I remember in particular was a photographer's brainstorm. We had gone behind the scenes at the circus to get an animal story. At that time I had never been nearer an elephant than to feed him peanuts, carefully extended at arm's length. I saw the photographer mutter behind his hand to the mahout, who barked something in Hindustani to the biggest elephant I had ever seen. The next thing I knew that elephant had picked me up with his snout and, carrying me through the air, had deposited me on his head. I found myself frantically holding onto his ears with both hands—just in case he decided to drop me as suddenly."

These were some of the adventures humorously recalled by Peggy when she dropped by the Magazine office recently and found the staff on the brink of moving into roomier quarters in preparation for the enlarged Magazine, of which this is the first issue. She recalled too that not long after she came to work in 1922 the Magazine moved to larger quarters and was increased in size.

But it was from the Magazine's first crowded office that the future author of *Gone With the Wind* went forth to cover her first assignment. Except that she weighed only about 90 pounds at that time, she looks very little older today. She was given then to wearing tailored suits which made her look even more diminutive and her reddish brown hair was long and done high on the back of her head. Her dark fringed Irish blue eyes may have been a little more serious with that all-fired determination to become a newspaper reporter.

She had been a debutante not so long before, and I remember there was some skepticism on the part of the rest of the staff as to whether she would get to the office on time. Debutantes slept late in those days and didn't go in for jobs. As it turned out, Peggy, who rode the street car to town from the white-columned house of her father, Eugene M. Mitchell, prominent Atlanta attorney, at 1401 Peachtree Street, usually beat the rest of us to work.

From first to last she was a good reporter in the traditional sense that she never made excuses and never fell down on a story. She was more than a good reporter in that her work was definitely creative and had that extra something which gives life and color to the simplest story.

"On my first morning," Peggy recalled the other day, "the Magazine editor sent me out to get a story about whether skirts were going to be shorter. World War I had brought short skirts, but in 1922 they were fairly long again. Mary Hines Gunsaulas (later Mrs. Sidney Daniel), was back from a three-month stay in Europe with a lot of Paris clothes. Would skirts be short again any time soon? That was the story I was told to get and I darn well got it. Mrs. Gunsaulas posed for photographs in her Paris frocks and mentioned incidentally that she had been in Rome the day the Fascisti marched in, black shirts and all, and Mussolini took over the government.

"Mussolini was not even a name to me then," Peggy says, "but it sounded interesting and I listened and asked questions while Mrs. Gunsaulas told more. I came back and wrote my story about skirts and tacked all this other incident onto the end."

Peggy grinned. "You know what happened. Angus—I .called him Mr. Perkerson then—turned the story hindside before and featured the eyewitness account of Mussolini taking over the Italian government."

Peggy and I got down some of the bound files of old Journal Magazaines and found that first story. Sure enough, in the pictures, skirts were about a foot above the floor. Most of the story was concerned with something else.

"A lot of the things we wrote about were topical, of course," Peggy mused, turning pages. "Could a girl be virtuous and bob her hair? Could she have a home and husband and children and a job, too? Should she roll her stockings, park her corsets, be allowed a latch key? These questions are all as dead as the bloomer girl now, but they were hot stuff then. Between the younger and older generation swords were drawn. Practically anybody could get publicity by criticizing young people. There was a passionate interest on the part of both old and young as to what prominent people had to say on these issues. They aren't issues any longer and they are dead because they are victories won by the younger generation of the 1920's."

We came to one of her early stories recounting a visit with a group of geologists to Salt Peter Cave near Kingston. Peggy told how the guide tied a string to a rock near the entrance and unwound the ball as he went along, cautioning them not to step on the string, or they might not find their way out. "That was before Floyd Collins was trapped in that cave in Kentucky," Peggy remarked feelingly, "or they'd never have got me into this one."

The story tells how they proceeded into the darkness through narrow passages, holding tight to their flashlights. There were stalactites and stalagmites and the sound of rushing water. Finally they came to a room which even the guide had not previously explored. To reach this room he had to inch himself up a 20-foot practically perpendicular plank, slick with accumulated slime. "Afraid to come along?" he called back to Peggy.

Her story confesses: "Afraid, no. Only terror-smitten." But the return trip was worse. "Seating myself on the board," she wrote, "I was preparing to edge my way down when my grip slipped and away I went whizzing, landing at the feet of the waiting group and knocking the ball of twine from Mr. Sperry's hands."

In spite of Mr. Sperry's scramble for the dropped ball of twine, Peggy remembers that her descent greatly enlivened the party.

Another early story finds Peggy arrayed in a pair of Size 40 overalls, ready to try out Borglum's swing. "One doesn't feel so very good when one is shoved out of a window of a skyscraper," she recorded, "especially when one has never been shoved out of any window before. A dizzy whirl, buildings, windows, a glimpse of the sky, anxious faces at the windows, all jumbled up for an instant of eternity, a feeling of nausea, then a bump completed the first swing in the air and brought me up against the side of the building with an awful wallop.

" 'Hey,' shouted a distant voice, 'look down this way and smile.' "

That cheerful greeting came from the photographer, of course.

Next we turned to Peggy's interview with Rudolph Valentino. He had wowed the ladies in the movie role of *The Sheik* only a couple of years before and was still wowing them. In order to get away from admiring fans at the Georgian Terrace, he and Peggy and the photographer retired to the graveled roof opening off the mezzanine floor. "In each window," Peggy recalled, "there were about 55 women all calling out to me to make him wave at them."

Peggy's own reaction is given in her story. With the interview ended, the only way back to the hotel corridor was through a window about four feet above the roof. She was preparing to chin herself up. Then—" 'Allow me,' breathed a husky voice in my ear and as masterfully as he sheiked Agnes Ayres, he picked me up and lifted me through the window. As he stood there with me in his arms, one girl gasped, 'Oh, the lucky little devil.' And then he deposited me on the floor. All aglow, wondering whether I had better register deep emotion, thrills or say, 'Sir, how dare you?' I ended by registering a world-beating blush, dropping my vanity case, pulling the hem out of the back of my dress with my heel as I bent to retrieve it and bumped heads with Valentino."

Looking again at Valentino's picture, there on the Magazine page, Peggy said, "He was a plain, nice spoken, very weary sort of person. I don't think he quite understood why ladies acted the way they did."

One of Peggy's many interviews was with Harry K. Thaw, who had made a study of American history while in Matteawan, where he was confined after the fatal shooting of Stanford White. "He would not give an interview to anyone at first," Peggy remembered. "He was tired of having his private life discussed, of having something dragged out that had happened twenty years before. But he told the editor that if anyone on the staff knew anything about the Battle of Atlanta, that person might accompany him on his tour of local battlefields.

"We saw the battlefields, we saw Stone Mountain and the Cyclorama," Peggy says. "He knew more about Confederate history than anybody I ever saw." How much Peggy herself knew came out later in *Gone With the Wind*. "Late that afternoon," she remembered, "in his Rolls Royce with a white, liveried chauffeur, we swept out Peachtree Street past the Georgian Terrace, where my grandmother, Mrs. John Stephens, was sitting on the terrace. When I waved, grandmother said to the other grandmothers also sitting there, 'That's my granddaughter in that Rolls Royce.' She lost no time in telephoning me to ask, 'Who was the gentleman, dear.'

" 'Harry Thaw, grandmother,'

"She was horrified, of course, and made me promise never to tell any of the other grandmothers. She enjoyed the excitement of hearing about the things that happened on my job, but she never quite approved of it."

One of Peggy's most charming stories dealth with her visit to Mrs. W. E. Baker, in Roswell. Mrs. Baker, then 87, was the last surviving bridesmaid of Mittie Bulloch who married Theodore Roosevelt at Bulloch Hall in 1854. They were the parents of President Theodore Roosevelt and grandparents of Eleanor Roosevelt. Peggy remembers her trip as a harrowing experience.

"A sandy-haired young photographer, named Pat, and I set out in his car about midmorning of a wild rainy day to drive the 20 miles to Roswell. The roads were not paved and we got stuck in the mud a number of times and had to be pulled out by farmers. That cost money. Just before we reached the covered bridge which then crossed the Chattahoochee River we had a blow-out. When the tire was fixed we had 10 cents between us, it was late afternoon, we had had nothing to eat since breakfast and were practically starved. Lunch was long over at Barrington Hall, where Mrs. Baker lived, and when the door was opened we were greeted by the delicious odor of collards or turnip greens already cooking for dinner.

"More vividly than anything else, Mrs. Baker recalled the great quantities of food served at Mittie Bulloch's wedding," Peggy said. "She talked about baked ham, shaved so thin it curled like a lady's hair, about chicken and turkey and roasted meats and about the icing parties the girls had where they all gathered to ice cakes for the wedding. Finally the starving photographer could stand it no longer. He moved beyond the sound of Mrs. Baker's voice and leaned his head against one of the white columns. But, weak with hunger, though I was, I had to listen to her tantalizing description of that wonderful collation. When we got away from there the photographer and I took our remaining dime and bought a hot dog and a glass of milk which we split between us."

In contrast to the ordeal endured on her Roswell story Peggy recalls: "I never ate better victuals than at Mt. Gilead camp meeting. The photographer and I sang through the morning services, with the congregation, and were invited to join them when dinner was spread under the trees. We met some people named Mitchell who said they were sure we were kin. We had such a good time we stayed and sang through the afternoon service, too."

In 1925 Peggy did a series of biographical sketches of Georgia Confederate generals. These, she says, and a few other stories are all she kept for her scrapbook. The stories signed by Peggy Mitchell ran out about midway of the 1926 file. Closing the big book, she said:

"Being a reporter was a liberal education. If more women, when they were girls, were in a position to see—as a newspaper girl is—the inside of jails, the horrible things Travelers' Aid discovers, the emergency rooms of Grady Hospital and those sad, desolate sections which used to be fine homes but now are rookeries and rabbit warrens—if more people knew the sad things and the horrible things that go on in the world, there would be a darned sight less complacency and probably not so many of these sad sights and horrible things. It is not so much that people are cold-hearted and selfish. It is just that they have not seen. And what eye has not seen, heart cannot feel. Nowadays girls do get out more, people do know more, but even so, one good whiff of the police station on a hot July day would do a lot for a lot of people."

Because she genuinely liked people, they opened up and gave her the stories she wanted. For the same reason she was popular with everyone in The Journal Building. I was just learning to drive a car when we journeyed to Clarkston at great risk of life and limb to the funeral of a Journal proofreader. Peggy particularly wanted to go because he had given her many kindly and helpful suggestions in her early days on the paper when she was ignorant of her new job and anxious to conceal this ignorance from other reporters. Only last year I saw her at the funeral of an old-time Journal photographer. In spite of her great fame she still finds time for the friendly, thoughtful things so many of us fail to do.

Because of ill health, she gave up her newspaper job in 1926 after four years as a star feature writer but for some time continued to write a column begun in the Magazine by the late Frances Newman, "Elizabeth Bennet's Gossip." As her health improved, she began the book that was to shatter all publishing records. Seven of the years between 1926 and 1938 were more or less devoted to writing that book, for which she received the Pulitzer prize. In 1939 most of Hollywood's important stars came to Atlanta for the world premiere of the movie version of the book which has been translated into nearly every known language and to date has sold approximately 5,000,000 copies.

When we closed the old files, Peggy got up from the same chair she had sat in back in her newspaper days. "Will they move that to the new Magazine office?" she wondered smilingly, remembering how the legs had to be sawed shorter because it was too high for her. "That carpenter had a dreadful time," she said. "First one leg would be longer and then another, but he finally got them even and I had a chair low enough to let my feet touch the floor." She wrote more than Magazine stories while sitting in that chair. She wrote love letters that began, not "Dear John," but "14 ems 8 pt. sun mag." That is the way Magazine pages are marked for the printer. "If I began my letters like that and Angus caught a passing glimpse, he would think I was hard at work on a story," she grinned.

Even before America entered the war Peggy gave the greater part of her time to Red Cross work. Both she and her husband have been tireless in civilian defense, bond selling and other wartime efforts. She was the sponsor of the first Atlanta cruiser. When it was sunk in the Solomons, she helped raise funds for the new Atlanta, which she also christened.

Is she writing another book?

"Definitely not."

Will she ever write one?

The answer was, she hoped so.

When? What will it be about? If I had been able to get the answer to that I would have put it at the beginning of this story—not at the end.

The Private Life of
Margaret Mitchell

By Edwin Granberry

Edwin Granberry wrote in the New York Sun *June 30, 1936, one of the first reviews of* Gone With the Wind, *one of which Margaret Mitchell was especially proud. "We can think of no single American novelist," he said, "who has combined as has Miss Mitchell all the talents that go into the making of the great panoramic novel such as the English and the Russians and the Scandinavians have known how to produce."*

Granberry was one of the few reviewers to perceive Rhett Butler as he would affect thousands of adoring readers. Most reviewers dismissed him as a stock character. He was, but a stock character with added dimensions. Miss Mitchell used him as a focus of recognition and—a very important and—as a focal point for characterization, not only of himself but also of the other principals of the story. Granberry's review says:

> *The greatest triumph of the book has been left for a final mention—the creation of the character of Rhett Butler. We feel fairly certain that the unforgettable quality of this book is occasioned by the scenes over which this scornful, swaggering devil (he never meant it) presides like a mundane Mephistopheles. He is one of the great lovers in all fiction, and no man ever had his heart more broken than he. Miss Mitchell's objective handling of him rivals Sigrid Undset's way with her Erling. As we remember, we are never—even in his worst moments of torment—let directly into the mind of Rhett Butler; the author is always able to find an action or a speech which reveals the havoc. (Watch for the moment when Butler opens his shirt to show his step-son the scar.)*

Miss Mitchell met Granberry shortly after GWTW was published. Over the years the Marshes and the Granberrys became even closer friends than did the Marshes and the Brickells. Granberry was one of the few people Miss Mitchell ever encouraged to write an article about her. His piece in Collier's *and an article in* Pictorial Review, *"The Woman Who Wrote 'Gone With the Wind,' " by Faith Baldwin, both appeared in issues for March 1937.*

In a department store in a large Southern city a tiny, though sturdy, young woman with blue eyes and dark auburn hair was trying on dresses in the privacy of a fitting booth. It was no longer a simple matter for her to buy a dress. In fact, it was not a simple matter for her to do anything unless she was willing to do it under the eyes of the world. She liked the world, this intensely active young woman. But she thought, nevertheless, that the fitting of a dress should be carried on with as little ado as possible, and for the moment, therefore, was happy in the seclusion offered by the fitting booth. Busily putting on and taking off, she was suddenly interrupted by the sound of women's voices in the aisle. Abruptly the curtains of the booth were drawn aside and there, peering at her, was an excited crowd. *"Isn't* she tiny!" exclaimed a woman. And a second voice: *"I* don't believe she wrote it—she's too little!"

Gazing back at them—with a look which was neither angry nor upset but full of amused understanding—were the wide blue eyes of Margaret Mitchell, author of Gone With the Wind.

Do not judge these ladies too harshly. They but typify the pressure of public interest which at the moment beats so fiercely on Miss Mitchell. And they are but a few of the millions who have fallen under the seemingly overwhelming spell of her great story of the Civil War—the novel which is no longer just the record-breaking first novel in history but one which has become instead a phenomenon, a movement, a sort of rallying flag for the emotions of a whole people. As a result, Miss Mitchell stands at the moment in such a spotlight of public attention as no American, excepting the President, has known since Colonel Lindbergh flew the Atlantic.

Born in Atlanta, of parents and grandparents who also were born in or near Atlanta, she has lived there all her life. All of her people have lived in the South since they first came to America. When they were not cotton planters, they were lawyers, doctors and ministers. The tradition not only of education but of extensive reading is in them. Even those in past generations who lived on remote plantations, far from towns, had large libraries, made a habit of reading aloud at night to the assembled families, ordered the newest of the good books—frequently those printed abroad—and subscribed to French and English periodicals. Excellent memories were a family trait of the Mitchells and their kin and the practice of committing long poems to memory was encouraged—such as Lalla Rookh, Marmion, Horatius at the Bridge, The Lady of the Lake.

In the neighborhood where Margaret Mitchell was reared, there were many old folks who had lived through the war and reconstruction. Along about twilight on summer afternoons when the children were tired of playing, they'd sit down on the front steps or around the fire on winter evenings, and listen to the old folks as they sat rocking and talking and reminiscing. Old ladies and old gentlemen both loved to talk those days, "recalling (as Miss Mitchell expressed it in Gone With the Wind) the fierce heat of their midsummer in this forlorn sunset of their winter." She heard endless discussions about whether General Johnston was a better general than General Hood; how ambulances had no springs and a man with a broken bone—unless it was in his leg—was a sight better off walking fifty miles to a hospital than riding in an ambulance; how a man was as good as dead in some hospitals because of the wild-fire way erysipelas spread, how hard it was to march on an empty stomach, and how far you had to march on an empty stomach if you happened to be in Stonewall Jackson's outfit.

And the ladies talked of how they used gourd seeds dyed red for buttons during the blockade, and plaited hats of straw and trimmed them with corn shuck rosettes, and made shoes with soles whittled from wood and tops made of carpets and shawls and, finally, of homespun. All spoke of the war as though it had happened only the week before, and the deaths of friends who fell at Shiloh and Gettysburg were as fresh in their memories as though they had happened recently. The old folks sang the war songs of their youth, Lorena and Maryland and many others, and if the children were extra good they recited poems such as "I'm a good old Rebel and that's just what I am."

"And then," Miss Mitchell tells us, "I used to go horseback riding with veterans before I was five years old. All were old cavalrymen and I heard about Forrest and Stuart and Joe Wheeler from them and how to use a saber, too . . . On the shelves of our bookcases at home were books about the war period and I read them by the time I was seven—Surry of Eagle's-Nest and Mohun by John Esten Cooke, Mrs. M. L. Avary's Virginia Girl in the Civil War and Dixie After the War; Two Little Confederates, by Thomas Nelson Page, and Diddie, Dumps and Tot, by Louise-Clarke Pyrnelle.

"And sometimes on Sunday afternoons when I had been arrayed in my best and taken calling on elderly relatives, if I was very good and did not get my dress messy and sat quietly on a footstool and listened to the battle of Gettysburg and the Valley Campaign without interruption, I was richly rewarded by being permitted to put my two thumbs into the two dents in the skull of a veteran where a Minié ball had gone in and out."

Miss Mitchell has already told somewhere of the shock it gave her when at ten years of age she learned that General Lee had been defeated. At this time she was attending the Atlanta public schools, skipping a few grades. Thereafter came Washington Seminary, in Atlanta, and then one year at Smith College, from which she withdrew to return home on the death of her mother. From 1922 until 1926, Miss Mitchell was on the staff of the Magazine Section of the Atlanta Journal. A sprained ankle that would not get well caused her retirement from the Journal and not—as rumor has it—"an automobile accident which left her in a plaster cast for three years." This heroic nonsense about having written her book while flat on her back in plaster amuses Miss Mitchell, for she is unable to compose except on a typewriter and she has never heard of any way by which a typewriter can be operated by one so bedridden. The truth of the matter is that at this time, 1926, her normal activities were greatly restricted by her bad ankle; she had more spare time on her hands than was pleasant for one of her energetic disposition; therefore, chiefly for the diversion it provided, at this time she began writing the novel which ten years later was to electrify America and a good part of the entire world, as well as set a record as the fastest-selling novel in the annals of publishing.

A first novel does well if it sells five thousand copies in a lifetime. Gone With the Wind has run up such unprecedented sales as fifty thousand copies in a single day, a half-million in less than one hundred days, more than a million copies in six months. Anthony Adverse, its nearest rival in the history of publishing, amassed but 18,474 copies in its best week, less than four hundred thousand in eleven months. Copies of the first printing of Miss Mitchell's novel commanded fifty dollars at the last quoting. Its fame has spread throughout the civilized world, with requests for translation rights from practically every country where books are published.

Word of it has seeped into the farthest out-of-the-way hamlets and into strata of society where one would suppose there was little time for the reading of novels. Standing recently under the steel girders of a railroad shed, discussing Miss Mitchell's book with a friend while waiting for a midnight Pullman to start, I suddenly realized that standing near us in the dim light were two men, their faces blackened with coal smoke, tools swinging in their hands. They were trainmen of some sort, and they were listening to what we had to say. I asked of one of them if he had read the book. He grinned in the affirmative, adding: "And I hope she never gets him back." And whether Scarlett ever got Rhett back has become well-nigh a major issue with the American people.

It is interest such as this in the characters of Gone With the Wind, coming from people in all walks of life, which has overwhelmed Miss Mitchell with such a pressure of notoriety. The millions who have lived its drama vicariously seem unable to shake off its grip. It "does something" to them and they turn instinctively to the one person who can lift the spell she has put on them—Margaret Mitchell herself.

As a result, Miss Mitchell is besieged in her Atlanta home. If she ventures out on a shopping expedition, she is surrounded by eager questioners and returns home hours later with the shopping still undone. The purchase of a dress, as we have seen, has become a problem, unless she wishes to try it on in public. Autograph hunters spring out from the most unexpected places. Yet to remain at home is to be overwhelmed by a barrage of letters, telegrams, calls by wire, calls in person, pouring in upon her from early morning until late at night. There is no secret about Miss Mitchell's address. Her telephone is listed. It is but part of her determination to continue to live her life as she has always lived it, and, as yet, she has not even considered "refugeeing" from Atlanta to some secret retreat. Atlanta is her home; it is where she belongs; it is where her husband lives and works; it is where her people have lived since before the city was born. It is where she has remained except for brief visits since *her* "Siege of Atlanta" began, and it is where she intends to live always, unless the pressure of public attention should force her to seek a hideaway elsewhere.

In one of the dramatic passages in her novel, besieged Atlanta takes comfort from General Johnston's stout declaration, "I can hold Atlanta forever!" Margaret Mitchell, besieged, likewise takes comfort from her hope that she, too, can hold on to her Atlanta residence forever. It is a strange situation which confronts Miss Mitchell, one that few people are ever called upon to face and one she little dreamed would be her lot. She is doing whatever she can to meet a well-nigh insuperable problem.

This problem is simply one of volume—a volume of invitations to attend meetings and make speeches, so great that she could not accept them all even if she did nothing but attend meetings and make speeches; a volume of callers, and persons seeking to call, so great that she could not receive them all if she devoted twenty-four hours a day to this one phase of her activities alone; a volume of requests for autographs so great that she would be suffering from acute writer's cramp long before she could comply with even a small fraction of the requests; and a volume of mail so large that practically her entire time is taken up with answering the thousands of letters.

Until the printings of Gone With the Wind passed the half-million mark, she was as generous with her autograph as any author, but after that, she was forced to call a halt. The printing presses were turning out copies of the book faster than she could put her name in them, she explained. Now that more than a million copies have been printed, the requests for autographs have run into the hundreds of thousands. She knows that autographing so many books in so short a time is beyond her strength, beyond anybody's strength, and if she cannot autograph for the humblest, she will not do it for the highest.

In one respect, however, she has not spared herself—the answering of the stream of letters that flood her apartment. Her mail has mounted to such a volume that when she returned home recently from a short trip, she found something over twelve hundred letters awaiting her. Does she read them, answer them all? To the last one of them she reads them and answers them herself. She has a secretary—sometimes two, one during the day and one at night—but every letter receives Miss Mitchell's personal attention. No form-letter replies are sent.

The majority of the letters are of a kind that could not be answered with stereotyped politeness, even if Miss Mitchell were inclined to handle them in that easy way. Many of them, written under the fervency of emotion aroused by the novel, have the tone of the confessional about them. Miss Mitchell knows as well as anybody that she could ignore them, but having unwittingly been the cause of the desperate note of some of them, she feels an obligation she cannot evade.

Wives write that the tragedy of Rhett and Scarlett has opened their eyes to similar tragedies under their own roofs and has moved them to correct estrangements from their husbands before it is too late. Husbands write that Rhett's separation from Scarlett after he has loved her so many years has kept them awake at night, fearful that they also might lose beloved wives. Letters come in, hardly legible, so shaky are the hands that wrote them, asking God's blessing on the young author for picturing so truthfully the war days through which the writers lived. Others, in the painfully precise handwriting of youth, thank Miss Mitchell for having given them their first real understanding of the Old South's gallantry and chivalry that is a part of the heritage of us all. Men broken by the depression—idealists who could not survive change and upheaval—pour out their hearts to Miss Mitchell in sympathy for Ashley, who also was broken by change and upheaval of war and reconstruction. Proud wives whose men have been thrown out of work write her letters filled with bitter compassion for Scarlett, for they have learned that no woman knows the degradation she will stoop to until she needs to defend her home and those she loves.

Reaping their share of attention, also are the scenes and characters of Gone With the Wind. Miss Mitchell has not drawn her characters from life. Believing it impossible to know completely another's mind, she filled the pages of her book with people of her own creation. Thousands, nonetheless, are identifying Scarlett, and the hunt for Rhett Butler proceeds at a frenzy. Tourists swarm through Atlanta looking for the house where Aunt Pittypat lived and through Clayton County looking for Tara. Neither Aunt Pittypat nor her house ever existed except in Miss Mitchell's imagination, and there is, alas! no Tara. Alas, indeed, for its halls and red fields have become as real to millions of people as their own firesides and lawns. To find there is not and never was a Tara is like the sadness for the vanished scenes of a dream. Not since Dickens have people so allied themselves with the joys and sorrows of fictional characters and the scenes where they played out their stories.

This clamor for the characters of Gone With the Wind and the impulse on the part of people to see and hear Miss Mitchell arises, it would seem, from a desire to prove to themselves that she *does* exist, to convince themselves that there *is* a person capable of producing singlehanded a novel of such breadth and emotional power, to satisfy themselves that she is, or is not, all that rumor has made her.

These rumors reach Miss Mitchell by every known channel of information—through the press, through the mails, over the wires, by word of mouth. Her impersonators are springing up all over the land. One appeared recently on a fur farm in the far, frozen North, willing to tell all, to sign autographs, to sell her confessions. It was too good to be true.

An alert newspaperman made a quick telephone call to Miss Mitchell's publishers in New York. They knew nothing of Miss Mitchell a-prowl so far in the North, certainly not on a fur ranch. More quick telephoning and Miss Mitchell was located asleep in her bed in faraway Atlanta, Georgia. And, again, this one, still more recent: A lady with two escorts appeared at a Florida airport and requested accommodations on a plane just leaving for Havana. The officials were sorry but the plane was full. Full, was it? stormed the temperamental lady. Did they know who she was? She was Margaret Mitchell and she would get accommodations, or know the reason why, for her bodyguard as well as for herself. At the very time when the impostor was storming about, advertising

Miss Mitchell as a person with very bad manners, the real Margaret Mitchell was several hundred miles away on a short vacation trip, seeking rest from her notoriety and moving quietly among strangers who never suspected that the small person in unassuming dress was the author of the book they carried under their arms and discussed so avidly on hotel porches.

It is not to be wondered at that the author of Gone With the Wind thinks the price of fame comes high at times.

Much of the mystery which surrounds Miss Mitchell arises from her refusal to be lionized. Except for her many friends in Georgia who knew her before she was catapulted to such sudden, dizzy fame, few people have ever seen her, those in the literary capitals of the North not at all. And the fact that she has not come to New York to receive the acclaim the book world is so eager to give her has helped to create a feeling toward her almost of awe.

The most humorous bit of disbelief Miss Mitchell met with in her own state. Clayton County, as you may recall, is the county in which much of the action of Gone With the Wind takes place. Soon after the book was published, tourists began halting at Jonesboro, hunting for the landmarks of the novel instead of speeding southward from Atlanta. If that young woman back in Atlanta, thought some of the local citizenry, had written a story about a house called Tara, and if tourists wanted to see Tara, then the least they could do to show their hospitality to strangers was to find them a Tara.

And so Taras came into being, many Taras. There was no intention to deceive; the county folks were simply being accommodating to strangers within the gate, while standing by one of their own. Not knowing Miss Mitchell's passion for accuracy—she has the dress of her characters and the houses they live in correct to the last minute detail—how could they be sure that one of the houses they had picked wouldn't suit her for the house in her story?

Thinking to look into these rumors, which were gaining in circulation, Miss Mitchell put off alone one day in her car and traveled to Jonesboro. Stopping at a filling station, like any good tourist, she inquired of the attendant as to the whereabouts of Tara. Would he direct her to the former old house? He would, with pride! and did—in the polite and hospitable manner native to Georgians.

Being shown a road, Miss Mitchell followed it some five miles into the deep country and came upon a very nice piece of architecture, done in the noblest period of Victoria, obviously in the eighties, but not at all like the rambling, ante-bellum, whitewashed brick structure Gerald O'Hara had built and called Tara, with its avenue of cedars and its hilltop eminence one quarter of a mile from the river. Wending her way back to the filling station and its attendant, Miss Mitchell began to pick at his Tara, in deft phrases such as come to no tongue but Miss Mitchell's.

Feeling he should speak up for the county, and sure that here was a tourist who in her heart really *wanted* to believe, he began to strive with her to help her believe. But she was a strange miss—conversion came hard for her; the more he strove, the deeper grew her doubts.

Miss Mitchell, meanwhile, was herself trying to show the young man that she felt sure the author of Gone With the Wind would rather that strangers not be told there was a Tara, since there wasn't and never had been.

Nothing would suffice, however, but that she play her last card—Miss Mitchell confessed her name, that she wrote the book, that she had herself made Tara and was sure she knew best what it would look like if there were one. Now what did he think of that?

What he thought made Miss Mitchell turn wan at the mouth and left her sunk in her seat—it was the old, old story. Even before he opened his mouth, she saw it written on his face: "Why, lady"—he was genial and polite to the end—"you're not big enough to write a book. That's a famous book—making a lot of money."

Reaching for the first thing that came to mind which would serve as identification, she was about to pass over to him an old savings account book which happened to be in her purse when, there on the first page, she saw accredited to her name the handsome balance of seven dollars. And he had said "a lot of money."

To this day Miss Mitchell would have been thought an imposter by one young defender of Tara had she not been able to produce somewhere from the car a copy of General Sherman's huge map of military operations in and around Jonesboro. Nobody would carry a map of its size but the author of Gone With the Wind.

She ran down four other such houses that day, underwent four similar experiences. After the fifth one, firmly letting in the clutch, Miss Mitchell fled the county of the Taras.

No one is more puzzled than Miss Mitchell that she should be made a mystery and the center of legends. For Margaret Mitchell is the most normal, balanced author you will likely ever see. She is not affected by stampedes. Awards, college degrees, recognition from distinguished societies throughout the nation are held out to her, but she has accepted none of them. Faced with the major temptations life has to offer—wealth, honors, international acclaim—she still retains her grip. The events of the past six months are like a tale from the Arabian Nights, but through it all she remains calmly at home, unflustered by the tide of public attention swirling at her from all sides. She likes to work without intrusion, play without interruption, to be herself and live casually in whatever manner she choses. She is a trained psychologist and knows in a scientific way what alterations sometimes happen in the personalities of those who are caught in a violent upheaval of circumstances. She fears that the intense glare of the spotlight beating down upon her, month after month, may eventually drive her into complete seclusion, in the hope of salvaging some remnant of her private life; she fears that she will lose touch with the world she loves because of this seclusion; she fears that people may think her hard and unappreciative and unsociable because of her enforced necessity of refusing the public demands upon her; she fears to be set apart, to lose the easy friendships she cherishes, to be put on an eminence from which she will not be permitted to descend.

And thus it is that she and her husband, Mr. John R. Marsh, advertising manager of the Georgia Power Company, continue to live in their five-room apartment in Atlanta just as they have always lived—with the comfort, simplicity, and modest good taste which comes natural to people of supreme common sense. They wear the sort of clothes they have always worn, eat the same food. Instead of the limousine with the foreign name they are reported to have bought, they ride in a modest coach of a type used by millions of normal everyday Americans.

Within the circle of her close friends, Miss Mitchell has long been known for the force of her conversation and for a type of humor which is wholly her own. It is utterly impossible to give the essence of this humor, which springs suddenly without the least hint of premeditation. There are no analogies to fall back on in describing it—there is nothing quite like it on the stage or in print, except the flashes of it in Gone With the Wind. And those who know her well will tell you that Margaret Mitchell herself is the principal key in answering the question heard on all sides: "What is the explanation of this book's power over readers and its record-breaking sale?" The force of her mind and the charge of her personal magnetism are so strong that they leap through the pages of her book to the reader, like the play of electricity between poles. The same excitement you get from those dialogues between Scarlett and Rhett Butler you will get from Miss Mitchell's private conversation. Her speech, however, is not excited, and is accompanied by none of the gestures of a nervous person.

Now all the foregoing, and a great deal more, is what has happened to Gone With the Wind and its author. To repeat, it "does something" to readers and like the Ancient Mariner, they wander through the streets, through drawing rooms, places of business, ready to lay a hand on any who will listen. The time has come when, by the look of a man's eye, you can tell how recently this book has been at him.

All of which needs explaining, for in the furor for both book and its creator is the presence of something strange, something headlong and desperate which was missing in the rage for other books of recent times.

Could the answer be Gone With the Wind itself, and the exceptional force of Miss Mitchell's personality which like a galvanic charge electrifies the drama of the story?

Certainly no American novel has ever before compressed within its pages such a wide range of feelings. The four principal characters of the story—Scarlett, Rhett, Melanie, Ashley—run the whole scale of human emotions, birth, love, marriage, death, the four great elemental experiences of life. And between these major emotions, these four characters together at some point in the drama subject the reader to all the other physical and spiritual pangs which rack mankind—hunger, jealousy, hate, greed, joy, loneliness, and on through to the last note of the emotional scale.

Because of the leanness, apparently of the modern novelist's imagination—perhaps because the over-refinements of modern civilization are sapping our vitality—readers have been taught to accept but one or two currents of feeling running through a story. Miss Mitchell overwhelms and sweeps the reader on in a multiplicity of emotional torrents unknown since the great days of novel writing.

And how does Miss Mitchell herself account for the phenomenal sale of Gone With the Wind? When asked the question, she parried it by asking us to answer it ourselves. We fell back on the word "genius," telling her there was no other way to explain the stupendous currents of thought and emotion which are driven under complete control through the book; no other way to explain its prescience, its intuition and the excitement it has imparted to an entire nation. We added that we thought she had been moved by impulses greater than she knew, and that like Joan of Arc—

But here Miss Mitchell stopped us with a smile. That incorruptible intelligence of hers will listen to no such stuff, for she does not feel at all that way about herself or her book. She regards Gone With the Wind as the product of hard labor and sweating, and its amazing success continues to be so mystifying to her that, in the words of Gerald O'Hara, she can attribute it only "to the mysterious kindness of God."

The Story Begins at a Luncheon Bridge in Atlanta

By Lois Dwight Cole

Lois Dwight Cole (Mrs. Allan Taylor) can aptly be described as the godmother of Gone With the Wind. *She learned of Margaret Mitchell's work on a novel while in charge of Macmillan's office in Atlanta. After being transferred to New York she kept in touch with her Atlanta friend and it was Miss Cole who urged Harold Latham to seek out Miss Mitchell when he went on his famous scouting trip to Atlanta. At the time Miss Cole wrote this twenty-fifth anniversary piece about* Gone With the Wind *and its author she was a senior editor at G. P. Putnam's Sons.*

The first time I met Margaret Mitchell was at a luncheon bridge, not long after I moved to Georgia to run the office end of the Atlanta branch of The Macmillan Company's trade department. In the flutter of hurried introductions, no names stayed in my mind and no individual stood out clearly. After luncheon, when we drew for bridge tables, I found my partner's name was Margaret Mitchell. She turned out to be a small, rather plump person with reddish brown hair, very blue eyes, and a few freckles across a slightly uptilted nose.

As the cards were dealt I asked, as one did, "Do you follow any particular conventions, partner?" Our opponents stared, and my partner said solemnly, "Conventions? I don't know any. I just lead from fright. What do you lead from?" "Necessity," I told her, at which she gave a sudden grin.

On the first hand our opponents bid four spades. My partner held six; I had two and two aces, and we set them five; whereupon we rose, solemnly if improperly, and shook hands across the table.

As there was more conversation than bridge, it was soon established that I was the Yankee who had come down to work for Macmillan (everyone knew but it was manners to ask) and that I had gone to Smith, where Miss Mitchell had been for a year. During refreshments she edged around to me and asked if I would come to supper the following Wednesday with her and her husband, John Marsh.

In those days the Marshes lived in a small, dilapidated, two-story apartment house known as "The Dump" on a narrow street once known as "Tightsqueeze" behind Peachtree Street at Tenth. To the delighted and never-ending shock of Atlanta there were two cards tacked to the front door. One said "Margaret Munnerlyn Mitchell" and the other "John R. Marsh." The apartment consisted of two, small square rooms and a tiny kitchen.

Over fried chicken and hot biscuits I discovered that evening that Peggy was one of the best conversationalists and storytellers one could find. Not that she monopolized the talk; she was, as she said, "a good ear," as genuinely interested in what other people had to say as she was skillful in luring them to talk.

Since "The Dump" was situated between the Macmillan office and the house where I boarded, I fell into the habit of stopping by after work once or twice a week for tea. Sometimes other friends would be there; sometimes Peggy and I would be alone and would happily compare opinions on books and people. There was a bay with tiny high windows in the living room and beneath it an old-fashioned sewing table that held a portable typewriter and stacks of paper.

Once, when I came in with a friend, Peggy, in shorts, blouse and eyeshade, was at the typewriter. She got up and threw a bath towel over the table. "Well, Peggy," said the friend, "how's the great American novel coming along?" "It stinks," Peggy said with a half-laugh, "and I don't know why I bother with it, but I've got to do something with my time." "When's it going to be done?" I asked. "Macmillan would love to see it," "At this rate it won't ever get done, and no one's going to want to see it."

It is difficult to put Peggy on paper, to convey her gaiety, her interest in and profound knowledge of people, her range of interests and reading, her devotion to her friends, and the verve and enchantment of her talk. Many Southerners are born storytellers, but Peggy told her tales with such fun and skill that a whole roomful would stay quiet all evening to listen to her.

During my years in Atlanta we saw a great deal of each other and became good friends. These were depression times, and sometimes, while our husbands were working late, we would have supper together. We both loathed sewing, and sewed badly; but it was easier to turn the collars on our husbands' shirts if we were discussing books, poetry, history, and people past and present.

Her friends knew, vaguely, that the book she was writing had something to do with the Civil War and Atlanta, for she would complain that the bound copies of the old newspapers in the basement of the Carnegie Library were so heavy she couldn't throw them around or hold them, and the only way she could read them was to lie on the floor and prop them on her stomach, which wore out her stomach.

When Macmillan closed the branch offices of its trade department, I was offered a place as associate editor in New York. In December, 1933, I wrote Margaret Mitchell a formal letter saying that Macmillan would like very much to see her novel, either when it was finished or in its present condition. She wrote me, just as formally, that the book was not finished, that she doubted if it ever would be, or be worth seeing—but that if she ever did bring herself to show it to a publisher, Macmillan would have first look. Aside from that, our correspondence was informal.

Then, in the spring of 1935, Harold Latham, the editor-in-chief of the Macmillan trade department, made his first scouting trip to the South. I wrote to Peggy and to Medora Field Perkerson, of the Atlanta *Journal,* asking them to do what they could to make his stay pleasant and turn up manuscripts. I told Mr. Latham about Peggy's book—that no one had read it except her husband John, but that if she wrote as she talked it would be a honey.

In Atlanta, Peggy and Medora took Mr. Latham to lunch, for a drive, and to a Georgia Writers' Club tea at Rich's Department Store. When he reached Charleston [New Orleans], he wrote to me thanking me for what my friends had done for him and going on to say that Mrs. Marsh had delivered to him the rough draft of an incomplete manuscript that she felt was in need of rewriting. She wished to know if it was worth working on more. The manuscript was so large he could not carry it with him across the country. He was sending it to me to read, so I could talk with him about it when he returned to New York.

Some eight months later Peggy wrote me telling how and why she had given him the manuscript. I had revealed to a mutual friend, who was being catty about Peggy's never-finished novel, that she had been given a contract. This I had confessed to Peggy, since she wished no one to know until the revision was finished. She wrote that she understood, adding that friends and acquaintances had kept her from finishing the book long ago. She told how she had seen one friend "through three psychiatrists and a couple of neurologists, a divorce and a happy new marriage." Later, at a party, when the book was mentioned, the happy bride had said, "Book, pooh! Peggy will never finish it. She's too fond of playing."

Peggy went on: "I've gone through deaths and handled funerals and the very people who call on me for these things are the very ones who say, in all affection, 'Isn't it a shame that somebody with a mind like Peggy's hasn't any ambition?' It never made me especially mad—until the last straw came. After all, when you give your friends something, be it money, love, time, encouragement, work, you either give it as a free gift, with no after remarks, or you don't give it at all. And, having given, I had no particular regrets. But this very same situation was what really made me turn over the manuscript to Mr. Latham. He'd asked for it, and I'd felt very flattered that he even considered me. But I'd refused, knowing in what poor shape the thing was. And that day he was here, I'd called up various and sundry hopeful young authors and would-be authors and jackassed them (that is a friend's phrase) about in the car and gotten them to the tea where they could actually meet a live publisher in the flesh.

"One of them was a child who had nearly driven me crazy about her book. I'd no more than get settled at my own work than here she was, bellowing that she couldn't write love scenes and couldn't I write them for her? Or she was on the phone picking my brains for historical facts that had taken me weeks to run down. As twilight eve was drawing on and I was riding her and some of her adoring girl friends home from the tea, somebody asked me when I expected to get my book finished and why hadn't I given it to Mr. Latham.

"Then this child cried, 'Why, are you writing a book, Peggy? How strange you've never said anything about it. Why didn't you give it to Mr. Latham?' I said I hadn't because it was so lousy I was ashamed of it. To which she remarked— and did not mean it cattily—'Well, I daresay. Really, I wouldn't take you for the type who would write a successful book. You know you don't take life seriously enough to be a novelist. And you've never even had it refused by a publisher? How strange! *I've* been refused by the very best publishers. But my book is grand. Everybody says it'll win the Pulitzer Prize. But, Peggy, I think you are wasting your time trying. You really aren't the type.'

"Well, suddenly, I got so mad that I began to laugh, and I had to stop the car because I laughed so hard. And that confirmed their opinion of my lack of seriousness. And when I got home I was so mad still that I grabbed up what manuscript I could lay hands on, forgetting entirely that I hadn't included the envelopes that were under the bed or the ones in the pot-and-pan closet, and I posted down to the hotel and caught Mr. Latham just as he was about to catch the train. My idea was that at least I could brag that I had been refused by the very best publisher. And no sooner had I done this and Mr. L. was out of town than I was appalled both by my temper and by my acting on impulse and by my giving him the stuff when it was in such sloppy shape and minus so many chapters."

The manuscript arrived, and I spent evenings reading it, breaking off late and reluctantly. It was, physically, one of the worst manuscripts I have ever seen. There was no first chapter (Peggy had tried six or seven and liked none), but Chapter Two was neatly typed on white paper. So was Chapter Three. Then came pages and pages of yellow paper, written over in pencil, and often three or four different versions of one scene. Then came more final chapters, then some would be missing entirely. There were two entirely different accounts of Frank's death. The last chapter was in final form, for that, she told me later, was written first. (When Peggy was on the staff of The Atlanta *Journal* magazine, she was famous for writing her stories backward, starting with the last paragraph and working forward.) In spite of the difficulties of reading the manuscript, I knew it was one of the most fascinating novels of all time.

Mr. Latham read it on his return, and so did Professor Charles Everett of Columbia, who occasionally advised us about novels. Our enthusiasm carried the Editorial Council, and Macmillan offered Peggy a contract. Here is how she received my wire.

"Lois, your telegram just came and I am overwhelmed! It came at a grand time for I was just limping home from Grady hospital to lick my wounds, having been scragged by a young intern whom *I* have scragged several times in the course of Bessie's illness. (Bessie was her cook.) Do you really mean they like it?

You wouldn't fox an old friend, would you? I don't see how anyone made heads or tails of it. I am very twittery about your wire and, having phoned John and read it to him, he said, 'You'd better sit down quietly so you'll have less distance to fall when the realization comes over you that someone besides me likes the damn thing.' Well, John was right. I think I had better sit down quietly. I shall fall down in another minute. You are a lamb to send me such a swell telegram and I shall frame it."

In the manuscript the name of the heroine was Pansy, and the title was "Tomorrow Is Another Day." Macmillan asked Peggy to change the heroine's name and the title, for there were thirteen books in print with titles beginning "Tomorrow. . . ." She offered "Scarlett" for "Pansy" and sent me a list of twenty-two possible titles. Number 14 was starred. It was "Gone With the Wind," with the source and a penciled note saying, "I'll agree to any one of these you like, but I like this the best." So did we.

Peggy Mitchell never felt that her book deserved all the praise it received, and never, or for a long time, had any confidence it would sell. "I wrote it for fun, for my own amusement. If enough people want to spend $3 so that Macmillan won't lose the money they've paid me, that will be fine."

When she saw an advance copy of our spring announcement list, she wrote:

"Lois, I was overwhelmed when I saw the catalogue, my position in it and my distinguished company. And seeing the opus listed as one of 'four great novels' got me into a proper state. I know it's all due to you, and I'm torn between gratitude and a sense of guilt that I certainly shouldn't be rubbing shoulders with Charles Morgan and Phyllis Bentley. Good God, this book isn't good enough to be there. I know you know your business—but I hope you haven't made an error in judgment because of a kind and loving heart."

Even after the book was taken by the Book-of-the-Month Club and sold to David Selznick for the highest price ever paid up to that time for an unpublished first novel, she still had no faith it would sell.

One of the best things about Margaret Mitchell was that to her true friends she never changed. She resented the multitudinous attempts to invade her privacy, to make use of her, and she was annoyed by the myths circulated about her and by sudden claims of hitherto nonexistent friendship. But to her friends she was always the Peggy we had known when she lived in "The Dump" and covered the stacks of manuscript with a bath towel.

Two years after publication of "G.W.T.W.," when my son was born, Peggy came north to see him since she was his godmother. One afternoon during that visit I was giving her another fight talk about writing another book—anyone who had given so many people so much pleasure had a duty, etc. Peggy said she probably would some day, when the fan mail had fallen off (she answered every letter and thanked every reviewer) and the foreign editions were all published and if her family and friends stayed well.

Then a faraway look came into her blue eyes. "You know, I always liked the book I wrote before 'Gone With the Wind' better." I took a firm clutch on the arm of the sofa and said as calmly as I could. "How nice. And where is the manuscript now?" "Oh, I burned it up when it was finished. I just wrote it for fun. I never thought of having it published."

People on the Home Front: Margaret Mitchell

By Sergeant H. N. Oliphant

One of Margaret Mitchell's many correspondents in the Armed Services was an old friend, Leodel Coleman, a Statesboro, Georgia, newspaperman who had become a Combat Correspondent in the Marine Corps. In a long letter of January 4, 1944 she wrote him about wartime shortages on the home front:

There are all types of shortages, few of them so serious as to cause actual suffering (except coal and oil heating). Most of them simply cause dismay and force some rearrangements in living. For instance you might think the rubber shortage would affect civilians mainly in the matter of automobile tires. But a recent survey showed that anguished mammas and pappas cried out that their main need was rubber pants for junior. Of course people got along since the beginning of the world without rubber baby pants and they can get along without them now, but a new technique in baby-holding (or an old one) must be developed.*

It was to Coleman she sent scarce peanuts and a hard-to-find harmonica at Christmas. And to him she sent the parcel of plug tobacco for distribution among his fellow Marines that is mentioned in this story by Sergeant H. N. Oliphant of Yank.

Atlanta, Ga.—Reporting for chapel on Guadalcanal one Sunday morning early in 1943, an Army chaplain was elated to find a full house, the biggest GI congregation he had faced in nearly two years' service. "I am deeply moved to note," he said, "that the heavenly light of true religion has at long last found this outfit."

Unhappily, as the disillusioned chaplain discovered in the near-stampede to the bamboo altar which took place immediately after his final prayer, "heavenly light" had nothing to do with it. It was chewin' tobacco. It seems some zealous civilian back in the States, worried over what was happening to quid-

---

*Editor's Note: Margaret Mitchell to Leodel Coleman, TLS, January 4, 1944. Georgia Southern College Library, Statesboro, Ga.

loving GIs who couldn't get anything stronger than Juicy Fruit in Red Cross packages, had dispatched a big box of scrap and assorted plug to the chaplain's assistant. This T-5, knowing which side his duty-bread was buttered on, had explained to the boys that all they had to do to get an honest chew was to sweat out a few hymns and prayers and then file piously to the altar.

The zealous civilian who authored the idea of sending GIs honest chewing tobacco is a half-pint-sized, blue-eyed female from Dixie named Margaret Mitchell. Miss Mitchell also authored, a few years back, that Civil War novel called "Gone With the Wind" and more familiarly known as GWTW, a long, rambling book about a dame named Scarlett O'Hara and a gent named Clark Gable—or maybe it was Rhett Butler.

According to Miss Mitchell, the novel's ending, which leaves the fate of the hero and heroine somewhat unsettled, may have been a happy inspiration in the literary sense, but its results in real life, especially her own, have been anything but happy. She has received millions of letters—many thousands from GIs, she says—and in almost every one of them there is either an earnest plea or a downright demand that she disclose what finally happened to Rhett and Scarlett. These demands haven't been confined to letters. One day not long ago when she was window-shopping on Atlanta's famous Peachtree Street, a somewhat wild-looking matron, recognizing her, rushed up and gave Miss Mitchell a kind of half nelson treatment, threatening her with bodily damage if she didn't reveal the ultimate fate of the star-crossed lovers. Regrettably, Miss Mitchell is unable to satisfy either her restrained correspondents or her would-be public assailants on this issue simply because she herself doesn't exactly know what finally happened to her on-again, off-again pair.

"For all I know," she says, her Irish eyes sparkling slyly as she mouths the words in an accent that combines the best features of cotton fields, magnolias in bloom and the last four bars of "Swanee River," "Rhett may have found someone else who was less—difficult. Why, honey, just think of it, out of this hypothetical union may have come a strapping fellow who grew up to be a dashing second lieutenant."

Another thing that GIs and other GWTW fans are always writing Miss Mitchell about is her next book. When is it coming out and what will the story be like? Miss Mitchell can't answer that one, either.

"I am writing every chance I get," she says, "but for the last four years or so I am afraid that hasn't been very often. We've been too busy with the Red Cross and Home Defense."

Margaret, who is known as Peggy to practically everybody in Atlanta's super-swank Piedmont Driving Club, has no illusions about the importance of her contribution to the late war effort.

"Actually, my efforts have consisted only of sewing thousands of hospital gowns, putting suitable patches on the behinds of GI trousers and, alas, playing dummy for the Home Defense fire-and-rescue department. In this last job I seemed invariably to be chosen for the practice sessions because of my four-foot-eleven height. I was tossed unceremoniously out of two-story windows, grabbed in the most monstrous places and thrown about as if I had been an acrobat's stooge. It was positively frightful."

Peggy is a little concerned over the accumulative effect of that striking phenomenon of the second World War, the pin-up. "Why, my goodness, honey," she says, "after looking at all those pictures of seraphic and perspirationless babes for so long in the privacy of a foxhole, what is a poor doughfoot going to do when he comes home and discovers that American women are, after all, biological and given, under stress, to shiny noses?"

The bulk of Peggy's GI mail in the past four years has been along the same lines as the mail she got in the late 1930s, except that soldiers, she finds, are, if anything, more curious than civilians about her personal life.

"Are you really like Scarlett?" one moonstruck Infantryman in Italy wrote, adding provocatively, "If you are, I think I know how you could be tamed. Please answer by return mail."

Peggy, as a matter of fact, is a lot like Scarlett in that she is extraordinarily energetic, intelligent, witty, attractive and—practical. But there the similarity ends. Peggy, unlike her mercurial and green-eyed heroine, is a home-loving, kind-hearted person and not by anybody's standards can she be tagged a fickle adventuress, or as "changeable," as one critic described Scarlett, "as a baby's underwear."

Miss Mitchell, it turns out, is strictly an enlisted-man's girl, having married a sergeant from the last war. Her husband is the man, incidentally, who is most responsible for The Book, which, when last heard from, was well over the 3,500,000 mark in sales. Some years ago Miss Mitchell was laid up with an auto-crash injury that refused to heal. Day in and day out, her husband, ex-Sgt. John R. Marsh, had to traipse to the public library, gather up an armful of books ("I have always been an omnivorous reader," Miss Mitchell says) and carry them home. After a couple of years of this routine, John got sick of the whole thing and, in a moment of desperation, said, "For God's sake, Peggy, can't you write a book instead of reading thousands of them?" Something clicked, and the result was "Gone With the Wind."

Peggy's present-day, GI fans, she says, are just as susceptible to the old rumors about her as were the readers of the first edition. One rumor has it that Peggy was married at the scarcely nubile age of 6. This, she says emphatically, is not true. "When I sidled to the alter," she continues, "I was in all respects a woman—and I sidled." Another persistent rumor that won't be laid is that she is going blind. Recently, she got a telegram from a solicitous GI who said, "Hear you're going blind stop wire me at once if there is anything I can do." Peggy answered, "Nothing you can do stop read your wire without a struggle." There is one fairly well-known story about her, however, that is true. She was ten years old before she knew that Robert E. Lee had surrendered to Grant. Up to that time she had always believed that the Confederacy had won the war. "It was a crushing blow," she says.

On the question of sectional differences, Peggy is liberal, reasonably impartial and optimistic. She feels that the collection of so many men from so many parts of the country into the Army and Navy has rubbed out a lot of the old vexatious, Rebel-Yankee stuff. She also feels that, due in part to an unfortunate Northern press, the South of today is not properly understood by many Northerners. "The spirit of liberalism has taken deep root down here," she says. "One symptom is our newspapers. Where can you find two more fair and forward-looking newspapers than the Atlanta *Constitution* and *Journal?*"

The climax of Peggy's career probably occurred when GWTW copped the Pulitzer Prize for the best novel of 1936. But the climax of her popularity was certainly reached during the run of the motion picture, which, incidentally, is still playing, or was until recently, in London.

Despite nearly ten years of almost suffocating publicity, enough to wreck most public figures, Peggy is still the modest, dynamic lady she was before The Book. In fact, she insists that she never really achieved fame until last summer when Bill Mauldin drew a cartoon in which a dirty soldier is shown holding a copy of GWTW with a neat shrapnel-hole through its center. The soldier is writing a letter addressed to "Dear Miss Mitchell."

"All the kids know me now," she says.

Little Woman, Big Book: The Mysterious Margaret Mitchell

By Ralph McGill

Ralph McGill came on the Atlanta newspaper scene after Margaret Mitchell had left her job on the Journal, *but, of course, he knew her. McGill moved from sportswriter to editor and eventually became one of the South's finest newspapermen and, in the eyes of many, Atlanta's leading citizen of the years after World War II.*

The article McGill wrote for Show *in 1962 is based on his own knowledge of Margaret Mitchell's years of fame. Information about her in her earlier years came from fellow newsmen and, especially, from notes supplied by Norman Berg.*

Berg was the young man in charge of Macmillan's office in Atlanta during the months Gone With the Wind *was being readied for publication. He later declared that he held the mother's hand during her pregnancy with the big book.*

The McGill-Berg combination was a great one. Berg knew certain facts better than just about anyone else in Atlanta and McGill could write better than just about anyone else in Atlanta.

"Peggy's book is coming out on June 30th," said the book buyer at Davison's, "and the publisher is allowing us to release it a bit earlier; so we are having a luncheon for some of her friends. . . ." (It was 1936.)

At lunch that day Peggy was excited; she had been for months. She was keyed to laughter and a sort of role Don Marquis's cockroach Archy would describe as *toujours gai.* She was weary from weeks of reading galley proofs with her husband. If Macmillan was going to publish the novel, then, by damn, there would be no errors in it.

There were friends around the table, and some of them were a bit resentful because she hadn't told them she was writing a novel. "Why *didn't* you tell us, Peggy? We'll never forgive you."

"Me? Tell secrets?" she replied, and laughter went about the table. Anything and everything was gay and bright that day because Peggy was there and her book was ready. There were copies of it on the table, side by side with the flowers—big fat books with dark yellow dust jackets, with an Old South scene on them, and the large letters GONE WITH THE WIND at the top.

"Any news from the publishers about the advance?" asked the man to the right of Peggy, while the eager gabble of conversation went on. ". . .Honestly, you'd think she would have told *some*one. . . ."

"They're pleased," she said. "Pleased. I don't know exactly what that means. I've read about first novels. If you sell 2,500 copies it's average. I have hopes this one may go at leat 5,000 copies." She paused and her face lighted up. "If all the Southern lending libraries buy a couple of copies," she said, grinning, "it may go 10,000. Wouldn't that be grand?"

It was an innocent luncheon, an innocent author and guests. In two months, "Gone With the Wind" was a runaway best seller. The Book-of-the-Month Club took it for July. Macmillan added 50,000 copies to a planned first edition of 10,000. In a little more than three months, it sold over 500,000 copies.

Those of us who gathered for lunch that day to celebrate Peggy's novel did not know it, but that was the last time we'd ever see the complex little woman of many paradoxes whom we knew so well. "Gone With the Wind" was to fall in on her. The weight of success became heavier. She made a gallant fight to remain Peggy Mitchell. She and her husband kept the same apartment, the same cat and servant. They held fast to the old friends and rather wistfully sought to retain the simple routines. But it was not to be. A new image grew of Peggy Mitchell. Her health and that of her husband became a problem. Success did not spoil her, but it changed her life.

"Gone With the Wind" was issued against the background of a savage depression. It was a time in which the nation was surfeited with the corrosive sorrows, frustrations and the griefs produced by economic defeat. But it also was a time of resolution in the face of disaster and need.

The world was as badly off. There were civil wars and rebellions. There was the sound of collapsing thrones; the creaking of others could be heard. Mussolini and Hitler were making the trains run on time and preaching a super race and a master philosophy. There was something in "Gone With the Wind" for all who read it, and European editions, both pirated and legitimate, soon were appearing. Tough and secular Scarlett O'Hara, endlessly resourceful; compassionate, gentle Melanie; and Rhett Butler, the gallant blackmarket operator of 1861–65 and the Reconstruction, who had turned to "the cause" in its death struggle; all these, and others, were akin to persons everywhere in the sick and hurt world of the 1930's. Letters were to come from Poland and Spain saying "We have lived the things which you have written."

The book kept selling. In mid-1961, Macmillan announced that more than 10,000,000 copies had been sold, not counting paperback or pirated editions. "Gone With the Wind" had been printed in twenty-five languages. These included Chinese, Japanese, Czech, the Scandinavian languages, Arabic, Slovak, Polish and, of course the less exotic languages of the world. Thirty foreign countries have accounted for sales of almost 5,000,000. (English-language editions have sold more than 5,000,000.) A number of countries pirated editions.

Peggy Mitchell, daughter of a lawyer, fought these with some success, winning royalties in Holland, Chile, Yugoslavia and Japan. In time she developed a grudging admiration for their brazen knavery. "The bastards always send me copies of their illegal editions," she said. "Usually, there is a letter telling me how much they liked the book."

Years ago, a critic who didn't care for the Mitchell writing style and who thought the plot commonplace, confessed to having been overwhelmed and silenced by the huge success and perpetual momentum of the book. " 'Gone With the Wind' " said the critic, "is not a book, but a phenomenon."

It is both book and phenomenon. It is no exaggeration to say that if all the stories and articles on Margaret Mitchell and the book (factual, fantastic and false) were published, they would make half a dozen or more volumes as thick as the novel itself. That deluge of interest and curiosity in her, and it has never halted, is eloquent evidence of the book's healthy longevity. It is a geriatric literary curiosity, a veritable Methuselah insofar as life is concerned.

The young woman who wrote it has been dead since 11:59 A.M., August 16, 1949. She died in Atlanta's Grady Hospital, to which she had been taken five evenings before after having been struck down on Peachtree Street, just a few blocks from her home, by a speeding automobile driven by Hugh D. Gravitt, aged twenty-nine, an off-duty taxi driver in a hurry. Margaret Mitchell Marsh and her husband were crossing the street to attend a neighborhood movie. Gravitt later was tried and convicted on a charge of involuntary manslaughter and sentenced to twelve to eighteen months imprisonment.

Margaret Michell was born on November 8, 1900. Her father was Eugene Mitchell, a highly competent and esteemed attorney. Two years after the birth of his daughter, who was christened Margaret Munnerlyn Mitchell, he purchased a 12-room, two story Victorian house near the corner of Jackson Street and Highland Avenue. It was here she spent her childhood; it was in this house she began to "write" impressions of her childhood. It was here, also, that she was interested enough to sit quietly in a corner and listen to the conversations of old lawyers and guests, men and women, who had lived through, or been soldiers in, the Civil War. She developed, or had, a retentive memory, and she unquestionably had an instinctive ear for colorful speech.

Her brother, Stephens Mitchell, has said of those young days on Jackson Street that his sister was a very much alive and energetic girl. She put down thoughts in writing. She rode a bicycle, climbed trees, roller skated, played baseball, participated in the mudball battles and ran foot races with the boys. She and brother Stephens built a tree-house. She remembered how they lifted up kittens in a basket. She and he took turns riding a pony named Nellie. Later, with father's permission, they swapped the pony for a horse.

The horse introduces an element which some psychologists find of interest. Are some persons "accident prone"? Whether they are or not, injuries were influential in Margaret Mitchell's life. One led her to make the decision to settle down and write a novel. Another accident brought her to Grady Hospital and five days of coma and delirium before death came for her. When she was eleven years old, her horse fell, pinning Margaret beneath. Her left leg was severely injured; her face was cut; a tooth was chipped. But she liked horseback riding and stubbornly continued on other horses.

In 1911, when Margaret was eleven, her father built a house on Peachtree Street. (It was this house, the center of what was a happy growing-up with no Freudian feeling of being unloved, that the complex woman of many paradoxes would direct, in some of her last instructions, be torn down.) There she was to grow through her teens to womanhood. She wrote plays which were acted out, with a community cast, in the living room.

In 1918, she was graduated from Washington Seminary, a school for young ladies of the gentility, and that fall went to Smith College. Friends often have wondered what Peggy Mitchell might have become, or done, had she stayed on four years at Northampton. But the death of her mother caused her father to suggest that she return home and become the head of the house. Her father wished her to become a proper Southern lady, and she herself was drawn toward this image.

It was in these years that the paradox of Margaret, or Peggy, Mitchell began to show. Perhaps it had been apparent all along in the life of this happy, enormously energetic, ebullient, tomboy-lady-girl. In 1920, the contradictions were plain to observing friends. But paradox merely added to her charm. She was very much the unreconstructed Southerner, and was to die unreconstructed. She had almost a reverence for the Old South traditions and legends, though sometimes, to be sure, she mocked at them. But she also was a rebel.

Peggy Mitchell was considerably influenced by Frances Newman. This Old South lady was the first Deep South literary feminist and rebel. She was twelve years older than Peggy and also a success. "The Hard-Boiled Virgin" was a shocker to proper ladies and gentlemen. Even so, Frances Newman, for all her rebellion, was "Old South," and believed that young Southern ladies from the right side of the tracks could do no wrong in the company of young Southern gentlemen from the right side of the tracks. Looking back at those years, it is possible to say, and believe, that Peggy Mitchell and Frances Newman saw no contradiction in that attitude.

Scarlett O'Hara emphatically was not an autobiographical character. But Peggy Mitchell was a part of Scarlett. She was harum-scarum and rebellious, but intensely feminist. She liked parties; she enjoyed hearing and telling bawdy stories; she was the natural life of any gathering of friends. There was nothing studied about her joy or verve. She was right out of the Southern Scott Fitzgerald era. She was a John Held girl. If, as Atlanta folklore has it, she went to a dance with small jingle-bells on her garters, everyone would laugh and say, "Isn't that just like Peggy?" It was the time of flasks and corn liquor, of a joyous freedom from the old Calvinist restraint. *"Toujours gai, toujours gai,"* as Archy would say.

There was the second accident in 1920; another horse fell with Peggy. She suffered injuries which were to trouble her the rest of her life.

In 1922 a big love came. There had been an earlier sentiment, but no one really knew the truth of it. A young man was killed in France with a picture of Peggy in his wallet and heart. However, they both were young, and if there was an engagement it was tenuous. But in 1922 she and a merry young man, Berrien K. Upshaw, were married. A friend of Upshaw's, John Marsh, was at the wedding. Marsh was a quiet man, and had never told his friend Upshaw, or the blue-eyed Peggy, that he, too, had been smitten.

The newlyweds needed more income. Peggy had a friend who was quitting a job on the Sunday Magazine section of the Atlanta *Journal;* she talked herself into the job; the salary was $25 per week.* She weighed then about ninety pounds, wore a beret and looked like a little girl playing at being grown-up.

Peggy loved the work. Her energy exploded. She climbed out on window-washers' platforms, had herself let down in a sling from the top of a seventeen-story building, rode elephants at the zoo. She interviewed Rudolph Valentino; she had a photographer snap the Great Lover lifting her in through a window.

Margaret Mitchell was a scrupulous and tireless correspondent, and it is from her letters as much as any other source that we learn of her remarkable character. In her letters to Paul Jordan-Smith, a West Coast critic, Peggy reveals wit, sensitivity, spontaneity and an irrepressible love of life, tempered by her sense of responsibility to the beloved literary behemoth her book had become. . . .

Atlanta, Ga.
May 27, 1936

My dear Mr. Jordan-Smith:

I am Margaret Mitchell, the author of "Gone With the Wind" which the Macmillan Company is bringing out at the end of June. Mr. Latham and the Atlanta branch of Macmillan's told me of the kind things you had said about my book and I took the liberty of autographing a copy for you, which I hope you have now received.

I could not let the book alone tell you how grateful I am to you for your praise and I had to write you this letter. When Mr. Latham was in Atlanta a while back I was talking with him about the probable reception my book would have in the South and at the hands of Southerners. I told him that I was a little frightened because, while I had written nothing that was not true, nothing that I could not prove and much that I had heard, as a child, from eye witnesses of that era, I feared some of it would not set well upon Southerners. I suppose Southerners have been lambasted so often and so hard, in print, that they have become unduly sensitive. With some types of Southerners, nothing pleases them about the South, no matter how laudatory or how well intentioned. . . .

Then Mr. Latham spoke of you and said that you were from Tennessee and that you had not denounced me as a traitor to my section and that you had liked the book. I was happy enough to stop the car and embrace him violently, right in the shadow of Stone Mountain. Then sometime later Mr. Berg, at the Macmillan

---

*Editor's Note: This is a mis-statement. Upshaw had left the Mitchell household before his wife was hired by the *Journal* in December 1922.

office here, told me of other exciting things you had said and when he came to the part about you comparing me with Mary Johnston, I had to go home and take a luminal and lie down with a cold towel on my head.

Mary Johnston was a school mate of my mother's and before I could read, I had her books read to me. Mother was strong minded but she never failed to weep over "The Long Roll" and "Cease Firing," and I always bellowed, too, but insisted on her not skipping sad parts. . . . While in the process of checking the part of my book about the campaign from the Tennessee line to Atlanta, I was very bothered about the weather during the fighting. . . . But I didn't want to trust my memory on such matters so I began trying to find out about the weather, for like as not, if I didn't get it right, seven hundred old vets would rise up out of Soldier's Homes and denounce me.

So I reread Generals Hood, Johnston and Sherman and several other reference books but got little satisfaction. Then I remembered "Cease Firing," which I had not read in many years. I knew it to be the best documented novel ever written so I consulted it to see about the weather. And unfortunately I became so engrossed in the story that I read on through till the tragic end. And when I had finished, I found that I couldn't possibly write anything on my own book. I felt so childish and presumptuous for even trying to write about that period when she had done it so beautifully, so powerfully—better than anyone can ever do it, no matter how hard they try. It was weeks and weeks before I could go back to work and then I went back pretty humble. Her book was so marvelous. . . . So, you can see why your comparison pleased me. . . .

Mr. Berg said that you had said my characters were real and how happy I was to hear that from a born Tennessean! For I know they are different from the usual Civil War characters. They aren't lavender-and-lace moonlight-on-the-magnolias people. But, as I recall from childhood, the survivors of that era were remarkably tough. I mean tough in the old sense of the word, not the slang meaning. I figured out they had to be tough or they'd never have survived. I'm sure, if you are Southern born, you must have seen many of the old ladies who had lived through that era who could scare the liver and lights out of you with one word and blast your vitals with a look. They owned their negroes still and their children and their contemporaries' children, too. And they were the bossiest, hard boiledest bunch of old ladies I ever saw. And they could be so plain spoken, upon occasion, that they made the brashest flapper blush. But they never got to be too old to be attractive to the gentlemen. . . . I felt certain that people who were like that in old age couldn't have been completely Thomas Nelson Page in their youths. And I am very glad that you liked them.

I have inflicted an awful long letter on you when I could have merely said "thank you." But your words made me far too happy to let it go at that.

Atlanta, Georgia
May 5, 1942

Dear Mr. Jordan-Smith:

Since 1936 I have been called upon to do many things—so many, in fact, that I have become like Alice's Queen and am able to deliver six impossible things before breakfast. Yesterday I had a new experience and I only wish all experiences could be equally happy. I attended Elizabeth Babcock's wedding, representing Mr. Paul Jordan-Smith. Going to a wedding in place of a male guest was new to me and I only hope I conducted myself in a manner that you would approve. . . .

There was a large bowl of punch and no one was pouring, so, as your representative, I presided at the bowl. (Honesty forces me to state that I would have presided anyway, for the sight of a tea tray or a punch bowl acts on me like a fire alarm on an old fire horse. Being the oldest girl in the family connection, I was brought up to such duties and can never restrain myself in the presence of an inactive punch ladle.)

I think it was Chatham Artillery punch, so I took only half a cup. Chatham Artillery punch is the lethal weapon with which the Chatham Artillery, of Savannah, Georgia, won the Civil War after the Surrender. The boys used to invite the outfits of their former enemies, such as the Hartford Rifles and the Pennsylvania Greys, to Savannah and feed them this innocuous concoction and lay them out in windrows before twelve o'clock.

I have done no writing since "Gone With the Wind" was published and do not know when I will have the opportunity to write again, much as I would like to. You know a great deal about what happens to people who write successful books, how the world crowds in, innumerable business details which come up, *et cetera*. Then, living so close to Hollywood, I know you realize that anything about the movies gets people into frenzies, and during the years before the release of the film of "Gone With the Wind" I hardly drew a free breath. I didn't have a thing to do with the film and wouldn't even go to Hollywood but, in spite of that, I was pulled and hauled for several years. . . . For one reason I am sorry I didn't get to Hollywood. I would have met you and that would have been fun. Should you ever come East, please stop in Atlanta and see us. My husband and I would like to really know you. I shall never forget your kindness to "Gone With the Wind" when it was freshly hatched and I would like to say "thank you" in person some day.

Old-timers recall that Peggy would come from the magazine offices to the city room to use the big dictionary which was on a stand by the city desk. (She was a stickler about spelling and the use of words.) There are two stories. One is that she was so tiny she stood on tiptoe to look up a word; this caused the short skirts of that time to lift and two or three inches of white skin would show above her stocking, to the great distraction of the city room copyreaders and rewrite men. The other is that Peggy would say, "I think I'll go in and give the middle-aged men a thrill."

In 1924, she and Upshaw were divorced. It had been a sad mistake. On July 4, 1925, a date deliberately selected as symbolic of independence, she and John

R. Marsh, a young Kentuckian and a newspaperman, who had been present at the first wedding, were married. They were not really independent. John had a lot of medical debts, the inheritance of an earlier illness. But Peggy Mitchell, for all her *toujours gai* qualities, had a never-failing ability to discipline herself.

"John and I are poor so we will live poor as hell until we get out of debt," she said.

They moved into a small, shabby apartment which Peggy soon made bright. They called it "The Dump."

Friends thought this marriage to solemn, slow-talking, serious John Marsh would not last. It did. Perhaps modern psychologists would say he provided the father image. Whatever it was, they got along. There were parties. "The Dump" was a favorite gathering place. But they got out of debt.

The injured leg and ankle were a bother. In 1926 John had a better job and more money, in the advertising department of the Georgia Power Company. Peggy, heeding a doctor, quit work. For a time she was on crutches. She began to write; there was nothing systematic about it; nor was it her first writing. This was a mysterious and complex little woman who never, at any time or to anyone, fully revealed herself, not even to John Marsh. She was never the marble statue of the symbolic Confederate woman. She always was flesh and blood. But she could keep her counsel and be as reticent as ice.

Once she was to say, in irritation at all the queries about whether she would write a sequel to "Gone With the Wind," "I have written a lot of novels."

That she did write one other is known. It was based on the establishment of an officers training station, Camp Gordon, on the outskirts of Atlanta, at the outset of the First World War. There came to Camp Gordon men from all over the nation. They entered into the social life of Atlanta. They brought cultures, ideas and attitudes. They fell in love and married Atlanta girls. Peggy destroyed this novel.

"Gone With the Wind" was not germinated until Peggy Mitchell sat down to write it. She had, of course, thought for years of the historical background of that period, but never in connection with writing a book. Nor had she really "thought" of the background. She had been raised on it, or absorbed it. In 1926, having quit her job because of the old injury, she determined to write a novel. She sensibly used what she knew.

She did not know—and therefore did not follow—any technique. The last chapter was written first. From then on she wrote whatever chapter was uppermost in her mind. As each was written, it was placed in a separate, labeled envelope, along with any rewrites she had made. Some chapters were rewritten many times. This did not, however, involve any change of plot, characterization or scene. The alterations were aimed at a better telling of the story. By 1929 the novel was practically completed. There are interviews in which Peggy Mitchell says she spent ten years on the book; this includes the background years. The slow writing of it took a little more than three years. For the next three years the novel remained almost untouched. It had not been "polished."

Only a few friends knew she had been working on a novel. One of these was Lois Cole, who had been in the Atlanta office of the Macmillan Company. In 1932, Miss Cole was transferred to the New York office. In the spring of 1935, Harold S. Latham, trade editor and vice president of Macmillan, set out on a trip to the larger cities of the South and West in search of manuscripts. Miss Cole wrote her friend Peggy, urging that she show Latham the manuscript. She wrote also to a mutual friend, Medora Perkerson, assistant editor of the *Journal's* Sunday Magazine, and asked her to see that Latham saw Peggy. Peggy met the distinguished publisher. She drove him about to see the dogwood and the residential area. But, she said, she had no manuscript worth showing to him.

Late in the same afternoon John Marsh called home. He was the only person who had read the manuscript. Peggy related Latham's request. John persuaded her to let him have it so that a professional opinion might be had.

Peggy Mitchell put down the receiver and bundled all the many dusty envelopes, with their several versions of chapters, into a great package. The first chapter was not ready; she sat down at her typewriter and did a synopsis of what she had in mind. She then drove to Latham's hotel and called from the lobby. He came down to see a tiny woman sitting by a pile of envelopes which reached to her shoulder. He went to a nearby luggage shop and bought a large suitcase; the manuscript filled it. He was leaving for the West Coast. He read it—with growing excitement—on the way.

The rest is history. A contract was signed. A few weeks later, so the story goes, Peggy Mitchell opened a letter. Her eyes widened.

"Let me lie down," she said to her husband. "Here is is a check for $500."

He took it and looked.

"Move over," he said. "It's for $5,000."

The presses could not print pages fast enough. A unique publishing phenomenon had moved onstage.

On the night of August 11, 1949, Margaret Mitchell failed in a desperate attempt to dodge the speeding car.

A human being is a many-sided prism, reflecting many lights, but also changing inside itself. It is difficult, perhaps impossible, to know another human being—be it wife or husband, mother, father, son, daughter, friend or lover. No one will ever be able to pin down, or gather, all the complexities of life that were in Peggy Mitchell. Many persons have sought to understand or "know" her. This was the more difficult because there were two images of her—one before publication and the other after the immense and overwhelming success of the book.

The surprise of that success, the many silly and baseless rumors that someone else must have written the book, all helped to reveal one of Peggy Mitchell's deep and dominant traits. Not one of the merest handful of persons who knew she had written a book had seen it or had the faintest idea of what it was about. Candor compels one to say that the most loyal friend would not have believed that even by rubbing an Aladdin's lamp could she have written the book. She hid herself completely, inwardly, and in many things, from her best friends.

What was she like? It is perhaps easier to look into the soul and mind of a creative artist than of those who are not. An author, in a very real sense, is what he or she writes. So we turn to "Gone With the Wind." There is much bitterness in it, and violence, too. Those characters in it who love are never understood. Not only that, they are, with the exception of Rhett, weak in the eyes of Scarlett, the central character. Those who have tried to pick the locks of the armor of reticence and reserve with which Peggy Mitchell covered herself think often of two telling scenes in the novel. One is when Scarlett is foraging in the fields, hungry, weary, almost defeated. But she shakes a defiant fist against a hostile sky and cries out that she will never be hungry again. Was it hunger mere food would satisfy? The other scene is the death of Melanie. Ashley says, when his wife dies: "She is the only dream I ever had that lived and breathed and did not die in the face of reality." Once, in 1936, Peggy Mitchell suddenly and inexplicably broke into tears when a friend quoted that sentence. Nor did she explain why she wept. Was she never hungry again? Did she ever realize the dream? Was there ever fulfillment? There are no answers.

Her will was a simple thing. She, daughter of a lawyer, sat down one day and wrote her last will and testament. It began very simply and directly: "I want John, Steve Mitchell, and the Trust Company of Georgia to be the executor of my will. I want Bessie Jordan [her long-time Negro servant] and her daughter, Deon Berry, to have the house and lot at 446 Ripley Street, N.E.—which they now occupy. . . ."

This was her first concern. This was in the old tradition—Peggy Mitchell almost certainly would have been greatly disturbed by the 1954 U.S. Supreme Court decision, and those following, voiding segregation in education because of color. People, of course, change. Had she lived, she might, too, have developed new attitudes. But she was always the unreconstructed Southener, with a fierce pride in, and loyalty to, the old code that a Southern white person scrupulously "looked after" servants and decent colored persons in distress.

The will carefully disposed of all real and personal properties. Her husband inherited the copyrights. They were, in turn, left to her brother, Stephens, in John's will.

Sometime before her death she had exacted two promises. One was that the old home place on Peachtree Street, in which she had grown up, would be torn down. The other was that the manuscript of "Gone With the Wind" and all her papers would be burned. Why? There are surmises, but no answers.

John Marsh, ailing and grieving, said that he had burned them all, save for a few pages of the manuscript, with his wife's handwritten changes and notes. He made a statement about it in a codicil to his will:

"My wife, Margaret Mitchell Marsh, wanted her private papers destroyed. She did not wish them to fall into the hands of strangers. . . ."

"Peggy left me discretion as to the disposal of her papers. I have decided that some of the "Gone With the Wind" papers should be saved, as a means of authenticating her authorship of her novel. If some schemer were to rise up with the claim that her novel was written by another person, it would be tragic if we had no documentary evidence and therefore were unable to beat down the false claim. So I am saving these original 'Gone With the Wind' papers for use in proving, if the need arises, that Peggy and no one else was the author of her novel. . . ."

The fact that there is so little religion in the book is curious and speculative. The Civil War had aroused a fervent, nationalist revival of religion. Yet, the novel does not touch on it. Peggy Mitchell was separated from her church. This was a blow which deeply affected her, through she never made talk about it.

She had no children. How badly this hurt no one knows. She was a warm, friendly, loyal person, fiercely devoted to her friends—who could do no wrong. What loneliness, regrets or unfulfillment she knew, she never discussed. She strove mightily publicly to be what she always had been. Neither she nor her husband piled up possessions, nor made any grand tours. Neither was well, but neither complained. John was husband, father, business manager, friend and watchdog.

We know a great deal about him and her—But the first person singular, Margaret Munnerlyn Mitchell . . . ?

Mr. Mitchell Remembers Margaret

By Keith Runyon

Keith Runyon's article about Stephens Mitchell in the Louisville Courier-Journal *is the most succinct, least inhibited of a number of feature stories published about the author's brother during the 1970s.*

In another excellent article about Mr. Mitchell (in Atlanta *for July 1974) Martin Shartar summarized:*

> *Stephens Mitchell is committed fiercely to truth, justice and order, underpinned by law, brotherhood and clarity. Since his sister's accidental death in 1949—25 years ago—and the death of John Marsh in 1952, Stephens Mitchell has been guardian of her rights and keeper of her memory. As executor of her estate he renegotiated a more profitable film contract with MGM (to whom Selznick had assigned his rights) when* Gone With the Wind's *copyright was renewed in 1964. The estate will receive an undisclosed percentage of NBC's reported $5 million payment for one-time TV rights to the film, scheduled for airing in 1976.*
>
> *As loving brother who shared more than royalties, he has fought to keep the real Margaret Mitchell separate from rumor-become-myth. He reads current articles and books engendered by* Gone With the Wind's *enduring gust, writing letters of correction when inaccuracies occur.*

Margaret Mitchell, once perhaps this city's most famous resident, has been dead for twenty-three years, but the book she wrote forty years ago is still big business.

"Gone With the Wind" sold 130,000 copies around the world last year, and in the thirty-six years since it was first published, the sales total has reached twenty million. The 1939 MGM movie based on the novel had grossed $73 million at the end of last year.

Tending the lucrative royalties from the book, and the healthy share of revenues from the motion picture, has become the job of Miss Mitchell's only surviving heir, her brother and lifetime confidant, Stephens Mitchell.

At seventy-six, Mitchell is a lively gentleman with snowy hair and a white, Teddy Rooseveltian mustache. Even though he's been seriously ill on several occasions, he is in good health today, exercises with weights at his home and takes brisk walks between his two offices in downtown Atlanta. He divides his working days between his law office and his "literary rights" office—where he looks after the interests of "Gone With the Wind."

Mitchell has always been the legal adviser for "Gone With the Wind"—since the days before it hit the bookstores in the mid-1930s. In a recent interview at the literary rights office on Atlanta's Luckie Street, Mitchell recalled how business was managed when Margaret Mitchell and her husband, John Marsh, were still alive.

"Margaret called us together and said, 'John, you be the businessman, and Steve, you're going to be the lawyer. I'll say what's what.' So she ran it like an executive.

"I would look up the law about whatever, and John would take care of business things. Every night we'd meet at their apartment and go over what we'd done in the day. John and I would argue about what to do, and Margaret would give out the decisions."

Marsh, a native of Maysville, Kentucky, died in 1952, less than three years after his wife was killed by a speeding taxicab which ran her down as she walked across Peachtree Street, only a few blocks from the apartment where "Gone With the Wind" was written. Since his brother-in-law's death, Stephens Mitchell has made all business decisions too, and when the time came to negotiate a new movie contract in 1964, he injected a clause which gave the Mitchell estate 10 percent of all further film rentals.

That little deal, Mitchell said, has given him a tidy nest egg worth several million dollars. It more than rectified the original deal, which paid Margaret Mitchell only $50,000 for rights to film her book. "I've made the thing really much more profitable than Margaret and John ever did," remarked Mitchell. "I ought to have been the businessman and John the lawyer."

The Mitchells are one of Atlanta's "oldest" families. Their ancestors helped settle and build the city, and consequently, both Mitchell and his sister always felt a proprietary interest in local affairs.

"Gone With the Wind" was Margaret Mitchell's valentine to Atlanta, picturing her city at its best and its worst in the years before, during and after the Civil War.

Preparations for writing the novel, her brother claims, began in her early childhood, when Margaret collected plenty of anecdotes while propped up on the knobby knees of relatives who happened to be old Confederate veterans with colorful war stories to tell. Like the characters in her novel, these people fought the battles, guarded the plantations and lived in the city during the long siege of Atlanta before Georgia fell to the Union armies.

In addition to having a retentive mind, young Margaret Mitchell also had a talent for writing, and from her youngest days she composed short stories and plays. The manuscripts are now housed with her personal papers in the Margaret Mitchell Collection at the University of Georgia.

"I knew Margaret liked to write," her brother said. "She was writing from the time she could hold a pen. When she was about seven or eight, she wrote a story about Mr. and Mrs. Drake. And it wound up that Mr. and Mrs. Drake were ducks!"

Her ambitions weren't always directed toward becoming a novelist.

"At first she wanted to be a doctor," Stephens Mitchell said. "She had read about a new form of doctoring called psychiatry."

In 1918 she headed north to begin pre-med studies at Smith, but a combination of bad luck, which included the deaths of her fiance in World War I and her mother in the 1918–19 influenza epidemic, brought Miss Mitchell home to Atlanta for good at the end of her freshman year. At that time, according to her brother, she surrendered any hopes of becoming a psychiatrist.

Instead she became a debutante, and entered Atlanta society in 1920. Stephens Mitchell proudly boasted that his little sister was "the best dancer in Atlanta."

She also had a string of male admirers—and a chorus of female enemies as well.

Miss Mitchell was "like most of the girls who have lots of boys around them," her brother said. "Most of the other women hated her guts." That animosity remained for the rest of her life, and her adult friends were mostly members of Atlanta's literary set.

"There are women in Atlanta today—old biddies—who are just waiting for me to die so they can write reminiscences of 'Me and Margaret Mitchell.' For those old cats, she was not what you'd call a 'popular' young lady," Mitchell estimated.

Like her heroine Scarlett O'Hara, parties and beaux weren't enough to satisfy Margaret Mitchell. She went looking for a career and landed a job as a reporter on The Atlanta *Journal* in 1922.

"She succeeded right from the first," said her brother. "She was their star writer in the Sunday Department. The best-known story she ever wrote at The *Journal* was on account of the headline.

"You see, some woman had shot her sweetie, and Margaret interviewed her. The headline came out: 'Shot Him Because She Loved Him.' I can remember those big, loud-mouthed newsboys hollering, "Read it and weep!' "

Margaret Mitchell's marriage to John Marsh in 1925 spelled a temporary end to her literary career. For a few years the thin, dark-haired woman who stood just under five feet, settled into the role of housewife and hostess, while her husband—a public relations executive with the Georgia Power Co.—served as breadwinner.

During her spare time in the late '20s and early '30s, Margaret Mitchell was spending a lot of time behind her portable typewriter on a project most of her friends didn't know much about. Stephens Mitchell heard about it one day when his first wife, Carrie Lou (who died just a few months after his sister), came home from the Marshes' apartment after lunch. "Margaret's working on a book," he was told.

The book wasn't finished until 1935, and it came out in the spring of 1936.

When Macmillan printed it, critical acclaim also came its way—followed by the Pulitzer Prize for fiction in 1937.

Since her first novel was so popular, why did his sister never write another book?

"When you consider now—forty years later—that the book has a full-time secretary and a man who spends nearly half his time with it," her brother explained, "well, you can imagine what it was like when it first came out."

For many years, the Mitchells operated three offices (two of which were filled with file cabinets). Most of those papers are now at the University of Georgia.

Margaret Mitchell insisted on answering every complimentary letter separately, so much of her time was taken with correspondence. In the early '40s her husband suffered a serious heart attack. "Then she laid everything else aside and said, 'Steve, you're my secretary. You've got to run everything you can. I'm going to nurse John.' Which is what she did."

In the years between 1936 and her death at forty-eight in 1949, Miss Mitchell also became one of Atlanta's most sought-after guests, even though she rarely went to parties. She worked for charities and sold bonds during World War II.

"You don't realize my position," she once told her brother. "It's something like Stone Mountain. I'm just here to be shown off. And everybody who's invited to town wants to see me."

While David O. Selznick was filming the movie version of "Gone With the Wind" in Hollywood, her phone rang constantly with questions about how things should be handled.

Reporters tried to get the author to say which movie stars should be given roles in the film.

"One man was trying to get her to commit herself about who would play Rhett," said her brother. "She just turned to him and said: 'My favorite movie actor is Groucho Marx.' Which he was. She was a great Groucho fan."

Clark Gable, rather than Groucho Marx got the part, and Miss Mitchell was delighted with his performance, as she was with Vivien Leigh's Scarlett, Hattie McDaniel's Mammy and Olivia de Havilland's Melanie. But, her brother said, she didn't like the way Leslie Howard portrayed Ashley Wilkes, Scarlett's lover who was married to her best friend.

"The part of Ashley was the part of a very smart, very discerning man. He had exquisite feelings and saw everything that was going to happen to everybody and to himself, but he couldn't do anything about it.

"He wasn't just a dumb clod like Leslie Howard played him."

Mitchell recalled that some people have tried to place historical ties to his sister's story which really never existed. Like the story about a famous madam in Lexington, Kentucky, who was reputedly the inspiration for the fictional bordello operator, Belle Watling.

"Margaret just made [Belle] up, and people have attributed all sorts of stories to her. Nobody in the book except the historic characters (like Civil War generals) are taken from life. Margaret had imagination enough to make greater characters than life could have provided."

Since he is now getting up in years, Stephens Mitchell understands that "Gone With the Wind" will some day be looked after by someone else. His family will continue to have a financial interest until 1992, when the copyright expires and the novel falls into the public domain.

Mitchell's second wife, Anita (who was once the head nurse at the polio hospital in Warm Springs, Georgia, where she knew President Franklin Roosevelt), and his two sons will handle matters well, he believes. "I've really got it down now to where there is not going to be so much. It will only take 'yesses' and 'noes,' coming mainly from my eldest son, Eugene, who is an economist."

Mitchell believes that his work to preserve his sister's work and uphold the novel's interests in the best taste has been successful. He's turned his thumb down on some projects—like one to build an Atlanta amusement park, a "Gone With the Wind Land," with the original movie-set Tara as a centerpiece, or the suggestion that a famous writer be hired to write a sequel to the book.

"You see, the theme of the book, which a lot of people don't really catch, is that many a woman has a good man but doesn't know it until it's too late.

"And then the book ends, of course. You don't go beyond the closing of the theme."

Margaret Mitchell did do some other writing before she died, but all the manuscripts were burned, at her request, by her husband in an incinerator in their back yard just after she died. So there will never be a "lost" Margaret Mitchell manuscript discovered and published posthumously, her brother said.

As he indicated, Atlanta won't soon forget his sister. An elementary school, a street, an emergency clinic at the hospital where she died and a room at the public library have all been named in her honor.

The area bounded by the public library—where she spent long hours in the basement reading dusty old newspapers printed during the Civil War—and the Loew's Theatre—where "Gone With the Wind" had its world premiere in December 1939, is known as Margaret Mitchell Square. There, a gas lamp burns in "perpetual shining light" as a memorial to her.

But if she were living here today, her brother doesn't think she would like Atlanta very much.

"You see, things have changed since she was here. The basis of Atlanta, the people who own the town, are descendants of the reconstruction "nobility" that she wrote about, that assembled in the town then. She made a historical misstatement in the book, giving the idea that most of them left town. Most of them didn't leave town. They live in town, they ran the town and they still run it.

"They call themselves 'old families' but the people who are really old families are those who were here sixty years before [reconstruction], like mine."

According to Stephens Mitchell, the best memorial to his sister is her novel, which is available in thirty-one countries and translated into twenty-five languages. It explains her views, he believes, about people and the way life should be lived.

"Our family was always an extremely reactionary family," Mitchell said.

"And I would say that Margaret was also a reactionary. Now by that, I don't mean a conservative. We are not conservative.

"She believed that there are certain principles we've always got to go back to. In any era, until the second coming of the Lord, there will be things that are bad. So you'd better go back and look for the things that were good in the past."

THREE

Are We Still Fighting the Civil War?

By Clifford Dowdey

The Great Depression was not an isolated event of the early 1930s, as most people born after World War II seem to believe. It was a decade-long climb from a disaster that permeated every fiber of life during the thirties. Southerners were all too conscious of the Depression, of their plight as "the nation's number one economic opportunity," of such books as The Collapse of Cotton Tenancy, Preface to Peasantry, *and* Tenants of the Almighty, *and, more importantly, of the very real economic advantage the rest of the country held over the South because of differentials in freight rates. Margaret Mitchell wrote her good friend Clifford Dowdey, August 22, 1938:*

> *There is a good paragraph on this subject in Jonathan Daniels' "A Southerner Discovers the South." It's where he compares the South with Carthage and remarks that the Romans, after all, were politer than the Northern conquerors, for after they had sown Carthage with salt they never rode through it on railroad trains and made snooty remarks about the degeneracy of people who liked to live in such poor circumstances.*

In a statement even more pertinent to Dowdey's article she said:

> *Of course I'm interested in the piece you are writing for* [The Southern Literary Messenger] *and I only wish you had told me more about it in your letter. When I read the title, "Are We Still Fighting the War?", I laughed aloud. Ever since Roosevelt's Barnesville speech Senator George and his supporters have been on the air. I have heard so many yells of "states' rights" and "Northern oppression" and "sinister centralization of power" and so many bands playing 'Dixie' that I have wondered whether this was 1938 or 1861. I feel that if I look out of the window I will see the Confederate troops, headed by General John B. Gordon, marching toward Washington. When I read Heywood Broun's sneering remarks about Senator George "arousing sectionalism" and his other remarks about some Southerners acting as if Appomattox had never occurred I wondered whether he was just plain dumb. His ideas, and those of a number of Northern commentators of pinkish tinge, seem to be that Appomattox settled beautifully and peacefully and justly all the problems, economic and social, for which the South was fighting. Their idea seems to be*

that might made right in 1865. Common sense should show that many of the problems that sent us to war have never been settled, and the same injustices persist—tariff, freight rates, et cetera. As far as I can see, Appomattox didn't settle anything. We just got licked. Our situation is, in spots, much worse than it was then and the problems are raising their heads once more. This seems to annoy Mr. Broun and his playmates. After all, when a section has been held in economic slavery for over seventy years that section should have the delicacy of feeling not to squawk.

Virginian Dowdey *wrote pungently and not without bitterness of the attitudes of and towards the South in the decade of* GWTW's *first popularity. An understanding of those years of the Depression is a great help in understanding the initial impact of* Gone With the Wind. *In her brilliant* Race and Region in American Historical Fiction *(Oxford: 1979), Willie Lee Rose errs in saying "Margaret Mitchell's fictional New South of the 1870's was influenced to a considerable degree by the experience of the 1930's depression" for the novel was a product of the Boom Era, not of the Depression. She is very right, however, in declaring: "Themes of hardship and survival had special appeal to the depression generation who could understand without prompting how it was to be penniless and confused in the middle of a rich and fallow land. There had to be a little bit of Scarlett and a little bit of Melanie in those who came through that troubled time."*

If, as a Southerner, you have lived in the north at all, you have been asked countless times, "You still fighting the Civil War down there?" You are asked it in derision, in tolerant amusement, in contemptuous impatience. You are asked it by people who weep over the hapless Chinese in their war with Japan, who denounce bitterly and at length the exploits of Franco in Spain. These people study those wars, cheer over the victories of their side and brood over the defeats.

Now these people are not military students. Their interest in the current wars is not because they are now happening, while other wars are dead. (In fact, students of military science particularly study dead wars, because there one learns lessons of warfare.) Their interest is presumably based then, not upon the contemporary wars as warfare, but upon the effects of the wars and their outcome on civilization. If Japan reduces China to the position of a dependent state, this situation will affect America. If the Fascists conquer in Spain, it is natural to expect a shift in European balances which will affect America.

Yet, it is not the direct effects upon America of these wars that their anxious followers usually discuss; it is the effect upon the growth of Communism, as practiced, to whatever extent, in China and Loyalist Spain. Apparently, then, these people are concerned with the ultimate effects of these wars on forms of government and economic systems. What they fail to see is that *they are now living in the midst of the effects of the Confederate War for Independence on the*

American government and economic system. Our answer to the stupid question
is, "Yes, we and you and America are still fighting the war!"

Here, then, is a war that stands as the greatest calamity, the most ghastly
and unnecessary tragedy, that America ever suffered. A large section, geo-
graphic, cultural and economic, was invaded by the rest of the country; its
culture was destroyed, its economic system ruined; its geographical unity
isolated in the bitter pride of defeat and the hatred of unjust humiliation. This
section was pillaged by its conquerors and excluded from financial expression,
in forming and developing the economic systems of the rest of the country, until
today the national President can say it constitutes the nation's number one
economic problem. Through the poverty and broken spirits caused by its
oppressors, this section fell so far behind the country in educational advance-
ment and the use of modern appliances of living that it became a subject of ridicule
to the country which fattened, certainly to some extent, on its subjugation.

In its defeat the South formed such intense sectional-consciousness and
loyalty that today, when the country desperately needs a solid front of national
interests, we have pronounced sectionalism over the whole country and passionately held individual interests. People who pride themselves on their interest in national and world affairs ask if we are still fighting the war!

A columnist, proud of his liberalism, asks: "Does the South not remember
Appomattox?" Does he ask: "Do the Jews remember Hitler?" Does he think
disfranchisement solved any more for the South than for the tragic German
Jews . . . and now Italian Jews? Does he ask Hitler doesn't he remember the
Versailles Treaty? He does . . . and so does the South remember Appomattox!

Some book reviewers, whose task supposedly is to inform America of books
contributing to its understanding of itself, write zealously of China and Spain
and Russia, and say they are bored with the Civil War. Are they bored with the
protests of New England States' governors against the lowering of freight rates
in the South because that will sound the knell of the Northern textile and other
industries? Are they bored with the congressional squabble over wages and
hours in the South, that makes it possible for Southern industries to increase
five-and-a-half times from 1900 to 1935, while those of the country as a whole
have increased four times? What do they think caused that situation except the
effects of the war?

The financial industrial North wanted to crush the agrarian South; and did.
So the South, of necessity, turned industrial. Now the industrial North is
reaping the fruits of its victories, and they taste bad. The greed of Northern
politicians and industrialists and financiers, their vindictiveness toward the
fallen South, created the situation which has boomeranged. The thoroughness
with which they subjugated the South created the living conditions out of
which low wages and low standards of living became inevitable. Now the South
is accused of low living standards by the sections which devoted themselves in
the time of living men to establishing those standards. Are we still fighting the
war? We are fighting it with the only weapons we have.

However, let us look carefully at what we are fighting for. It is true that living standards are low in the South, that our fine industrial spurt leaves vast segments untouched, that many of our people are afflicted with chronic and acute poverty, and our sub-marginal population is huge. Our chosen representatives in the national government have drafted a list of recommendations for our ills. *The Herald-Tribune* found this list suspect of playing politics, of having—along with its honest intent—the secondary intent of liquidating from the ruling political party the old-line leaders. *The Herald-Tribune* stated editorially that, whatever the virtues of the list, the South would find its prosperity when the nation returned to prosperous, productive manufacturing. It so happens, that the South's darkest days were lived during the nation's greatest expansion of prosperous, productive manufacturing. Attribute that to the aftermath of the war, if you like; it is still true that our sub-marginal population and our vast poverty did not spring into being in 1929. It existed during the boom; and while it might be worse now, the situation is old . . . as old as the war. In fact, except for excoriating us for our handling of the Negro problem which they threw in our laps, the North paid us little attention until our economic plight began to affect the whole and our surging textile industries affected their prosperity.

It seems not unreasonable to assume that their interest in the South as a section is no greater than it was before, and both from their absence of inherent interest and their long neglect they are scarce fitted to deal with our problems. So we are fighting, as we fought before, essentially alone—however much we might be part of the whole. And we are fighting, again, for our economic security and our way of life.

Now, let us recognize, for the lovely legends that they were, some of the values we supposedly fought for in the war itself. There is the moonlight and magnolia plantation-life ("You can hear the darkies singing"); the aristocrat civilization (with the attendant and indignant denial that a middle-class ever existed); and all the comic-opera costuming of chivalry and honor and deathless devotion to the Confederacy. Statistics abound, and are easy to come by, proving the small minority of anything approaching the plantation-life of poem and song; proving the existence of a very large and very important middle-class which produced, among many another of our leaders, "Stonewall" Jackson; proving that the South suffered from its own deserters and criminals and profiteers; proving, in short, that the South was not very much different from what it is today in its basic pattern of classes and peoples.

Only one-fourth of the whole population of the South had any association with slavery whatsoever, and this means men, women, and children. Three out of every four Southerners, then, did not own nor belong to an immediate family which owned a single slave. Of the one-fourth, over half owned from one to four slaves, obviously being small farmers whose additional help came from slave labor in much the same manner that small farmers employ hired help today. Of the remaining half of slave-owners, a small percentage held the great plantations, much the same percentage that today controls great wealth.

Those legends were useful to us in defeat, especially as few Southerners knew then or know now what we fought for. We fought because of a deep antagonism between the sections, economic in basis and personal on the surface. Fundamentally, despite the clearer understanding between sections and the leavening of sectional characteristics by the march of American "civilization", that is still our fight. We can be most effective without false legends and phoney ideals.

The war, as such, is over. The fight still goes on. Let us cease weeping over vanished glories, which in large part were never ours; let us cease eulogizing our heroes as men apart, whose like we will never see again. Let us return to the war as the beginning of our fight, return to our great men and women, and their great deeds, as a source of inspiration for today: let us remember their courage and fortitude and stouthearted convictions as sources of strength for us to draw upon. Let us remember their deeds as ideals to emulate, not to rest upon.

The last days of the old *Southern Literary Messenger,* before its revival, served a magnificent purpose in re-creating the glories and the details of the life that was lost with the war. Today we know more of that life; today we know the fight did not end at Appomattox. Today our writers turn increasingly to the bodies of people who form most of the South, for their subject material. Gone are the days when we weep in print for the goateed colonel and his julep, little missy and the gallant young gentleman whose eyes flashed at the slightest imputation to his honor and rushed for his dueling pistols. (Alas, a brief study of the duels in Virginia will produce a dishearteningly few recorded ones . . . disheartening, that is, to the lovers of legends. A far greater number of these dashing gallants are recorded to posterity because of unpaid debts.) Gone are the days of writers bemoaning the passing of the plantation-life, with the darkies singing. Today they write of convicts singing (who probably sing for much the same reason, in spite of the authentic mammies who remained faithful). They write of the sharecroppers and the sub-marginal population, of thieves and murderers and sex criminals, of the shabby genteel poor and the flashy ungenteel rich, of the happenings that concern, and always have concerned, the vast numbers of Southerners who actually fought the actual war, and are still fighting this one. It is time for a magazine in Virginia to allow them a voice.

If we bring the realism of vision and the hardihood of spirit to bear in this fight, as did our dead soldiers (and I mean the ones in the ranks, the ones who walked barefooted and ran on empty bellies in those charges for which our leaders are justly famous) we can win more lasting victories than did they, and make their sacrifices not in vain.

Introduction to
Kiss the Boys Good-Bye

By Clare Boothe

Heywood Broun was certainly not Margaret Mitchell's favorite commentator. He said of Gone With the Wind in his column "It Seems to Me" in the New York World Telegram, September 19, 1936:

Am I wholly alone in thinking that the book is just a shade too sweetly Southern? It will be said that I am traditionally Yankee-minded and a blind-baiter of the dear old Southland. . . . As far as the binding force of the Constitutional argument went, I think the South could make a good case for itself. But I do not mean to say that the war was unjust when I say that its roots were economic. Roots have a habit of being that. Economically the South was wrong, and that is vital. It is more vital than charm or the fragrance of the flowers.

Mr. Broun was not Miss Mitchell's favorite, but he stood high in the estimation of the accomplished playwright Clare Boothe. Not only did she regard him as a brilliant writer, she thought that Broun should be allowed "to defend himself" on the charge that in her Kiss the Boys Good-bye "the character of Madison Breed was intended as a thinly disguised portrait, or rather a bold and vulgar caricature of Mr. Broun." Miss Boothe considered her comedy "a parable" and "a political allegory about Fascism in America."

The Atlanta Constitution recorded September 6, 1941, an interview of Inez Robb with Miss Mitchell in New York. In it Miss Robb reported: "The Atlanta author said she had seen Clare Boothe's 'Kiss the Boys Good-bye' and 'just whooped with laughter' over it. But she was at first incredulous and then doubled up with merriment when told that Miss Boothe regarded her play as a serious exposé and indictment of the south as the stronghold of Fascism." Margaret Mitchell saw the play when it was performed in Atlanta in the spring of 1939. Before that time, she had written her friend Colonel Telamon Cuyler November 9, 1938: "Friends [Clifford and Helen Dowdey] who came through here last week-end had seen 'Kiss the Boys Good-bye.' They said it was a burlesque on Selznick's search for Scarlett. They said that it was amusing in spots but that the author evidently hated every one of her characters so much *that it was impossible to feel any sympathy for them. It was a malicious comedy all the way around."*

Clifford Dowdey *wrote of one aspect of the ideology of the South in the 1930s. Miss Boothe wrote of another. An understanding of her point of view is as necessary as an understanding of his in knowing how to interpret* Gone With the Wind *in its own time. But one needs to read Miss Boothe bearing in mind her admonition: "Certainly one cannot either clearly understand or condemn 'Southernism' by simply slapping on it the black Fascist tag."*

This play was meant to be a political allegory about Fascism in America. But everywhere it has been taken for a parody of Hollywood's search for Scarlett O'Hara. As such it has had a good measure of success with the public, far less with the critics—and none at all with myself, its author. For once again I have quite missed my target.

I say "once again" because I had this same humiliating experience with *The Women.* There I had thought to satirize a very small, special group of female parasites. My aim, clinical and specific, was at a sober-sided if impolite *genre* study of Manhattan manners. But judging by the fact that two million-odd playgoers have paid to laugh at dubiously translated versions of it in eleven languages, I must have achieved a goal commensurably as large as their laughter. The very size and catholicity of the audiences it drew is probably a proof that the New York critics' first-night accusations were true: no matter what my original intent, I had penned a hilarious lampoon on *all women.*

Now, in *Kiss the Boys Good-bye,* I did design the characters for their broadest values as class symbols. Whereupon they were reviewed both publicly and privately as petty caricatures of my personal acquaintances. And when I deliberately sought to build a satirical plot on a national thesis, then I merely succeeded in fashioning a burlesque on a highly topical and (I think) rather footling subject—a casting crisis in Hollywood.

On the record, it would seem that as a playwright I suffer from a bad case of artistic negativism. Therefore, it is a little heavy-heartedly, and somewhat apologetically, that I put down here a few thoughts which inspired what I had hoped would be the apparent thesis of this comedy. But now I only hope that in *Kiss the Boys Good-bye* I have not fumbled this purpose so badly that even after reading the book-play itself, this preface will seem like a totally irrelevant essay.

There are lies so simple and lovely that saints may speak them gracefully. One of the pleasantest falsehoods we mouth as a nation is this: that liberty is part of the inalienable genius of the American people and is therefore secure in the traditions and institutions of our land. Actually, perhaps, we have suffered and fought too little for liberty. There are certainly other countries which have fought more ardently and desperately for the sum total of their national interests; and there are also other peoples who have fought more passionately for their liberties. Having suffered so little, it may be we have yet to discover in the storm's test whether we have sufficiently developed on this raw continent those unwritten laws of social discipline and personal responsibility which, equally with any Bill of Rights, are the necessary conditions of liberty in civilization. Because we, as a people, have always demanded an ever-wider franchise, we believe we have therefore always demanded our liberty—and always will. We confuse the democratic habit of sticking into a slit in a box a piece of paper (marked with a name from a circumscribed list of names committed to circumscribed policies) with the love of civil rights and liberties. That "more and more democracy" is not necessarily the same thing as "more and more liberty" is perhaps too obvious to mention in this day of political slogan-busting. But certainly, in the past seventy-five years, outside of the South, we as a people have been far more concerned with the benefits of expanding capitalism, and latterly, with the penalties of its crises, than we have with the simple human virtues of liberty.

Another highly passable piece of political counterfeit is the current belief that Fascism is an evil of such baneful weight as to be unendurable to decent men and needs only to be experienced briefly. I am certainly no expert on the affairs of the collectivist nations, but I harbor the suspicion that Fascism for *most* of those who live *in* it, as opposed to those who live *under* it, is not as onerous and ugly as it is made to seem in the more hysterical departments of the American press. Indeed, those who are more intent on guarding us against its growth in this country than on "sicking" us into a war (itself an essentially Fascist undertaking) on its exponents abroad, are those who warn us frankly that Fascism once experienced may quickly become a tolerable if not a pleasurable sensation. Of all national ways of life, it is, perhaps, the most quickly habit-forming. It is the alcohol and the opium of political systems; it will rob us eventually of our physical and mental and even moral powers, but it gives us a temporary illusion of escape from an inimical world, a lift of the spirit, a feeling of superiority, of power. . . . Also, we are warned (though not loudly, not often enough!) when—or if—Fascism comes to *all* America, she will come so prettily costumed in red, white and blue as to be practically indistinguishable from a music hall's Fourth of July performance "Rockette," than which nothing could look more charmingly, happily, uniformly American. Only the most vigilant and even suspicious critics of our national manners will then see that this bunting really adorns somebody else's baby doll.

So in the popular parlor game of searching for the vanguard of American Fascism, it seemed to me that the hunt had best be directed first, not at those elements in our nation which we most regularly criticize as dangerously alien, but rather at those which we most eagerly gloss with the sentimentality of the familiar. Thus, I chose to construct a fable about the first coming of Fascism out of Dixie.

Now to abuse and vilify the South has been for over a decade the fashion among the intellectuals, and to abuse "Southernism" by calling it "Fascism" is

certainly not original in a time which may go down in history as the Era of
Political Abuse. But, curiously enough, to call "Southernism" "Fascism" conveys to many people the idea that if both are the same, both are therefore a new
fact, or a new threat in our American world. That is, doubtless, because "Fascism" is a comparatively new word invented to describe what we believe to be a
new ideology marked "made abroad." We are not, perhaps, sufficiently aware
that "Southernism" is a particular and *highly matured* form of Fascism with
which America has lived more or less peacefully for seventy-five years.

Indeed "Southernism" may possibly have been the inspiration or forerun-
ner of Fascism. At any rate, those who like to draw political analogies, which
means all those of us whose intellectual ability to cope with historical processes
consists in reciting innumerable rather too pat analogies between "Then and
Now," "Over Here and Over There," may surely with profit trace the Black or
Brown Shirt Idea to the White Shirts of the Ku Klux Klan. And, although
"industrial capitalism" had relatively little to do with their problem, the White
Shirts, like the Brown and Black Shirts, also brought order out of a post-war era
of chaos. The Southern chaos of 1865 being worse than the German chaos of
1932, it is notable that the order was even more quickly and brutally brought.
The carpet-bagger-inspired Communism of the Negro was ruthlessly and passionately stamped out, even as the "Jew-inspired" Communism of the laborer in
Germany has been. Indeed the swastika never burns more brightly or savagely
in the *Schwarzwald* than the Fiery Cross of the Klan once burned in the bayous
and cypress swamps of Dixie. To be sure, practically all of the more spectacular
outward, and most of the more vicious inward, manifestations of this
pyrotechnic night-shift *Kultur* have long since passed overseas, where it is not
for me to prophesy, but merely to hope, they will stay.

So long as there is industrial and agricultural peace in the South, it is likely
that they will stay exported. The terms of this peace are not severe enough, just
barely enough for the black man to eat and a little less than enough for him to
wear. (The black man—no Oliver Twist is he!) The vital difference between
Southern Fascism and the Germanic variety is that the Southern Fascist has so
far consolidated and battened down his victory over his domestic political
enemies, the sharecropper, the po' white and the Negro, that he need never don
his White Shirt publicly (though even the most liberal of Southern statesmen
find it politically expedient to do it secret lip service, as Chief Justice Black will
be the first to deny). The brutality inherent in all Fascisms is only rarely evoked
in the present-day South—usually in those extreme instances of the Negroes'
frenetic attempts to sin in the white man's way. What follows are known as
lynching-bees. The ritualistic terror, the Fascist fury with which some of these
little "purges" are conducted, quite make up for their fortunate infrequency.
But on the whole, over a period of seventy-five years, the Southerner has evolved
a benevolent Fascism, which is to say, a *relatively* tolerable, politically pragmatic form. His Jim Crow laws and his Jim Crow spirit have, on the whole, been
accepted as the moral and political norm even at last by the North, where

Southern Fascism, though frequently condemned morally, has seldom been viewed with militant alarm—chiefly because it has to date produced no Hitler. "Every [white] man his own Dictator" is a fact, let it be confessed, more often recognized by Northerners with envy than distaste. In short, as long as the Negro is willing to remain mentally, spiritually and politically enslaved, he has nothing to fear (of his *life*) from Southern Fascism, because it will then have nothing to fear from him. (Of course, both white and black continue to be *subconsciously* afraid of one another: the black of the terrorism that might wipe him out in a night blacker than he, if there came a widespread recrudescence of American Fascism; the white of the revival of Northern-agitated Communism among the numerically superior blacks.) Moreover, the South, grafted Siamese-twin-wise to the body of the North by the surrender at Appomattox[1] has to endure a certain amount of moral and political policing from its brother. (This is of course a mutual affair.)

Here, further analogies concerning Fascism in the South, based on its cultural, labor and political organizations, I leave to those who have made more detailed study of them than I. For these matters should be given great care. In our present ideological tussles Fascism has been too commonly diagnosed simply as an advanced phase of industrial capitalism. Perhaps it *is* safer to examine each Fascism separately, as a special case, before one attempts to state what they all have in common. Certainly one cannot either clearly understand or condemn "Southernism" by simply slapping on it the black Fascist tag. I am persuaded that it still remains for us of the North to understand much better than we do, not only what Southern Fascism is, but what has made it work as long—if as "po'ly" as it does, and most importantly what it offers that makes it tolerated, accepted, admired, even *loved* by millions of sane people, and in succesive generations.

Something of all this I had hoped lightly, even gaily, to suggest in this play. I have most miserably failed. But others, I know, will succeed. For it is, finally, my guess (if I were wiser and braver I could call it a conviction) that America will be in our time sufficiently forewarned—forewarned against the attractive, as well as the ugly, guises of Fascism. This country does, I believe, possess one peculiar native trait which can be counted upon to react with instinctive repulsion to the authoritarian theory or practice—that is the trait of independence. It is notable in this connection that the ideal of personal independence ("rugged individualism" will still do) is *least* of all associated with the South, where family ties ("kin"), allegiance to small localisms and parochial insolvencies, where archaic manners and mass hypnotism by Things Past give the predominately uniform gray color to the social landscape. Independence in one sense—intellectual and financial solvency—we associate with New England. In another sense—enterprise—with the Middle West; in another—adventure and self-reliance—with

---

1. In current ideology, the South "lost" its Fascist war, the North "won" a democratic victory.

the Far West. But in no sense with the "Southernism" of the South—unless it be that curious sense of its own geographical apartness, its moral unreconstructed Rebelism, its spiritual independence of *the rest of the* U.S.A.

To be sure, there are alarming reports that the great difficulties and complexities of modern industrial life have beaten down this new continent's spirit of self-reliance. Nevertheless, there is something deeply and realistically American about the word "independence," and the end of that word on our continent has not come yet. Even if we go to war again, at home or abroad, our armies will again be composed of officers and men who regard the hand-salute as a mere temporary, private joke between them. The American, like other men, is gregarious and patriotic; but he is not yet the *creature* of any state. The nation, the state, loom larger and larger in the background of his mind; but in the foreground, thank God, there is still predominately—himself.

Now what on earth has all this to do with little Cindy Lou?

This, precisely: that I deliberately chose that most exportable, highly praised and consistently sentimentalized of Dixie products—the Southern Belle—to examine her, not only for her own Fascist leanings, but for her potentialities as a proselyter to the Cause. In satiric terms she is an American version of a Brown Shirt street brawler from Munich, in a swank Berlin coffee-house, *circa* 1930. Cindy Lou Bethany, the hoop-skirted menace in Westport, satirically but honestly conceived as the symbol of much that is worst and some that is best in "Southernism." Cindy Lou, who not only feels but thinks and acts entirely with her heart—that is to say, her emotions. . . .

For perhaps it may be said that "Communism" originates in the bowels (add "of compassion," if you will) of "Capitalism" in the cold, gray cells of the brain, the Fascism in the heart, the veins, the sinews. (Liberalism, such as we sorely need today, would be the only "ism" animated by all three.) It is not without significance that the country where the "heart" is the most touted organ, and the most frequent motif in ornament and design, where even day laborers wear cute little red-felt replicas of that vital organ on the sleeves of their sweaters, is Greater Germany. Most of Cindy Lou's "rationalizations," her "opinions," her "convictions," her "beliefs," are all simply emotional, sentimental or, more accurately, *physical* reactions which she has translated into the rather meaningless symbols of words. They pour from her in a steady stream of gentle, though none the less hysterical, blather. When they fail to conquer her listeners by sheer weight and numbers (Cindy Lou makes no intellectual effort to *convince*) she retranslates them, with no sense of strain whatsoever, into immediate physical action—tears, laughter, screams or direct bodily assault. It never seems to occur to her (nor for that matter to the audience!) that a butt in the stomach carries no *intellectual* conviction at all. But Cindy Lou's desire (a truly infantile, and yet recognizable Fascist one) is not to convince, but to *silence* her opponent. And one must admit that her technique is brilliantly adapted to her purpose. Cindy Lou (as Fascism will itself if it ever really sweeps the land) arrives in the still liberal Northeast, on a high patriotic mission, for which no one can honestly condemn her. Indeed, she is searched and *sent* for! She comes perfumed with the odor of jasmine and magnolia, dripping honeyed words, appealing to the chivalry in every man who meets her, with her false, yet native, air of "helplessness" (too soon to be abandoned!), so that Youth will rally to her, and "sensitive" people will not like to see her ridiculed. She, romantically enough, portrays the "pure white race" standing firm against the "corruption" of the mind, the manners, the blood of her fathers. . . . Who are they who try, for such ignoble reasons, to do in this sweet, tender girl? Why, the Intellectuals, of course. First, the profit-pinching, right-side, bread-buttering controller of public opinion, the tycoon pressman. He is the first to ridicule, then to condemn her—until he sees that she is willing to put her honey on the same side he puts his butter on; the cheap, wisecracking jokesmith, who so fondly believes that he is a Liberal simply because he demands every license; the flesh-potters, oblivious to everything but their own gnawing fleshly needs, the "slumming" social-register aristocrats, now a little wearied of Marx's "shocking-pink" which goes so badly with complexions that are beginning to be a touch green; the cultural czar, and high-priest of propaganda, the Hollywood-Boy, who, seeing her box-office value, seeks both to exploit and seduce her, brashly unaware that he will most certainly be *her first real victim*. And, alas, the good Liberal, the weak Liberal, the verbose Liberal, a bit debilitated in his old age from too much "flirting" or too little honest cohabitation with Communisms. . . . The Liberal— the gentleman! He who refrains with questionable squeamishness, not from insult, not from ridicule, but from giving Cindy Lou that honest reciprocal klug-on-the-mush or (as in this case she *is* a pretty baby) spank on the bottom without which she *must* conquer after all. How easy it is for her to finish off these top-drawer custodians of American traditions! By charm, by flattery, by trickery, by force. When all else fails, let them finish themselves off, which, in any intellectual or emotional crisis severer than criticizing some *other* Liberal's "integrity" or seducing their neighbors' *fraus,* they are certain to do. Does it all seem *too* easy for Cindy Lou? Perhaps that is because she wears an impregnable armor against which one cannot talk—one can only act. She cannot be humbled or insulted or convinced by words, since she feels essentially and immutably "superior" to them all. She is passionately aware that her "culture," like her complexion, is a super sort. Above all, she never stoops to think! She is, *herself,* an act of faith. Against her, the Tall Talkers of the World are helpless as chained fools. Therefore, all things are possible to her, providing always that when honesty or trickery fails, she can lay hand to the proper force-technique. And "all things" are what she wants, whenever she can get them. She feels no qualms in taking them all, the T.T.W., in examining them in the light of her ideology, in keeping that which she can use, and spewing forth the rest. Such is the fulfilment of her Destiny. That is what God made her so superior *for.*

Thus, everywhere, proceed the baby-steps, the first tactics of Fascism. But what of the American people? What will *they* be doing? For the first round (in "Westport"), they will be sitting in the audience, laughing *at* her and, alas, *with* her, and not recognizing her for what she is at all, and simply tickled to pieces to see her finish off those smug, self-appointed upper-crusters, those holier-than-God and ruder-than-Satan Intellectuals. The people will be applauding, and quite properly too, the strength that a simple honest belief in the worth of *any* tradition and the importance of *any* ideal gives one. And they will, again quite properly, be forced to admire our heroine's unswerving loyalty to the fact or fiction of her own class's inviolability. Single-minded loyalty and belief, though they be to dreams and in nonsense, are never without a human dignity which makes intellectual contempt in any form look cheap and feeble. This dignity, this strength, is the "ole Cunnel's" real sword, his shield, and his *panache* too. . . . Thus, the people perhaps will vicariously begin to experience the dangerous nostalgia of the North for the white South's passionate and radiant acceptance of its own Supremacy.

So that is all. That is, perhaps, enough. Probably it is too much. And I wish with all my heart I could have got this properly said in *Kiss the Boys Good-bye*.

Reflections of Theology from Gone With the Wind

By The Rev. Howard Tillman Kuist

It has often been remarked that religion plays only a small part in Gone With the Wind. *Nevertheless it was the subject of sermons in Atlanta's First Christian Church, before the interdemoninational congregation of Dr. Preston Bradley in Chicago, and doubtless others. Dr. Kuist published the following article in* The Union Seminary Review, *October 1939.*

There is far more theology in great fiction than this world dreams of, for man is a moral being, and every man at heart is a theologian. There is a hidden shrine in every human breast, which veils or unveils an image of God. It may be the vague image of the savage, or it may be the distorted image of the pagan, or it may be the exalted image of the Christian: "the image," as Paul put it, "of the invisible God" in the face of Jesus Christ. But every man at heart is a theologian. His ideas of the Deity may never be formulated, but, high or low, they remain nevertheless as potent factors which influence his actions, and thus pass into character, and so out into the broad avenues of human life.

It follows that every book which deals with living men and women will reflect a theology. This is bound to be true just as long as man is human; as long as the mind of man is the home of great issues; as long as the heart of man is the meeting-place of the seen and the unseen; or as long as the will of man struggles, as John Hutton has put it, between "the occupations of time and the recurring preoccupation of eternity." Since man is "incurably religious," every document, whether explicit in statement or implicit in the situations it records, is the carrier of a theology. Or, to change the figure, this theology, good or evil, ripe or rotten, is like a fruit which makes known the manner of tree on which it grew.

This is where the theology of the Bible comes in. It has been said that "the Bible is the unveiling of the divine heart and the mirror of the human heart. It has hands which grip you, eyes that pierce you, a voice which thrills you, and feet which carry you." This is so because its knowledge of man is as broad and deep as the virtues and vices of the human race. Therefore this book of books holds its unique distinction in relation to the records of the race. Its authentic disclosure of the divine heart and its equally authentic reflection of the human heart have won for it a place of solitary preeminence in literature. It is far more than a mere source-book of theology. It is theology fanned into flame. It is the inspired product, as Lynn Harold Hough has declared, of "centuries of intense religious experience made poignantly articulate."

This is the supreme distinction of the Bible as a literature. And this is why it is qualified to function as the moral norm of all literature. In the Bible we find not only prototypes of ourselves in relation to the divine but fields where the masters of literature have discovered the vital springs of thought and action for their characters. "Shakespeare leaned on the Bible," said Emerson. What great literary artists have not drawn inspiration from it? Robert B. Pattison, (*Religion in Life*, Summer Number, 1938, pp. 439–450), lists 235 books, including a few plays, with Biblical titles. "The surpassing picturesque expressions of Biblical phraseology rightly reflect vital qualities and experiences of the human spirit," says he, and as such they "correctly justify Heine's characterization of the Psalms: 'sunrise and sunset, birth and death, promise and fulfillment, the whole drama of humanity.' "

It has long been recognized that the Bible is the world's best seller. The American Institute of Public Opinion has announced the results of a two year poll of "men and women in all parts of this country, and in all walks of life, asking the question: 'What is the most interesting book you have ever read?' " Nearly 20 percent, or one voter in every five, named the Bible, making it by far the leading choice. The only other book which at all approaches the Bible in the actual number of mentions is Margaret Mitchell's *Gone With the Wind*. While about 12 percent, or one in every eight, acclaim this book as leading choice, *Gone With the Wind* is actually named more often than the Bible in New England and other eastern states. This naturally raises some intriguing questions about America's phenomenal best seller.

How are we to account for the vital, wide-spread and sustained interest in this ponderous book? What places it so far ahead of all other books and so near to the Bible in its popular appeal? One reviewer, Edward Weeks, (*New York Times Book Review*, Dec. 20, 1936), analyzed *Gone With the Wind* as follows: Emotional content, 25 percent; Characterization, 15 percent; Invention, 10 percent; Publisher's advertising, 5 percent; Timeliness, 45 percent. In other words, Mr. Weeks attributed the magnetism of the story to the fact that the book arrived precisely at the moment when men were ready for it. The book apparently speaks directly to a mood in which present-day people find themselves, a wistful mood, perhaps best epitomized by the suggestion of the title, "gone with the wind."

What is gone from life today for which men are earnestly groping? And with what sinister wind is it gone? This question brings us face to face with the function of the Bible we are considering. From time to time, some gifted, clear-eyed genius like a Hugo, an Ibsen or a Dostoievski appears who deals so intimately and decisively with the heart problem, which is but another way of saying the sin problem, that for generations men see reflected as in a mirror what the Bible has already declared permanently and finally about the whole human race. Or, to change the figure, this literary artist offers a current diagnosis of that chronic mortal malady from which the generation suffers and for which the Bible has already prescribed a cure. Is this why *Gone With the Wind* is so timely?

John Chamberlain has written a chapter on Literature in the Symposium entitled *America Now* in which he describes "The central problem of the 30's, as 'the relation of the individual to the mass,' " and dismisses *Gone With the Wind* as but another example of the literature of escape. But this view will hardly bear scrutiny. However else you may describe what has been transpiring in this old world of ours during the past decade or more, you can certainly put it pictorially in terms of wind. Mankind has been experiencing not only a wind but a whirlwind, not merely a local tempest but a universal hurricane. And the end is not yet!

The title *Gone With the Wind* is drawn immediately from the third stanza of Ernest Dowson's poem written to a lost love, which reads:

> "I have forgot much, Cynara,
> gone with the wind—."

But where did Ernest Dowson get this figure? Presumably from the 103rd Psalm, verses 15 and 16: "As for man, his days are as grass: as a flower of the field, so he flourisheth. For the wind passeth over it and it is gone, and the place thereof shall know it no more." This reminds us that there is much in the Bible about wind. A concordance reveals many discerning passages—for instance: "The speeches of one that is desperate are as wind" (Job 6:26). "The wicked are as stubble before the wind" (Job 21:18). "The wicked . . . are like the chaff which the wind driveth away" (Psalm 1:4). "He that troubleth his own house shall inherit the wind" (Proverbs 11:29). "They sow the wind and they shall reap the whirlwind" (Hosea 8:7). "All our righteousnesses are as filthy rags, and we all do fade as a leaf, and our iniquities like the wind take us away" (Isaiah 64:6). Who can forget the hot wind, the full wind, the whirlwind of Jeremiah? (4:11). Or who has not heard the immortal words of Him who spake as never man spake?—"Therefore whosoever heareth these sayings of mine, and doeth them, I will liken him unto a wise man, which built his house upon a rock: And the rain descended, and the floods came, and the winds blew, and beat upon that house; and it fell not: for it was founded upon a rock. And every one that heareth these sayings of mine, and doeth them not, shall be likened unto a foolish man, which built his house upon the sand: And the rain descended, and the floods came, and the winds blew, and beat upon that house; and it fell: and great was the fall of it."

Pictorially, then, according to the Bible, wind is what tempers and tries life;

wind is what winnows and sifts the souls of men. Experience teaches us that there are two kinds of wind: the winds which blow from without and the winds which blow within. The winds from without are adversity, war, pestilence, famine, calamity, misfortune: winds over which men have little control. The winds from within are passion, uncleanness, enmity, strife, jealousies, malice, factions, parties, envyings, revellings. These are winds (the Bible calls them lusts) over which men may have control. Human beings are strange creatures. The winds from without, men cannot control, but they do resist them. But those winds within, which men have been made to control, they often fail to resist. It is into such a mortal setting as this that the present study introduces us.

There is no more revealing passage in *Gone With the Wind* which describes this mortal malady of man than the scene at the funeral of Gerald O'Hara, characterized as a "Fightin' Irishman and a Southern gentleman." His friends and neighbors have come to pay their last respects. His prospective son-in-law delivers the eulogy:

". . . There warn't nothin' that come to him *from the outside* that could lick him. He warn't scared of the English government when they wanted to hang him. He just lit out and left home. And when he come to this country and was pore, that didn't scare him a mite neither. He went to work and he made his money. And he warn't scared to tackle this section when it was part wild and the Injuns had just been run out of it. He made a big plantation out of a wilderness. And when the war come on and his money begun to go, he warn't scared to be pore again. And when the Yankees come through Tara and might of burnt him out or killed him, he warn't fazed a bit and he warn't licked neither. He just planted his front feet and stood his ground. That's why I say he had our good points. There ain't nothin' *from the outside* can lick any of us.

"But he had our failin's too, 'cause he could be licked from the inside. I mean to say that what the whole world couldn't do, his own heart could. When Mrs. O'Hara died, his heart died too, and he was licked. And what we seen walking 'round here warn't him.

". . . All you all and me, too, are like him. We got the same weakness and failin'. There ain't nothin' that walks can lick us, any more than it could lick him, not Yankees nor Carpet-baggers nor hard times nor high taxes nor even downright starvation. But that weakness that's in our hearts can lick us in the time it takes to bat your eye." (Pp. 710, 711.)

What a lay sermon on Isaiah's memorable words: "And our iniquities, like the wind, have taken us away!"

Another passage which reveals what the winds of the world without and the winds of the world within do to the souls of men is found in the words of old Grandma Fontaine who had lived through not only one war but many: the Mexican War, the Indian War and the War between the States; a rugged type of the sturdy American pioneer. She speaks to a girl of younger and comparatively tender years. She says:

". . . And when it comes to something that's unpleasant but can't be helped, I don't see any sense in screaming and kicking about it. That's no way to meet the ups and downs of life. I know because my family and the Old Doctor's family have had more than our share of ups and downs. And if we folks have a motto, it's this: 'Don't holler—smile and bide your time.' We've survived a passel of things that way, smiling and bidding our time, and we've gotten to be experts at surviving. We had to be. We've always bet on the wrong horses. Run out of France with the Huguenots, run out of England with the Cavaliers, run out of Scotland with Bonnie Prince Charlie, . . . and now licked by the Yankees. But we always turn up on top in a few years. You know why?"

. . . "Well, this is the reason. We bow to the inevitable. We're not wheat, we're buckwheat! When a storm comes along it flattens ripe wheat because it's dry and can't bend with the wind. But ripe buckwheat's got sap in it and it bends. And when the wind has passed, it springs up almost as straight and strong as before. We aren't a stiff-necked tribe. We're mighty limber when a hard wind's blowing, because we know it pays to be limber. When trouble comes we bow to the inevitable without any mouthing, and we work and we smile and we bide our time." . . . (Pp. 716, 717.)

How far can a man, how far can a woman, bend without breaking? Ask Job, ask Ruth, ask Jeremiah, ask the Psalmist, who declares, "Bless the Lord, O my soul. O Lord, my God, thou art very great. . . . Who walketh upon the wings of the wind, who maketh winds his messengers, flames of fire his ministers. . . . Yea, the trees of the Lord are full of sap. The cedars of Lebanon which he hath planted" (Psalm 104).

The plot of this book turns primarily about the vital relations of four characters: two men, Ashley Wilkes and Rhett Butler, and two women, Melanie Hamilton and Scarlett O'Hara. The two women, Melanie and Scarlett, are depicted in a way to show how differently they reacted to the winds which blow from within. Melanie Hamilton is a thin, steel blade of righteousness, who endures all the sufferings of her contemporary womanhood and who bends but never breaks. She is described as follows:

In her small face, her eyes were too large for beauty, the dark smudges under them making them appear enormous, but the expression in them had not altered since the days of her unworried girlhood. War and constant pain and hard work had been powerless against their sweet tranquillity. They were the eyes of a happy woman, a woman around whom storms might blow without ever ruffling the serene core of her being.

How did she keep her eyes that way, thought Scarlett, looking at her enviously. She knew her own eyes sometimes had the look of a hungry cat. What was it Rhett had said once about Melanie's eyes—some foolishness about them being like candles? Oh, yes, like two good deeds in a naughty world. Yes, they were like candles, candles shielded from every wind, two soft lights glowing with happiness at being home again among her friends. (P. 732.)

How did Melanie Hamilton keep her eyes that way? A literary artist can describe the eyes, but that is as far as the artist dare go. And this is where the function of the literature of the human heart is most clearly seen in its relation to the Bible's. The one is descriptive, the other revealing. The one points to effects, the other to first causes. The one analyzes motives, the other discloses sources. And this is why the reading of a great novel like *Gone With the Wind* becomes not only an experience to be enjoyed. For when it is read with the Bible at hand, or, better yet, with the Bible in mind, it becomes instructive with respect to those affairs of the soul which are highest or deepest. Scarlett's question about Melanie's eyes becomes the reader's question. And he is carried in thought to what the Bible declares about the true light which lighteth every man which cometh into the world. Here he himself is introduced to the source of light which does not fail in the person around whom storms may blow "without ever ruffling the serene core of her being."

The main character of this book, the person about whom the whole stirring narrative turns is Scarlett O'Hara, who might be described as a vain, selfish, quick tempered social belle, who thinks she knows what she wants but never gets it; a woman within whose soul the winds of elemental passion blow a perfect hurricane. She is best described by her contrast to her mother, Ellen O'Hara. To her daughter

> Ellen O'Hara was different, and Scarlett regarded her as something holy and apart from all the rest of humankind. When Scarlett was a child, she had confused her mother with the Virgin Mary, and now that she was older she saw no reason for changing her opinion. To her, Ellen represented the utter security that only Heaven or a mother can give. She knew that her mother was the embodiment of justice, truth, loving tenderness and profound wisdom—a great lady.
>
> Scarlett wanted very much to be like her mother. The only difficulty was that by being just and truthful and tender and unselfish, one missed most of the joys of life, and certainly many beaux. And life was too short to miss such pleasant things. Some day when she was married to Ashley and old, some day when she had time for it, she intended to be like Ellen. But, until then . . . (P. 60.)

Scarlett loved to do as she pleased. She is the type of person whose prototype we see in certain characters in the Bible who will never come to grips with life. Scarlett is the type of person who will never come clean on any moral issue but will always go around it. Whenever a matter becomes too hot for her kind, they simply leave it by putting it off until another day. "Tomorrow." And this is where Scarlett's theology expresses itself. Three outstanding characteristics of God, as Scarlett thinks of Him, may be mentioned.

In the first place Scarlett's God is a bargaining God.

> . . . Scarlett felt that the time for prayer had passed. If God had seen fit to punish them so, then God could very well do without prayers. Religion had always been a bargaining process with Scarlett. She promised God good behavior in exchange for favors. God had broken the bargain time and again, to her way of thinking, and she felt that she owed Him nothing at all now. And whenever she found Carreen on her knees when she should have been taking an afternoon nap or doing the mending, she felt that Carreen was shirking her share of the burdens. (P. 510.)

Scarlett's God a bargaining God! How far does such a view influence a person's behavior?

But Scarlett's God is also a God of wrath (p. 829). When her conscience torments her over the cold, bald way in which she has used Frank, she sighs to herself:

Oh, if only God did not seem so furious and vengeful! Oh, if only the minutes did not go by so slowly and the house were not so still! If only she were not so alone! (P. 822.)

And when she confides her fear and remorse to Rhett:

"I'm afraid I'll die and go to hell," (p. 826).

He reads her mind relentlessly and declares:

"Your ethics are considerably mixed up too. You are in the exact position of a thief who's been caught red-handed and isn't sorry he stole but is terribly, terribly sorry he's going to jail" (p. 829).

Since Scarlett's type holds low ideas of God, consequently her remorse is low: Love God for what you can get out of Him. Get away with all that you can, and when life goes against you, read Him out of your universe by relegating Him to tomorrow.

And Scarlett's God is also an absentee God. When Mammy, her old colored slave, remarks:

"Ah doan know whut de Lawd thinkin' 'bout, lettin' de bad women flurrish lak dat w'en us good folks is hongry an' mos' barefoot."

"The Lord stopped thinking about us years ago," said Scarlett savagely. "And don't go telling me Mother is turning in her grave to hear me say it either." (P. 557.)

What happens to people who value everything, even God, in terms of their own self-centered needs or desires? What does a theology based on belief in a bargaining, vengeful, absentee Deity do to a person? What did it do to Scarlett? When upon one occasion Rhett rebukes her, to use his own words:

"How clever of you to rook the helpless and the widow and the orphan and the ignorant!" (P. 774.)

Scarlett replies:

". . . I know I'm not as—scrupulous as I should be these days. Not as kind and as pleasant as I was brought up to be. But I can't help it, Rhett. Truly I can't. What else could I have done? What would have happened to me, to Wade, to Tara and all of us if I'd been—gentle when that Yankee came to Tara? I should have been—but I don't even want to think of that. And when Jonas Wilkerson was going to take the home place, suppose I'd been—kind and scrupulous? Where would we all be now? And if I'd been sweet and simple-minded and not nagged Frank about bad debts, we'd—oh, well. Maybe I am a rogue, but I won't be a rogue forever, Rhett. But during these past years—and even now—what else could I have done? How else could I have acted? I've felt that I was trying to row a heavily loaded boat in a storm. I've had so much trouble just trying to keep afloat that I couldn't be bothered about things that didn't matter, things I could part with easily and not miss, like good manners and—well, things like that. I've been too afraid my boat would be swamped and so I've dumped overboard the things that seemed least important.

"Pride and honor and truth and virtue and kindliness," he enumerated silkily. "You are right, Scarlett. They aren't important when a boat is sinking. But look around you at your friends. Either they are bringing their boats ashore safely with cargoes intact or they are content to go down with all flags flying."

"They are a passel of fools," she said shortly. "There's a time for all things. When I've got plenty of money, I'll be nice as you please, too. Butter won't melt in my mouth. I can afford to be then."

"You can afford to be—but you won't. It's hard to salvage jettisoned cargo and—if it is retrieved, it's usually irreparably damaged. And I fear that when you can afford to fish up the honor and virtue and kindness you're thrown overboard, you'll find they have suffered a sea change and not, I fear, into something rich and strange. . . ." (Pp. 774, 775.)

Not only is there a relation between the theology and the ethics of the Scarlett type but this relation becomes particularly pointed with respect to motive. And it is here that the gifted artist who gave us *Gone With the Wind* has painted her most telling portrait of the human heart under the urge and quiver of motive. Having jettisoned her cargo of the things that matter most, Scarlett finally arrives at the moment of supreme confession. It is her subconscious self which is now speaking, when she awakes from a dream cold with sweat.

. . . She was running, running, till her heart was bursting, running in a thick swimming fog, crying out, blindly seeking that nameless, unknown haven of safety that was somewhere in the mist about her (pp. 855, 856).

And she confides to her husband:

"Oh, Rhett, I just run and run and hunt and I can't ever find what it is I'm hunting for. It's always hidden in the mist. I know if I could find it, I'd be safe forever and ever and never be cold or hungry again" (p. 856).

And then comes the key question of the book, and its revealing answer. Rhett asks:

"Is it a person or a thing you're hunting?"

Scarlett replies:

"I don't know. I never thought about it" (p. 856).

Ah, there's the rub. Suppose the Scarlett type did think seriously or deeply about what they are hunting? This is where theology passes almost imperceptibly over to religion and then into life. Here is where the veil is withdrawn and the Image within the human breast is revealed: Hunting a thing or a Person? It is here that "God's fresh heavenward will, with our poor earthward striving" receives a decisive answer. And it is here too that a man or a woman learns that heart's full scope "which we are hourly wronging," when like Augustine he quits the search for things and turns gratefully to the Person, concerning whom he declared: "Thou hast made us for Thyself and our hearts are restless till they rest in Thee," or when he hearkens to the words of Him who said: "Seek ye first His kingdom and His righteousness and these things shall be added unto you."

But Scarlett and her kind will never think seriously about moral issues, and *Gone With the Wind* traces with unerring skill this central urgency and its inevitable consequence. Over and over again Scarlett chants her most characteristic theme-song; and with what a variety of moral issues it is associated!

"I won't think about it any more" (p. 445).

"I won't think about it now" (p. 541).

"I won't think of Tara now. I'll think of it later when it won't hurt so much" (p. 590).

What would Mother say? . . . "I'll think of all this later" (pp. 662, 663).

"Oh, I'll think of them later" (p. 787).

"I won't think of it now. I'll think of it later when I can stand it" (p. 928).

Tomorrow—well tomorrow was another day. Tomorrow she would think of some excuse, some counter accusations . . . (p. 932).

"I won't think of it now. I can't stand it if I do. I'll think of it tomorrow at Tara. Tomorrow's another day" (p. 967).

"Not tonight! Tomorrow morning I'll come early and do the things I must do, say the comforting things I must say. But not tonight. I can't. I'm going home" (p. 1019).

"I'll think of it all tomorrow, at Tara. I can stand it then. Tomorrow, I'll think of some way to get him back. After all, tomorrow is another day" (p. 1037).

Unhappily in the moral universe the morrow of opportunity never dawns. Character is only formed in the realities here and now. And our choices and our decisions today are reaped by their consequences tomorrow. The only morrow which ever dawns is the morrow of reckoning, the morrow of judgment. It is not without significance that the stern requirements of moral urgency are prescribed in the Bible:

"Today, if ye will hear His voice
Harden not your hearts."

Today, Today, Today! So at the end of the book Scarlett is alone. She is almost desperate in her aloneness. She is alone with the red earth of the old plantation. In the presence of that scene the reader can almost hear the voice of the Prophet: "She obeyed not the voice, she received not correction. . . . Her princes in the midst of her are roaring lions. Her judges are evening wolves, they leave nothing till tomorrow." This is the tragedy of the nation as well as the person who seeks things at the expense of the Supreme Person: to face-up to one's inexorable tomorrow alone! And this also was Scarlett's tragedy:

> She had never understood either of the men she had loved and so she had lost them both. Now, she had a fumbling knowledge that, had she ever understood Ashley, she would never have loved him; had she ever understood Rhett, she would never have lost him. She wondered forlornly if she had ever really understood anyone in the world (p. 1036).

Everything she had counted precious had gone with the wind. Or had it?

Gone With the Wind is much more than a stirring narrative of the War between the States in a new setting. It is rather in this setting a vivid and timely transcript of the elemental human soul experiencing the hurricane which blows more violently within than from without. In the realistic words of Will Benteen: "There ain't nothin' *from the outside* can lick any of us. . . . But that weakness that's in our hearts can lick us in the time it takes to bat your eye" (p. 711).

But there is not only a weakness in our hearts—there is also a strength. The instinct of the race for God, in spite of sinister winds within, still dares hope for tomorrow. Yes, tomorrow *is* another day.

> "It is God's day, . . .
> A lavish day! One day, with life and heart,
> Is more than enough time to find a world."

Our Second Reconstruction

By Westbrook Pegler

Margaret Mitchell was certainly no Fascist. Neither was she a liberal in any political sense. In a letter to Herschel Brickell she described her friends Mark and Willie Snow Ethridge as "Liberals" and called them "strange bedfellows for such Tory Conservatives as John and me." World War II proved her to be intensely patriotic and the postwar years show her as staunchly and consistently anti-Russian.

Less than three weeks before her death she wrote Dr. Wallace McClure, her particular friend at the State Department in unraveling her foreign entanglements concerning copyright, on July 26, 1949:

As I look back over the years since the day Senator George introduced my brother and me to you, I realize I have had a box seat at the world's biggest show from 1936 until now. . . . I realize now that my book has taken me to many countries and made many friends for me. I realize it all the more now when I lie awake at night wondering about the publishers, agents, newspaper critics, and just plain letter-writing friends who have suddenly become silent and disappeared as Russia rolled over their countries—Bulgaria, Roumania, Hungary, Poland, Yugoslavia, and now Czechoslovakia. The Communists have attacked "Gone With the Wind" in this country and in every other country. . . .

At night I pack food and vitamins and clothing boxes, always wondering if they will ever reach the people to whom they are sent. Sometimes when I am out in crowds I find I do not have too much conversation about what is going on in Georgia because I have been wrestling with international financial regulations and wondering about people who cannot possibly escape from the encirclement of Russia.

In *Show* magazine for last October, Ralph McGill, the Atlanta journalist, offered an affectionate requiem to Peggy Mitchell; the Margaret Mitchell who wrote the greatest American novel, *Gone With the Wind*. He conjured a mischievous little flirt in the office of the Atlanta *Journal*, at a time when he was a cub in general practice but with a tendency toward sports. This was my own bent in New York, in the first few years after the First War, when many of us gallus expense-account tramps of the World Series and the Big Fight had a loosejointed fraternity reaching down to Nashville, Augusta, and New Orleans. Ralph presently dropped out of sports, probably because Atlanta was, in the baseball rating, a minor league town. But he had a belligerent, wrong-side-of-the-tracks attitude in social and political matters, and undoubtedly would have marched off to the Revolution behind the Pied Piper of Hyde Park—or his to reason why. Sport would have staled with him even in New York in the Era of Wonderful Nonsense. I had never heard of Margaret Mitchell in those days—but who had?

I

Gone With the Wind came out in 1936; and by the time I made pilgrimage to her knee-sprung little flat in Atlanta, near the end of the Second War, she was not seductive but "settled" and even rather dumpling. She was so earnest, worried by her knowledge of the past in the midst of the swirling present of a country again beset by scoundrels, that I caught no glimpse of the happy nature that McGill had known. I faintly envy his earlier friendship with the sly little scamp who, in those days, wore her skirts up to here, in the mode preserved for the Ages by John Held Jr. Ralph startled me with a report in his tribute that in those days, before Success and her foresight subdued her, she sometimes whipped out of the Sunday Department of the *Journal*—where she wrote "feature" stories—into the City Room: to paw the big dictionary on the conventional wobbly stand for the precise meaning of some word, and standing on tip-toe, "give the middle-aged men a thrill." That girl who clearly gave Ralph, himself, a thrill, was gone with the wind when I drove up to her door and discovered a henchman on My Side. She was anti-Roosevelt but asked me to spare her the suffering that would have been inflicted by McGill's Side for having truck with me. Once, back there, I did venture to indicate in print that she was still Unreconstructed and in fear of a hell of retribution for our folly in following Roosevelt down the bloody path of glory, greed, and corruption. And I believe Ralph will agree with me that his admonition to let Peggy speak for herself was rather waspy. He seemed to assume that he could speak for her, though. But he did not know she had already spoken; so he may have thought she was a covert scallawag silently biding her time to go out barn-burning with the pickets of Roosevelt's New Ku Klux Klan. She would have been a comfort for My Side for she had moral influence and devotion, as I shall persuade you when I come to the hour of her death. She was a comfort to me. Even then, she was eyeing the grafters in the very White House itself; more impudent and crude than any in the household of General Grant—profiteers, carpet-baggers, union racketeers, and Reds. They were swaggering even in her own Atlanta.

II

Ralph wrote me a letter along in there declaring that he knew of no wrong that Eleanor Roosevelt ever had done. We were imbedded in our principles so neither one could win the argument. We could only destroy a friendship founded in an ancient respect and watered by similar experience and personal hurts.

I last saw him in the awful Ukraine Hotel in Moscow during Dick Nixon's 1959 trip. It had been some years then, so I felt caution, but he readily told me that he and his wife, who then was toward death, had been put to terrible hurt by dirty phone calls in the night during the Roosevelt Years. This cowardly business clearly was the work of persons on My Side who, of course, were unknown to me. But His Side had called My Side *Fascist-Minded Copperheads*, if you remember. We were *hatemongers*. We had rejected Roosevelt's National Recovery Administration as Star-Spangled Hitlerism. We had snarled our malicious devotion to the Constitution at New York bar-room patriots, procurement colonels buying uniforms for WACs, lawyers, and strident entertainers sacrificing their talents for Our Brave Boys. The *New York Post* was Roosevelt's bugle, bravely furious at Americans who doggedly remembered the true story of St. Petersburg in 1918. Lindbergh was an evil man in many and many a New Deal night club.

Nevertheless, the McGills kept their phone alive, whereas I shut ours off at night. But who could suppress the radio night after night for years as vicarious commandos bawled and shrieked at us Labor Baiters, Roosevelt-haters, and Fifth Columnists: from a boozing-den run by two Bessarabians under a Scottish name, where great, luscious steaks went to the garbage smothered in the soggy butts of dollar cigars and blankets of ashes? They couldn't speak English very well there. Red Points were a smutty joke. These members of His Side had no personal endorsement from McGill, either.

Ralph believes Peggy Mitchell held out against "Integration" but he forgives her though she had to be wrong because he was right. She never got Reconstructed but out of his bigness he forgives her that, too.

The food in the Soviets' Ukraine Hotel was the worst in all my travels. "Steak" was about an ounce of un-bled bluish dark meat off anonymous critters, cleavered with jagged chips of bone, from wherever the broad-axe fell. When I came out of Russia and caught up with some of Ralph's essays in the papers, I had to wonder whether he wrote his rhapsodies to mock me.

At meals, we hedged away from our little asperities about Peggy Mitchell. I had none of her letters with me and I wasn't sure that I ever could find them again.

III

But when Ralph wrote his recent memorian for *Show* I went to the jumble and passed a miracle. There were her letters, and in the one of September 7, 1944, she had said:

"I'd like to make a request of you and, to someone with your experience as a reporter, it may not seem an unusual one. Please keep my connection with all this confidential.

"I have never been averse to controversy but at this stage of my life, my greatest wish is to avoid anything that would focus public attention on me. Since 'Gone With the Wind' was published, I have had too much public attention. The problems that it brings have kept me busy for eight years and left me no time even for trying to write. In addition, my father was seriously ill for several years and needed constant care until his death in June.

"Now that he is gone, I am trying to catch up on things I left untended during the years before and recapture some part of a normal life. If it became public that I had 'collaborated' with Westbrook Pegler by supplying you this information it would stir up a flurry that would disrupt my life for two or three months at least. At this time, I would like to avoid all flurries and disruptions and live as quietly as possible.

"Please feel free to call on me for any information I can supply but just keep me out of it. I am glad to uphold your hand in this courageous work you are doing but, right now, I prefer to do it from the sidelines."

She knew the terrors of "Democracy." She knew Danny Kaye was a great American. It said so in the papers and on the air.

I had asked her for information on two individuals who became great scavengers in Reconstruction. One was Columbus Delano, an Ohio political hack who became Commissioner of Internal Revenue and Secretary of the Interior, under President Grant. The other was Rufus Bullock, the Governor of Georgia during Reconstruction. Miss Mitchell soon sent me thirty-six lines of single-space, mostly references, on Columbus Delano and more than three pages of single space on Bullock.

Delano's rascality was not local but widespread. The notorious Whiskey Revenue Frauds, originally disclosed in St. Louis, continued "to blacken the record of the national government." She directed me to many authorities out of the abundance of her information, earned by study in the writing of her master-work. Columbus Delano was one of the great looters in the Georgia railroad conspiracy. He became rich enough to bequeath to Kenyon College at Gambier, Ohio, an edifice called Delano Hall. The destitution of the Indians wrought by Delano's ignorant, predatory reign was one of Grant's awful failures. Other Delanos have tried to ennoble the scoundrel but he remains one of the great rogues of an era which, until the present, stood apart from less majestic perfidies. The New Reconstruction levelled Columbus Delano to the stature of his peers. He had a son whom, Peggy Mitchell wrote, "was definitely mixed up in the finagling of the railroads."

IV

The cautious historian speaks in the first paragraph of her letter of September 7, 1944 where she begins: "Before I start riding off in all directions to try to dig up some information you need, I want to set you straight about a matter which could cause you much embarrassment—your natural mixing of the names Bullock and Bulloch. Perhaps only born Georgians and historians can keep them straight. They are mixed so often, especially by Northerners and unfailingly screams of protest arise from the South."

The only protest I ever heard, however, came from Archie, a soldier son of

Theodore the President, who noisily lost patience forgetting, no doubt, that his own Cousin Eleanor had balled-up the names and characters of William E. Dodd, a second-rate historian, and Harold W. Dodds, the double-dome President of Princeton. Her husband sent Dodd to be his Ambassador to Hitler, thinking Dodd was Dodds. The results were worse in that case, for Dodd had a son, a Red, who was legally forbidden to be hired in any job by the Washington Bureaucracy, and a daughter who made herself notorious in Germany and later absconded to the Soviet Empire with a sympathetic spouse. Doctor Dodds of Princeton made no scream of protest, though.

"Rufus Bullock was Governor of Georgia during part of the Reconstruction Period," Miss Mitchell continued. "I made mention of him at some length in 'Gone With the Wind', for he was a colorful figure. This Rufus Bullock came from upstate New York, I believe Albion. Someone in Albion recently offered to sell me a desk which belonged to Rufus Bullock's father. I am practically certain that this Rufus Bullock came to Georgia in the early fifties and was employed very respectably by some express company. He fought in the Confederate Army and I believe was mustered out as a lieutenant colonel. I think he was not in a line regiment but I am not certain of this. So far this is a perfectly respectable record. Many men of Northern birth fought for the Confederacy. At some time during Reconstruction, Rufus Bullock suddenly emerged as a close friend of the Northern troops then garrisoned in the South and a close associate of Republicans, Carpetbaggers, and Scalawags. The scandals of this period in Georgia are incredible and the history of them is so tangled and hidden and confused that it is difficult to say what is what. I think it is the most confused period of American history." Of course the girl did not know the truth about Yalta then or the UN. She knew little about Lend-Lease. The Truman Administration, the Bay of Pigs, and the abduction of General Ted Walker to a stinking Bedlam by order of an impudent plug-ugly who had never tried a case in court, lay in the future. But she was beginning to see dark figures hiding in the shadows of Tomorrow.

"When this present war is over it will be difficult to straighten out in France just what the political, social, and business relations were between the German conquerors and the collaborationists. So, with Reconstruction in Georgia.

"The railroad scandals smelled worse than any other scandals of the period. It has been so long since I did any work on them that I cannot even recall the names of the books I read but I will hunt them up today. However, you will not find the truth about these railroad scandals in any one book. The truth is that once Reconstruction was over and the troops were taken out of the South, everyone was so worn and weary from War and Reconstruction, turmoil and bitterness, that by common consent the people agreed to forget, at least publicly, a great many things. Governor Bullock hastily left, safeguarded by Federal troops, to the great pleasure and relief of all.

"That is Rufus Bullock. Now let me tell you about the Bullochs, one of whom, Mittie (Martha) married into the Theodore Roosevelt family.

"There is no more respected, or looked-up-to family in the history of Georgia than these Bullochs. The Bullochs lived at Bulloch Hall in Roswell, Georgia, an old and lovely settlement twenty-nine miles from Atlanta. One of this clan had been famous in the Revolutionary War. Another, E. M. Bulloch, was an admiral in the Confederate Navy. He stayed in England after the war and never returned to this country.

(Eleanor Roosevelt disagreed with popular legend and perhaps with the truth in her first book of memoirs entitled *This Is My Story,* published in 1937. She wrote: "There was one mysterious visitor that winter (1891), Uncle Jimmie Bulloch, who came over from Liverpool where he had lived ever since the Civil War. On account of the work he and his brother had done for the Confederacy they had not been included in the general amnesty and so had to settle in England instead of returning. He was, of course, entirely safe, but he had come over under an assumed name, and there were many people in New York who would not receive the man who had succeeded in getting the *Alabama* out to sea to prey on Northern ships and had actually sailed in her as a junior officer. I remember a very vital, big man in my mother's sitting room playing with me, giving me a strange sense of adventure even though I knew nothing of the reasons for it.")

"This Admiral was an uncle of Theodore Roosevelt the elder. Mittie Bulloch of this fine family, married the father of Theodore Roosevelt, the elder, in Roswell in the 1850's and went North to live. Many years after, President Theodore Roosevelt returned to Georgia and went to Roswell to visit his mother's old home. I go into these details so that you will not mix these two families for if you made this seemingly small error it would give Southern people the right to say that nothing you wrote was correct."

V

This and other letters from Peggy Mitchell were signed *Margaret Mitchell Marsh (Mrs. John R. Marsh)* in honor of a husband who had been a genteel journalist and who, in his last years, was a publicity man. He was failing with heart disease when I last saw them in a modest hotel in New York. She had phoned me to come over, for she would not risk the wear and tear, on John, of an evening in a restaurant or among strangers in their small suite. She wanted my opinion of the politics of a New Deal book-writer for the advice of a publisher, whom she did not name. I told her honestly and the subject closed. I never learned why the publisher wanted to know or what influence my opinion had on him. We had one drink each of bourbon and I then conveyed an offer from *King Features Syndicate* of the Hearst outfit of $1,000 a week for the rest of her life for permission to use her name over a feature—a comic strip was the idea in mind—to be called "Gone With the Wind." She might either write or veto the ideas and text or simply cash her checks. The offer came from Ward Greene, our editor who had been an elder among the city-side reporters in Atlanta when she was a girl. He rejoiced in her great success and probably bore her a degree of love, as most of her colleagues did. And he was a great writer, himself, though one of many fine writers who never caught the brass ring.

Peggy asked me to thank Mr. Greene and tell him she was resolved never to accept any pay for anything she did not write herself. She had no intention just then of writing anything at all as long as she might live. She never did, for she was fatally hurt in a traffic accident while she and John Marsh were strolling to a movie on August 11, 1949.

VI

On December eighteenth, the Sunday magazine section of the Atlanta *Journal*, a home talent color press production, consisted almost entirely of bravely restrained but nevertheless almost tearful memories of the girl who had made her start in its pages interviewing Rudolph Valentino; and, more notably, Mrs. William Baker, of Roswell, who had been a bridesmaid at the wedding of Miss Mittie Bulloch to young Theodore Roosevelt, and became the mother of President Theodore Roosevelt. Mrs. Baker was eighty-seven years old at the time of this routine "feature" in 1923, and Peggy wrote that her hair was still black with only a few faint threads of silver. The Sunday magazine tributes to Peggy were written by members of the Sunday magazine staff.

Ward Greene, in New York, suggested this spread to Angus Perkerson, the Editor, and Ward sent me a copy. There I find the story of "Margaret Mitchell's Last Hours" at Grady Memorial Hospital by Marguerite Steedman who began thus:

"Please, how is Miss Mitchell? I'm calling for the folks at my boarding house. We don't know her but we're SO worried!"

"No'm, I don't know her but I'm praying for her!"

"Isn't there anything I can do? Run errands? Give blood?"

"Hour by hour the calls floated into an office at Grady Memorial Hospital—a small room ironically full of sunlight. On the desk beside the never-silent phone were flowers and stacks of telegrams, letters pouring in from a stunned, incredulous world. . . . If you telephoned for news and someone asked your name, your message, to be sure that neither was lost or forgotten. Both were written down so that Margaret Mitchell, if she lived, or her family, in any case, might be able to thank you, silently, even if you never knew."

It is just as well that this great soul did not go brawling in the riots kicked up by the New York Influence which held Roosevelt and his wife above the United States. What could she have done?

The Hysterical Personality and the Feminine Character: A Study of Scarlett O'Hara

By Charles E. Wells

Responding to an Illinois doctor (Mark A. Patton) who had written her a fan letter, Margaret Mitchell noted on August 22, 1936:

Nothing could have pleased me more than have a psychiatrist praise the pattern of Scarlett O'Hara's emotional life. I am one of those people who are disliked by all real psychiatrists. I am a layman who knows just a little about abnormal psychology. I started out to be a psychiatrist, but, unfortunately, was forced to leave college when my mother died . . . I hoped for years to go back to medical school, and with that idea in view kept up my studies. I realize that I know all the tops of abnormal psychology—and have none of the basic and rudimentary knowledge. It's like knowing geometry and never having known the multiplication tables. Perhaps you can understand, after this explanation, why your words of praise about "The accurate description of human emotions" pleased me so much.

How well Miss Mitchell understood the basis of Scarlett's personality is discussed in an illuminating article by Dr. Charles E. Wells of the Vanderbilt University School of Medicine.

Hysteria and hysterical have for many years been words in search of a meaning, at least within the discipline of psychiatry. The spectrum of definitions has ranged from the notion that the meaning is so specific that the "hysteric" patient can be recognized at a glance to the opinion that the words are nothing more than terms of opprobrium designating particularly trying patients.

For slightly over two decades, however, there has been a move toward refining the meaning of these words in their psychiatric use. Hysterical neurosis, conversion type,*(1)** hysterical neurosis, dissociative type, *(1)* and hysterical psychosis *(2)* have been separated from the mass of conditions called hysterical and have been defined with considerable precision. The former two have attained the status of specific diagnostic entities in the *Diagnostic and Statistical Manual of Mental Disease.* *(1)* It is generally agreed that these three disorders are not dependent upon a substructure of a specific personality type. *(3)* What remains is a group called "hysterical personality" that has proved especially difficult to limit and define.

In 1958 Chodoff and Lyons *(4)* published a classic description of the hysterical personality, limiting their description entirely to observable behavior. According to them, "hysterical personality is a term applicable to persons who are vain and egocentric, who display labile and excitable but shallow affectivity, whose dramatic, attention seeking and histrionic behavior may go to the extremes of lying and even pseudologia phantastica, who are very conscious of sex, sexually provocative yet frigid, and who are dependently demanding in interpersonal situations." These words are echoed almost verbatim in the definition of the hysterical personality offered in the DSM II. *(1)* Placing total reliance on behavioral characteristics has, however, proved unsatisfactory, and others have sought to add depth to our understanding by viewing the hysterical personality in different perspectives.

Psychoanalysis has tried to define personality types in terms of the ego defense mechanisms habitually employed. Hysteria has traditionally been associated with over reliance on the defense of repression, and indeed the diagnosis has often rested upon the recognition of dependence on repression as a defense mechanism. Others, taking account of the emotionalism prominent in most individuals called hysterical, have conceived emotionality as such to be a defense mechanism, *(5)* and one perhaps more characteristic of the hysterical personality than repression.

Psychoanalysts have sought to understand the hysterical personality beyond merely identifying and elucidating defense mechanisms. Psychodynamically it has been suggested that the genesis of the hysterical personality rests in a disturbed mother-daughter relationship. The girl child destined to be a hysteric suffers a deprivation of maternal love and nurturance. She then turns to her father for such, but to her father not as father but as a substitute mother. "Since they barter sexual attractiveness, they grow up to be women who use sex as a means—often the prime means—of obtaining maternal gratifications from men. The only change is the person from whom closeness and love are sought; a suitor or husband is substituted for father."*(6)*

Although persons having hysterical personalities often do employ repression to a striking extent, Shapiro *(7)* has pointed out that this fails to explain many commonly observed features. He sought further understanding in styles

---

*Editor's note: Italic numbers in parentheses indicate reference at end of article.

of cognition, describing hysterical cognition as "impressionistic," i.e., "global, relatively diffuse, and lacking in sharpness, particularly in sharp detail." Moreover, he emphasized the hysteric's incapacity for intense intellectual concentration, lack of detailed factual knowledge, impressionability and distractibility, and lack of logical organization of facts and feelings. According to Shapiro these cognitive features favor the use of repression.

More recently questioned is the extent to which social factors lead to the development of the hysterical personality and whether the hysterical personality can be separated from the "normal" feminine character. Shapiro wondered if some aspects of hysterical cognition might not represent "a certain cultural image of femininity, now somewhat out of date except, perhaps, among some classes of Southern women." Hollender *(6)* later suggested that "the ideal climate for the production of hysterical personalities existed in the plantation society of the antebellum South, epitomized in Margaret Mitchell's *Gone With the Wind*." More recently, Lerner, *(8)* focusing on Chodoff and Lyons' observation that the hysterical personality is a "caricature of femininity," has questioned whether it is possible to separate the hysterical character from the normal female character. She suggests that in American society "a girl's immediate social environment puts enormous pressure on her to develop a style of cognition and personality that will lend itself to this diagnosis [hysterical personality]." This possibility had been suggested earlier by Halleck.*(9)*

There seems to be general agreement that social forces play a major role in fostering the development of the feminine character and feminine characteristics (as well as defining them). The importance of social forces in shaping the hysterical personality is much less certain and more difficult to establish. One approach to this problem is to study fictional Southern female characters raised in this "ideal climate for the production of hysterical personalities" to see if they satisfy the various criteria of the hysterical personality enumerated above. Scarlett O'Hara, as described by Margaret Mitchell in *Gone With the Wind (10)*, remains four decades after her creation the prototype of the Southern belle.

The study of Scarlett that follows seeks to answer three questions: (1) To what extent were Scarlett's behavior and personality consonant with our present concepts of the hysterical personality? (2) To what extent were Scarlett's behavior and personality a reflection of or a result of the culture in which she was born and raised? (3) Does a study of Scarlett cast any light on the relationship between feminine character and the hysterical personality?

In appearance and behavior, Scarlett O'Hara fulfilled almost exactly the criteria for the hysterical personality offered by Chodoff and Lyons.*(4)* Sixteen years old at the beginning of the novel, she was "not beautiful, but men seldom realized it when caught by her charm." Katie Scarlett was the oldest and clearly the favorite child of Gerald and Ellen O'Hara; two other daughters chafed in her shadow, and three sons lay buried in the family graveyard. When she was first met "in the cool shade of the porch of Tara, her father's plantation," on the eve of the Civil War, she was "a pampered child who has always had her own way for the asking." "Born to the ease of plantation life, waited on hand and foot since infancy," Scarlett appeared prepared for nothing more challenging than the next day's barbecue. Yet the novel closed twelve tumultuous years (and three husbands) later with Scarlett preparing to meet yet another crisis.

Let us look at the individual criteria of Chodoff and Lyons *(4) to weigh how precisely Scarlett fit each. Egoism, vanity, egocentricity, self-centeredness,* self-indulgence—she had all these in abundance. Her whole life centered around her own wants, and what she wanted foremost was attention and adulation in a setting of comfort and security. She "was, in reality, self-willed, vain and obstinate; . . . she could never long endure any conversation of which she was not the chief subject." Even in mourning for her first husband she could not forego wearing a new bonnet to make herself pretty (and noticed).

Her dramatic, attention-seeking, and histrionic behavior indeed went to the extent of lying to achieve her aims. Seeking attention was a way of life to Scarlett, and if she had to exaggerate, act, or even lie, these acts were merely tools, used by her with an artisan's skill. Her unbridled and labile display of affects, emotional capriciousness, and excitability were notorious, and as tools of her egocentricity, they too served her well. "When Scarlett gets mad, everybody knows it. She don't hold herself in like some girls do."

She sexualized all relationships; coquetry and sexually provocative displays were never far beneath the surface. "She was constitutionally unable to endure any man being in love with any woman not herself." She consciously employed all her beauty and charm to attract men's attention, then for her attention she usually made them beg and plead "laughing if they sulked, growing cold if they became angry." "She had never had a girl friend. . . . To her, all women, including her two sisters, were natural enemies in pursuit of the same prey—man." This "predatory nature" was by no means unnoticed by other women, her boyfriend's mother openly regarding her as "that sly piece."

Chodoff and Lyons(4) emphasized the sexual apprehensiveness, immaturity, and frigidity of the hysterical personality—and here one cannot be quite certain of Scarlett. Her sexuality was not so clearly spelled out in this novel of the mid-thirties. It appears likely that she remained sexually frigid throughout her first two marriages, but since she married each of these men with full awareness that she felt no sexual attraction for them, this might be expected. She clearly was not frigid in her sexual relationship with Rhett Butler, her third husband, though even here sex does not seem to have been greatly valued by her. It seemed likely that, in Chodoff and Lyons' terms, she did experience "failure of sex impulse to develop toward natural goal," for in fact sexual fulfillment seemed never to have mattered very much to Scarlett.

The "demanding, dependent" quality of the hysterical personality is the last behavioral characteristic emphasized by these authors. That Scarlett was demanding cannot be doubted; that she was dependent cannot be believed. Often, particularly in her relationship with men, she gave the appearance of dependency; but in fact, after the death of her mother Scarlett never depended on another human being other than herself.

From this descriptive-diagnostic standpoint, Scarlett fulfilled almost perfectly the criteria for the diagnosis of the hysterical personality proposed by Chodoff and Lyons *(4)* and officially sanctioned in the DSM II. *(1)* Furthermore, as drawn in the novel, there is little question that Scarlett was one of those women who would be diagnosed at a glance as a hysterical personality by many psychiatrists today (and diagnosed correctly according to the standards of the DSM II). However, let us look beyond these behavioral characteristics to see how she fits the other features described for this diagnostic grouping.

Repression and perhaps emotionality have been identified as the defenses most reliably and consistently employed by the hysterical personality. Throughout this long novel, which centers on Scarlett's perceptions, feelings, thoughts, and behavior, there is no suggestion that her ego utilized repression to an excessive or even to a significant degree. Similarly, although her emotions were frequently painful and intense, there is no suggestion that emotionality as such was serving a defensive function. On the contrary, as will be considered later, Scarlett's perception of herself and of her environment was usually precise despite the access and excess of her feelings. The two ego defense mechanisms most openly recorded in the novel are suppression and anticipation, both rated high-level mature defenses in Vaillant's hierarchy of ego defense mechanisms. *(11)* In fact, Scarlett's reliance on suppression has become almost an American cliché:

> "I won't think of it now," she said desperately, burying her face in the pillow. "I won't think of it now. I'll think of it later when I can stand it."

Equally important to her was anticipation, her awareness of and planning for the future. "Scarlett was never to look back." Even at the book's end, deserted by Rhett Butler, the only husband for whom she had cared, Scarlett said to herself: "I'll think of some way to get him back. After all, tomorrow is another day."

Nor does Scarlett satisfy the dynamic constellation proposed for the hysterical personality. She was clearly the favorite child, and equally the favorite of her mother and of her father. The relationship with her parents was intense, meaningful, and lasting; in fact, throughout the story, her relationships to Ellen and Gerald were the only ones that really seemed to count in her life. Even her relationship with Rhett lacked meaning and permanence. Throughout Ellen's life and even after her death, Scarlett's thoughts were haunted by her desire to return to the state of perfect love and security under her mother's care: "She wanted the very comfort of her mother's presence. . . . She always felt secure when Ellen was by her." Though Scarlett saw all women as natural enemies, it was always "all women with the one exception of her mother." And she knew with absolute certainty, "No woman ever really liked me, except Mother." Even as the narrative closed she was planning to return to Tara, her parents' home, seeking the security lost since the death of her mother many years before.

The relationship with her father, although different, was no less warm and genuine. Her three brothers dead, Scarlett to some extent took their places in her father's life. A tomboy in her early years, she grew into an attractive and seductive woman, but even so Gerald treated her "in a man-to-man manner which she found most pleasant." She and her father were united in their mutual dependence on her mother. With Ellen's death, Gerald disintegrated, and Scarlett never depended on anyone again.

To what extent was Scarlett's style of function consonant with hysterical cognition and dominance of emotions? Her cognition was in fact never impressionistic. With a sharp eye for detail, she saw the features of her world with striking clarity. She had an intense curiosity and hid "a sharp intelligence beneath a face as sweet and blank as a baby's." She suffered none of the insufficient organization and integration of mental contents said to be typical of the hysterical personality; with "singlemindedness of purpose, her eyes were centered on the goal and she thought only of the most direct steps by which to reach it."

With a particularly good head for figures, she computed probable profits and losses with a swiftness and precision that defeated her competition. Though admittedly remarkably deficient in general knowledge, it was a deficiency based on disinterest, not on inability. General information simply had no usefulness for Scarlett, who was supremely utilitarian. Even though it was said that she "would never be able to understand a complexity," in fact the only complexities she failed to understand were those that had no practical usefulness to her, with one major exception—people. She was not "a speck smart about folks." It was not, however, their complexity she didn't understand. Her life being dominated by "shrewd practicality," it was purely beyond her ken that people could allow themselves to be guided by their feelings and by their standards. It is hard to know which of these features was more perplexing to her.

She experienced affects vividly and at times gave vent to her feelings in a seemingly unbridled fashion; but her actions were not dictated by her emotions, nor in their display was there lack of control. In the middle of the battle of Atlanta, her very world disintegrating, with fire and explosions on every side, "into her swaying, darkened mind, cold sanity came back with a rush."

Even while she felt the hot blood of wrath still in her cheeks, something in Scarlett's practical mind promoted the thought that what this man said was right, and it sounded like common sense.
But so well did she conceal her feelings, so well did she enact her role. . . .
Raging as she was . . . the cold hand of common sense held her back. She swallowed her anger.

Even Rhett, so often the target of her rages, admired her self-control and admitted: "I know the practical in you will always win." In Scarlett, liability of emotion did not lead to its domination, and she had little understanding and no sympathy for people whose actions were determined by affects.

Even less did she comprehend morality and the strictures of the superego. The only limit to her shrewd practicality was what she thought she could get away with. Those guided by higher motives garnered only her contempt.

Romance and fantasy dominated only one segment of her life—her fantasied love for Ashley Wilkes. Ashley was in many ways the antithesis of everything she valued in life, but he was unobtainable, and this her vanity could never tolerate. But her fantasy was sharply circumscribed and could coexist alongside her practicality. In the end even this fantasy was dispelled as she came to realize Ashley's true nature.

To what extent did social forces mold her behavior and her character? There can be no question that social forces fashioned the hysterical carapace regarded as femininity in that age (and perhaps not greatly modified in our own). The subject of role-playing to attract a man to marriage was a major requirement in each girl's curriculum. Young girls before marriage had to be sweet, beautiful, gentle, ornamental, helpless, and clinging.

"I wish to Heaven I was married," she said resentfully. . . . "I'm tired of everlastingly being unnatural and never doing anything I want to do. I'm tired of acting like I don't eat more than a bird, and walking when I want to run and saying I feel faint after a waltz, when I could dance for two days and never get tired. I'm tired of saying, 'How wonderful you are!' to fool men who haven't got one-half the sense I've got, and I'm tired of pretending I don't know anything, so men can tell me things and feel important while they're doing it."

But as Scarlett shrewdly realized, "Really it took a lot of sense to cultivate and hold such a pose." The pose was acknowledged by all concerned, but it was recognized as being strictly time-limited. Its curtain descended with the marriage vows, for "after marriage they were expected to manage households that numbered a hundred people or more" with responsibility, orderliness, and devotion. The demands of each role (maiden and wife) in this society were explicit, and there was little overlap. Both roles were feminine, but only the maiden's is likely to be considered a manifestation of the hysterical personality. Even here, as seen in the study of Scarlett, the evidence for diagnosis of hysterical personality was limited to the spheres of appearance and behavior. Scarlett did not manifest the defensive structure, psychodynamic relationships, or cognitive style characteristic of the hysterical personality.

The hysterical personality has been studied and defined in terms of behavior, characteristic defenses, psychodynamic structure, and cognitive style. Recently the identity of the hysterical personality type has been questioned, and it has been suggested that social forces bend the female child into a feminine character style that is indistinguishable from the hysterical personality. Further, it has been suggested that the plantation society of the antebellum South might have been the most fertile climate for the growth of such personalities.

Scarlett O'Hara, as the prototype product of this environment, has been studied to evaluate *(1)* to what extent she represents the hysterical personality as generally understood today and *(2)* to what extent she represents the typical feminine character resulting from the social forces of her age and culture. While by appearance and behavior Scarlett fulfills almost perfectly our requirements for being labeled a hysterical personality, she does not at all fit our understanding of the hysterical personality in terms of favored defense mechanisms, psychodynamic forces, and cognitive style. Scarlett's appearance and outward behavior (her hysterical carapace, that is) are clearly presented as the product of social forces then extant. Social forces, however, failed to mold in her the other features typical of the hysterical personality. Indeed, they failed to mold in Scarlett even the expected features of femininity below those apparent on the surface. In fact, the study of Scarlett suggests, in answer to the third question posed at the outset, that while social forces may produce the appearance of a feminine character or a hysterical personality (which might be confused), appearance is the sole result, not the rigid underpinning, of character structure.

While the conclusions that can be safely drawn from a study of fictional characters are limited, fictional characters often have psychologic and social validity reflecting the genius of their authors. That Scarlett has such a validity is attested to by her having become almost a figure of folklore in the decades since her creation. A study of Scarlett suggests that although social forces may produce characteristic appearance and behavior that might be termed typical of the hysterical personality or of the normal feminine character as judged by different observers, the same social forces do not necessarily create the characteristic defenses, psychodynamic forces, and cognitive styles generally found in hysterical personalities. Lack of attention to these other features leads to confusion of the feminine character with the hysterical personality.

References

1. American Psychiatric Association: Diagnostic and Statistical Manual of Mental Disease (ed 2). Washington, DC, APA, 1968

2. Hollender MH, Hirsch SJ: Hysterical psychosis. Am J Psychiatry 120:1066–1074, 1964

3. Chodoff P: The diagnosis of hysteria: An overview. Am J Psychiatry 131:1073–1078, 1974

4. Chodoff P, Lyons H: Hysteria, the hysterical personality and "hysterical" conversion. Am J Psychiatry 114:734–740, 1958

5. Siegman AJ: Emotionality as a character defense. Psychoanal Q 23:339–354, 1954

6. Hollender MH: Hysterical personality. Comments on Contemporary Psychiatry 1:17–23, 1971

7. Shapiro D: Neurotic Styles. New York, Basic Books, 1965

8. Lerner HE: The hysterical personality: A "woman's disease." Compr Psychiatry 15:157–164, 1974

9. Halleck SL: Hysterical personality traits. Arch Gen Psychiatry 16:750–757, 1967

10. Mitchell M: Gone with the Wind. New York, Macmillan, 1936

11. Vaillant G: Theoretical hierarchy of adaptive ego mechanisms. Arch Gen Psychiatry 24:107–118, 1971

FOUR

News From Selznick International Pictures, Inc.

Decisions concerning the sale of the film rights to Gone With the Wind *had to be made just at the time Margaret Mitchell was suffering most from what her husband described as the "strain of becoming too famous too suddenly." In mid-August 1936 she summarized in a letter to Harold Latham:*

Yes, the moving picture deal was closed up about two weeks ago. However, I was ill at the time, and as my eyes were going bad on me I made a quick two-day trip to New York with my brother, who is a lawyer. I went off in a lather of rage about the contract, all ready to throw it in the movie company's face. It was the stupidest contract I ever saw, a contract that no rational person could sign, regardless of the amount of money involved....

The Selznick lawyers were mighty nice. So were the pretty young ladies in the Selznick office. They smoothed me down. They made concessions and I made concessions and the contract was rearranged so that it was possible for me to sign it.

Before the contract was signed Russell Birdwell had issued a release for Selznick International Pictures saying a deal had been made. From New York Virginia Nixon, who worked for United Artists, the film through which SIP's films were expected to be released, gleefully sent the novelist a copy of UA's brief news story. Mrs. Nixon, as Virginia Morris, had been one of Peggy Mitchell's roommates at Smith College nearly twenty years before.

NEWS

from
SELZNICK INTERNATIONAL PICTURES, Inc.

FOR IMMEDIATE RELEASE

DAVID O. SELZNICK OUTBIDS ALL
PRODUCERS FOR "GONE WITH THE WIND"

———

MARGARET MITCHELL BOOK ON SELZNICK
SCHEDULE FOR COMING SEASON

———

David O. Selznick announces the purchase of the screen rights to Margaret Mitchell's "Gone With the Wind," following a bidding contest into which nearly every producer in Hollywood entered. The film will be one of major items on the Selznick schedule of productions, all of which will be released through United Artists.

The story of "Gone With the Wind" is laid in Georgia's red clay hills, and takes the Civil War as the background of its action. It is not a war story, but a tale of society torn by the war between the states and is climaxed by the dramatic period of reconstruction which followed.

According to Macmillan, the publishers of "Gone With the Wind," the book, a first novel, passed the 100,000 mark of sales even before it was placed on the bookstalls. In its first two weeks, it sold 140,000

# # # #

Released through UNITED ARTISTS • 729 Seventh Avenue, New York City • BR-9-7300

For the Defense

By David O. Selznick

The creator of Gone With the Wind *wisely stayed away from involvement in the making of its film version. In the fall of 1936 the Atlanta* Constitution *ran a long—very long—interview Margaret Mitchell granted to Lamar Q. Ball. In the fifth (November 12, 1936) of the six parts in which this interview was published she discussed the making of the film:*

> I sold the moving picture rights to Mr. Selznick. Rhett and Scarlett are his to have and to hold and to cast as he sees fit. If he should botch the job that will be his worry. I have made up my mind very definitely about that movie version—I'll have nothing to do with it. . . .
>
> Now "Gone With the Wind" is a mighty long book. No one knows that better than I. No one knows better than I the movie men will have to whittle that book down to normal movie size. Something must go. I don't know much about moving pictures, but I have a feeling that war scenes thrill directors and probably this one will be far more interested in those war spectacles than he will be in the reconstruction periods that come after. He will have the lust of battle in his nostrils if he is human, and I am afraid the aftermath of war will bore him to death. . . .
>
> Mr. Selznick has assured me he will see that the whole spirit of the movie is carried into the moving picture. He did a very good job on "David Copperfield." I am hopeful about "Gone With the Wind," but not confident. . . .
>
> I am dragged into argument after argument as to whether I believe Clark Gable should play Rhett or Joan Crawford should play Scarlett or do I believe this actress should play Scarlett and that actor should play Rhett. I tell them I don't know—and I don't. The moving picture people know what makes good pictures and they live or die by their ability to cast their roles properly. . . .
>
> My movie tastes run to Donald Duck and the four Marx Brothers, none of whom, I believe, could portray the role of Scarlett or Rhett.

Nearly two years later preparations for filming GWTW were still going on. Gable had been signed to play Rhett, but the search for a Scarlett seemed never ending. Selznick explained his side of things in an open letter dated "Hollywood, Sept. 30" published in Ed Sullivan's column "Hollywood" in the New York Daily News, *October 1, 1938.*

Dear Ed: I haven't commented upon the thousands of mistaken items that have appeared throughout the country in connection with "Gone With the Wind." However, in view of what I had thought was a friendship existing between us, I want to put certain things squarely up to you, so that you can determine whether your comments are fair. Let's review the history of exactly what I've done: We bought the book from the galleys, paying $50,000 for it. So far, I think you'll agree, nothing wrong, nothing stupid. Second, I assigned George Cukor to direct the picture. I have stubbornly held to this decision through difficulties which you cannot imagine, because I felt that Cukor was the ideal man to do it.

I engaged Sidney Howard for the script. He is one of America's most distinguished playwrights, a Pulitzer Prize winner among other things. I have personally spent four or five hours a day for a period of about twenty-five weeks on the script, in close collaboration with Howard and Cukor. We have been as rigidly faithful to the book as possible—although you understand that putting the book as written, on the screen, would make about a 100-reel picture. However, I have insisted, in all my dealings on the picture for release, on the privilege of making the picture as long as sixteen or seventeen reels—the longest picture ever made, because I want to give the public as much of the book as is possible at one sitting.

Before going into the unavoidable delays, let us say that all of them could have been avoided, which is, of course, not so. What of it? Why shouldn't the book be picturized a couple of years after it first appeared? I made "Little Women" sixty-five years after it was published. I made "David Copperfield" eighty-six years after it was first published. I made "The Prisoner of Zenda" forty-three years after it was first published, and the same applies to "A Tale of Two Cities," "Little Lord Fauntleroy" and "Anna Karenina."

Now as to the casting. You've been in Hollywood a year, long enough to realize that players under contract to a studio cannot be secured by another studio just for the asking, even for such a project as "Gone With the Wind." The public's choice clearly was Clark Gable for Rhett Butler. But you must have a rough idea as to how willing M.-G.-M. would be to give up Gable for a picture to be released by another company. Accordingly, the only way I could get him was to distribute the picture through M.-G.-M., and this meant I had to wait to start the picture until my contract with United Artists had expired, which it does when I finish my present picture. Therefore, I couldn't start "Gone With the Wind" one day sooner.

Now as to Scarlett. Please believe me when I say that I have at my disposal more information as to whom the public wants in this picture than any one else. The public's choice is clearly and very strongly for a new girl as Scarlett. I have spent a fortune trying to find this new girl—not $500,000 as reported, but actually very close to $50,000, and that buys a lot of talent searching. I had the best talent scouts in the country; I sent Cukor and a whole crew through the South; between Cukor and myself, we have seen personally every available player and young actress that was even remotely a possibility. We have had readings, tests; we have trained girls, we've done everything conceivable. Other studios helped me, as I promised them that if they found a girl, they could use her in an occasional picture. The search is on again with renewed vigor—and the best Scarlett that shows up by the time Gable is available to start work will play the role, willy-nilly.

Warner Brothers offered me Errol Flynn for Rhett and Bette Davis for Scarlett. But the public wanted Gable. There is no point in going through the strings tied to other stars who might have played Scarlett, because either they were choices whom the public would have hopped all over, or it was utterly impossible to get them. We played around with the idea of having Norma Shearer do the role. You know the outcry that was raised. Mind you, I think the outcry was unfair, and off on the basis of demonstrated versatility. I think she might have been treated with more consideration.

Please bear in mind, Ed, that I'm not seeking publicity on the picture. You know that to be so. In two years, this letter to you has been my only statement on "Gone With the Wind."* The only stories we have sent out have been definite announcements such as the purchase of the book; the assignments of Cukor and Howard; the decision to make it in Technicolor, and the deal with M.-G.-M. for Gable, and its distribution. We have refused $100,000 to put it on the air, we have turned down newspaper chain tieups. Therefore, when I'm belted by a nationally syndicated writer such as you, especially when that writer is to the best of my knowledge a friend of mine, I am grieved and mystified. Having laid my cards on the table, don't you think you owe it to me to straighten this out?

Cordially and sincerely,
DAVID O. SELZNICK.

---

*Editor's note: Actually Selznick had previously written at least one letter to a news columnist. In his column Tradeviews in the *Hollywood Reporter* March 24, 1937, W. R. Wilkerson responded to a rumor that Norma Shearer would play Scarlett by arguing for the casting of new faces. Selznick answered Wilkerson in a long letter published in the *Reporter* March 25. "I have decided," he wrote, "to clarify our objectives on the casting of this picture, especially since this casting has turned into a national game. If this letter does nothing else, it should relieve me of the necessity of long-winded discussions on this subject with everyone I meet socially and professionally."

Of Shearer he said: "This great artist and beloved star has flattered me by publicly expressing pleasure over the prospect of doing 'Gone With the Wind' or another picture for me. She has, at the same time, publicly expressed what she and I have privately agreed: that a new star should and could be made by Scarlett—as, indeed, could others of Miss Mitchell's brilliantly drawn and already-celebrated characters." He went on to point out that he had introduced Freddie Bartholomew, Katharine Hepburn, and others as new faces.

He reinforced the authenticity of his search for Scarlett as a genuine hunt for a new face and not just a publicity stunt. "At the very moment of your paternal suggestion," he declared, "George Cukor was preparing [for] an extensive southern trip to look for new personalities: Oscar Serlin was doing the same in the sticks up north; and Charley Morrison the same out here—all searching for Scarletts and Rhetts and Ashleys and Melanies and Bonnies and Pittypats. If they find them, grand! So far, no luck. The scouts for every other company haven't just skipped over them so they'd be left for us. But, hopefully, we'll find them. If we do, we'll take a chance even with comparative amateurs, for I am fortunate in having in Cukor as fine a director of new personalities as exists, in my opinion, anywhere in the world."

Studies in Scarlett

By Gavin Lambert

The search for Scarlett kept publicity about GWTW *alive during the long wait for filming to begin. Gavin Lambert masterfully recounts the story of that search and of the actresses who aspired for the most coveted role of the century in his article "Studies in Scarlett." "Studies in Scarlett" was published in London's* The Sunday Times Magazine *December 30, 1973, as a teaser for the British publication of Lambert's* GWTW: The Making of Gone With the Wind *in 1974. (The book had already been serialized in* The Atlantic Monthly *and published in the United States by Little, Brown and Company.)*

Early in 1936 David Selznick received from his story editor in New York a long synopsis of a long forthcoming novel. It was called *Gone With the Wind* and nobody had ever heard of the author. The story editor, Kay Brown, strongly urged him to buy the rights at once.

He didn't. Although tempted by the material, he knew that movies about the Civil War were usually commercial failures. He turned it down, then had second thoughts for six weeks. Finally he made an offer which was accepted, went to Hawaii for a vacation with his wife and read the novel he'd bought. He returned to Hollywood to find it a runaway best seller and already part of the national psyche.

Having decided that George Cukor should direct the picture, Selznick's first thoughts about casting were directed toward Rhett Butler, not Scarlett O'Hara. He wanted Clark Gable, but the star was under contract to MGM. His father-in-law, Louis B. Mayer, was still angry because Selznick had previously left the studio to form his own company and refused a sumptuous offer to go back. Reluctant to deal with this difficult potentate again, Selznick fell back on his second choice, Gary Cooper. He approached Sam Goldwyn, to whom the actor was under contract, and met an unblanketed refusal. He next thought of Errol Flynn, at that time the movies' top swashbuckler. Warner Brothers, who owned his contract, offered a package instead of a refusal. Bette Davis, also owned by the studio, had begun an ardent campaign for the part of Scarlett the moment she heard that Selznick was going to produce the movie. Jack Warner was prepared to make her part of the deal.

Selznick was seriously tempted, but not Davis. Desperate though she might be, she wouldn't play Scarlett to Errol Flynn's Rhett. Jack Warner broke off negotiations; Selznick, after considering Warner Baxter and Ronald Colman for a few minutes, reluctantly admitted to himself that Gable was a necessity. He went back to MGM, faced his triumphant father-in-law, and was met by some not unexpectedly stiff terms. MGM would lend Gable at a figure considerably above his usual salary, and provide half the financing in return for world distribution rights and half of the total profits.

Since Selznick's company had a contract with United Artists to distribute all his pictures until the end of 1938, *Gone With the Wind* could not be released by MGM until after that time. It was now October, 1936. Selznick's next problem was how to keep public interest alive in his project for the next two years.

Out of this dilemma came the idea of a nationwide talent search to find an unknown to play Scarlett O'Hara. When he thought of it, Selznick was certainly not convinced that he *wanted* an unknown—even after shooting began he was still considering stars for the lead—and the search in the end yielded nothing except a girl in Charleston, Alicia Rhett, to play the part of India Wilkes, Ashley's unpleasant sister. But as an attention-getting device it was brilliant. The search for a girl to play the most popular heroine of the decade received a gratifyingly wide national coverage, and was the subject of editorials from the *Times* of Los Angeles to the *Times* of New York.

Today, when the casting of unknowns in leading roles is hardly revolutionary, it seems almost inconceivable that such a simply ploy should have worked so well and for so long. But Selznick was handling a very special property at a time when the *mystique* of Hollywood and the star system was at its height. The formation of the Rome-Berlin axis, the Moscow spy trials, the German occupation of Austria and the Munich Conference were comparatively minor events to an isolationist public holding its breath while 1400 candidates were interviewed and 90 tested as potential flesh and blood of an instant legend.

Later, and privately, both Selznick and Cukor admitted that the results were simply awful. And the possibility that an unknown might be chosen to play Scarlett also had its effects on the stars and their fan clubs. Letters poured in from all over the country—from Europe, too, since the novel was repeating its triumph there—suggesting almost every leading lady of the moment. Of the write-ins, Bette Davis was easily the most popular candidate, with 40 percent of the vote, but her refusal to play opposite Flynn had taken her out of the running. The loss of the role haunted her for years. Convinced that a deal could have been made but for Cukor's opposition, she gave out interviews claiming that he thumbed her down because he favored Katharine Hepburn from the start.

But Katharine Hepburn, her imagined downfall, was in fact a self-announced contender, one of several stars who either suggested themselves to Selznick or put their agents to work. Because of her previous association with Cukor and Selznick on *A Bill of Divorcement* and *Little Women,* she was thought for a while to have the inside track; but although Cukor was receptive, Selznick doubted whether she had the sex appeal to enthrall Rhett Butler for so many years. He was also worried because at the time exhibitors were labeling her "box-office poison". He offered to test her, however, but she refused. Although officially out of the running, she remained a strong possibility in Cukor's mind, and he thought that if the search should fail to yield an 'ideal' Scarlett, Selznick would reconsider.

Another widely publicized candidate was Norma Shearer, with whom Selznick had discussions concerning the part. But her fans created an outcry at the thought of an actress renowned for her sweet and ladylike qualities playing a southern minx. Ed Sullivan, then a powerful columnist, joined the protest. In the end, in spite of encouragement from a *New York Times* editorial, Shearer withdrew from the race.

The list of actresses who wanted to play Scarlett, or were touted for it by the fan magazines, press and radio commentators, and their agents, is amazing not only for variety but incongruity. Remembering that the story begins with Scarlett at the age of 16, it seems extraordinary that among the serious contenders were Shearer (37), Miriam Hopkins (35), Tallulah Bankhead (34), Joan Crawford, Jean Arthur and Irene Dunne (all 33). Some of these were actually tested. This is a comment, of course, from a society that is much more conscious of age (or youth) than were the Thirties. The most popular figures of that time were women rather than girls.

In Jean Arthur's case, one suspects the test to have been partly a sentimental gesture, since Selznick was in love with her before he married Mayer's daughter. An original and charming actress, she was clearly too old for the part, with no hint of the southern belle in her temperament. The test looks strained and embarrassing, and nervousness pushes the lovely husky voice to a series of grating rather than girlish squeaks. Bankhead's test is equally uneasy. Although a southerner, demureness was never her stock-in-trade, and in trying to recapture the innocence of the early Scarlett her memory clearly fails her. Miriam Hopkins, who read for the part but didn't make a test, also came from the South and had recently starred in the movie of *Becky Sharp;* the similarities between Thackeray's and Margaret Mitchell's heroine had been pointed out in several reviews. She had a strange, powerful intensity and like Shearer could create the illusion of physical glamor. You feel she might have got away with Scarlett on the stage. Joan Crawford was Louis B. Mayer's own personal choice, but in spite of his powerful promotion Selznick never asked her to read or make a test.

Other actresses tested were Joan Bennett (from *Little Women*), Paulette Goddard, the young Lana Turner, who had just attracted attention in her first, small movie role in *They Won't Forget,* and a New York model called Edythe Marriner whom Selznick's wife had spotted at a fashion show. To see the film on the contenders is to see why Selznick and Cukor continued to hold out. Some are instantly out of the question. Lana Turner at sea, dazed and ringleted. "If I can understand it, I can do it," she told Cukor years later, working with him as an established movie queen. At the time she made this test the moment had not yet arrived. Edythe Marriner—who changed her name to Susan Hayward after the test—looks right; she was 19 then, with a slight resemblance to Vivien Leigh, but there's already a career-girl toughness in her screen presence.

Paulette Goddard, recently launched by Chaplin in *Modern Times,* is the only one who comes close. Chaplin had sensed her *gamine* quality and brought it out very effectively in his film; in the test it is still there, lively and appealing but somehow too redolent of city sidewalks for the daughter of Tara. Still, for a while she was under the most serious consideration, and then almost signed.

Of all these, Hopkins was the most hotly tipped by the press; but Cukor, although he admired her talent, says he never felt she was right for the part. Nor was he particularly enthusiastic about Loretta Young, who interested Selznick for a while. There was talk of asking her to do a reading, but it never happened. Other names tossed into the arena were Carole Lombard, Margaret Sullavan, Claudette Colbert, Ann Sheridan and Jean Harlow, but here we seem to enter the land of delusion and publicity gimmicks. And when Selznick asked the other studios to suggest any actresses they might have under contract, RKO came up with a 27-years-old unknown called Lucille Ball. "Are you kidding?" was her forthright reaction, but the casting agent pressed a vocal coach on her and arranged a reading for Selznick. He was polite but noncommittal.

By November 1938 there was still no Scarlett, but Selznick had announced that a single sequence of *Gone With the Wind,* the burning of Atlanta, would be shot during the following month. The deal with MGM specified that Gable had to begin work during the second week of February 1939, and there was no guarantee that he would be available for more than 20 weeks, which was less than the established shooting schedule. Selznick had to rearrange it so that he could use the months before Gable became available on this big spectacle scene and on other scenes that didn't involve him.

Reviewing all the known and unknown actresses under consideration for Scarlett, he had also narrowed down the final list to Katharine Hepburn, Joan Bennett, Jean Arthur and Loretta Young. As usual, second thoughts occurred, and he asked Cukor to make another test of Paulette Goddard. He viewed the result several times and found himself increasingly impressed. Third thoughts occurred. Cukor had also tested an unknown actress called Dorothy Jordan, the wife of Merian C. Cooper, producer of *King Kong.* Selznick now ordered another test of her; it was promising, but it never quite caught fire. Finally he came to a decision. Paulette Goddard would be his Scarlett O'Hara, and her agent was contacted.

At this time Chaplin and his star were publicly living together, and no-one was certain whether or not they were married. In more paranoid circles of the industry and the middle classes, Chaplin's alleged Left-wing views in *Modern Times* had caused the first stirrings of the unpopularity that was to drive him out of the country ten years later. Now the cry of an 'immoral' private life was raised. When it became known that Goddard was on the verge of being signed, women's clubs all over the United States fired salvos of protest. Such things were far more serious then than now, and Selznick felt obliged to ask his Scarlett whether she was Chaplin's wife. Goddard insisted that a ceremony had occurred at sea, in the harbor of Singapore, while they were on a cruise to the Orient. Unfortunately Goddard couldn't produce a marriage certificate or any official evidence that the wedding had taken place. Deciding not to risk a scandal, Selznick reluctantly ordered the search to continue.

On December 10, the night of the second burning of Atlanta, there was still no Scarlett. Cukor called the first "Action!" on *Gone With the Wind,* and the doubles of Rhett and Scarlett made their escape past the blazing exterior sets of *King Kong* and *The Garden of Allah,* dressed with false fronts for the occasion. To some Los Angeles residents, always fearful of natural disasters such as earthquakes and holocausts, the overpowering glow in the sky announced that the city itself was on fire. A few dozen people hastily packed suitcases and started driving towards the desert.

As the fire began to wane and the shooting ended, Selznick's brother Myron arrived, slightly drunk. A leading Hollywood agent, he'd been entertaining some clients at dinner. "I want you to meet your Scarlett O'Hara!" he said loudly, causing everybody to turn around. Selznick looked from the acres of burning rubble to a young actress standing beside Laurence Olivier. Firelight seemed to accentuate the hint of pale green in the light blue of her eyes, the green that Margaret Mitchell had ascribed to the eyes of her heroine. He knew that she was Vivien Leigh, an English actress, and that she and Olivier were in love. He also knew that several months ago he'd screened two picture she made in Britain, *Fire Over England* and *A Yank at Oxford,* thought her excellent, but in no way a possible Scarlett. Seeing her now, the moment turned into a scene from his own *A Star Is Born.* "I took only look and knew that she was right—at least right as far as her appearance went," he said later.

Behind this legendary moment lies a contrivance of reality. Vivien Leigh had read the book in London when it first came out, and she was eager for the role. With an intuition and courage that were typical of her, she even thought she would get it. When she went to Hollywood early in December 1938, it was on a sudden impulse, very Scarlett-like in its mixture of romance and ambition. Laurence Olivier and she were in love, although both were still married to others. Olivier had already gone to Hollywood several months earlier to play Heathcliff in *Wuthering Heights.* He wrote unhappy letters to Vivien—he had athlete's foot and was hobbling around on crutches; the film was going very badly; he felt he was not getting any help from the director, William Wyler, who gave all his attention to Merle Oberon; and this was naturally affecting his relationship with his leading lady. He implied that she might even walk off the picture, and there was a chance of Vivien replacing her. So Vivien joined him because he was unhappy and because she might get the role of Cathy.

The chance of replacing Merle Oberon did not in fact exist; but Scarlett O'Hara was still not cast, and Myron Selznick was Olivier's agent. Knowing how much she wanted the part, he asked Myron to introduce her to David. At first Myron was tentative, then at the burning of Atlanta the moment suddenly arranged itself. When they met, Selznick was so electrified by the look of Vivien that he asked her almost at once if she'd like to make a test. She was clever enough to express surprise, then agreed.

Next day Selznick took her to Cukor's office. The director also knew very little about her at the time, but with his acute nose for talent felt something 'exciting' in her presence. He asked her to read one of the test scenes and was immediately disconcerted by her English accent. "She began reading this thing very sweetly, and very, very clipped . . . So I struck her across the face with the rudest thing I could say. She screamed with laughter. That was the beginning of our tender, wonderful friendship."

He arranged to shoot a test the next day. Vivien always remembered that when she got into Scarlett's costume it was still warm from the body of the hopeful actress immediately preceding her. The test was in black-and-white, and she played two scenes, with Hattie McDaniel as Mammy lacing up her corset for the Wilkes's barbecue, and with Leslie Howard as Ashley, when she first declares her love for him during a siesta at the barbecue. A few days later she made a third test, coached in the meantime for a Southern accent. This was a later scene with Ashley; she makes another, even more passionate declaration of love and suggests that they run away together.

To see these tests is to witness one of those instantaneous understandings between actress and part. The Southern accent hardly exists in the first two, but it doesn't matter. In every other way Vivien Leigh *becomes* Scarlett, and the boldness and confidence of an actress only 25 years old, required to show her grasp of a role with hardly any preparation at all, is extraordinary. In contrast to all the others who tested, what is unique and immediately striking is her passion. "There was an indescribable wildness about her," Cukor remembered later. She is never coy or tentative or strained, and instead of playing the first scene with Ashley like a schoolgirl with a crush, she is direct in her desire for him, dangerously impatient. In this alone she reveals a feeling for the character far in advance of the other actresses tested. The Jean Arthur-Tallulah Bankhead-Lana Turner approach involves excessive fluttering of eyelashes. Susan Hayward and Paulette Goddard tend to play it conventionally sexy. Cukor said he was always looking, in the actress who should play Scarlett, for someone "charged with electricity" and who seemed "possessed of the devil". In these tests Vivien Leigh seems endowed with both qualities.

The third test is the most highly charged of all. Within a few days she has basically mastered the Southern accent, which slips away only now and then, and since Leslie Howard was not available that day is playing with another Ashley, but the woodenness of Douglas Montgomery in no way deters her. Now she presents a woman instead of a girl, hardened by experience, with an underlying panic and desperation; the scene becomes a fierce, disturbing appeal to Ashley to save her life. The performance here is in fact more striking than when she repeats it in the film under Victor Fleming's direction, after Cukor has been fired.

Both producer and director were convinced they had found their Scarlett. The only dissenting vote came from Alexander Korda, from whom Selznick had to buy Vivien's contract. He told his young star that she was making a mistake. "You are quite wrong for the part . . ."

How Hollywood Built Atlanta

By Wilbur G. Kurtz

Margaret Mitchell aided and abetted the appointment of Atlantan Wilbur G. Kurtz as "historian" on Selznick's staff for the making of Gone With the Wind. *Mr. Kurtz; his wife, Annie Laurie Fuller Kurtz, who served as his assistant; and Susan Myrick, a Macon newspaperwoman for whom the novelist maneuvered a place as an adviser on Southern manners and customs, served as Margaret Mitchell's eyes and ears in Hollywood. Through them and Kay Brown, who was Selznick's Assistant in Charge of the Author, Miss Mitchell kept much more in touch with what was going on at Selznick's studio than she was wont to admit.*

In a letter in anticipation of George Cukor's visit to Atlanta in the early spring of 1937, Miss Mitchell wrote Miss Brown, March 8:

So tell Mr. Cukor to come on at any time convenient to him and let me know as far in advance as possible. . . . If he wants to see the line of old fortifications between Atlanta and Dalton or those at Jonesboro, I want to get hold of Wilbur Kurtz who . . . is about the only living authority on these campaigns. He knows every foot of ground in two hundred miles, the old houses, who lived in them, what generals died in them, et cetera. As a matter of fact, if you wanted an honest to God expert on the War part of the picture, you couldn't do better than kidnap Mr. Kurtz and take him to Hollywood.

Not only did Mr. Kurtz help show Mr. Cukor the Atlanta area, he had two long stays in Hollywood working on the details that give GWTW *its air of authenticity. For the Atlanta* Journal's *Sunday Magazine* two Sundays before *Gone With the Wind's premiere at Loew's Grand he told for his and Miss Mitchell's hometown audience "How Hollywood Built Atlanta."*

The mention of Atlanta's old carshed in "Gone With the Wind" was meaningless to the picture people until I showed them photographs of it, together with measurements taken from the original plans of the edifice as drawn in 1853 by Edward A. Vincent, architect and engineer, which plans are now in possession of the Atlanta Historical Society. Since much of the action of the story takes place in and around this structure, it was decided to erect it as one of the sets. Here Ashley arrives on furlough from Virginia—his leave of absence signed by Jeb Stuart himself—to be greeted by Melanie and Scarlett. The railroad settings were carried out only as far as picture requirements dictated. The combination of moving trains, loaded to the guards with soldiers, smoking locomotives and the added illusion of sound would make an old-time Atlantian almost detect the odor of the famous institution as embodied in a later but similar structure.

The carshed, together with a section of downtown Atlanta as of the period, was visualized for the art department by a water color bird's-eye view which I prepared. There was ample photographic data for this. Working from this layout, the art department drew plans for structures along Peachtree, Marietta, Decatur and a few of the other streets, and by the end of February, 1939, the Atlanta of the 1860's assumed full form and visibility.

It was odd to hear all these well-known street and location names bandied about by persons who never had been in Atlanta, or Georgia, either. I was asked by someone if there really was a street called "Peachtree" in Atlanta—the questioner probably surmising that the name was merely fictional, like Tara.

As to Tara, Twelve Oaks, Aunt Pitty's house, Dr. Meade's and Mrs. Merriwether's residence, and the exotic house that Rhett built for Scarlett—the lumber mill, Frank Kennedy's store and the engine house, these are pure fiction, unless one insinuates that the engine house was the old Mechanics' Fire Company No. 2, which stood on Washington Street just north of the site of old St. Philip's Cathedral.

All of these places were designed in keeping with the architecture of the period, and of the place, with perhaps one exception: the post-war mansion which Rhett built for Scarlett being rather the sort of thing Scarlett would demand—and get!

Tara, Twelve Oaks and Aunt Pitty's house are largely symbols. Tara represents the sturdy, rambling rural homes of the Piedmont section of the state; Twelve Oaks, the glamorous estates of the Old South of story and song; Aunt Pitty's town house, the snug, respectable, straight-front architecture of the cast-iron statuary era. The plank sidewalks and the white picket fences are all in place, and the never-to-be-forgotten red dirt is in evidence everywhere, whether one is at Tara, Twelve Oaks or in Atlanta.

I worked in an advisory capacity on all these edifices, also making numerous sketches and diagrams, from which the outbuildings and the like were assembled, the covered way, and kitchen—the well with the hipped roof, the ginhouse, the cotton press, the slave quarters, the blighted cotton patch and kitchen garden, the makeshift fences and distant pine woods, and the contour plowing on the red hills.

Beyond the glimpse of a few newsreel cameras in action, and a brief movie shot made on the vacant lot where now stands the Rialto Theater in Atlanta, I had up to December 10, 1938, never seen a camera crew in action. My first glimpse was far from being a trivial one, indeed; my introduction to this amazing form of artistic creation was attended by what is admitted to have been the most awe-inspiring spectacle ever staged in this land of magic lanterns.

I refer to the scene in the screen version of "Gone With the Wind," where the Confederates of General Stewart's Corps, and the Georgia militia abandon the city the night of September 1, 1864, after the disastrous defeat of Hardee's troops at Jonesboro. Unable to remove eighty-one carloads of fixed ammunition standing on the tracks of the Georgia Railroad, the military authorities set them afire, together with certain warehouses in the railroad yards. That which resulted was pure motion picture material. It so happened that certain personages known as Rhett Butler, Scarlett O'Hara, Mrs. Ashley Wilkes (Melanie) and a little loquacious Senegambian maid who answered to the name of "Prissy," left the city at the same time the big fireworks began. Of course they became involved in it, and just how much they were involved the grandeur—screen-invoked for this particular scene, will reveal.

As for myself, I was one of that spellbound throng who watched the roaring flames devour the buildings and explode the cargoes of the boxcars. So this was Hollywood! Here upon the flat shelf which borders the Pacific Ocean, was recreated an episode of those far-gone days in old Atlanta, and I pinched myself to ascertain if I were awake or only dreaming.

Since this scene comes nearly midway of the picture and was the first to be filmed, certain types, props and costumes which would become standard for the rest of the picture, had to be fixed. Here we saw for the first time that light purple dress which Scarlett wore. The wardrobe department reasoned that by September, 1864, Scarlett would be emerging from the sombre black of her mourning for Charles Hamilton, and the purple would be proper. Scarlett in later affluence, appears in creations that would make a Parisian couturier retire to a cave for fasting and prayer; but there was a period between the time she was a hospital nurse and the moment when she appropriated the green window curtains for a costume, that this purple dress became a symbol of the decline and fall of the Southern Confederacy.

It began as a demure street costume, but several cataclyomic events contributed to its disintegration. First there were the red mud and dust of Atlanta streets—then the hospital nursing, followed by the stress of shell-fire from the Federal siege guns. By this time Rhett Butler was twitting her about her resemblance to a rag-picker. On that fatal September 1, when she went upon the fruitless errand to the carshed only to find that Dr. Meade was up to his elbows among the wounded soldiery from Jonesboro, and therefore could not come to Melanie, the purple dress was just something to wear. Back at Tara, the dress becomes a suit of armor for the embattled Scarlett, who vows that she will win through in spite of perdition, highwater and the Yankees!

She drives Suellen, Carreen and even Mammy and Pork to the cotton patch; sans hoops, she stands in this dress upon the stairs with a smoking revolver in her hand; she cooks up a mess of soft soap in the back yard, and—her big moment—again wearing this dress, she hurls the red soil of Tara full in the face of Jonas Wilkerson!

When Selznick International Pictures, Inc., acquired screen rights to "Gone With the Wind," book sales had not then mounted to the amazing figures of a later date, but they were on the way up. By the time picture production began, Mr. Selznick knew there was no alternative but to make the picture conform to story and setting. The Atlanta of the 1860's was a definite place with a peculiar history; the Piedmont section of Georgia possessed a characteristic terrain, fauna and flora. As an endeavor to secure this authentic background—a physical entity as well as an historic one—a technical adviser was indicated. It was not a matter of having some one familiar with motion picture technique, but some one who might be presumed to know the background of the story. That I was elected to do this work was to me a complete surprise. My record for knowing nothing about picture technique was perfect; as for the other, I was merely using some facts picked up during several years of indulging in a hobby—a study of Atlanta's colorful past, its beginnings, its growth, its tragic war history, together with its place in relationship to the Atlanta campaign of 1864.

Several factors contributed to the furtherance of this hobby. I found a number of others who were interested in the same subjects and without them I never could have ranged far afield.

For eight years a trio consisting of Beverly M. Dubose, Franklin M. Garrett and myself combed the Piedmont section of Georgia in weekly jaunts over the red hills, largely in the country where embattled forces of Sherman, Johnston and Hood made history.

On one such afternoon jaunt we found in a pocket of hills near High Shoals, in Paulding County, a group of farm buildings that must have seen or have been seen by the marauding out-riders of Sherman's legions. Here also was the old wagon that served as the type for the "escape wagon" in "Gone With the Wind." In December, 1938, I found its counterpart at the Cameron Ranch near Culver City, Cal., and it made its debut in the big fire sequence mentioned above, the night of December 10. This wagon carried Scarlett and the others from Atlanta to Tara. Since this picturesque journey is a prominent feature in the production, we see the old wagon in practically all the vicissitudes of that trek.

The horse, an abandoned equine, stolen by Rhett and christened "Marse Robert," was all that its designation, "woe-begone," implies. It was on its way to the glue factory when promoted to the movies, and its subsequent elation when placed upon a diet of oats, occasioned much comment.

As my first work in connection with the picture I was directed to write schedules of personnel and properties for the barbecue at Twelve Oaks; the bazaar where Scarlett defies Mrs. Grundy and dances with Rhett, and the crowded street scenes in Atlanta as of the different periods.

I was called upon to select all the wheeled vehicles demanded by the story. This list embraced the carriages, buggies, farm wagons, coaches, fire engines, ambulances, army wagons and the artillery. A lot of these items of a bygone period and still practical, were museum pieces. They had circulated among most of the producing studios, and before numberless cameras. "That carriage," remarked a dealer, "worked in 'Juarez'—that one in 'Dodge City,' the other one in 'Man of Conquest.' " I visited one dealer who had everything on wheels from a Roman chariot to a carriage of the gay nineties. Of course, we had an unlimited choice among the horses, and the long-eared mules were no less in evidence.

The famous cow which Scarlett picks up en route to Tara was discovered at sundown in a pasture in Burbank. It had a disconsolate moo, and the right length of horns for the attachment of the string with which it was led. Ashley's single footer, Gerald's white jumper, and the Yankee cavalryman's steed, together with the "woe-begone" Marse Robert, made a quartet not envisioned by the prophet of the Apocalypse.

Then there were the dogs! No rural domicile in Georgia is complete without a pack of long-legged, long-tailed, lop-eared hounds. Even Grimalkin was represented, but the long-haired parlor type was rigorously excluded. Chanticleer had one brief moment in the back yard at Aunt Pittypat's when Uncle Peter, "chop-axe" in hand, chased it through the mud and rain that it might grace Ashley's Christmas dinner.

Bonnie's pony was a problem only in that it had to jump hurdles, but the hurdle was successfully made.

The artillery units represented a combination of cannon of the period, of horses, and artillerymen. We found what was required in the way of authentic field pieces, with 1862 stamped on the muzzles. Two caissons were constructed in the carpenter shops, and the ancient artillery manuals supplied by the Army War College gave us all that was needed in the way of data on personnel, rank, equipment, guidons, bugles and formation. One of the property men, at my insistence, did not forego a search until he had found several genuine metal artillery buckets of the period.

Indeed, the military sequences of the picture launched me into a welter of arms, uniforms, general equipment, and to some extent, into maneuvers. While no battle scenes are shown, we see a lot of the embattled defenders of Atlanta, and a conglomerate back-wash of military activity generally. The spic and span uniforms of the Confederacy in its earlier stages inevitably give way to the tattered and torn habiliments of the "thin gray line."

The canvas-topped army wagons emerged from the paint shop with the proper lettering on them—Hardee's Corps, Stewart's Corps, etc. The ambulances were likewise the recipients of last-minute attention by the sign painters.

My work with the wardrobe department consisted in advising with them about what was proper in clothing for the Georgia scene, as of definite periods. The bazaar scene called for a colorful display—hence the gay cadet uniforms of the youngsters in the Home Guard. This brave display of gold lace, of red and of blue, seemed to strike the right note of gaiety and optimism which marked the first year of the war.

Only too soon does that gaiety vanish, and with it the vari-colored uniforms, for the brave lads are swept into the gray ranks by time and the conscript law.

The costumes of the Negroes were matters of close scrutiny. The field hand and the house servant were known by the clothes they wore, and in nearly every instance where the coachman or carriage driver appeared, he was clad in what might have been the cast-off frippery of his master—and he always knew when or when not to wear his tall hat—and as a sign manual of his duties, he never left the carriage box without taking his whip along. The costumes of the white convicts leased by Scarlett to run her sawmill were made according to the legal specifications of the period, as adduced, at my request, by Col. Walter McElreath, of Atlanta.

Among the other and varied items assigned me were the text for the printed posters and proclamations seen on the Atlanta streets and in the hospital; the text of the various inserts like Ashley's furlough, Charles' death message, and the check with which Scarlett paid the taxes on Tara; the specifications for and the inscriptions on the markers in the O'Hara family cemetery, the trestles used for Frank Kennedy's coffin where Rhett picks up the rose!

With the script writing, the historical references were mine to watch as to sequence and accuracy; the titles—unusual for length and vigor in this picture—were scrutinized for accuracy of reference and statement. All flags and guidons were drawn in color and to scale, for the manufacturers; the old lamp posts were reproduced in the shops from measured drawings of the originals.

Even the finding of certain typical items constituted a problem. I recall a search made at several dealers' establishments before I found the right iron kettle or "clothes pot." Certain of those crude yard benches made of slabs, were fabricated by the prop maker, as was the paddle with which Scarlett stirs the soft soap.

Since the picture is in Technicolor, a lot of care had to be given to color selection. White, for instance, appeared in front of the camera as gray, and great pains were exercised never to allow Scarlett's famous green dress to show against a green lawn.

It has become an old saying by now that this picture represents all that care, time and patience were able to give it. I have been out here one year with nothing to do but answer questions and volunteer suggestions about it. Everyone who worked on it seemed to take a pride in his or her endeavors, and as for the technical part of the work—the part that has had to do with historical accuracy, mode of living and traditions in the South, the studio has been in a mood entirely receptive thereto.

I have had in this work, as my assistant, my wife, whose knowledge of the country of "Gone With the Wind" was hers as a birthright. To some good purpose did she spend her childhood holidays on her grandfather's plantation in the county of Clayton, at the headwaters of the Flint River.

Three Years of Hullabaloo

By Newsweek

Atlanta's great day finally came. Here is how Newsweek *reported it under the headline " 'Gone With the Wind': After 3 Years of Hullabaloo, It Emerges a Great Picture."*

On July 30, 1936, David O. Selznick, who had read an advance copy of Margaret Mitchell's *Gone With the Wind,* paid $50,000 for the right to screen the first novel of an unknown author. Next day the president of Selznick International Pictures, Inc., sailed for a Honolulu vacation. When he returned, the 1,037-page story of the South in Civil War and Reconstruction days was a sensational best seller.

Later Selznick was to turn down a $1,000,000 offer for the book's screen rights, but the first inkling that he was holding a bear by the tail came when America's movie fans took over the job of casting the film for him. Clark Gable was the almost unanimous choice for Rhett Butler—that hard-boiled iconoclast who became Scarlett O'Hara's third husband—but as the book's popularity grew by phenomenal bounds and thousands of letters flooded the studio, the casting of the fiery, calculating Scarlett became the chief storm center.

Letters vociferously and variously demanded Miriam Hopkins, Bette Davis, Katharine Hepburn, and a host of other favorites for the role. Selznick sent three talent expeditions—as well as George Cukor, slated to direct the film—all over the nation in search of an unknown Scarlett. The search lasted more than two years, reaped acres of publicity, engendered as many comic allusions as arguments, and was burlesqued in the Broadway success "Kiss the Boys Goodbye."

Finally, when his movie public began showing signs of apathy, Selznick announced, on January 13, 1939, that the O'Hara sweepstakes were over. Some 1,400 candidates had been interviewed and 28 screen tested at an estimated cost of $92,000, but Scarlett had been found in Hollywood—and she was an English girl to boot.

The girl the lightning struck was Vivien Leigh ("Storm in a Teacup," "A Yank at Oxford"), a talented actress but comparatively unknown in this country. The choice of an English girl (born in Darjeeling, India) to impersonate a

Southern belle aroused a storm of protest, particularly in the South. Speaking for the defense, Selznick pointed out that Miss Leigh, like Scarlett, was green-eyed, wasp-waisted, and of French-Irish stock. But the official seal of approval was awarded by Mrs. Walter D. Lamar, president-general of the United Daughters of the Confederacy, who emphasized the resemblance between the language of cultured England and of the South.

The summer before Selznick had signed Clark Gable on a releasing deal with Metro-Goldwyn-Mayer. Sidney Howard, noted playwright who recently met death in an accident, had been slaving on the script since 1936. And finally, on January 26, 1939, "Gone With the Wind" went before the Technicolor cameras.

Even in production the Selznick epic met with delays. After serving a few weeks as director, George Cukor resigned, to be replaced by Victor Fleming ("Captains Courageous," "The Wizard of Oz"). But eventually, after 140 shooting days, the most talked of and anxiously awaited film in Hollywood history was ready—except for the job of cutting 225,000 feet of printed film to the approximately 20,000 that run 3 hours 40 minutes on the screen.[1]

By this time West Coast cynics were convinced, that Selznick had stalled too long for his own good. After three years of delay and publicity that had overreached itself, public and critics alike were prepared to meet the film in a challenging mood. But last week, at a special press preview in Hollywood and later at the Atlanta premiere, "Gone With the Wind" rose from the adjectival ashes of its past to rank as one of the foremost films in screen history.

Except in telescoping its Reconstruction period problems, Sidney Howard's fine script is a faithful transcription of the Margaret Mitchell novel. The first half of the film—there is an intermission after 1 hour and 45 minutes—is especially notable, capturing perfectly the feeling of Southern hospitality and charm before the Civil War. In these sequences the characters are all part of a larger theme—the Old South that crashes with the utter ruin of war.

After the intermission the film becomes a drama of persons rather than people and, in accenting Scarlett's battle against the world and her ruthless domination of everything about her loses its epic quality. Nevertheless, in its magnificent production, its superb Technicolor, and in the power and integrity of a story that combines a vivid personal narrative with such superlative screen spectacle as the burning of Atlanta by the Yankee troops and its evacuation, "Gone With the Wind" is a triumph for Selznick and everyone concerned.

Perhaps of first interest to the book's admirers is that fact that Vivien Leigh,[2] bringing to life with thorough conviction the mercurial and unpredictable character Scarlett O'Hara, gives a flawless performance in the screen's

---

1. The longest film ever released, "Gone With the Wind," costing $3,957,000, is also one of the three most expensive. "Ben Hur" and "Hell's Angels" cost approximately the same sum.

2. The day following the Atlanta premiere, Miss Leigh flew to New York, where she announced her engagement to Laurence Olivier, British star of "Wuthering Heights."

most sought after role. The choice of Clark Gable as Rhett Butler—the realist who mocked his class and turned the war to his own profit by blockade running—is perfect type casting, as is Leslie Howard's assignment as the weak, gentlemanly Ashley Wilkes. Probably the most impressive member of the cast, aside from Miss Leigh, is Olivia de Havilland, who reveals histrionic finesse with her sensitive interpretation of the gentle Melanie. As the bossy Negro Mammy, Hattie McDaniel turns in a first-rate job that frequently amounts to scene stealing; and Laura Hope Crews (Aunt Pittypat), Ona Munson (Belle Watling), Thomas Mitchell (Gerald O'Hara), Rand Brooks (Charles Hamilton), Carroll Nye (Frank Kennedy), and Harry Davenport (Doctor Meade) are outstanding in a splendid cast.

Although "Gone With the Wind" opens this week simultaneously in two New York theaters—the Astor and the Capitol—Atlanta saw the film's world première on December 15 amid enthusiasm unequaled since the opening of the Cotton States Exposition there in 1895. Gov. E. D. Rivers of Georgia proclaimed Friday, the day of the premiere, a public holiday throughout the state; all state buildings were closed and the Confederate banner flew from the Capitol masthead beside the flag of the United States. Atlanta went the Governor two better; Mayor Hartsfield declared a three-day festival. Furthermore, for more than a month the city's butchers and bakers, businessmen, Junior Leaguers, housewives, and children had been dressing up the city for the big event.

And a big event it was, for if "Gone With the Wind" is a new high for film making, Atlanta's première out-Hollywooded Hollywood and all points east. When the film's stars and feature players, accompanied by Carole Lombard, Claudette Colbert, and studio executives, arrived last Thursday, they found a city facaded in the architecture and finery of the '60s, its citizens dressed in the hoop skirts and claw-hammer coats of a more colorful and prosperous era. Half of Atlanta's 300,000 population turned out to greet the motorcade that carried the film folk from the airport, down Peachtree Street, to the Georgian Terrace Hotel; but Thursday's high light was the charity ball at the City Auditorium.

For the ball Gable and the other Georgians-by-proxy donned the most colorful costumes they had worn in the film; five Governors—Rivers of Georgia, Prentice Cooper of Tennessee, Frank M. Dixon of Alabama, Burnet Rhett Maybank of South Carolina, and Fred Cone of Florida—and the Atlanta elect who were fortunate enough to snap up the 5,200 $10 tickets to the affair matched the stars' attire with their own colorful costumes. Gable escorted Miss Mildred Hartsfield, the Mayor's daughter; the Mayor returned the compliment by escorting the star's wife, Carole Lombard. In the auditorium the grand march was led by Miss Margaret Palmer, chosen by The Atlanta Constitution from the unmarried Junior Leaguers as "Atlanta's Scarlett."

Friday's luncheons, tea, and cocktail parties were climaxed by the pièce de resistance—the unreeling of "Gone With the Wind" at Loew's Grand Theater while 400 Guardsmen, details of State Troopers, and police held back the thousands of curious who milled around the theater's rebuilt entrance, a reproduction of Twelve Oaks, the Greek-pillared mansion in which Ashley lived. The studio had reserved 700 seats for guests and the press; an estimated 25,000 people scrambled for the remaining 1,300 tickets—again priced at $10 and donated to the city's Community Chest.

Because of illness, the Atlantan responsible for the fireworks—Margaret Mitchell (Mrs. John Marsh)—was unable to attend the ball. But Friday night, in one of her rare public appearances, she watched the screen re-create the glory and sorrow that was Georgia's while the select audience, weeping, cheering, alternately applauding "Dixie" and hissing Sherman's celluloid army, took the Selznick drama to their hearts. In a shaking voice Mayor Hartsfield called the actors to the stage at the close of the film. Finally he called Margaret Mitchell. She, too, seemed overcome with emotion.

Although the author of the book that has passed 2,000,000 copies firmly refused to take any part in the furor that attended its filming, she could not escape repercussions of the excitement she had created. Long before the frenzy of fiesta that rocked Atlanta last week, a Selznick representative had telephoned Miss Mitchell on business. In passing he asked the author if she were writing another book. Miss Mitchell's reply, though soft in Southern intonation, was unequivocal. "Law—*zee!* Look what *this* one's done to me!"

Atlanta's Most Brilliant Event

By Harold Martin

One of Atlanta's finest reporters wrote the main story about the premiere for the Atlanta Georgian *of December 16, 1939. In it he wisely quoted Margaret Mitchell's simple and effective curtain speech.*

Choked by emotions too deep for tears, Atlanta watched Friday night as at last upon the screen of Loew's Grand the storm wind blew until an empire fell and its broken fragments tumbled before the hurricane into the mists of time.

Men and women who had never understood quite rightly what the old folks meant when they told in trembling voices their passionate stories of those days knew at last what their grandfathers fought for, what their grandmothers suffered for—and what mingled streams of gallantry and folly and courage blend in their own blood today.

It was being said Saturday that the world premiere of "Gone With the Wind" was the grandest first showing any picture ever had. It must be true, for surely, nowhere in the world, was a picture shown to an audience more spiritually suited to receive it.

It was not the glitter and the fanfare that made it great. Nor the array of visiting dignitaries who came from everywhere to share the celebration. It was the spirit which gripped the crowd from the moment that grand foreword, beginning "There was a land of cavaliers and cotton fields . . ." on through the four soul-stirring hours to the end, when Scarlett lay crumpled on the great stair, remembering the feel of Tara's red earth and brokenly repeating, over and over, the name of her girlhood home.

When it all was over, and the applause and the cheering had died away, Julian Boehm stepped to the microphone to speak the words which were in the hearts of every man and woman there.

Quietly he said:

"God bless our little Peggy Marsh."

Then he turned the microphone over to the Mayor, who brought down the stars, and the acclaim they got as they came down to stand in the white glare of the spotlight, looking out into the darkness of the audience, was deservedly great, for all of them had lived the parts in which they were cast.

Then he paused a minute and the place tightened up till you could hear the breathing, and he asked Margaret Mitchell to come down.

She came, with Rhett and Scarlett, a tiny little woman in a simple pink dress, with a tiny pink rose in her hair, and the applause that went up was not for Gable and for Leigh, magnificent as they had been, but for her alone.

Her face was white and her eyes were big, and you could tell she was under a strain almost unbearable. But her voice was steady as she stepped to the microphone to make a simple little speech.

"Friends," she said, "and I know that more than three fourths of you here tonight are friends of mind, I want to say just this. Nobody needs to be told the value of friendship and consideration, shown to one in adversity.

"But from my heart I tell you that its value can be greater to one who has experienced the incredible success that I have. To all of you here—and to many who aren't, to the man at the grocery, the boys at the filling station, the folk on the newspapers—I want to say, thanks for your kindness.

"Of this picture, I feel that the only expression adequate for use is that one made trite by usage many times. We have just come together through a great emotional experience.

"I know it was to me. And I know I'm not the only one whose eyes have been wet tonight."

So tiny, she came only to the shoulder of Clark Gable, standing beside her, she went on:

"I want now to say a word about the man who made this picture. All of you, I know, heard the jokes about the search for Scarlett—'I'll see the picture when Shirley Temple gets old enough to play the role,' and all that sort of comment.

"But I want to pay my tribute to David O. Selznick, for his stubbornness and determination in getting the Scarlett he wanted. He wanted a perfect cast, and to my mind, he got it.

"You've all been most kind to me. Now, please that the picture's here at last, be kind to my Scarlett."

That was all. A great bouquet came down, from the Loew management, and another, of red roses, from the City of Atlanta. And the light dimmed into darkness about Peggy Mitchell.

Somehow, watching her there, one was reminded of the grand speech made by John Marsh, as coming in, a radio announcer stopped him to ask:

"Aren't you proud of your wife?"

"I was proud of her," said John, "long before she wrote a book."

The lights flashed on. The great crowd rose to go.

Down near the front, close up to the screen that they might see and hear, tall state troopers helped from their seats four bent old men in Confederate gray.

One straightened, waved a cane, toward the screen on which Atlanta had burned.

"That's what I've been trying to tell 'em," he said. "That's what I been trying to tell 'em all along."

He told a few and they didn't quite understand.

Peggy Mitchell "told 'em," and now the whole world knows.

Overview of Civil War Atlanta painted by Wilbur G. Kurtz.

Disorder of Atlanta just before its fall to Sherman's troops in 1864 as it was minutely reconstructed in April 1939.

Victor Fleming's retake of the opening scene, March 1939.

Preparation for scenes of Confederate wounded at the Atlanta depot, May 20, 1939.

The studio's version of a Confederate ambulance and some of the dummies used when needs exceeded Central Casting's resources, May 20, 1939.

CLASS OF SERVICE

This is a full-rate Telegram or Cablegram unless its deferred character is indicated by a suitable symbol above or preceding the address.

R. B. WHITE
PRESIDENT

NEWCOMB CARLTON
CHAIRMAN OF THE BOARD

J. C. WILLEVER
FIRST VICE-PRESIDENT

WESTERN UNION

1201 P-2

SYMBOLS

DL = Day Letter
NL = Night Letter
LC = Deferred Cable
NLT = Cable Night Letter
Ship Radiogram

The filing time shown in the date line on telegrams and day letters is STANDARD TIME at point of origin. Time of receipt 1939 JAN 15 PM at point of destination

Received at **Atlanta, Georgia** ALWAYS OPEN

S4 TWS PAID 3=WUX TDS CULVERCITY CALIF 13 650P

MRS JOHN R MARSH=

4 EAST 17 ST NORTHEAST ATLA=

DEAR MRS MARSH: IF I CAN BUT FEEL THAT YOU ARE WITH ME ON THIS, THE MOST IMPORTANT AND TRYING TASK OF MY LIFE, I PLEDGE WITH ALL MY HEART I SHALL TRY TO MAKE SCARLETT O'HARA LIVE AS YOU DESCRIBED HER IN YOUR BRILLIANT BOOK. WARMEST REGARDS=

VIVIEN LEIGH.

THE COMPANY WILL APPRECIATE SUGGESTIONS FROM ITS PATRONS CONCERNING ITS SERVICE

CLASS OF SERVICE

This is a full-rate Telegram or Cablegram unless its deferred character is indicated by a suitable symbol above or preceding the address.

R. B. WHITE
PRESIDENT

NEWCOMB CARLTON
CHAIRMAN OF THE BOARD

J. C. WILLEVER
FIRST VICE-PRESIDENT

WESTERN UNION

1201 P-2

SYMBOLS

DL = Day Letter
NL = Night Letter
LC = Deferred Cable
NLT = Cable Night Letter
Ship Radiogram

The filing time shown in the date line on telegrams and day letters is STANDARD TIME at point of origin. Time of rec 1939 JAN 15 at point of destination

Received at **Atlanta, Georgia** ALWAYS OPEN

S6 TWS PAID 3=WUX TDS CULVERCITY CALIF 13 650P

MRS JOHN R MARSH=

4 EAST 17 ST NORTHEAST ATLA=

DEAR MRS MARSH: THIS NEWS THAT I AM TO PLAY MELANIE MEANS A LONG CHERISHED DREAM REALIZED. NOW I HOPE FOR ONE THING MORE IMPORTANT, THAT IS TO PLAY THE ROLE TO YOUR SATISFACTION.=

OLIVIA DE HAVILLAND.

THE COMPANY WILL APPRECIATE SUGGESTIONS FROM ITS PATRONS CONCERNING ITS SERVICE

WESTERN UNION

1201

S5 TWS PAID 3=WUX TDS CULVERCITY CALIF 13 650P

MRS JOHN R MARSH=

4 EAST 17 ST NORTHEAST ATLA=

DEAR MRS MARSH: I AM NOT AT ALL ENVIOUS OF RHETT BECAUSE
THANKS TO YOU, IT WAS MELANIE, MA'AM, THAT I WANTED. BUT
SERIOUSLY, I FEEL IT A GREAT HONOR TO HAVE BEEN SELECTED
TO ENACT ONE OF THE ROLES OF YOUR BOOK, THE TITLE OF WHICH
ESCAPES ME AT THE MOMENT.=

LESLIE HOWARD.

Twelve Oaks set with its curving stair ready for action under the direction of Victor Fleming.

Vivien Leigh, Olivia de Havilland, and Ona Munson: Belle Watling gives Melanie Wilkes money for the Confederate hospital.

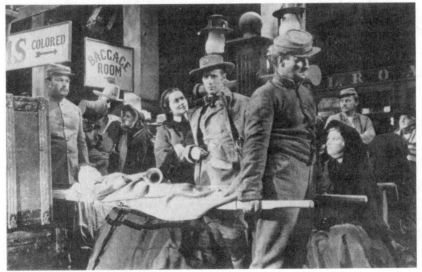

Ashley Wilkes (Leslie Howard, with Olivia de Havilland) arrives at the Atlanta depot, Christmas, 1863.

Rhett and Scarlett (Clark Gable and Vivien Leigh) in happy days of their marriage.

David Selznick's Film Is World's Greatest

By the *Hollywood Spectator*

Reviews of Selznick's Gone With the Wind *were almost universally enthusiastic, notable exceptions being Carlton Moss's vitriolic review in the* New York Daily Worker *of January 9, 1940, and Lincoln Kirstein's attack on it and on Hollywood in general in the spring 1940 issue of* Films. *Jesse Zunsser wrote in* Cue, *a magazine less prone to unmerited praise than most of the review media of the thirties, for December 23, 1939:* Gone With the Wind *is one of the most spectacular, thrilling, beautifully photographed, and consistently entertaining pictures the screen has seen in years. . . . To put it as briefly as possible,* Gone With the Wind *is a glorious show. You must see it."*

It was no surprise that Southern reviewers reacted favorably to the film. E. D. C. Campbell, Jr., points out in his The Celluloid South *(Knoxville: 1981), however, that film-goers everywhere had been so conditioned by forty years of cinematic glamorization of the Old South that they were completely taken in by the producer's claims of historic and social accuracy.*

One day after Selznick wired Jock Whitney that the film was finished he screened it for 750 press representatives. An early and ecstatic review of Gone With the Wind *is that of the* Hollywood Spectator, *December 23, 1939. Despite its excesses of enthusiasm, it is notable as an immediate reaction to the film among Selznick's Hollywood public and for its attention to the fine craftsmen and technicians who participated in making the film.*

Mightiest achievement in the history of the motion picture.

Superb entertainment which will hold the close attention of audiences for every minute of its long running time.

A production which gives David Selznick undisputed right to recognition as the greatest producer motion pictures have developed.

A great novel becomes a great screen offering without sacrifice of any of the values which made it notable as literature.

When it was announced that David Selznick had purchased *Gone With the Wind* for the purpose of making it into a motion picture, even his friends in the film world felt he had bitten off several hundred pages more than he could chew. Many more outside his circle of personal friends were quite satisfied the purchase was an unwise one, that he never would be able to make a picture which would meet with the favor of the many million people who had read the book—many million if the reports of libraries and individual sales are to be relied upon.

But dubious head-shaking did not dampen Dave's enthusiasm nor dull the lustre of what his imagination saw as the pictorial presentation of the book. With complete confidence in his estimate of the screen possibilities of the story material, he organized his forces, worked with them, imparted his enthusiasm to them, selected wisely the experts to do the expert work, the people to play the several parts, the director to make the whole thing live on the screen.

Not with as much confidence or assurance of making it worthy of his inspiration, can a reviewer approach the task of estimating the values of the picture. He can sum it up by saying the film version of *Gone With the Wind* is a screen presentation one cannot afford to miss if he takes an intelligent interest in the development of the screen or is merely looking for an evening's entertainment, but to enumerate the features which justify such summing up, he would have to write a review proportionately as long as the book.

The picture is breath-taking in its visual beauty, for once Technicolor having justified its use in a dramatic multiple-reel production. There are hills of velvety softness and warmly rich hues which roll back from the foreground action, sunshine sifting through trembling tree leaves, hoe armed men tilling the soil of tilted fields—a succession of Corots, Van Dycks, Rembrandts, serving as backgrounds across which a gripping story moves, a story of a selfish, designing girl, and a distressed, tortured people.

I was one of an audience composed of all the motion picture critics there are in Hollywood, writers who are aware film entertainment is only photographed fiction, that the players are their carefree neighbors, friends and acquaintances, yet there were few dry eyes and fewer unchoked throats among these appraisers of screen values as scene after scene moved across the screen. And all the critics realized they were viewing a picture to which the most eloquent pen could do faint justice.

Extraordinary skill was exercised by the late Sidney Howard in making his script faithful to its source. The picture as a whole is truly the book in pictures and dialogue; it glorifies the book, makes it live before our eyes; animates its comedy, its drama, its tragedy, recreates the Old South for us, then shatters it. And through all the scenes of tremendous sweep, of thousands of people in action, the thread of the story glides without breaking the continuity of our interest in the little group of people upon whom it so deftly fastens our attention as each makes his or her first appearance on the screen.

Gone With the Wind is the biggest motion picture ever made, the most overpowering, the best entertainment. And, at the same time, it is the greatest purely cinematic triumph of all time, a picture which will delight the student of screen art, which marks the farthest step the screen yet has taken toward the fulfillment of its artistic destiny. From the outset it pays the viewer the compliment of presuming he has intelligence: it lets him discover the leading characters, each of whom is seen first in the background and is drawn to our immediate attention only when the story demands it. Scarlett, for instance, is but one of a large group of girls in her first scene, and by a gradual process is brought to the foreground.

All the other characters are treated in the same manner. That is logical screen procedure, based upon the obviously sensible presumption that a reason for our interest in a character must be created before we can become interested.

The picture could not be made on the assumption that all who would see it had read the book and therefore knew the people in it. If it is to be successful financially, it must be seen by scores of millions who have not read the book, who never heard of Scarlett, of Rhett Butler and the rest.

But if I were to treat all the cinematic virtues of the picture with as much detail as the above, I would write a review which would match the book in bulkiness. There are many other points upon which I would like to dwell, but I will leave them for future *Spectators* and after I have seen the picture again. It is too overwhelming to be seen only once.

On the whole, the screen version of the book is a sociological document of tremendous import. It is the strongest plea for peace ever made by man. It does not argue against war. It shows us war, acres of dead, dying and tortured victims of man's most depraved and vicious manifestation. There is no flag-waving in the picture. It takes no sides in the controversies it records, preaches no sermons, points no morals—just lets us see humanity in action and uses a little group of wholly unimportant people as the symbols of what it wishes to express.

Scarlett, of course, is the centre of our attention: her whims and fancies are what holds the intimate story together.

The moment he selected Vivien Leigh to play the role of Scarlett, was the moment David Selznick reached the peak of his discernment as a motion picture producer. He never again can do anything so spectacularly brilliant. With millions of dollars, as well as his career, at stake, he selected a girl he spied in a crowd, a girl unknown to American picture audiences, and, so to speak, put the millions of dollars on her shoulders, depended upon her to bring them back with added millions to justify his choice.

Vivien Leigh does not *play* Scarlett. She *is* Scarlett—even to the green eyes. That is all I need say about her performance. What I may say about her next, I do not know. I am not sure she will be convincing in any other part, for I do not see how Scarlett O'Hara can make me believe she is some other person. But perhaps Vivien Leigh can surmount even that big difficulty.

Another performance which does not inspire comment is that of Clark Gable. I can praise Rhett Butler, but not Clark, whom I did not see on the screen.

I liked Rhett for his honesty, his lack of pretense, his philosophy and his unuttered yearnings. And thanks to Clark Gable for all that, for the most discerning performance he has given us.

Olivia de Havilland's contribution to the picture is a tremendous one. She moves through it like a breeze scented by apple blossoms floating through a stuffy room. She gives the picture what it needed—a strain of sweetness sifting in and out through the story's ugly phases, through its bickerings, deceits, jealousies, tragedies—something to clear our nostrils of the stink of rotting flesh, something for our eyes to rest upon when they turned from war's horrors. It is a great performance that Olivia gives, one which gives her rating among the screen's most important actresses.

Only by the excellence of all the performances could *Gone With the Wind* achieve the excellence it has as a whole. There are scores of bits in it done as well as the biggest scenes of the leading players. It is impossible to give praise to all who deserve it. Some of those who figure most prominently in providing the feast of superlative acting are Leslie Howard, Thomas Mitchell, Ona Munson, Hattie McDaniel, Barbara O'Neil, Evelyn Keyes, Ann Rutherford, Laura Hope Crews, Harry Davenport, Carroll Nye—but look down the list presented with this review and credit each name with a job done well.

When you pause to consider that all the millions Dave Selznick spent in making the picture could have become wasted money by poor direction, you get some realization of the responsibility which rested on Victor Fleming. Viewed from one standpoint, all the credit for a great picture belongs, in the final analysis, to the director, for he is the only man in a position to nullify all the other contributions to it. Victor comes through with flying colors, realizes fully all the possibilities of his material. A striking feature of his direction is the manner in which he keeps his backgrounds alive, has motion in the extreme up-stage end of every scene. His vigor in scenes filled with action is a far cry from the tenderness of such scenes as that in which Scarlett bids farewell to the dying Melanie, yet the direction is supreme in each.

Fleming presents us with no flat groupings, does no given thing in a certain manner because it always has been done that way. He does not sacrifice composition to unnecessary close-ups. But most of all does he keep his characters human and consistent, and get emotional reponse by the very simplicity of his appeal for it, such as in the scene in which the gracious lady (Olivia de Havilland) steps into the carriage of the prostitute, (played brilliantly by Ona Munson) and the two have an intimate talk: if you see that scene without being moved profoundly, you will prove yourself a peculiar person.

There must be some end to this review, so I can do but scant justice to the other geniuses who had a hand in its making and whose names appear on this page: William Cameron Menzies, for designing the extraordinary and pictorially rich production; Lyle Wheeler, for his art direction; Ernest Haller, Ray Rennahan, Wilfrid Cline, for their superb photography; Jack Cosgrove, for outstanding photographic effects; Lee Zavitz, for his thrilling fires; Hal Kern and James Newcom for their masterly film editing—but I am embarking on another excursion it will take too long to finish. There are so many who deserve praise.

But it all sums up to David Oliver Selznick, to whom this picture gives rating as the world's greatest motion picture producer. When some other producer faces such odds and gives us a greater picture than *Gone With the Wind*, I will shift the crown to his brow.

Study groups and schools must prepare for the showing of this supreme screen masterpiece. My review does scant justice to it. My task was about as hard as it would be to describe the Grand Canyon. But before the picture reaches most houses I hope to discuss it further for the benefit of motion picture appreciation classes and others interested in the screen both as an art and as a medium of entertainment. I wish I had time to write a book about it. To exhibitors everywhere: Get it.

An Open Letter to Mr. Selznick

By Carlton Moss

At the other extreme in reviews of Gone With the Wind *is Carlton Moss's. It appeared in the* Daily Worker, *New York, January 9, 1940, under the title "An Open Letter to Mr. Selznick." An editor's note introduced the reviewer: "Carlton Moss, the author of the accompanying open letter, is a gifted young Negro dramatist. Collaborating with the Negro composer, William Grant Still, he wrote the opera, "Blue Steel." He authored two productions for the Federal Theatre and is at present a radio script writer for the National Broadcasting Company."*

Careless (or distorted) in some of its facts as Moss's review is, it represents a point of view among Blacks that was incomprehensible to Miss Mitchell and most white Southerners of her generation. Their feelings towards Blacks may have been, individually, kind and generous, but by the 1930s Negro leaders regarded such attitudes as degrading and patronizing.

Margaret Mitchell contributed to scholarships for premedical students at Morehouse College and made generous gifts for special facilities for Blacks at Atlanta's Grady Hospital. Her personal relations with individual Blacks cannot be faulted, but her attitudes towards race relations in general belonged to an era that was rapidly passing. She wrote Susan Myrick April 17, 1939, concerning comments made by some Blacks during the filming of GWTW: "I do not need to tell you how I and all my folks feel about Negroes.... I have paid for medical care and done the nursing myself on many occasions; all of us have fought in the law courts and paid fines.... Shortly after the book came out the Radical and Communistic publications, both black and white, began to hammer, but all they could say was that the book was 'an insult to the Race.'... Of course you know how happy it made me to have the Radical publications dislike 'Gone With the Wind.' I couldn't have held up my head if they had liked it, but the Negro angle bothered me, for Heaven knows I had and have no intention of 'insulting the Race.' Recently the Negro press has discovered the way in which they have been insulted. It is because I had various characters use the terms 'nigger' and 'darkey.'.... Regardless of the fact that they call each other 'nigger' today and regardless of the fact that nice people in ante bellum days called them 'darkies,' these papers are in a fine frenzy.... I have had enough twisted and erroneous and insulting things written about me and 'Gone With the Wind' to make me sore on the whole Negro race if I were sensitive or a fool. But I do not intend to let any number of trouble-making Professional Negroes change my feelings toward the race with whom my relations have always been those of affection and mutual respect. There are Professional Negroes just as there are Professional Southerners and, from what I can learn from Negroes I have talked to, they are no more loved by their race than Professional Southerners are by us."

Dear Mr. Selznick:

Whereas "The Birth of a Nation" was a frontal attack on American history and the Negro people, "Gone With the Wind," arriving twenty years later, is a rear attack on the same. Sugar-smeared and blurred by a boresome Hollywood love story and under the guise of presenting the South as it is in the "eyes of the Southerners," the message of GWTW emerges in its final entity as a nostalgic plea for sympathy for a still living cause of Southern reaction.

The Civil War is by no means ended in the South, Mr. Selznick. It lives on and will live on until the Negro people are completely free, until the infamous poll tax is eradicated, until the starvation and misery of millions of poor blacks and whites is wiped out, and most important, until the sons and daughters of the GWTW aristocracy, the Bilbos, the Garners, the Cotton Ed Smiths, and the Martin Dies are eliminated, together with their anti-Negro divide and rule policies.

*   *   *

I saw this much heralded "epic" of the old South. I saw Sherman's army pictured as a band of invaders, bent on murder, rape and plunder. (Sherman himself is never shown on the screen but his name is flashed in menacing letters against a background of ruin and there are several references to him and his army of "destruction.") I saw homes, churches, hospitals and Atlanta streets crowded with wounded and dying Confederate soldiers, while one doctor, with insufficient equipment and medicine tried vainly to aid them. I saw helpless men, women and children frantically seeking refuge from the constant cannon fire of the Union Army. I saw scores of negroes leisurely saunter along the roads (while the whites were hurrying to escape), concerned only with the welfare of their "kind" masters. I can still see Scarlett O'Hara as though she were crying hysterically: "Give us back our liberty! Give us back our peaceful parasitic existence, you damned Yankees! Give us back our slaves to exploit! Give us back our right to trade and profit in human flesh!"

A glance at history, Mr. Selznick, will tell you that when Sherman made his heroic march to the sea, there were with him two regiments of white men from Alabama and Georgia. That throughout the war thousands of whites kept deserting to the Northern forces, while thousands of Negroes escaped across the lines to the Union Army, or became active in a general strike behind the lines. History also tells that the southern aristocracy comprised the bulk of the Confederate Army. That Sherman's special field order No. 119 read:

"Soldiers must not enter the dwellings of the inhabitants, or commit any trespass. . . . In districts and neighborhoods where the army is unmolested, no destruction of property should be permitted; but should guerrillas or bushwackers molest our march . . . then army commanders should order and enforce a devastation more or less relentless, according to the measure of such hostility. As for horses, mules, wagons, etc., belonging to the inhabitants, the cavalry and artillery may appropriate freely and without limit, discriminating, however, between the rich, who are usually hostile, and the poor and industrious, usually neutral or friendly."

*   *   *

The entire casualties for the Union Army throughout this march were 103 killed and 428 wounded. Along the route, more than 25,000 Negro refugees joined the march. Sherman wrote: "One poor creature, while nobody was looking, hid two boys five years old in a wagon, intending, I suppose, that they should see the land of freedom even if she couldn't." He further wrote that he found the Negroes "simply frantic with joy." This, Mr. Selznick, certainly refutes the myth put forward by your picture that all the people were solidly behind the Confederate cause, throughout, and that the Union Army was a ruthless gang of invaders.

If for nothing else but its distortion of the reconstruction period, GWTW ranks as a reactionary film, and there is plenty else. For years, this deliberate falsification of a progressive era in American life has been fed the American schoolboy and to the American people through the stage and screen. The most repeated lies about the Civil War and the Reconstruction period are:

1. That the Negro didn't care about or want his freedom.

2. That he had neither the qualities nor the "innate" ability to take care of, let alone govern, himself.

In reproducing the period of Reconstruction in GWTW, you have the newly freed Negroes idly walking the streets, dressed in natty outfits, wearing jaunty loud colored derbies and exaggeratedly puffing long cigars. The Negro Union soldiers look on approvingly at street crap games while white Union officers gamble with "gentlemen prisoners" and carouse with the city's "madams." A Northerner tells a crowd of Negroes that they are going to get 40 acres and a mule. They look at him with little comprehension and no enthusiasm. In the midst of this "after the war setting" Scarlett passes through on her way to the countryside. She is accosted by a white man who tries to rob her. Big Sam, her former slave, saves her. Following this a Negro attempts to rape her. Big Sam battles him off too. Scarlett goes home and tells her husband, and he and his friends go off to take vengeance. Where and how we are not shown, but the implication is clear. It is the justification of the KKK.

Again let us look at the actual historical facts. This is a period in American history when black men played leading roles in the state and local governments and fought vigorously for the rights not only of their newly freed brothers but for the rights of the poor whites, who, too, were denied the balllot and who were victimized by the slave-owning reactionaries. Much of the legislation of the "black Parliaments" still stands. Possibly their chief remaining contribution was the establishment, for the first time, of a free public school system for the people of the South. These black parliaments would have grown and flourished, carrying out their program "of greater democracy to all people regardless of color," had not Southern reaction been permitted to reorganize and consolidate its forces to crush them in their infancy. The terroristic, hooded KKK paved the way by armed struggle against the Negro population, by raiding of Negro territories, and by literal threats of death to Negroes who sat in legislative seats to which they had been legally elected. The terror of the KKK was legalized by the Southern bourbons who slowly recaptured the power, against the stiff resistance of forward thinking Negroes.

*   *   *

The press reports your meticulous concern for accuracy in this $3,700,000 production. There are reams written about how you guarded against errors such as "a misplaced, 'you all,' a petticoat with inappropriate lace, the wrong style of waltz, an error in an army uniform; no mistake, it was known, would be too small to bring indignant protests from some eagle eye in the South." You have done all this and won a clamorous applause from Mrs. Walter D. Lamar, president-general of the United Daughters of the Confederacy and the class she represents. It is also reported that you personally told a Negro organization that there would be no scenes offensive to the Negro people in the picture. Let us examine the Negro characters. I have already alluded to the lopsided treatment of the Negro people in the mass scenes. Then there's that bourbon belly-chuckle, the scene with the Negro chasing the chicken, and numerous little scenes with the Negro slaves hopping up supplying "master's" wants before they are even asked for.

As to the principal Negro characters, they follow the time-worn stereotype pattern laid down by Hollywood. There is shiftless and dull-witted Pork, Young Prissy, indolent and thoroughly irresponsible, "Big" Sam with his radiant acceptance of slavery and Mammy with her constant, haranguing and doting on every wish of Scarlett. It is made to appear that she loves this degrading position in the sevice of a family that has helped to keep her people enchained for centuries. This false collection of two-dimensioned Negro characters is insulting to the Negro people. Especially is this so since history provides us with such positive Negro characters as Nat Turner, Denmark Vesey, Gabriel Prosser, Fred Douglass, Harriet Tubman, Sojourner Truth, etc., and thousands of others who participated in the operation of the Underground Railroad, unflinchingly sacrificing their lives for the eventual freedom of their people and the ultimate completion of American democracy.

Very truly yours,
CARLTON MOSS.

Max Steiner Establishes Another Film Music Record

By Bruno David Ussher

In the torrents of words that have been written about Gone With the Wind *the music of the movie has been relatively (and strangely) neglected. Max Steiner's score is a masterful accomplishment, yet William Pratt devotes less than two pages to it in* Scarlett Fever *(New York: 1977) and Roland Flamini barely more than a page in* Scarlett, Rhett, and a Cast of Thousands *(New York: 1975). In* GWTW: The Making of Gone With the Wind *(Boston: 1973) Gavin Lambert gives Steiner and his work only one paragraph, but a highly laudatory one. He declares in his summary sentence to that paragraph: "Quintessential Hollywood 'prestige' music, the score fits Selznick's conception perfectly, narcotic, quivering, or rousing as occasion demands."*

Steiner began work on the score for GWTW in the late summer of 1939. Under great pressure of time he composed (or arranged and scored) three hours and twelve minutes of music for the film. This was cut for use to two hours and thirty-six minutes. When Steiner's preparation of the score seemed to lag, Selznick hired Franz Waxman as a back-up and discussed with another composer, Herbert Stothart, the possibility of taking over if necessary. The film uses two brief compositions by Waxman, and Steiner was aided in the scoring by him, Adolph Deutsch, and Hugo Friedman. Pratt asserts that "Heinz Roemheld composed all the music for the escape from Atlanta and the burning depot scenes." This claim is not borne out by the film's credits nor by the more detailed "Music Report" appended to the "Dialogue Cutting Continuity" issued by Loew's Incorporated in 1939.

The "Dialogue Cutting Continuity" is meticulous in giving the sources for the music not by Steiner to composers ranging from Dan Emmett (for "Dixie") to Richard Wagner (for the "Bridal Chorus" from Lohengrin*). These credits show that, next to Steiner himself, the most extensive composer of music for* Gone With the Wind *was Stephen C. Foster. Steiner used no less than eleven of Foster's tunes in his score: "Beautiful Dreamer," "Camptown Races," "Dolly Day," "Jeanie with the Light Brown Hair," "Katie Belle," "Louisiana Belle,"*

"Massa's in de Cold, Cold Ground," "My Old Kentucky Home," "Old Folks at Home," "Ring de Banjo," and "Under the Willow."

Bruno David Ussher wrote in the Hollywood Spectator for December 23, 1939: "Steiner's Gone With the Wind music is infinitely more than a folksong fantasy. It bears his own screen-musical physiognomy which anyone will recognize who is familiar with his film music style. Yet he does not intrude. . . . [He] indeed listened to the 'wind' of which Margaret Mitchell's book tells. He has distilled it into a beautifully balanced score, which rises to hurricane strength and which is again soft and soothing. Here is a score which blows greater life into a great motion picture."

Ussher expanded his comments on the music of GWTW in a pamphlet issued a little later by Fox West Coast Theaters. It is the text of that pamphlet that is reprinted here.

Long before film producer David O. Selznick announced that Max Steiner had been invited to contribute the background music in, "Gone With the Wind," it had been a foregone conclusions in Hollywood that the choice would fall on this pioneer among film composers.

When one thinks of music in the films, today or as it was in the early stages of the sound-film ten years ago, the name of Max Steiner comes to mind immediately. The fact that he happens to be one of the early and most resourceful pioneers in this field of music—dramatic music is not sufficient reason for his name coming up whenever film music is being discussed. Nor is the circumstance of his having set music to more than 170 films of varying lengths sufficient reason for such high and general regard. Steiner has earned his position by the remarkable and consistent qualities of his film-scores in which dramatic fidelity of expression, the fitness of general musical ideas is accompanied by a fresh and versatile sense of tonal beauty where beauty is appropriate.

Long ago, Hollywood became convinced—and ten years are a long time in Hollywood—of the artistic usefulness of Max Steiner, first as an orchestrator and conductor of recordings, then as a composer who could deepen, quicken, in brief, could vitalize a single important episode in a film, or add emotional strength to an entire film production. He has demonstrated this ever-flowering gift, and it has never flowered more extensively than during Selznick's production of "Gone With the Wind." This longest of all motion pictures made so far—three hours and 45 minutes to be exact—is accompanied by more than three hours of music. The picture itself has been compared to an historical mural, to a photographic panorama in Technicolor, and Max Steiner's music adds motion and emotion to this long narrative of Civil War Days in Georgia. It sets the atmosphere melodically and motivates the action before the picture itself flashes on the screen. It serves as a frame for sections of this long panel of pictures, giving individual scenes rhythm and a combining unity to their total of varied impressions. The score tells of battle where the spectator is spared the implied horror even of make-believe death and vast devastation.

There is music which has the shrill, brash mirth of human unripeness and echoes the characteristically leisured, quaintly confident tone of upper-class Southern life before the terrible winds of war began to blow.

Painstaking research has gone into the preparation for writing the longest background score in motion picture annals. Margaret Mitchell's book is not a novel of frontier life, of how men and women risked their lives in pushing westward to win another harvest-acreage from a Western no-man's land where Indian arrows or bullets from white outlaws were a daily menace. "Gone With the Wind" was a polite society which cherished manners and traditions, which threw nonchalantly heedless bravery against the raking superiority of armament. The book and the motion picture tell of the doom of civilization which had its heart roots so deeply in the soil of plantations, owned generation after generation by the same families. The action plays in Georgia only, and the men of Georgia died, the women of Georgia suffered more ardently, more bitterly for that very soil that had given such individual character to the lives of their fathers and of their children. Here was a real task, then, for a musician, to make his share of this mammoth production pregnant with the spirit of a people as of an age.

One can almost claim that Max Steiner was predestined to compose the score for "Gone With the Wind," not only by talent and technique, but by the very experience which brought him to America twenty five years ago. Two years ago he brought over his father, Gabor Steiner, for many years owner-director of the celebrated "Theater an der Wien" in Vienna.

For that matter, the Steiners have always belonged to the theater in one capacity or another. Grandfather Maximilian Steiner was one of the principal producers of operettas by the older Johann Strauss and by Offenbach. His father, Gabor Steiner, carried on the best conventions of musical theater life in Vienna, producer for Johann Strauss, the son and his successors. Love for the music-theater was a natural possession of the boy, Max Steiner. Although showing unmistakable artistic gifts, his father wished him to follow a less hectic calling than that of the theater, that of engineering. Young Max, however, had a will of his own. When only fourteen years of age, he presented his parent with an operetta score and lyrics of his own creation, "The Beautiful Greek Maiden." Turned down by his father but still endowed with the parental energy, he submitted the work to one of his father's competitors, the owner of the Orpheum Theater in Vienna, who not only allowed the youngster to conduct the premiere, but found it profitable to keep the opus in the repertoire for an entire year.

That defeated Gabor Steiner's plans to make his son an engineer. Still in his 'teens, Max Steiner was enrolled at the Imperial Academy of Music in Vienna, where he studied under such celebrities as Fuchs, Graedener, Mahler and Rose, leaving that institution with exceptional marks of distinction, including the coveted gold medal. Doblinger, the long-renowned Viennese publisher, accepted a number of his symphonic and lighter compositions, but rehearsals and performances left little time then for creative work.

In 1904 young Max Steiner was called to London to take charge of the music at Daly's Theater. The young Viennese created a furore which led him in turn to the Adelphi Theater, the Alhambra, the Pavilion, including cross-channel engagements under the management of Alfred Butt in Paris and at the London Opera House, which was then owned by Oscar Hammerstein. It was a decade of successes. It would, no doubt, have lasted, but the glory and the gayety of those days were soon "gone with the wind" blowing across the North sea in August, 1914, from a war-torn continent.

A special passport, procured for him by the Duke of Westminster (brother of the King of England), who admired the Austrian composer-conductor, saved him from internment and in the fall of that year the name of Max Steiner appeared on the programs of various Broadway productions as conductor and musical collaborator on the scores. The list of shows is too long to mention here—long enough and so successful as to command the attention and interest of Hollywood. The sound-film had come to stay and musicians of experience, yet of flexibility, were needed badly. William LeBaron (now in charge of productions at Paramount) was managing director at RKO, and in 1929 Max Steiner came to that studio, soon to take charge of the music department as general music director and composer.

It is obviously impossible to do more than sketch hastily Max Steiner's musical activities these last ten years. Background scores in pictures as well as "musicals" were still in an experimental stage. Max Steiner is the last person to overrate his contribution to the proper technical, music-dramatic and financial solutions of these problems.

As a matter of fact, by the end of the 1920's, music was out of favor in Hollywood. It had no pull at the box office. Those were humble beginnings then in 1930, when Steiner wrote the music for "Cimarron," RKO screen credits not even so much as mentioning the music. Public curiosity, however, had been aroused even by that brief score. The first battle for musical recognition had been won with the score for "Symphony of Six Millions." "Bird of Paradise" was accompanied by music from beginning to end.

Followed "Little Women," "Lost Patrol," "The Informer" (bringing the Academy Award), "King Kong," "Little Minister," "The Fountain," "Of Human Bondage," "She," "Jezebel," "Zola," "White Banners," "Dark Victory," "Garden of Allah," "A Star Is Born," "Charge of the Light Brigade," "Daughters Courageous," "Old Maid," "Dr. Clitterhouse," "We Are Not Alone," and one of the most recent, "Four Wives," a Warner Brothers film containing a modern tone-poem of seven minutes length, during which the chief production emphasis is laid on the music performed by a full-sized symphony orchestra.

For the last three years, Max Steiner has provided background music for an outstanding array of the principal Warner Brothers productions. Before taking up his present studio affiliation (Warners), he was principal composer for David

O. Selznick, after leaving a musical regime at RKO made notable by his creative and administrative results. For "Gone With the Wind," the Steiner pen and imagination was "loaned" by Warners to Producer Selznick. A complete account of the work and the honors which have come to Max Steiner will perhaps never be told.

One reason is that Max Steiner is too busy composing and conducting recordings; too busy digging in his garden surrounding a quietly furnished villa in Beverly Hills; too busy with taking camera shots or shooting at a target. He collects old guns and enjoys home life with Louise Steiner, a brilliant harpist, and his father. He does not talk about his various medals and distinctions, which include the rank of Officer in the "Academie Française" in recognition of his international services on behalf of screen music. He takes genuine satisfaction in his large fan mail from screen music lovers and when he talks to music clubs about film music, one realizes again how true a servant he is in this democratic medium of art and entertainment.

"I have been thinking a long time about the music for 'Gone With the Wind,' " he told me while turning on the water under several fruit trees on his 2½-acre flower and vegetable garden. "I came to the conclusion that it took a Georgia woman to give certain intimate touches to this great novel. I think you will understand why I have used a number of American songs belonging to the time and country with which Margaret Mitchell's novel deals. Of course, I have my own music, and enormous quantities, in this score which is the length of a big opera. In the main I have worked with seven principal character motifs of my own, and supplemented these with traditional folk-songs which I use in part or entirely, or again in some varied shape adapted by me to suit the situation."

Twice, Steiner has felt the withering blasts of war, which sears the souls of men if it does not consume them as well as their possessions. Once, when he escaped the European crucible, a quarter of a century ago to become an American. The second time he experienced that onrush when the Austria of old days went down and lost its autonomy. (Before that had come to pass, he had sent for his old father.)

"I think I can experience what has happened to the people of Georgia and to the O'Hara family and their friends at 'Tara' and 'Twelve Oaks.' Some people have referred to Mr. Selznick and his director, Victor Fleming, as having made a great mural. Others have referred to this film as an enormous narrative. It is enormous, but more than a mural and more than narrative, although huge action scenes, colossal action episodes with immense quantities of men in action have been avoided.

"To me, it is tremendously dramatic as it pictures the passing of an era of graciousness and loveliness. I am not qualified to evaluate the sociologic, economic and historic causes of the civil war. This book and this film, very faithfully tell of the suffering of a great community of Southern men and women; the whole tragedy is silhouetted in the fine and at times highly self-willed lives of certain individuals suffering through the events of those days.

There was no need to re-stage battles to show tragedy. The great scene showing a plaza filled with wounded, the fire scenes, the pictures of burned houses and trampled fields symbolized enough."

Steiner paused long enough to point out the artichoke and strawberry beds which he and his father are fond of tending. He showed me some trees given him by different friends. It looked like rain and he covered up two sandstone figures near a little waterfall.

"So it was not a question of a war film and a piece of war music. 'Gone With the Wind' on the screen is a human document, dealing with white people, and with four people in particular, with Scarlett O'Hara, Rhett Butler, with Melanie and with Ashley Wilkes. There are other salient figures, but they are really secondary.

"And, more important than all these individuals is 'Tara,' the O'Hara family plantation. Having felt the 'wind,' I can grasp that feeling for 'Tara,' which moved Scarlett's father and which is one of the finest instincts in her, that love for the soil where she had been born, love of the life before her own which had been founded so strongly. That is why the 'Tara' theme begins and ends the picture and permeates the entire score."

Steiner's own and original themes for the principal dramatic characters are those for Scarlett O'Hara, for Rhett Butler, for Melanie, a theme denoting the love of Melanie for Ashley Wilkes and another one for Scarlett and Ashley, the theme for Scarlett's father. Last, yet in some respects most important, is the theme for "Tara," unmistakable in its broad, nostalgic mood, powerfully appealing in its warm, lingering touch that betokens love of home, and ground, and tradition. Here is a theme filled with Southern flavor, with beauty, strength and affection.

As Steiner says, " 'Tara' is more than a plantation, more than a fine old house, saturated with proud, and sad, and always loving memories. 'Tara' is a living thing giving and demanding life. 'Tara' is an idea which keeps Scarlett on her unrelenting quest to preserve with it the spiritual heritage of the O'Haras and of the Old South."

Great care has been taken by Max Steiner not to commit anachronisms. That is to say, every traditional theme is historically and geographically justified. It is music of the time and of the place, of Georgia. Such tunes as "Dixie," "Bonnie Blue Flag" (the national anthem of the South), and "Maryland, My Maryland" serve to denote the cause of the Confederates. Northern soldiers are hardly seen on the screen and songs referring to them are hardly used. At the beginning of the second part of the film, when rising conflagrations and a bluntly laconic title denote Sherman's march to the Atlantic coast, he uses the strains of "Marching Through Georgia." Nor is there much justification for the use of voices, the picture rarely depicting negro life or work in the field. Steiner employs a vocal background when "Dixie" is first heard in the opening title sequence, but he has wisely refrained from stressing the words. The human significance of the tune is brought home by the very presence of the voices.

Stirring, too, is the uplifting, soaring choral ending of the film, like the magnificently radiant, ecstatic promise "of another day," on which prophetic words the entire film production comes to a culminating climax. Here again Steiner's eloquent "Tara" theme sets in once more, just as it has opened the picture, now tying together the threads of a stormy life, setting on them the binding seal of that musical symbolism of love for home and family and ancestral soil.

There is little reason then for using Negro spirituals. "Go Down Moses" is sung briefly during a scene in besieged Atlanta when a regiment of Negro soldiers marches by, on its way to the front. One other highly suitable vocal strain occurs during the honeymoon journey scene on board ship, when background singers are heard in J. E. Woodbury's much sung love-song, "Stars of the Summer Night."

Just as Vivien Leigh, the actress, perfectly is the type for Scarlett O'Hara, so Max Steiner has coined themes which, musically, bear the physiognomy of the characters. But Steiner has not limited himself to this one theme for Scarlett. In the barbecue scene, for instance, he characterizes her by means of Stephen Foster's "Katie Belle." Scarlett's father is of Irish stock, as name and personality convey. His musical theme, while Steiner's own, too, is in Irish vein. A typically Southern Negro melody has been given to Mammy, faithful factotum in the O'Hara household. There is a swagger and a brashness and a winsome recklessness in the Rhett Butler theme.

To the lover and student of American folk-lore, Steiner's "Gone With the Wind" score offers a rich and fascinating study. He demonstrates strikingly how much significant material can be derived from a period in which music was made by the people, rather than the professional musicians. Steiner's investigation into the music of the South brought various and interesting results. "Cavaliers of Dixie," sung in the Southern States, had not, as supposed, its origin below the Mason and Dixon line, but was imported from England where it was in vogue first. The composer is unknown. Steiner makes use of it in the early part of the film when news of the war brings the young Southerners together. Another English tune, "London Bridge Is Falling Down," occurs in the music box scene, and when Butler takes little Bonnie to the British Isles. "Dixie" is re-introduced poignantly during the famous scenes showing hundreds of wounded soldiers. Here, too, "Bonnie Blue Flag" waves its melodious flutter. Subtle indeed is employment of L. Lambert's "When Johnny Comes Marching Home," heard when Ashley is shown splitting fence rails.

Stephen Foster's songs provide apt material for a score so carefully aimed at the emotional expression of the period. His "Louisiana Belle" and "Dolly Day" fit well into the barbecue atmosphere, and the "Ring de Banjo" has been suggested by Margaret Mitchell's description of the party. J. Barnby's "Sweet and Low" passes through the score in the scene showing the three O'Hara sisters asleep. A bit of satire is implied, perhaps, when the colored Mammy remonstrates with Scarlett, who supposedly in mourning for her unloved husband who had died somewhat embarrassingly from measles and not while leading his men. Scarlett tries on a bright green hat, and the shocked Mammy reminds her that she is supposed to be a widow, the orchestra echoing her with "Massa's in de Cold, Cold Ground." Steiner loves to inject such bits of whimsical humor. "Maryland, My Maryland" lends deeper meaning to the scene when the women folk swell the exchequer of the Confederacy with their bits of jewelry. The author of the novel makes actual mention of the tune "Lorena" as being heard when, in the original story, the collection of jewelry has been completed.

Margaret Mitchell's young folk dance Virginia reels to such tunes as "Irish Washerwoman" and "Jerry Owen," and Steiner takes that cue. The bassoon adds a comic note in the "Chicken Reel" when the darky chases the rooster. Mendelssohn's "Hark, the Herald Angels Sing" makes the Christmas scene more plausible. Prissy, the light-headed negro girl, often sings "My Old Kentucky Home" in the Mitchell book on which the film is based.

"I have often wondered why Margaret Mitchell should have gone to the length of mentioning it, but in any case I knew it would not be amiss if I wove that melody into my score for scenes in which Prissy has a part," Steiner once commented, while pausing during a recording of this musical sequence. He has touchingly caught the weary spirit of the wounded when the music takes on the melodic mood of "Old Folks at Home" (known also as "Swanee River"), while endowing the very same scene, in turn, with a feeling of stoic heroism.

As those waiting anxiously for war news are shown on the screen, the gentle melody of "When the Cruel War Is Over" and the brisker "When Johnny Comes Marching Home" speak of the suppressed feelings of those left at home in suspense. "Yankee Doodle" accompanies the advent of the unwelcome purchaser of "Tara." Foster's "Camp Town Races" is heard garishly from the saloon when Prissy comes to fetch Rhett Butler. "Tramp, Tramp, Tramp," "Battle Hymn of the Republic" and again "Marching Through Georgia" are whipped together as the fire spreads through shell-torn Atlanta.

There are in this super-score not less than 282 definite musical episodes, an average of more than ten to each of the 25 reels forming the entire film production. It was a colossal task to find and to assign the proper music, traditional and original, for these 3 hours and 45 minutes of picturization of the story of a girl in a time of grave and hectic re-making of a state.

It would lead too far to spot the significant placement of all the traditional melodies interwoven with his own material. Max Steiner's research notes mention the following well-known songs as having been employed in one form or another, this grouping not enumerating those already pointed out.

"Beautiful Dreamer," "Jeanie With the Light Brown Hair," "Old Folks at Home," "Under the Willows" by Foster, "Deep River," "For He's a Jolly Good Fellow," "Ben Bolt" (by N. Knears), "Silent Night" (F. Gruber), all forming a natural, emotional and dramatic frame for an extraordinary succession of scenes which again often form most striking contrasts. Notwithstanding the diversity of locale, setting and tempo of action, Max Steiner has always found music of his own, or from the sources mentioned and kept abreast with the burden of the cinematic progress. Many times the music has lightened and speeded, added unobtrusive strength to conversation and action which might have seemed stale or long anticipated without his musical ministration. In short, Max Steiner's music has added a measure of Southern atmosphere and veracity of sentiment without which the film "Gone With the Wind" would not be a success.

Steiner's "Gone With the Wind" music, despite the "dimensions of time"— four hours almost—has achieved a work of moving unity. It is not a loud score, but it has strength from within. To repeat, Steiner's own experience includes those catastrophal, uprooting tornadoes of destiny which, when they have subsided, leave tragically little that is not "gone with the wind." That and his capacity for penetrating into the causal ramifications and inner complications of a story and story characters, long proven and proven admirably, must have moved Producer David Selznick to bespeak Steiner's services as a composer.

That is why Steiner could set as he did the bright, yet pathos filled, music for this picture. He could sense the great loneliness of this girl, Scarlett O'Hara. He could echo the throes of a cracked and crushed Georgia. That is also why he could find music which is drastic and hopeless, resolute and gay, infinitely tender, ruthless and filled with remorse. Music such as the scene when Scarlett shoots a maurauder and disposes of him demands mastery of understanding, of expression as of concentration, for it is not a long episode, deeply significant as the incident is as a revelation of that constant state of transition through which Scarlett O'Hara passes. It is a stage of transition constantly overshadowed by the threatened ruin, by the importance of "Tara," by the consuming, never to be denied claim made by "Tara" on Scarlett, and by Scarlett on that time hallowed possession of the O'Haras.

This theme of "Tara" is like a monumental, yet sweetly weaving tree which stands at the very entrance and exit to the house of "Tara." It is music as that of a deeply-rooted tree, earth bound by its roots and its roots holding together the very ground on which "Tara" rests. A great music symbol of a theme, grown from the very symbolism of the book and the film, "Gone With the Wind."

Somewhere it is written "that the historical play teaches history to those who cannot read it in the chronicles." There is more than actual history in this film and not all that was swept before the winds of war and the wars of desire could be told or held on the screen. Time and again, screen playwrights, producer and director have relied on the composer to convey what could neither be said nor shown, for reasons of time and tendency. If Oscar Wilde had lived to witness the growth of the screen he would have included it in that dramatic movement which "has the illusion of truth for its method, and the illusion of beauty for its result."

How often this double-fulfillment has been left to Steiner to verify and to ennoble or to strengthen. Again, it is beyond the limits of space to go into much detail, but to point out those episodes of Ashley's return, this inwardly torn

"Johnny" coming marching home to that very tune. The music tells of the dispute within himself, the break within him, and of the torture within Scarlett.

Infinitely much is said in the orchestra during the loving and the quarreling between Rhett Butler and his wife Scarlett, when Scarlett suffers the accident and when Bonnie dies. The musician here takes the place of the photographer as well as of the playwright.

There is music of pathos and death before the screen arrives at that intimately tragic scene, the passing of Melanie, of Melanie's dying as she has lived,—gently. It is again the composer's scene, and yet the musician, not for a moment, does more than express what Melanie means to the others, what her going means to those whom she leaves behind. Here and in other places, inescapable to the responsive film-goer, the screen not only speaks, but grows eloquent by virtue of an eloquence beyond speech,—the eloquence of music.

Scarlett Materializes

By Nell Battle Lewis

After her curtain speech at the premiere Margaret Mitchell never had a great deal to say publicly about the film made from her book. From public and private statements, however, one can make some fairly solid deductions.

The film more than lived up to her initial expectations. She felt Ben Hecht's flowery rolling titles lent a false note to her story and was dismayed that the upcountry life she had written about was seen through the camera's lens as that of a mannered enclave of a civilization that would have rivaled Blenheim Palace. Concerning the excess of white columns on Georgia homes that should have been "plantation plain" she wrote Virginius Dabney, July 23, 1942: "Many of us were hard put not to burst into laughter at the sight of 'Twelve Oaks'."

She was delighted with the performances of Vivien Leigh and Olivia de Havilland and never said a word to indicate that Clark Gable's performance had not completely overcome her initial wish for some other actor in the role of Rhett Butler. She had joined Susan Myrick in fearing that Hattie McDaniel had been too thoroughly typed by earlier parts to play GWTW's Mammy effectively but was delighted with her performance.

She was disappointed in the film's portrayal of Prissy. She felt that she had created a character who should be played as "shiftless" but not as "stupid." That change in interpretation could easily be a fault of direction rather than of acting. Her disappointment in the interpretation of Prissy was particularly strong for, as she had written Kay Brown, August 13, 1937: "I have been especially interested in who would play this little varmint, possibly because this is the only part I myself would like to play. For this reason whoever plays Prissy will be up against a dreadful handicap as far as I am concerned, for I will watch their actions with a jealous eye."

Her greatest disappointment was in Leslie Howard's performance as Ashley Wilkes. She felt—and strongly—that Howard played a much weaker character than she had written.

Margaret Mitchell had not time, nor energy, nor motivation to respond to movie reviewers as she had written to the early reviewers of her novel. She was, however, particularly pleased with Nell Battle Lewis's column in the Raleigh News and Observer *and on March, 15, 1940, wrote to tell her so.*

She noted especially Miss Lewis's comment on Susan Myrick's work with the actors' speech. "The best compliment," she said, "I heard about the so-called 'Southern dialect' was that no one was aware of it! And all of us would have been dreadfully aware had the actors spoken as if they had their mouths full of hot okra."

The most vital woman in American literature who heretofore has lived in the imagination of countless readers, the fighting O'Hara who wouldn't say die, has successfully materialized on the screen. For once a blurb turned out to be a statement of fact: "Vivien Leigh IS Scarlett," and Selznick's version of "Gone With the Wind," like another Southern saga of twenty-five years ago—"The Birth of a Nation," is "a milestone in cinema history." Beautiful in Technicolor, faithful in translation of Margaret Mitchell's dramatic story of the Confederacy and Reconstruction from page to screen, careful and accurate in manifold details of speech, costume and custom, the movie "Gone with the Wind" should satisfy even the most critical Southern audience.

If the book is Scarlett's, even more so is the picture. That tumultuous, driving, wayward, daring, unconventional, egocentric heroic personality which, in spite of war and desolation and poverty, "in spite of hell and high water," flatly refused to fail its rendezvous with life, dominates the picture from the first scene when the spoiled eighteen [sixteen] -year-old belle is flirting with the Tarleton twins to the final one when the twice-widowed, life-scarred, and finally deserted adventuress raises herself out of her seeming defeat with a surge of the old glorious courage, resolves to return to the beloved red hills of Tara and, still unbeaten, faces tomorrow as another day. My primary reaction to the picture was not, "What a fine movie!" but "What a gal! What a gal!"

There is no question that among the performances in order of excellence Miss Leigh's comes first. As "Gone With the Wind" is Scarlett's story, so its screen version is Miss Leigh's picture. And that, when it so easily might have been otherwise. The previously obscure British actress was a natural; a find, indeed.

Next to the acting of Miss Leigh, I put that of Thomas Mitchell as Gerald O'Hara. And probably of all the actors he looked most like the original as pictured in the reader's mind. As for me, I wouldn't change a hair of him. And third, to my way of thinking, comes Hattie McDaniel as Mammy, rotund, ebon and inimitable in speech and spirit, that dark duenna who strove so valiantly and so vainly to make a lady out of Scarlett. This trio, it seems to me, is well ahead of the field.

As for Rhett—he was Clark Gable in the raiment of the '60's; nevertheless, "adequate"—shall we say? Although never wholly satisfactory to me, he carried the part well and certainly with the requisite virility. Still, something was lacking, some finesse, some polished and subtle gentility which in my conception of the character survived all the rascal Rhett's nefarious doings. But perhaps I am still prejudiced. I heard numerous people say that they found Clark Gable entirely satisfactory—in fact, excellent—as the aristocratic Charlestonian black sheep. "De gustibus non disputandum."

Olivia de Havilland and Leslie Howard I thought better cast. Olivia was a sweet, consistent, convincing Melanie; and, in spite of his ineradicable and occasionally obtrusive Britishness, Mr. Howard was probably as nearly Ashley as any actor who could have been found.

As Dr. Meade, Harry Davenport gave one of the most successful interpretations of a minor part. The white-haired old-school medico was thoroughly authentic. Probably like you, I have known several Doctors Meade in and out of the medical profession.

Distinctly disappointing was Laura Hope Crews as Aunt Pittypat, but the picture's most conspicuous defect was in Prissy; for Prissy, alas, was little more than the black Butterfly from Harlem. Never once did Butterfly McQueen really get into this part, and I doubt that she ever understood what was expected of her. Even Miss Susan Myrick, who, like the rest of us down here, must be well acquainted with Prissy from encounters in real life, could not impart to the Harlem Butterfly the true conception of the lazy, triflin' Negro girl of Miss Mitchell's story. Though inevitably occasionally comic—for even a fluttery, too-stagey Harlem interpretation could not wholly devitalize the part—Prissy was a flat tire. I'm pretty sure that I could have walked through Oberlin and picked out a better Prissy myself.

As for the Southern speech in the picture that was just about what Miss Susan Myrick had prepared us for—and prepared for us. It did not offend. For the most part it was not in any way noticeable. You simply forgot all about it. Right at first, as Scarlett coquetted with the Tarletons on the steps of Tara, there seemed a faint artificiality, a suggestion of unnaturalness; but even then there was nothing approaching what we've had to endure in other Southern movies. Soon, as I say, through interest in the picture one forgot to listen critically. Occasionally and briefly Mr. Howard would seem linguistically some three thousand miles distant, but about the speech as a whole I repeat what I said last Sunday: I think it was extremely well managed. No one but a very carping critic could find anything to object about it.

One thing that struck me about the picture was the fact that obviously effort had been made to keep it as much as possible from reviving sectional animosity. True, the Yankee Army was the villain—there couldn't be any other and have the story at all—but the Northern villainy was not underscored, and the Union soldiers themselves seldom appeared. The one whom Scarlett shot, though in the book one of Sherman's raiders, in the picture was a deserter—of course, a sop to Northern self-respect. But although Mr. Selznick plainly did everything he could to keep his picture from inflaming old enemies against each other, there is really no way in which to whitewash very effectively Sherman's march from Atlanta to the sea.

I noted one odd phenomenon at the Raleigh showing which I am at a loss to explain. Over the big open square in Atlanta which during the siege was filled with the prostrate bodies of wounded Confederate soldiers—one of the most striking scenes in the picture—there floated the Confederate battle flag. For a good minute it fluttered before the audience in a close-up, covering about half of the scene. Expectantly I awaited the reaction. Not a sound from the Raleigh audience greeted it, not a single hand-clap, not even one faint cheer. I don't understand that silence, and I don't approve of it any more than I approve of our neglect of General Lee. Maybe we all are Americans now—though, frankly, I still feel pretty Southern myself—but I'm no more in favor of forgetting the old heroisms of our regional past which are symbolized by this most moving banner than I am of forgetting the brave and worthy things in one's own personal background. The Confederate flag is still to me the world's most beautiful flag, beautiful in symbolizing the extraordinary courage and devotion of my own people. I can't forget—and I don't want to forget—that one of my grandfathers died for it at Malvern Hilll; and I hope that never again will it wave in silence on a Raleigh screen.*

There was a substitution in the picture which I found regrettable. You remember that in the book Scarlett's original oath was "God's nightgown!" For some reason this was expurgated.** But who could have been corrupted by an expletive so amusing? In place of it, Miss O'Hara expressed her wrath and exasperation by "Great balls of fire!"—a very puny substitute, I thought.

I was quite surprised that at no point in the picture did I weep, rank sentimentalist and ardent Confederate though I am. I went equipped with a large clean handkerchief, expecting that at the end of the show it would be drenched with tears. But not so. When I left the theatre, it was as dry as when I had entered.

This worries me a little. What can be happening to me? Have the years afflicted me with some deplorable hardening of the arteries around the heart? I trust not, but it does look a little suspicious. I remember how openly and often I wept at "The Birth of a Nation"—but that was twenty-five years ago. Then I should have denounced in the most vehement terms any Southerner who,

---

*Editor's Note: In her letter to Miss Lewis March 15, 1940, Margaret Mitchell wrote: "I was especially interested in your paragraph about the lack of applause when the Confederate battle flag was shown fluttering over the acres of wounded Confederate soldiers at the car-shed. Here in Atlanta at the premiere there was a great deal of applause early in the picture, and later on where Scarlett shot the Yankee deserter on the stair the tense audience practically yelled. But during the scene you mentioned there was a deathly stillness, just as you noted in the Raleigh theatre. Afterwards a number of us were talking it over, each giving reasons why the audience had been so still. One man summed it up this way—'Have you ever felt like applauding in a Confederate cemetery on Memorial Day? No, you haven't; you feel something too deep for applause.' I think he was on the right track."

**Editor's Note: Writing to David Selznick for the Motion Picture Producers and Distributors of America ("the Hays Office") on October 14, 1937, Joseph I. Breen noted that "God's nightgown" was an expression that probably would be censored. Joseph I. Breen to David Selznick, TLS 7 p. (copy) Sidney Coe Howard Papers in the Bancroft Library, University of California—Berkeley.

dry-eyed, could watch Henry B. Walthall, the Confederate Colonel, return after Appomattox to his desolate home. Yet, with an unfolded handkerchief in my pocket, I watched the valiant Scarlett return to desolate Tara.

That, the return to Tara, to dead Ellen and to senile Gerald, was the best part of the picture. There Scarlett was really the heroine, at grips, at death grips with life in the raw. There she rose to something more than herself, the representative, the symbol of hundreds of other Southern heroines and heroes in the flesh who, not celebrated as the heroes in war, rebuilt with immeasurable suffering and self-sacrifice the New South on the ashes of the old. To me not even the courage of the Southern people in the four war years can equal that, for here is one of the most poignant and most inspiring records of valor in all history.

I consider the extraordinary popular interest in this movie, like that in the book, a very interesting social phenomenon, and I am sure that this interest is not merely a result of the dramatic quality of the story. It is compounded, I believe, of three elements: in the South, of pride in a heroic past; in other parts of the country and here also, of an unacknowledged and perhaps unrecognized yearning for some more gracious mode of life than the one which we follow at present, a graciousness which the Old South continues to represent in the popular mind for the defeat of all "debunkers"; and in all sections—North, South, East, West—of the need for the spiritual topic which a character like Scarlett furnishes us. You may recall that some time ago I quoted Henry C. Link who said that brave, undefeatable Scarlett represented something of a wish-fulfilment for us all. For here she is, standing stoutly on her own feet, though her whole world crashes around her, and then setting herself doggedly to its rebuilding, asking no odds of fate. Scarlett has life in herself; whatever else she is, always she is vital. The current decay in self-reliance has a by-product of wistfulness. Life presses upon us; its complexity confuses us; its tragedy appalls us. Too often we yield, but some of us still have manhood enough to wish that we didn't, to know that we shouldn't, and to admire someone, even a character in a book, who does not.†

The high-brow critics make me laugh. It is not comme il faut, you know, to consider "Gone With the Wind" a very good piece of literary work. It's really not so much of a book, it seems—except in the minds of several million readers with whose low-brow opinion no real critic could agree. But, regardless of such an estimate, Scarlett is not going down in literature any more than in life. Hear me turn prophet: Scarlett is going to survive the high-brow critics. For as long as life is a challenge which men must have courage to meet, the fighting O'Hara who wouldn't say die is going to live.

---

†Editor's Note: Dr. Link wrote in his *The Rediscovery of Man* (New York: 1938), pp. 23–24: "Scarlett, though in many ways not an admirable person, was a woman who remained forever the master of her world rather than its victim. Neither war, nor disappointment in love, nor scandal, nor starvation, nor the burning of her home, nor the pain of childbirth, nor bloodshed, none of the catastrophes could daunt her spirit. . . . Here was a woman who, to many suffering the comparative luxuries of a depression today, exemplified a personal triumph over social insecurity. Ten million readers! Ten million nostalgic gasps from the victims of a machine concept of social security, a people still protesting the loss of personal responsibility and power."

Gone With the Wind: The Old South as National Epic

By. Edward D. C. Campbell, Jr.

Writing in the souvenir program distributed to viewers of the first run of The Birth of a Nation *in 1915 Rupert Hughes, a highly regarded popular historian of the time, wrote enthusiastically of David W. Griffith's adaptation of Thomas Dixon's fiction. His praise might, very nearly word for word, have been for David O. Selznick's adaptation of Margaret Mitchell's fiction a quarter of a century later.*

"When a great achievement of human genius is put before us," wrote Hughes, "we can become partners in it in a way by applauding it with something of the enthusiasm that went into its making. . . .

"Here was a whole art gallery of scenery, of humanity, of still life and life in wildest career. Here were portraits of things, of furniture, of streets, homes, wildernesses . . . pictures of family life, of festivals and funerals, ballrooms and battlefields, hospitals and flower-gardens, hypocrisy and passion, ecstasy and pathos, pride and humiliation, rapture and jealousy, flirtation and anguish, devotion and treachery, self-sacrifice and tyranny. Here were the Southrons in their wealth, with their luxury at home, their wind-swept cotton fields; here was the ballroom with the seethe of dancers, here were the soldiers riding away to war, and the soldiers trudging home defeated with poverty ahead of them and new and ghastly difficulties arising on every hand.

"Here was the epic of a proud brave people beaten into the dust and refusing to stay there."

E. D. C. Campbell, Jr., *gives an overview of the Old South in film, from* Uncle Tom's Cabin *to* The Birth of a Nation *to* Gone With the Wind *to* Roots *and beyond, in his* The Celluloid South *(Knoxville: [1981]). This essay* is not a part of* The Celluloid South *but conforms to its point of view in relation to* Gone With *the Wind.*

---

*This essay is a revised version of *"Gone With the Wind: Film as Myth and Message,"* in *From the Old South to the New: Essays on the Transitional South,* edited by Walter J. Fraser and Winfred B. Moore. Reprinted by permission of the publisher, Greenwood Press.

Emerging from Loew's Grand Theater after the premiere of *Gone With the Wind* in Atlanta, an aged Confederate veteran exclaimed, "it's the gol'darndest thing I ever saw."[1] The production was far more than that. When Margaret Mitchell's novel was published in 1936 the United States was still in the midst of the Great Depression. By the film's premiere December 15, 1939 the nation was fully aware of the political turmoil and military ravages that were disrupting Europe and even threatening America.

The people watching *GWTW*, as it became known, saw an example of the fortitude and ideals of another civilization which had also faced monumental uncertainties and had survived in spirit. Though overdone, the film presented an example for Depression era audiences that few could ignore. The image of the vanquished took on a new luster; the picture became a national epic with contemporary meaning.[2]

The United States was not alone in perceiving *Gone With the Wind's* power and significance. In war-torn London it played for almost the entire Second World War, enthralling audiences eager for the reassurance of the film's obvious message of a society's emergence from the destruction of war. In 1945 liberated areas of Europe were wildly excited by opportunities to view a film of spiritual survival at any cost. Even though many of the prints first seen by European audiences were still in English and without subtitles, the movie was nonetheless a broadly popular tale to which the people could relate with ease.

As the culmination of the 1930's pictures with an antebellum theme, the film is hardly less romantic and certainly no less lavish in its praise of the prewar South than its predecessors. The decade began with productions such as the musicals *Hearts in Dixie* in 1929 and *Dixiana* in 1930. Other popular films included *Mississippi,* with Bing Crosby, and *So Red the Rose,* with Randolph Scott and Margaret Sullavan, in 1935. *Jezebel,* in 1938, starring Bette Davis and Henry Fonda, played heavily upon advance publicity about *GWTW*. Movies such as *Way Down South,* in 1939, with Bobby Breen, the male counterpart of Shirley Temple, continued the tradition of elaborate films with a conservative slant. The productions were escapist entertainment to be sure, but within each, significantly, lurk biased interpretations on many issues, the racial hierarchy for example. *GWTW* pointed better than any previous movie though to the possibility (and the dangers) of the plantation theme as more than entertainment. And the film was eagerly awaited. A Gallup Poll of December 1939 estimated that 56.5 million people planned to see it.[3]

---

1. *Nashville Banner,* Dec. 16, 1939.
2. As one Eastern reviewer stated, "the story of the Old South with its Cavaliers and cotton has given America its most eloquent and grandest film narrative." A Midwestern critic remarked that the drama of the plantation culture was for all, since it was a "story of great events in American history," not merely Southern. See Wilmington (Del.) *Journal-Every Evening,* Jan. 27, 1940; St. Louis *Post-Dispatch,* Jan. 28, 1940.
3. *New York Times,* Dec. 20, 1939.

Once David O. Selznick had purchased the film rights to the novel for $50,000 he determined that the film would be a sincere effort to portray the South as accurately as possible—at least as he saw accuracy.[4] He began appropriately enough. At the recommendation of Margaret Mitchell, Selznick hired various technical advisers to oversee production details. Wilbur G. Kurtz, an Atlanta artist and esteemed amateur historian, was employed as Historian. Will A. Price checked the cast's Southern accents. And Susan Myrick, styled "the Emily Post of the South," was hired as an expert on antebellum social customs.

The problem—one common to pictures of the Old South—was that the studio's penchant for accurate detail extended only so far. Whether oral thermometers could be used in the hospital scene had to be confirmed, but Selznick's sweeping interpretation of the South was another matter entirely.[5] Few dared contradict his perceptions. Margaret Mitchell, much to the producer's chagrin, wanted no part of the film adaptation. She was determined to remain aloof in the event the production disappointed her fellow Southerners. More importantly, sudden fame and the accompanying attention had altered her life so considerably that she did not wish to court further complications by working for Hollywood. As a result Selznick had relatively free rein over the general romanticism of the picture despite the criticism of his advisers.[6]

The producer's overwhelmingly romantic conceptions of the antebellum region were particularly evident in his instructions for the construction of the Tara set. Though researchers studied period photographs closely (as well as sketches and other documents) to achieve the right architecture for the set of 1864 Atlanta, the prewar O'Hara mansion owed more to imagination than to research. Consequently the set reflected the mythology built up by a long procession of earlier films and accepted, seemingly without question, by a film maker whose preciseness of detail had helped establish his reputation.

In the novel Tara is not a grand seat of plantation wealth and power but the home of a not particularly wealthy planter. In other words, it is a fairly ordinary home, especially in light of the cinematic presentations of Southern houses. But

---

4. For the best overview of the novel's creation, see Finis Farr, *Margaret Mitchell of Atlanta* (New York, 1965), especially 25–56, 99–147; see also Richard B. Harwell, ed., *Margaret Mitchell's Gone With the Wind Letters, 1936–1949* (New York, 1976), especially 1–2, 5–6, 61–62, 65–66, 71–72, 111, 118–20, 132, 219, 298–300, 357–58, 406. For the background of the adaptation to film, see Rudy Behlmer, ed., *Memo From David O. Selznick* (New York, 1972), 143, 159, 206, 235; Gavin Lambert, *GWTW: The Making of Gone With the Wind* (Boston, 1973), 16–17, 31–36; Roland Flamini, *Scarlett, Rhett and a Cast of Thousands: The Filming of Gone With the Wind* (New York, 1975), 3–5, 8–9, 12–13, 16; see also Bob Thomas, *Selznick* (New York, 1970), 155.

5. The anecdotes of the lengths to which the exactness of detail was carried are many; see for example Studio Press Book for *Gone With the Wind* (1954, re-release), in Museum of Modern Art Film Study Center, New York; Studio Press Book (1961, re-release), in Library of Congress Motion Picture Section Box C-109, cited hereafter as LC-MPS. See also Souvenir Booklet (1967, re-release), in LC-MPS Box C-41; and Studio Press Book (1967, re-release), in LC-MPS Box C-19.

6. Behlmer, *Memo*, 202; Harwell, *Gone With the Wind Letters*, 36, 137, 249–50, 358, 406–07; see also Lambert, *GWTW*, 69–70; and Flamini, *Scarlett, Rhett and a Cast of Thousands*, 146, 148, 210.

Selznick realized that such a structure comported neither with his idealization of the section nor—and far more importantly—with the public's. For the movie, Tara became quite unrepresentative of the class of which Miss Mitchell wrote, though she had given the O'Hara property an avenue of cedars and neatly ordered, whitewashed slave quarters. By the writer's own admission, it was "hard to make people understand that North Georgia wasn't all white columns and singing darkies and magnolias. . . ." Even Southerners questioned her as to why the novel's setting was not the mansion that they had come to expect. The picture achieved a view romantic enough to satisfy any and all of those disturbed at the book's lack of splendor on that point.

Selznick, production designer William Cameron Menzies, and art director Lyle Wheeler presented an architecturally grand house of white columns, handsome vista, and blossoming dogwoods. It was hardly the small plantation common to North Georgia in 1861. In fact, searching through Clayton County, which the author used for the novel's setting, Miss Mitchell had found but one columned house from the prewar era. But Selznick knew the nation desired the grand image and that the South would embrace it wholeheartedly, even to the extent of claiming Tara or Twelve Oaks as "just like the mansion my grand-pappy had that Sherman burned."[7]

Though she persisted in refusing to interfere directly, Miss Mitchell did express her fears upon occasion to Susan Myrick. Realizing Selznick's un-bounded enthusiasm and how warmly the South itself would receive the nostal-gic romanticism he was so carefully creating, she regretted the excesses. She especially feared that the opening scenes would include fields hands suddenly erupting into joyous song, as they had in many films. She and her husband, John Marsh, she wrote, were weary "at seeing the combined Tuskegee and Fisk Jubliee Choirs bounce out at the most inopportune times and in the most inopportune places. . .," as such groups had done from *Hearts in Dixie* in 1929 to *Jezebel* in 1938. Worse than the singing would be "the inevitable wavings in the air of several hundred pairs of hands. . .," a cliché born as early as the Thomas Edison Company's 1903 version of *Uncle Tom's Cabin.*[8] She was not far wrong; though the movie contains no mass chorales, every other stock ingre-dient is included.[9]

---

7. Harwell, *Gone With the Wind Letters*, 271–72; see also 406–07.

8. Ibid.; see also Richard Harwell, ed., "Technical Adviser: The Making of *Gone With the Wind*, The Hollywood Journals of Wilbur G. Kurtz," *Atlanta Historical Journal*, XXII (Summer, 1978), 7–131.

9. See Dialogue and Cutting Continuity of *Gone With the Wind* (1939), in LC-MPS Copyright File LP-9390. The romantic aura of the Old South was also brought out in the advertising, which pictured belles, gentlemen, and officers. See for example, Baltimore *Sun*, Jan. 26, 1940; *St. Louis Post-Dispatch*, Jan. 24, 1940; *Detroit Free Press*, Jan. 24, 1940; *Meridian* (Miss.) *Star*, Mar. 24, 1940; *Manchester* (N.H.) *Union*, Feb. 9, 1940; *Santa Fe New Mexican*, Feb. 20, 1940; *Newark Star-Ledger*, Jan. 25, 1940; Portland *Oregon Daily Journal*, Jan. 21, 1940; *Seattle Post-Intelligencer*, Jan. 24, 1940; *Providence* (R.I.) *Journal*, Jan. 25, 1940; Sioux Falls *Daily Argus Leader*, Feb. 25, 1940; Memphis *Commercial Appeal*, Jan. 26, 1940; *Pittsburgh Press*, Jan. 25, 1940. The more well-known poster of Rhett carrying Scarlett was actually developed for the later releases; see Poster for *Gone With the Wind* (n.d., re-release), in Library of Congress Prints and Photographs Division.

As the first portion of the picture attempts to demonstrate, the South was in Melanie Hamilton's words, "a whole world that only wants to be graceful and beautiful." If the region's physical beauty were to be destroyed, the changes wrought would threaten the South's basic ideals. And throughout the remainder of the film, the audiences are vividly shown the alternative—when a society's very foundations crumble. For viewers in 1940 the analogy to their own times was not easily missed. As a result, the Old South's position took on even more force.

The latter half of *Gone With the Wind* repeatedly accentuates the differences between the plantation world and the postwar society. One of the recurring symbols of the changes brought by the war is the use of the staircases of Twelve Oaks, Tara, and Scarlett's postwar extravagant home.

The grand, wide, beautifully curving stairway of the Wilkes home represents all that was gracious in the Old South. The passage is sparkling white, airy, full of the ebb and flow of refined society. There Rhett first spies Scarlett. There Scarlett ensnares various of her admirers. The stairwell area is the meeting place of bowing servants and their supposed betters. There Melanie displays her Christian charity in defending Scarlett's designs; there too Ashley Wilkes encounters the flirtatious O'Hara. One widely-used publicity still pictures the stairs full of belles descending to meet awaiting gentlemen. It is the plantation world at its best.

Such a world could not last. The war changed it all. The movie refrains from showing much of the actual fighting, confining the war to panoramic shots of a besieged or burning Atlanta and of Scarlett driving a wagon across a field strewn with the dead and the debris of defeat. But the horror and destruction of war are powerfully captured in the scene of Scarlett cornered on the staircase of Tara repelling the Yankee looter. In that moment the horrifying extent of the culture's alteration is depicted.

The region is no longer the same. Tara's once graceful interior is but a shell of its former self. Scarlett stands on a stairway, appearing confused within its war ravaged condition. This symbolic structure is dark, weakened, narrow, and leads to only further darkness and ruin in the once proud estate. At its bottom waits what appears to her to be the cause of all the destruction. The ensuing shot echoes the South's frustration; whatever price might be exacted upon the enemy, the culture's fate is already sealed.

But, the script emphasizes, perseverance will bring eventual recovery. Even though Scarlett and Rhett maintain a fortune built upon the former's new-found entrepreneurial skills and the latter's wartime blockade running, the lifestyle they enjoy can never match that which had been destroyed. Their new mansion does not reflect the refinement of the South but the materialism of a commercial society with which the cinematic South had been so unfamiliar. The red brick, Victorian style house seems out of place, and dominating its interior is a wide, dark-stained, garish red-carpeted staircase leading from a gloomy and foreboding hallway up to what often appears to be total darkness. The crass, overdone, and heavily ornate grandeur is in pointed contrast to the splendor of Twelve Oaks. This is the stairway over which rages many an argument, and it is the passage down which Scarlett rushes in pursuit of Rhett who has declared that even he—once viewed as an oddity for his prewar disregard of conventions—is "going back to Charleston, back where I belong" to find if there is not "something left in life of charm and grace." Down the stairs he retreats to a past. In the end, Scarlett follows the same course, going back to Tara where she belongs, to the land still dominated by a mansion and still tended by Hollywood's ever-present faithful blacks.

Audiences North and South flocked to the theatres to view the epic. Particularly in the South was there a sense of pride, even of vindication. Heralding the Atlanta premiere, a million people streamed into the city for what the Governor had declared a state holiday.

GWTW was hailed in the Georgia capital as a giant step towards the healing of sectional wounds. In an editorial in the *Atlanta Constitution*, Robert Quillen exclaimed that the story of the Old South "by the simple expedient of telling the truth, has won the admiration and affection of all America." Forgiven and finally understood, the spirit of the region would "march through all America, conquering hearts as it goes." A later editorial praises the tale's refraining "from caricature, either the romantic exaggeration of Southern partiality or the impossible nobility of visionary Northerners." As a result, the production would be viewed "as the historic recording of its place and time." The editor of the *Atlanta Journal*, the newspaper for which Miss Mitchell had once worked, agreed completely. The film chronicled an age that "seems never to have died—or, rather, to have died and risen in new strength and beauty."[10] Margaret Mitchell's fears of modern Southern romanticism had been well grounded.

Consistently, regional critics viewed the picture as a "superlative effort" which would withstand close scrutiny and the test of time. A Richmond commentator was especially pleased with the treatment of the slavery issue, as it was "in accord with all the stories and legends of slavery-time Negroes," and accurately depicted the planters and their ladies. Thus *GWTW*, as one reviewer phrased it, "should give the dream reality."[11]

Though one reviewer pointed to the issue of slavery and warned that in light of the world economic and political situation, the master-slave relationship was not necessarily a dead issue, such critical insights were rare. Several critics, however, perceived Scarlett's excessive business greed built upon sprawling urban growth as appalling. Henry Martin, a Memphis reporter, viewed Vivien Leigh's change in character as one which served as a "study of the South's descent into Gethsemane and its return from Calvary." And Gable's final aware-

---

10. Atlanta *Constitution*, Dec. 13, 14, 15, 16, 1939; Atlanta *Journal*, Dec. 14, 15, 1939.

11. See for example, Richmond *Times-Dispatch*, Feb. 3, 1940; Birmingham *News*, Feb. 4, 1940; Montgomery *Advertiser*, Jan. 28, 29, 1940; Little Rock *Arkansas Democrat*, Feb. 25, 1940; Meridian (Miss.) *Star*, Mar. 24, 1940; Raleigh *News and Observor*, Feb. 11, 18, 1940; Dallas *Morning News*, Feb. 7, 1940; Miami *Herald*, Jan. 18, 1940; Charlotte *Oberver*, Jan. 30, 1940; Louisville *Courier-Journal*, Jan. 27, 1940.

ness of the culture's significance was the "personification of man's regeneration through belated awakening to the call of a cause greater than one's own self."[12]

Though Southerners such as Mrs. W. D. Lamar, President-General of the United Daughters of the Confederacy, believed *GWTW* was "wonderfully faithful to the traditions" of the section, for national import the production had to prove popular and meaningful to the North and West as well.[13] Popular it certainly was. In Boston a record crowd of 17,000 persons viewed the film its first day; the line for tickets had formed at 6:00 A.M. and by the second day of the run over 50,000 advance bookings were sold.[14] But did non-Southerners grasp the theme of the plantation ideal and of spiritual survival?

Indeed, the reception was unanimous. In Los Angeles, the critics were particularly pleased with the detailed background. A San Francisco commentator marvelled at "how completely the gracious, patrician life of the Old South, the life of Tara and Twelve Oaks, has been shattered, never to be reclaimed." At times, there seemed genuine sorrow that such a culture had to die. Though regretting what he interpreted as the film's bitterness against Northerners, a Chicago reviewer remarked that the war was "in pathetic and terrible contrast to episodes of the lazy, carefree prewar era in a South of Cavaliers and ladies and gracious living. . . ."[15]

Particularly noteworthy about these reviews is the consistent perception of the South as a section overflowing with wealth and refinement, of Tara as indicative of the upcountry, middle-class planter existence and of the cotton planter class itself as representative of the region's populace as a whole. Selznick had firmly stamped his romantic view of the Old South on Miss Mitchell's that was already more romantic than even she realized. A Midwestern critic labeled the film as accurate; the atmosphere was "faithful" and "startingly beautiful in pastoral scenes." Practically all reviewers described the production's view as accurate in its recreation of the plantation setting as a "graceful culture" or a "gorgeous panorama." The myth was becoming harder to distinguish from fact. As the film is overdone, so too was the critics' acceptance of the "magnolia-scented days of the Old South." To non-Southerners its society was without doubt one of "wealth and distinction," with the attendant "hospitable manners, broad acres, beautiful women and chivalrous men and the faithful old mammies who served them."[16]

If the lifestyle had become so laudable, so fantastically alluring, it was but a

12. Dallas *Morning News*, Feb. 8, 1940; Houston *Post*, Feb. 11, 1940; Memphis *Commercial Appeal*, Jan. 27, 1940.

13. Nashville *Banner*, Dec. 16, 1939.

14. Boston *Daily Globe*, Dec. 22, 1939; see also Indianapolis *News*, Jan. 27, 1940; Butte *Montana Standard*, Feb. 22, 1940; Newark *Star-Ledger*, Jan. 26, 1940.

15. Los Angeles *Times*, Jan. 1, 1940; *San Francisco Chronicle*, Jan. 26, 1940; *Chicago Daily Tribune*, Jan. 26, 1940.

16. *Cleveland Plain Dealer*, Jan. 27, 1940; *Portland* (Me.) *Press Herald*, Feb. 9, 1940; *Detroit Free Press*, Jan. 24, 1940; Portland *Oregon Daily Journal*, Jan. 26, 1940; *Salt Lake Tribune*, Jan. 29, 1940; *Seattle Post-Intelligencer*, Jan. 26, 1940.

short step to grieve at its passing, to regret the treatment of the South by the victors, and finally to praise its determination and example. It was quite a turnabout only seventy-five years after the nation's bloodiest conflict.

Romantic films can take a great deal of the responsibility for the change. Movies aided enormously in the affirmation of the South as the most distinctive region of the country, with a rural character which increasingly served as an alternative to recall with fondness. So attractive was the section, especially as seen in *GWTW,* that non-Southerners continued to embrace the film's viewpoint with little hesitation or awareness of the social repercussions.

Many reviewers, as one in Topeka, insisted that *GWTW* presented its theme without undue favoritism towards the South, a judgment revealing the extent to which mythology had taken the place of reality. *Gone With the Wind* and its predecessors make a strong case that the South was not solely responsible for the war, that slavery was not all evil, and that both sides were defending a lifestyle, a mode of society. Pictures of the antebellum period make the point, as a Connecticut writer phrased it, that people "merely misunderstood the motives underlying two completely different types of people," of two "contrasting sets of ideals." Once the sincerity of the Confederate cause was understood and its way of life so lovingly recreated, even a Northerner could—as a Boston writer postulated—"rise up and whistle 'Dixie' along with rabid Yankee-hating Georgians."[17] That was unfortunate.

The film in its presentation of "the finest qualities of the Old South" indeed constituted to its first generation of viewers a strong argument that the section was misunderstood. What a Midwesterner termed the region's "dreamy appeal of the baronial magnificence" became a vision for Depression audiences. Viewers too faced what the defeated South had encountered, "the rise of a new and unhappy age" as a Cleveland writer described it. And in the defeated people's very survival as a unique part of the nation lay the lesson. A Philadelphia critic believed strongly that the example merited considerable attention, that "even a dyed-in-the-wool Yankee must—and can afford to—give a rebel yell for *Gone With the Wind.*" The epic served to demonstrate that one "courageously, stubbornly, and painfully built upon the ashes of crushed hopes and ruined lands. . .," a feat many hoped to duplicate.[18]

The romantic films of the Old South during the 1930's of course did not alone ameliorate the low spirits of numerous viewers, but their contribution towards such an end was considerable. Moreover, and more essential, releases such as *GWTW,* which praised the fortitude of the South, furnished to the country a popular example of recovery from adversity. For the region itself the movies of the Thirties verified legend and presented an apologia more sweeping

---

17. *Topeka Daily Capital,* Feb. 21, 1940; *Hartford* (Conn.) *Times,* Feb. 3, 1940; *Boston Daily Globe,* Dec. 22, 1939.
18. *St. Louis Post-Dispatch,* Jan. 28, 1940; *Cleveland Plain Dealer,* Jan. 27, 1940; *Philadelphia Inquirer,* Jan. 19, 1940; see also *Pittsburgh Press,* Jan. 27, 1940.

than any the section had previously constructed. By the outbreak of World War II the many myths, the racial and cultural conservatism, had reached an apex of cinematic reevaluation begun so humbly and unintentionally in 1903 with *Uncle Tom's Cabin*. The marvel was that the process was still so much one of innocence, the stories often simply the studios' reflection of a popular taste which craved romance. But what a message the surface innocence of pictures like *GWTW* bore! Their very acceptance reveals the persistence of a legend which decrees an opulent South and argues that its beliefs were to be praised at the expense of national progress towards a more accurate perception of the South's past and problems, particularly at the expense of progress towards better race relations.

FIVE

Tara Twenty Years After

By Robert Y. Drake, Jr.

One of the earliest academic evaluations of Gone With the Wind *was submitted as a Masters of Arts thesis at Vanderbilt University in 1956 by Reta Anderson. Miss Anderson set out to prove (and did so quite well) that GWTW "though not a great book, is a good and important one." She declared: "It is a view of the South and of the Civil War completely different from any other ever presented in fiction and is as near to realism as a view of those times and circumstances can successfully be." In her introductory remarks Miss Anderson commented on the reputation of Margaret Mitchell's novel twenty years after its publication: "I do not think that anyone, in the calm, clear light of reason and now that the furor has largely passed, would call* Gone With the Wind *a great book. . . . It has, in fact, been something of a tradition for critics to regard it, if at all, either with large-handed tolerance or a kindly sneer. It deserves better."*

Two years later Robert Y. Drake, Jr., published the first scholarly article about GWTW to appear in a general academic quarterly, his "Tara Twenty Years After" appeared in The Georgia Review *for summer 1958.*

I remember a conversation I had several years ago with a friend who, in addition to "creative writing," was teaching a course in the modern American novel. And although he taught Civil War novels by Allen Tate, Caroline Gordon, and others, not once did he allude to Margaret Mitchell's *Gone With the Wind.* When I asked him why he had excluded the novel which is, by all odds, the most popular Civil War novel ever written, he replied, "Well, it's just not good enough. I would like for it to be a good novel, I really would. But every time that woman gets up close to what the South and the War were really all about, she lets it slip right through her fingers." I, who was younger and had read Miss Mitchell's book and seen its fantastically successful screen version at a very impressionable age, countered with the suggestion that he had taught "creative writing" so long that he no longer knew a good story when he saw it. And, though I know now much more about the novel as an art form than I did then, I am still of the same opinion.

Miss Mitchell's work has little of the subtlety of presentation that characterizes the more "literary" Civil War novels, little of the "awareness" of reality that one finds in a novel like Stark Young's *So Red the Rose,* little of the complexity of the imagination of William Faulkner or the art of Robert Penn Warren. And yet I am inclined to think that its very lack of subtlety and self-consciousness is in its favor. For the society it presents (in an epic sweep, covering both War and Reconstruction) was essentially unself-conscious, as the life of tradition always is, as opposed to the analytic and introspective. And it seems to me that in a treatment as broad in scope as Miss Mitchell's is, it is altogether proper that its style maintain the detachment of the folk tale or the epic. For Miss Mitchell's novel is primarily a *story,* in which things happen to people, not, as is the case with so much modern fiction, a *study,* in which people happen to things. I am oversimplifying, of course; but the point I wish to make is that *Gone With the Wind* is an epic treatment of an epic theme. And we must not look for the subtlety or conscious craftsmanship in it that we demand in more "literary" fiction.

For, truly, Margaret Mitchell, who said she was ten before she knew the South lost the War, made no pretension to being a "literary" novelist. Brought up on Civil War tales, educated briefly at Smith, trained as a newspaper woman, she later retired into devoted wifehood, wrote her book; and there, as far as she was concerned, was an end on it. In some respects—and I say this in fear and trembling—she resembled the pre-Nobel Prize Faulkner, who disdained to talk or write "critically." But, in spite of all its "critical" weaknesses, her book has, in a little over twenty years, firmly established itself in the hearts of people everywhere as *the* Civil War novel. And it is the considered advice of this layman to the "literary" practitioners of the art of the novel that, since they cannot lick her and, for reasons of conscience or art, let us say, cannot join her, they had at least better give her another look.

The chief conflict in *Gone With the Wind* is essentially what Donald Davidson has elsewhere called the conflict between tradition and anti-tradition. This conflict appears in many different forms and focuses throughout the novel, and it is its principal unifying theme. The *status quo* is represented, of course, in the planter families like the O'Haras and the Wilkeses, along with all the other "county" families. I used to think it was a weakness in the novel that Gerald O'Hara should be an Irish Roman Catholic immigrant, married to a Roman Catholic Charleston aristocrat; surely, he was no "typical" Southerner. Miss Mitchell's artistic decorum is vindicated, though, by modern historical scholarship, which has shown that the Old South was a far more fluid society than was once thought—with greater "social mobility." Thus, I believe Miss Mitchell was bent on demonstrating that part of the Southern society's vigor and strength as a traditional society was derived from its adaptation and integration of diverse national stocks and traditions to serve a unified order. (It is to be noted that it is Gerald O'Hara's daughter who brings the more "typical," inbred Wilkes family through the War and Reconstruction). This is what Grandma Fontaine tries to tell Scarlett the day of Gerald's funeral, that their strength as a family lies in thieir adaptability. We're buckwheat, she asserts, not wheat; buckwheat can bend with the wind.

The old order, the life of tradition, is, of course, represented in Ashley Wilkes and his wife, Melanie Hamilton. The Wilkeses are always sending off for books of poetry, taking European tours, and marrying their cousins. Their plantation, Twelve Oaks, is everything romanticists would like to believe about the Old South. And yet when the War and defeat come, and with them a peace more terrible still, they are dependent on the kindness of others for very existence. Melanie, of course, is the ideal of Southern feminine graciousness, the great lady personified, as is Ellen O'Hara, Scarlett's mother; but there is a toughness in her that is surprising. She it is who, though she may starve, cannot compromise her principles. And though she is charity itself, she cannot forget what the Yankees, the foes of all tradition, have done to the tradition by which she lives. "I can't forget. I won't forget. I won't let my Beau forget and I'll teach my grandchildren to hate these people—and my grandchildren's grandchildren if God lets me live that long!" she says. And when Scarlett kills the Yankee on the staircase at Tara, it is the bed-ridden Melanie who comes to her aid with Charles Hamilton's sword. Scarlett is surprised. " 'Why—why—she's like me! She understands how I feel!' " And later, during the dark days of Reconstruction, it is Melanie who calmly takes command in the desperate "play" to fool the Yankees into thinking that Ashley and the other men, suspected of participating in a Klan raid, have spent the evening at Belle Watling's brothel. In the gentle Melanie's blood are "banners and bugles of courage" that the forces of anti-tradition—and Scarlett herself—find so paradoxical and so unyielding.

The tragic figure in the novel is Ashley Wilkes, the aristocrat who cannot function successfully once his traditional system is destroyed. He, like many another, has had his mainspring "busted"; and, as Grandma Fontaine observes, to Scarlett's annoyance, it will be Melanie who will pull the Wilkes family through the Reconstruction, if they come through at all. In the memorable scene at the mill Ashley talks to the uncomprehending Scarlett about the beauty of the old days, the life that had "a perfection, a symmetry like Grecian art." "The old days had no glitter but they had a charm, a beauty, a slow-paced glamour," he tells her. But with Ashley it always seems to be "dreams," and Melanie is the only dream he ever had that "did not die in the face of reality." Ashley is the actor who cannot play his part once his prepared script is destroyed. An idealist, he had planned to free his slaves when his father died; and yet he cannot operate outside a slave economy, it seems. But it is Rhett Butler who puts his finger on what is really wrong with Ashley. "He's only a gentleman caught in a world he doesn't belong in, trying to make a poor best of it by the rules of the world that's gone," he tells Scarlett.

But what really gives Ashley tragic stature is his self-knowledge. He knows he is finished; and that makes it all the worse, as Rhett says—Rhett, who in many ways seems to be the antithesis of Ashley but who is basically like him. Ashley knows this, too, as we learn from what he says to Scarlett.

We came from the same kind of people, we were raised in the same pattern, brought up to think the same things. . . . We still think alike but we react differently. As, for instance, neither of us believed in war but I enlisted and fought and he stayed out till nearly the end. We both knew the war was all wrong. We both knew it was a losing fight. I was willing to fight a losing fight. He wasn't."

This paradox, of course, is completely incomprehensible to Scarlett, who is now fully committed to the principle of anti-tradition—in her case, money-making. The trouble with him is that he is always seeing both sides of the question. "No one ever gets anywhere seeing both sides," she tells him. And Ashley replies, posing what is the fundamental question not only for Scarlett but also for anyone bent on "survival" at all costs, "That's true but—Scarlett, just where do you want to get?" But Ashley is weak. Although he knows of Scarlett's obsessive love for him, he cannot manfully take his family away from Georgia to New York, where he has been offered a job in a bank. And though his principles keep him from committing overt adultery with her, he lusts after her in his heart. In short, it is in Ashley that we see the tragedy of every man who cannot be what he was born to be or would be.

On the other hand, Rhett Butler has spent nearly a lifetime trying, it would seem, to destroy the system which bred them, not from without as the Yankees do but from within. When we first see him, at the barbecue at Twelve Oaks, he arouses the enmity of all the war-hungry hot-bloods by pointing out that, for purely economic reasons, the South cannot possibly win the war. Later, he blithely engages in wartime speculation and mocks constantly at the gallant boys in grey. And yet when Atlanta falls to Sherman, he leaves Scarlett and Melanie with her newborn baby on the road to Tara to join the remnants of General Hood's army. During Reconstruction he abets the activities of the Klan; and after his marriage to Scarlett, in an effort to attain social acceptance for their daughter, Bonnie, he becomes completely identified with the Southern or traditional "cause." At the novel's end he is thinking of going back to Charleston to try to make peace with his estranged family, to try to recapture "the calm dignity life can have when it's lived by gentle folks, the genial grace of days that are gone."

Rhett, as opposed to Ashley, is a man, not of principles but of pragmatism. When Scarlett first hears of him, in the delicious odor of scandal, she finds herself respecting him because he refused to marry a girl whom he had apparently but not actually compromised on the ground that she was a fool. It is Rhett who, in the engagement scene, soothes Scarlett's feelings of guilt about Frank Kennedy (whom she had taken away from her sister, Suellen) by saying that there is no Hell and maybe God understands why she did what she did, anyhow. And yet his anti-traditionalism is more therapeutic than destructive, aimed not at repudiating what is genuine and sound but at purging what is idolatrous and false. And at the end of the novel we see him for what he is—without his usual mask of irony—a strong and yet weak man who tried to find in his daughter the love he could not get from his wife. When Bonnie dies, he sees at last, perhaps, that he has nothing left to give his life meaning except the very tradition he once rebelled against; and he leaves Scarlett to go visit older countries and civilizations and perhaps to return at last to Charleston.

The chief focus of the conflict between tradition and anti-tradition is, of course, within the character of Scarlett O'Hara. From the very beginning we see this conflict beginning to emerge, growing in intensity until it reaches its climax in the rundown fields of Twelve Oaks, only to have its direction completely reversed at the end of the book. We know that Scarlett has a "sharp intelligence," which, in accordance with the precepts of Southern ladyhood, she struggles to hide under a countenance "as sweet and bland as a baby's." To all outward appearances she is the daughter of a coastal aristocrat, her mother; but, as Rhett tells her, to her indignation, the current that really flows in her vitals has its source in some not too remote Irish peasant ancestor. Pragmatic to the bone, she seems concerned with none of the Southern "principles" which Ashley, Melanie, and even Rhett would fight and die for. She is bent only on survival—at all costs. In the memorable climactic scene in the devastated grounds of Twelve Oaks she vows solemnly that she will never go hungry again.

Throughout the South for fifty years there would be bitter-eyed women who looked backward, to dead times, to dead men, evoking memories that hurt and were futile, bearing poverty with bitter pride because they had those memories. But Scarlett was never to look back.

She gazed at the blackened stones and, for the last time, she saw Twelve Oaks rise before her eyes as it had once stood, rich and proud, symbol of a race and a way of living. Then she started down the road to Tara. . . .

Hunger gnawed at her empty stomach again and she said aloud: "As God is my witness, as God is my witness, the Yankees aren't going to lick me. I'm going to live through this, and when it's over, I'm never going to be hungry again. No, nor any of my folks. If I have to steal or kill—as God is my witness, I'm never going to be hungry again.'

And then when she toyed with the idea of becoming Rhett's mistress in order to get the tax money for Tara, she shows her disregard for the Church. She knew the Church forbade fornication on pain of hell fire; but, if the Church thought that was going to keep her from saving Tara, "well, let the Church bother about that." And later, during Reconstruction, she flouts many of the proprieties of Southern ladyhood by engaging in business. And yet she is always *outwardly* a Southerner. Though she hobnobs with the carpetbag aristocracy, she goes out of her way to be rude to men in the blue uniform. And she will do anything to save Tara and what it means to her, though she does not grasp its full significance until the end of the novel. She wants the strength of the Southern tradition, though she does not realize it until the end; but she is not willing until then to bow to the exactions of the tradition.

There is little subtlety or complexity in Scarlett's character, but that is quite proper in the heroine of an epic. The conflict within Scarlett may well be characterized as one between simplicity (anti-tradition) and complexity (tradition), between her "romantic love" for Ashley and her real inclination toward Rhett. But, as the novel moves toward its close, she gains progressively in insight; and finally, at the death of Melanie, which is the book's "catastrophe," she learns what it is that she really wants, only to lose it at the moment of this realization. And the insight, toward which the novel has been moving, is thus achieved.

> She had never understood either of the men she had loved and so she had lost them. Now, she had a fumbling knowledge that, had she ever understood Ashley, she would never have loved him; had she understood Rhett, she would never have lost him. She wondered forlornly if she had ever really understood anyone in the world.

In the death of Melanie, who embodies a "living" tradition, Scarlett realizes at last that it is only "dead" tradition which she has loved in Ashley. It is only in Rhett that there is real vitality, as the dying Melanie makes her see. But now it is too late. Scarlett, who is only beginning to see life in its complexity, imagines that she can really start over again, that the past really can be wiped out. "My darling," says Rhett, "you're such a child. You think that by saying, 'I'm sorry,' all the errors and hurts of years past can be remedied, obliterated from the mind, all the poison drawn from old wounds. . . ." Ironically, it is now, when she is closer to reality than she has ever been, that she loses Rhett, the "reality" she has really been seeking in the "idealistic" Ashley. But in that loss there is a gain in maturity and a growth in spirit.

> For a moment she was on the verge of an outburst of childish wild tears. She could have thrown herself on the floor, cursed and screamed and drummed her heels. But some remnant of pride, of common sense stiffened her. She thought, if I did, he'd only laugh, or just look at me. I mustn't bawl; I mustn't beg. I mustn't do anything to risk his contempt. He must respect me even—even if he doesn't love me.
> She lifted her chin and managed to ask quietly.
> "Where will you go?"

And so at the novel's end Scarlett stands alone, having lost Melanie, "who had always been there beside her with a sword in her hands, unobtrusive as her own shadow, loving her, fighting for her with blind passionate loyalty, fighting Yankees, fire, hunger, poverty, public opinion and even her beloved kin." She has lost Ashley, whom she finds she has never really loved; and she has lost Rhett, on whose love she has unconsciously relied and whom she did not come to love until it was too late. But there is something left—Tara and all that it stands for, Tara and Mammy, "the last link with the old days." "We shall manage—somehow," she had told Ashley a few hours before when Melanie died. Now, again, she is ready to "manage," for "tomorrow is another day." But this catch-phrase is no longer a rationalization for a desire to escape the complexity of experience. She is now deliberately choosing to return to Tara and the life of tradition which she has loved all along, unconsciously, in Tara. Like Rhett, she has been redeemed into the life of tradition. In that context she will find solace and perhaps even some remedy for her griefs.

She had gone back to Tara once in fear and defeat and she had emerged from its sheltering walls strong and armed for victory. What she had done once, somehow—please God, she could do again! How, she did not know. She did not want to think of that now. All she wanted was a breathing space in which to hurt, a quiet place to lick her wounds, a haven in which to plan her campaign. She thought of Tara and it was as if a gentle cool hand were stealing over her heart. She could see the white house gleaming welcome to her through the reddening autumn leaves, feel the quiet hush of the country twilight coming down over her like a benediction, feel the dews falling on the acres of green bushes starred with fleecy white, see the raw color of the red earth and the dismal dark beauty of the pines on the rolling hills.

With the spirit of her people who would not know defeat, even when it stared them in the face, she raised her chin. She could get Rhett back. She knew she could. There had never been a man she couldn't get, once she set her mind upon him.

This, then, is what "happens" in *Gone With the Wind,* an epic treatment of the fall of a traditional society. It is structurally, by its very nature, one-sided. The Yankees are quite properly portrayed as deep-dyed villains, as in the case of General Sherman, whose machinations all occur off-stage but whose menace is distinctly and oppressively felt in the wartime chapters, or in the instance of Jonas Wilkerson, the former O'Hara overseer who marries the poor-white, Emmie Slattery, and ironically tries to become master of the acres he once rode as overseer. In this respect *Gone With the Wind* is no more nonpartisan than the *Aeneid.* But it dramatically demonstrates, as the *Aeneid* did before it, that you cannot destroy a traditional society simply by destroying its machinery. The strength of such a society does not lie, ultimately, in outward forms or institutions but, rather, in the "knowledge carried to the heart," the intangibles by which it lives. *Gone With the Wind* states once more, in dramatic terms, the hoary truth that, though you may lick a people, you cannot "reconstruct" them.

I know of no other Civil War novel with as much "breadth" in conception as *Gone With the Wind.* What it lacks in "depth" and in "art" it compensates for in the clarity and vitality of its presentation of the diverse and yet unified issues involved, in sustained narrative interest, and in the powerful simplicity of its structure. The conflict which it dramatizes is as old as history itself. It has been presented more skillfully before, and no doubt will be again. But it will never be done more excitingly or appealingly than it is here.

The Last of Its Genre

By Henry Steele Commager

One of the earliest, most thorough, and most laudatory reviews of Margaret Mitchell's novel was the one Henry Steele Commager wrote for the New York Herald Tribune Books *for July 5, 1936. Commager's review began with a short sentence that to the author was comparable only to Herschel Brickell's coupling it with Douglas S. Freeman's* R. E. Lee. *"This novel," said the reviewer, "is the prose to 'John Brown's Body,' and the theme is the same."*

Miss Mitchell sent Commager a long, enthusiastic thank-you for his review on July 10. In it she wrote: "What in the world am I going to say to you about the lead of your review, about my philosophy and my ability to create character and narrative vigor and all the other fine things you attribute to me?"

Commager's "Introduction" to the Limited Editions Club edition of Gone With the Wind *in 1968 is a briefer, soberer look at the novel which had moved him to over two thousand words of praise three decades before. Each in its own way is a fine assessment of the book. It is the latter that is included here.*

There are, in a broad way, two kinds of historical novel. First, and doubtless most familiar, the costume piece, picturesque and dramatic, consciously re-creating the past. Familiar here are such examples as *The Hunchback of Notre Dame* or *The Three Musketeers* or, in our own literature, *Hugh Wynne, Free Quaker* or the more recent *Oliver Wiswell*. The second type reflects, though not self-consciously, its own time and its own society, rather than some more-or-less remote past. It achieves history, as it were, through the passing of time, whereas the formal historical novels have history thrust upon them. Thus the novels of Jane Austen, not written as "historical novels," but clearly in that genre, or—more elaborately—those of Anthony Trollope or of Emile Zola; thus in our literature such novels as *The House of the Seven Gables* or *Huckleberry Finn* or *Barren Ground*.

But there is something in between. Commenting on his many imitators, Sir Walter Scott wrote, in 1826: "One advantage I have over all of them. They may do their fooling with better grace, but I . . . do it more natural. They have to read old books and consult antiquarian collections to get their knowledge. I write because I have long since read such works, and possess the information which they have to seek for." Where the historical romances of others were, in a sense, artificial and contrived, his—so he here implies—grew out of his own intellectual experience and, we may be confident, out of his psychological experience as well.

The distinction which Scott made persists sometimes in the same novelist. When Edith Wharton wrote that remarkable picture of eighteenth-century Italy, *The Valley of Decision*, she had to "cram," but *The Custom of the Country* and *Hudson River Bracketed* came out of her own background and were suffused with her experience. Willa Cather's story of seventeenth-century Quebec, *Shadows on the Rock*, was in a sense contrived, but *My Ántonia*, just as truly an historical novel, was born of her own experience in early Nebraska. So, even more obviously, with Mark Twain's *Prince and the Pauper* and his *Life on the Mississippi*, so with Cooper's medieval romances, *The Heidenmauer* and *The Headsman*, which were almost painfully artificial, and his Leatherstocking tales or his Littlepage trilogy.

Gone With the Wind is, quite clearly, a traditional historical romance—a conscious reconstruction of the past—but it has, just as clearly, some of the qualities which Scott claimed for his own novels. Though it is a costume piece, it is not a hothouse or library production but a book that grew out of tradition and inheritance; indeed—to invoke another literary analogy—it is rather closer to *Vanity Fair* than to *Henry Esmond,* as Scarlett is closer to Becky Sharp and Rhett Butler to Rawdon Crawley than either is to the somewhat cardboard characters of *Esmond*. For alongside the romanticism of the plantation scenes, of the war, and even of Reconstruction, there is a great deal of what we have come to call realism: fraud, hypocrisy, ruthlessness, and brutality. The Civil War—perhaps we should call it the War Between the States—as it is portrayed in these pages, is neither splendid nor heroic, and the clever men avoid it and profit from it. Only in the minds of infatuated Southerners can it be considered romantic and, as their society comes tumbling about them, they suffer for their illusions. Certainly there is nothing either romantic or heroic about the war to either Scarlett or Rhett Butler. It is this readiness to acknowledge the more sordid side of the war—and of human nature—that distinguishes *Gone With the Wind* from so many earlier novels about the Lost Cause—Mary Johnston's *Cease Firing,* for example, or George Eggleston's *Warrens of Virginia,* or the many novels by the indefatigable Charles King—and links it rather with such books as *Miss Ravenel's Conversion* or *The Red Badge of Courage.*

Miss Mitchell chose to write not about the low-country aristocracy but about middle-class up-country farmers—farmers on their way to becoming planters. The heroine, Scarlett O'Hara, is the daughter of an Irish immigrant, and she combines peasant cunning with her beauty and ruthlessness with her ambition. The hero, Rhett Butler, is a blockade runner and an adventurer. Both, in the end, get their comeuppance, but not because they are disloyal to their land or their flag—that is almost a side issue. Scarlett marries for money and to restore her paternal plantation; she marries Rhett largely to get revenge on him; she betrays her husband, and he deserts her. Altogether a sordid story. But then, Miss Mitchell is saying, that is what happens in a world turned upside down. It is Rhett Butler who is the mouthpiece of this philosophy:

> This isn't the first time the world's been turned upside down, and it won't be the last. . . .And when it does happen, everyone loses everything and everyone is equal. And then they all start again . . . with nothing except the cunning of their brains and the strength of their hands. But some people have neither cunning nor strength, or, having them, scruple to use them. And so they go under, and they should go under.

This is not designed as a plea for either ruthlessness or cynicism but rather for fortitude and endurance.

In this paragraph, Miss Mitchell has written,

lies the genesis of my book and that genesis lies years back when I was six years old and those words . . . were said to me. They were said to me not by a materialist, but by one of the most idealistic people I ever knew, but an idealist with a very wide streak of common sense, my mother. I didn't want to go to school; I couldn't work arithmetic, and I saw no value at all in an education. And mother took me out on the hottest September day I ever saw and drove me down the road towards Jonesboro—"the road to Tara"—and showed me the old ruins of houses where fine and wealthy people had once lived. Some of the ruins dated from Sherman's visit, some had fallen to pieces when the families in them fell to pieces. And she showed me plenty of houses still standing staunchly. And she talked about the world those people had lived in, such a secure world, and how it had exploded beneath them. . . . And she said all that would be left after a world ended would be what you could do with your hands and what you could do with your head. "So for God's sakes go to school and learn something that will stay with you. The strength of women's hands isn't worth anything, but what they've got in their heads will carry them as far as they need to go."[1]

The characters of the book represent, in many ways, the New South versus the Old, and it is not clear that one is better than the other. Miss Mitchell shows us the Old South in all its infirmity, its selfishness, and its hypocrisy, and she shows us the New in all its greed and push and vulgarity. And because the Civil War and Reconstruction lingered on in the South long after they had evaporated elsewhere in the country, *Gone With the Wind* is more nearly contemporary than are most historical novels. Time is, after all, a relative matter, and history has a way of telescoping. Besides, a triumphant past can be taken for granted and forgotten, but a past of defeat and humiliation has greater vitality. The pride and the defiance, the preconceptions, prejudices, and fears of the Old South persisted into the New—persisted, indeed, into Miss Mitchell's generation, so

---

1. Letter to H. S. C., 10 July 1936. [The complete text of Margaret Mitchell's letter of July 10, 1936, appears in *Margaret Mitchell's "Gone With the Wind" Letters, 1936–1949*, pp. 37–40.]

that she might feel that she was writing not about some remote past, but about her own present.

It all seems very far away—almost impossibly far away, and so difficult is it, now, to conjure up the South that Miss Mitchell describes that we are tempted to wonder whether it ever really existed or whether it was not merely the figment of her—and others'—imagination. It is hard to reconcile Scarlett's Georgia with the Georgia of Governor Maddox, for example; hard to reconcile even Rhett Butler's Confederacy with the Confederacy *redivivus* which Governor Wallace commands, flags and all. We no longer believe in the legendary South, the South of magnolias and of the Southern Lady, or in the life that was lived in the great houses, or in the happy Negroes; we are scarcely able to credit even the reality of the fortitude and courage that went into the War, or the sufferings of Reconstruction. Certainly we no longer believe in either of the things the war was about—States' Rights and Slavery. The Lost Cause may still stir the imaginations of the descendants of those who lost it, but not in any genuine fashion, for they themselves do not seriously believe in either States' Rights or Slavery, and both their enthusiasms and their loyalties are in a sense contrived.

What we have here is a legend that has gone stale, a myth that has been dispelled. The high point of the romantic view of the Lost Cause in our time came in that decade: *John Brown's Body* was published in 1928, *I'll Take My Stand* in 1930, *So Red the Rose* in 1934, Freeman's *R. E. Lee* in that year and the next, and *Gone With the Wind* in 1936—a cluster of celebrations of the Old South that owed something to disillusionment with the North and with an economy that had so palpably gone wrong. Yet a few more years and Gunnar Myrdal was to publish *An American Dilemma* (1944), and thereafter thinking about the South and the Negro could never be the same again.

Gone With the Wind was, in a sense, the last of its genre; it pushed the romantic theme of the Old South and the War about as far as it could go and was, at the same time, realistic enough to make clear the spurious quality of that romanticism. Not many years later (1950) William Faulkner was awarded the Nobel Prize for novels which depicted a South impossibly remote from that of *Gone With the Wind*. By the 1950's complete disillusionment with the claims of the Old South had set in, and because by that time so little of Miss Mitchell's South remained, the natural tendency was to wonder whether any of it had ever existed, even in the 1850's, or whether it was all a myth. It is one of the virtues of Miss Mitchell's book that she presents the myth without being taken in by it or asking us to accept it, and that she makes clear the reasons for both its vitality and its ultimate demise.

Gone With the Wind as Vulgar Literature

By Floyd C. Watkins

Miss Anderson found in GWTW that "the scent of magnolias and the soft touch of moonlight are noticeably absent." Floyd Watkins, a distinguished professor at Emory University and a widely recognized authority on Southern literature (and, like Miss Anderson, a product of graduate study at Vanderbilt), posits a view about as different as different can be. He declares: "Much in the novel is bad, false to history, and, worst of all, false to human nature." His was not a "kindly sneer" but a vigorous snarl. His view is, however, representative of that held by many academicians and professional critics.

At the end of a good historical novel, do the fiction and the reader discover the meaning of history as Jack Burden does in Robert Penn Warren's *All the King's Men*? Or do the mysteries of history remain undiscoverd, the private belief of different meditators as in William Faulkner's *Absalom, Absalom!*? How much history must a historical novel have? How much meditation? How much story? The practices of the best modern novelists present meditation above all other things. Story in the sense of a straightforward, chronological narrative may matter little or none. The popular and romantic novel like *Gone With the Wind* is written and then revered as a story; the folderol and paraphernalia of history are presented ostentatiously and defended vigorously as plain and true. But meditation? Who wants it? Leave that, they say, to the symbol-mongers, the pedants, and the myth-masters.

The best critical tradition in our time demands that the novel contain meditation; even if a writer like Faulkner in *Absalom, Absalom!* does claim that it is impossible to deduce the past, every man—and novelist or reader—must try for himself. According to Lion Feuchtwanger, creative writers who write about historical subjects "desire only to treat contemporary matters. . . ."[1] This theory

---

1. Lion Feuchtwanger, *The House of Desdemona: Or the Laurels and Limitations of Historical Fiction*, trans. by Harold A. Basilius (Detroit, 1963). p. 129.

has flaws: it denies the pleasures of antiquarianism and some of the accomplishments of the historian and the human imagination. When Feuchtwanger maintains that the "sole purpose" of a historical novel "is to enable the reader or the viewer to re-experience the author's immediate experience of history" (p. 142), he again excessively limits the human mind. But he does state the aim of the best kind of novelists. William Styron is thinking of a similar principle when he describes *The Confessions of Nat Turner* as "less an 'historical novel' in conventional terms than a meditation on history." The thinking of an author in our time may be of such value artistically and philosophically as to justify even the deliberate invention if not misrepresentation of history.

In a "Foreword" to *Brother to Dragons* Warren maintains that "the relation" of his work "to its historical material is, in one perspective, irrelevant to its value. I am trying to write a poem and not a history, and therefore have no compunction about tampering with facts." Warren continues by arguing that a poem cannot violate "what the writer takes to be the spirit of his history" or "the nature of the human heart." Here Warren is careful to distinguish his work from run-of-the-mill historical novels. Perhaps literature would be more blessed if the historical novelist would be willing to take some of Warren's risks in the hope of reaching some of his achievements.

The facts which are the proper subject of a meditator on history must be sufficiently complex to represent the human heart and the mortal condition in our time or any other. No one can defend chattel slavery now. Then how can a reader sympathize with a good poet like Henry Timrod, who defended slavery while in the process of sympathizing with the new Confederacy in the 1860's? Is it possible to shut out from the mind the ironies of Timrod's praise of a lost cause and to appreciate the poetry as poetry? Was the Southern white soldier so completely wrong that it is impossible to sympathize with him? If fiction is to be written about the Civil War in 1936 or 1970, the men on both sides must be human enough to be potentially tragic figures. Not many historical novels may attain such greatness. But the potentialities do abide in the genre, and a model in some respects is Styron's *The Confessions of Nat Turner*.

In *Set This House on Fire* Styron is at times purely antiwhite. But in the story of Nat Turner the intertwined moral and racial issues become so intricate that the reader can only stand amazed as he ponders the mysteries of person, race, and issues. A black man rather than a white returns a poor escaped slave to his evil master. A white man accuses Nat Turner's confederates of being cowardly and expands the generalization to include the entire black race; two pages earlier he had maintained that "the ordinary Negro slave . . . will leap to his master's defense and fight as bravely as any man." When these kinds of absurd contradictions come from the authority of the novelist, fiction must be bad. When they come from a confused character unaware of his own inconsistency, there are at least the rudiments of good fiction. Another instance: Nat says Negroes are "a people not notably sweet-natured around domestic animals." Obviously Nat regards his judgment as the prevailing view. His opinion may indicate his error, his unfairness to his own race, the black people for whom he sacrifices his life. Presumably, the Negro boosted his own ego by abusing "a poor dumb beast," the only thing he could "feel superior to." Other eyes than Nat's or Styron's, however, might argue that the Negro felt great love for dumb beasts because he shared their chattel status. In fiction of the plantation tradition Negroes are traditionally kind to beasts. The facts are not the point here. Somewhere in the depths of human nature there are facts; but in good fiction they are obscured by all the ponderables of human nature. In simple romantic historical fiction every fact is always weighted in the same direction: black and white Southerners are always good in older romances; in recent fiction white Southerners are bad unless they are radical. But in good art human nature seldom exists in absolute form. Judge Jeremiah Cobb in Styron's novel is the one good white man whom Nat promises himself to spare, but he is also the judge who sentences Nat to death. And as he passes the sentence, even the fanatical victim feels "a curious pang of pity and regret." Nat realizes that the judge is "close to death." This situation is human and complex. Compared to this, Scarlett O'Hara's killing of the Yankee soldier in the halls of Tara is as simple a drama as the wolf huffing at the door of the three little pigs.

Good historical novels in some way are meditative. They are not written merely to make history come alive.[2] Mere dramatization or fictionalizing of history may be a service to history—if it is accurate enough—but it is a disservice to literature. It is unnecessary because one may know much factual history without the embroidery of art. There must be, however, a limit to meditation. Obsessive interest in archetypes and mythology ruins the brew, and the contemporary and the humanity in the work are obscured. When a novel is false to historical fact and also false to the human heart in the contemporary age, then it must be simply a poor novel. Despite an immediate popularity which excelled that of all other books, that is the category of *Gone With the Wind*—a bad novel. It creates a myth which seems to ease the hunger of all extravagantly Southern and little romantic souls, but it propagandizes history, fails to grasp the depths and complexities of human evil and the significances of those who prevail. *Gone With the Wind* is what William Dean Howells called vulgar literature: "what is despicable, what is lamentable is to have hit the popular fancy and not have done anything to change it, but everything to fix it; to flatter it with false dreams of splendor in the past, when life was mainly as simple and sad-colored as it is now. . . ."[3]

Never has a book been more praised than *Gone With the Wind* for what it omits. A friend of mine in the business office of Emory University became heated in anger recently when I told him that *Gone With the Wind* is a bad book partly because of what it leaves out. It is a good book, he maintains, because it

---

2. Helen Cam, *Historical Novels,* Number 48. The Historical Association (London, 1961), p. 18.

3. William Dean Howells, "The New Historical Romances," *North American Review,* CLXXI (Dec. 1900), 943.

tells a good story and does not expose itself to the nit-picking analyses of scholars and pedants. As a child, Margaret Mitchell evaluated a book about the Rover Boys: "The story is all that matters. Any good plot can stand retelling and style doesn't matter."[4] And Stephens Mitchell, the brother of the novelist, asserts that she "repeated this early opinion, almost word for word," not long before she died.

The most laudatory article about *Gone With the Wind* praises it for its little subtlety, the lack "of the complexity of the imagination of William Faulkner or the art of Robert Penn Warren."[5] The "lack of subtlety . . . is in its favor," or said to be, because society was "unself-conscious . . . as opposed to the analytic and introspective."[6] "Story" is better than "study." Other critics praise the novel for the lack of obscenity and the failure to include "the inductive vagueness of the stream-of-consciousness school."[7] One who lauds the absence of subtlety later maintains that Ashley's "self-knowledge" gives him tragic stature; his is the "tragedy of every man who cannot be what he was born to be or would be."[8] And Scarlett, the same writer finally says, deliberately chooses "to return to . . . the life of tradition" and is "redeemed into the life of tradition" (p. 149). And the true conflict of this epic-like novel "will never" be presented "more excitingly or appealingly than it is here" (p. 150).

The real difficulty in criticizing *Gone With the Wind* seems to be coping with half-criticism. All it has to be is a good story. Now, the real question is whether this is possible. Ultimately, no one can prove the impossibility. Unfortunately, it is a matter of faith and taste rather than knowledge. That *Gone With the Wind* does need more analysis may be shown by claims for excitement, for tragedy, and for profound tradition and meaning—all these in what is said to be a simple story. How is one to judge whether these may be in a simple story if "story" and "simplicity" are the main characteristics? Obviously, one cannot. And that is why, perhaps, little direct frontal assault has ever been made on the novel which has outsold any other fiction. The critic faces a difficult task and a hostile audience of nations of readers.

When a critic ventures to say what a novel should have included, he has begun to write his own fiction—like the reviewer who says what a book should be without ever considering what it is. Perhaps the only way to avoid this arrogance is to turn to the writings of good novelists and good scholars and to see—in comparison—what greater literature and greater characters or human beings are. After all, isn't this the only real literary purpose of the discipline of comparative literature? (Isn't all else that is comparative really a study of the

4. William S. Howland, "Margaret Mitchell—Romantic Realist," *Margaret Mitchell Memorial of the Atlanta Public Library* (Atlanta, 1954), p. 5.

5. Robert Y. Drake, Jr., "Tara Twenty Years After," *Georgia Review*, XII (Summer, 1958), 142.

6. Drake, p. 142.

7. Belle Rosenbaum, "Why Do They Read It?" *Scribner's Magazine*, CII (August, 1937), 145.

8. Drake, p. 145.

fashions and trends of ideas and techniques?) What can history and myth be besides icing for the antiquarian, a sop for those looking for color and extravaganza, and escape to ardent romance for those wishing to forget the arduous moment? Myth for Robert Penn Warren is "a fiction, a construct which expresses a truth and affirms a value." When "history is blind," the individual "man is not."[9] History is where we find out what man is that makes God or even man mindful of him. A historical novel, if it wishes to claim as much greatness as it claims popularity, must present characters whose accomplishments, with the Hebrew prophets, we exalt to the heavens or whose shames, with Melville, we wish to cover with the "costliest robes."

There are many works about history and the Civil War which accomplish things that by comparison indicate *Gone With the Wind* is no better than it should be. The Pulitzer Prize Committee chose *Gone With the Wind* over Faulkner's *Absalom, Absalom!*, published in the same year; and Faulkner believed that *The Unvanquished* was used as a threat in Hollywood's maneuverings about the production and casting of *Gone With the Wind*. These two novels alone contain much which can never be found in the gaudier romance. There is history in the works of Faulkner and Miss Mitchell, but the depths of humanity appear only in Faulkner. In Scarlett's marriages and aspirations and Rhett Butler's ruthlessness there are parallels to Sutpen.[10] But no one in *Gone With the Wind* is capable of Sutpen's tragic failure. *Gone With the Wind* lacks true depth for one reason because it leaves evil out of the garden of Tara. The "clumsy sprawling building," the old oaks, the lawn "reclaimed from weeds," the "avenue of cedars," and the slave quarters have "an air of solidness, of stability and permanence" until the Yankees come. In shallow romantic fiction except for occasional bad manners all evils flow entirely from without. The houses of great literature fall before enemies, and usually they simultaneously crumble or at least struggle from within. Consider the complex forces in the Sutpen mansion as Sutpen builds it almost with his bare hands and as it is burned by its founder's mulatto descendant. And compare the house of the seven gables and even the establishments of the Montagues and the Capulets. It is almost as if *Gone With the Wind* shares the simplicity and the callousness of its heroine, who endured struggles which "passed over her without touching any deep chord within her. . . ."[11]

The determined and vengeful Drusilla in *The Unvanquished* is a greater enigma and tragedy than Miss Mitchell's willful and selfish Scarlett, and Bayard Sartoris's struggles in killing Grumby and renouncing the sword are deeper than any of the petty issues of the "sub-pornographic" romance *Gone With the*

9. See L. Hugh Moore, Jr., "Robert Penn Warren and History: 'The Big Myth We Live,' " unpub. doctoral dissertation (Emory University, 1964), pp. 13, 68.

10. W. J. Stuckey, *The Pulitzer Prize Novels: A Critical Backward Look* (Norman, Okla., 1966), p. 111.

11. Margaret Mitchell, *Gone With the Wind* (New York, 1936), p. 219.

Wind.[12] With Scarlett we enjoy being titillated by the hope of sexual promiscuities for the sake of material security, and then foolishly we are disappointed that she did not keep her Rhett in the end. Faulkner's Drusilla is unsexed by the loss of a lover in war; John Sartoris is violently destroyed with some justification and Bayard is redeemed by his courage and conviction in renouncing violence. *Gone With the Wind* has no character with their consistency, sacrifice, courage, and suffering. No prominent character except for the weak Ashley and the too-perfect Melanie is constant in depth and integrity. Romantic stereotypes cannot even confront the decisions of great characters created by a great and noble mind.

Movements through the city during the burning of Atlanta magnificently but superficially portray the shiftings about of small men caught in terrible forces, but *Gone With the Wind* never catches all the complexity of the Negroes marching for freedom and "homemade Jordan" in *The Unvanquished,* caught in a tangle of forces they cannot comprehend, rejected by the very soldiers who freed them, understood by some of the owners from whom they flee. The battle of Atlanta in *Gone With the Wind* is good pageantry, but its accomplishment stops precisely there. The victor is victor in romantic fiction, but Faulkner's greater work shows a victor overrun by those he liberated and harassed by those he defeated. In contrast, Margaret Mitchell's novel, in the words of her brother, "struck a blow for her Southland."[13] The freed slave here is just another mean nigger who causes an uprising by the Ku Klux Klan, punishment of Southern whites by the Yankees, and the death of another of Scarlett's husbands. In Faulkner, he is a massive physical force or a minor character and a political issue. The great drama of the forces of history appears in Faulkner's work, but not in Miss Mitchell's. This is negative criticism, almost pure judgment. But the wise critic can make it from a perspective and with taste which cannot be shared by the large popular audience which admired *Gone With the Wind.* In the final analysis, pure assertion must have some critical place. Fiction has often fought the Civil War, and the soldiers in Warren's *Wilderness* and *All the King's Men* and in Crane's *Red Badge* engage in profounder personal and massive struggles. It is possible to bury one's head among the rapidly shuffling pages and insist that *Gone With the Wind* is good because it is an engaging story, excellently told; but when proof is not forthcoming, the same claim can also be made about "Marse Chan." *The Little Shepherd of Kingdom Come,* and Thomas Dixon's *The Clansman.* Damning a novel with faint praise because of what it does not contain is inadequate criticism, but at least it is a beginning point.

But all the errors of *Gone With the Wind* are not of omission. Much in the novel is bad, false to the facts of rural and Southern life particularly, false to history, and, worst of all, false to human nature. Grandiloquent claims have

---

12. Stuckey, p. 111.

13. Stephens Mitchell, "Margaret Mitchell and Her People in the Atlanta Area," *Atlanta Historical Bulletin,* IX (May 1950), 22.

been made for the historical accuracy of *Gone With the Wind*. Miss Mitchell, we are told, "did write the truth, and because she did her novel is an authentic historical study as well as a fascinating love story."[14] And her biographer wrote in 1965 that "So far as can be determined, there is not even a minute error of fact in the novel."[15] Patently, such a claim may be wrong; Andrew Lytle believes that the novelist may create only "the illusion of past time . . . because finally . . . we must leave the truth to God."[16]

Factual errors in *Gone With the Wind*, however, do exist, though most of them are negligible. The most obvious mistakes lie in the field of pyronomics. One burning Southern plantation home has its fire remarkably extinguished: "The wooden wing of Mimosa had burned and only the thick resistant stucco of the main house and the frenzied work of the Fontaine women and their slaves with wet blankets and quilts had saved it" (p. 471). John Carter, a fire investigator for the city of Atlanta, comments that their methods of fire-fighting were "surely impractical" if not impossible. "Three years of stored cotton" go up in flame which lights "up the place lak it wuz day . . . , and it wuz so bright in this hyah room that you could mos' pick a needle offen the flo" (418). But loose cotton burns with a tiny blue flame, and baled cotton only smolders.[17] The statistics of slaveowning in Miss Mitchell's Clayton County do not conform to actuality. Poor white trash in *Gone With the Wind* never owned more than four Negroes (17), but in Clayton County only thirty-six farmers owned more than ten Negroes, and only 134 owned from one to ten. To reach even the lowly status of poor white, a man in this county in fiction would have to own as many slaves as a middling slave owner in fact. The Tarletons own one hundred Negroes (6), and apparently several other plantations in the novel are about that same size. But the census of 1860 lists no slave owner with that many slaves in Clayton County, and only one owned between forty and fifty slaves. The luxuriousness of class has been exaggerated for poor white and large plantation owner. False romance is created by increasing the number of slaves. In *Gone With the Wind* during the Reconstruction a citizen could not vote "if he was on the tax books for more than two thousand dollars in 'sixty-five" (523). Miss Mitchell exaggerated and dropped a digit. Those denied amnesty in fact were the ones whose taxable wealth surpassed twenty thousand dollars.[18]

The romance is also false because Miss Mitchell reaches too low into the barrel for her chief poor white family, the Slatterys. They own a "meager three acres," where they grow a "few acres of cotton" and a poor vegetable garden.

14. Marian Elder Jones, " 'Me and My Book,' " *Georgia Review*, XVI (Summer, 1962), 184.
15. Finis Farr, *Margaret Mitchell of Atlanta: The Author of "Gone With the Wind"* (New York, 1965), p. 104.
16. Andrew Nelson Lytle, "The Image as Guide to Meaning in the Historical Novel," *Sewanee Review*, LXI (1953), 410–11.
17. See burning cotton or consult with J. W. McCarty, of the Georgia Institute of Technology and consultant with the Georgia Department of Agriculture.
18. Alan Conway, *The Reconstruction of Georgia* (Minneapolis, 1966), p. 44.

Slattery begs cotton seed for planting or a side of bacon "to tide him over" (48–9). The economics and the culture are wrong. In 1860 only two farm families in Clayton County farmed as few as three to ten acres, and only seven as few as ten to twenty. Probably no one in life farmed as few as the three in fiction. When the poor white begged in the South, he asked only for those things his wealthier neighbor could not use—such as corn cobs which might be soaked and fed to the cows. Usually he begged for nothing, as is shown in Faulkner's more accurate representation of the yeoman farmer in the fiercely independent convict of *The Old Man,* and the Bundrens, who refused to be beholden.

But many errors are more serious than factual errors though less definite. Romances of the Civil War and Southern history and the admiration for romances have had a pernicious influence. Southern readers—and foolish romantic readers anywhere—dream of an impossible past, expect more of the present than can be realized, ignore an authentic culture while praising a false culture that never existed, foolishly defend themselves against attacks from the North, use false defenses of illogic and rhetoric, become vulnerable to attacks that could be avoided, fall victim to false and pretentious characters in dreamers and political demagogues, ignore and condemn the yeomanry and the peasantry. False history causes sentimentality about the past and hopelessness about the present. For other reasons false history can fail. Sheldon Van Auken has indicated that the old Southern way of life could be defended only after it "is no longer regarded as a menace" and that then "the North listens to its voice with interest and appreciation."[19] In part, of course, it has failed to continue to be a menace to Northern and modern culture because it has been falsely romanticized and made aristocratic. A true picture of the values of yeoman Clayton County might form a threat to the monolithic patterns of progress in our culture. *Gone With the Wind* is no menace to anything false. It has what Richard Chase calls a "fatal inner falsity."[20] It is like chamber of commerce advertising, which can sell almost anything but a true picture of the complexity of life in the South (or anywhere else, for that matter).

Formal manners and dress in *Gone With the Wind* give a false picture of the old South, idealize its flaws, and suggest that people who are perfect in the social proprieties are also perfect or nearly so in their human relations. Scarlett's "seventeen-inch waist, the smallest in three counties" (3), may be possible. But it surely is improbable considering her buxom flesh. Even on weekdays she wears stays "laced too tightly to permit much running" (24). Maybe on certain streets in older towns such as Charleston and New Orleans this might be the fashion, but so much style in Jonesboro, Georgia, seems most unlikely. The rather stereotyped Irish head of the O'Hara plantation, Gerald, wears a cravat when he goes on a trip to buy a slave—even on a weekday (29). And before he

19. Sheldon Van Auken, "The Southern Historical Novel in the Early Twentieth Century," *Journal of Southern History,* XIV (May, 1948), 175.

20. Richard Chase, *The American Novel and Its Tradition* (London, 1957), p. 20.

married, this rough, florid forty-three-year-old bachelor had a valet who served his "meals with dignity and style" (51). These formalities sit better in the *Ladies Home Journal* or with Peggy Marsh in Atlanta in the 1920's than with an Irish farmer in Clayton County before the Civil War. During the summers "the County averaged a barbecue and ball nearly every week . . ." (86), and lusty girls like Scarlett were supposed to "eat lak a bird" at the barbecues until their marriage. The intimate details of going to bed move almost with the formality of a barbecue. The chief Negro slave leads the family upstairs "with the pompous dignity of a first chamberlain of the royal bedchamber lighting a king and queen to their rooms . . ." (71). Presumably the social amenities and formalities reflect a society untroubled by most human frailties before it is destroyed by depraved Yankees. The problem is not that these things never happened. Southern society has its manners, even its going-to-bed rituals, but I suggest that these concentrations of formalities in Miss Mitchell's novel are propaganda instead of history. Social purpose is in control when Negroes come home from their field work and the whites hear "the shrill careless laughter of Negro voices" (8). There is no mention of sweat, of exhaustion, of the arduousness of field work. *Gone With the Wind* is a world without sweat, except for that caused by the Yankees.

The contrast in manners is completely apparent when women follow Northern soldiers into Atlanta. "They were so lately come from nothing and so uncertain of themselves they were doubly anxious to appear refined . . ." (879). Some have been chambermaids; some grew up in a room over the family saloon; and one "had come out of one of her husband's own brothels" (879). But they foolishly strive to be as gracious in their manners as ladies on a Southern plantation.

Perhaps *Gone With the Wind* is one of the last books to be openly patriotic and popular in our time. It defies all the lessons of restraint which Miss Mitchell could have learned from the early Hemingway, and it blatantly defends what Stephens Mitchell called "the Southland." It is sentimental and patriotic and melodramatic—and shallow, enough to make shallow readers, even radical modern integrationists, suspend their disbelief. The home guard, the militia, and home-front patriots sing the "Bonnie Blue Flag," and tears come with "a deep hot glow in eyes" (170). Ashley and Miss Mitchell define the Civil War and the cause of the war in a sentimental fashion which is altogether foreign to the twentieth century except among some readers of a vast popular audience: "Perhaps," Ashley says, "that is what is called patriotism, love of home and country. . . . I am fighting for the old days, the old ways I love so much but which, I fear, are now gone forever, no matter how the die may fall" (211). Sentimentally, but truly, they are gone with the wind; and not all the weeping and wailing can bring them back. Obviously, Miss Mitchell satirizes Scarlett's chivalric dreams, but by creating characters like Scarlett and Ashley and making them admirable, Miss Mitchell also is a victim of their sentimentality. Given the plot and characters, there is no way to make "Marse Chan" or *Gone With the*

Wind truly realistic. Ashley is "a young girl's dream of the Perfect Knight. . . ." (214). And every female heart that ever dreamed of Walter Scott or soap opera falls victim along with Scarlett.

The irony of defeat—an irony that could not be treated by a contemporary like Timrod—is conveyed mainly through the character of Rhett Butler. No patriot, Rhett predicts defeat. He even sees the flaws of the Confederacy, represented by the contract holders who sell "shoddy cloth, sanded sugar, spoiled flour and rotten leather to the Confederacy" (228). But Rhett is not enough to remove the stigma of sentimental patriotism. Truth breaks in to encourage the woebegone reader: "But even with this loss on the top of the others, the South's spirit was not broken. True, grim determination had taken the place of highhearted hopes, but people could still find a silver lining in the cloud" (278). Such triteness is followed by tear-jerking sorrow over the retreating army. Even the sardonic Rhett finally makes a patriotic speech (and it is only half-comic) before going to join the Confederate Army. There is a "malicious tenderness" in his voice as he speaks to Scarlett (389). Rhett is a tough guy who could get along well with the roughest of Hemingway's characters, but when he softens he is a blithering patriotic old sentimentalist, for all his rough ways with women. And his sentimentality is as false as the falsest thing of the sea. He goes to war purely for feeling, not because the South had any kind of true cause, Rhett and Miss Mitchell might have learned a great deal from a poem like Donald Davidson's "Lee in the Mountains."

An oversimplified regionalism in *Gone With the Wind* is the source from which nearly all evils flow. There has been all too much of this in Southern fiction. *To Kill a Mockingbird,* for example, a Pulitzer prize winner as was *Gone With the Wind,* divides humanity into good blacks and good white Southern liberals versus bad white Southerners. *Gone With the Wind* is on the opposite side. Yet both books take sides so superficially that one wonders if the authors would not have switched sides with the times. Nothing Southern is so inglorious as the Reverend Hightower's grandfather, shot while he was stealing chickens from a henhouse. No Northern soldier is so kindly as the Yankee officer who refuses to drag the children Bayard and Ringo from the protection of an old woman's skirt. No scalawag is so admirable as Redmond in Faulkner's "An Odor of Verbena." He refuses to shoot even to protect himself when the young Bayard Sartoris comes to see him apparently seeking vengeance. Instead, despite such foolish and extreme claims by historians as the contentions that slavery was the only issue or that it was not a main issue at all, *Gone With the Wind* is one of the most oversimplified treatments of the Civil War. The chief contention of the book and its author is that Yankees are bad and Southerners are good. Yankee soldiers burn and loot; Southerners visit folks on the home front and encourage them without taking their foodstuffs. The scalawag of *Gone With the Wind* is unalleviated evil. Mulatto babies increase after Northern soldiers come to town; Northern mothers refuse to trust their babies "to a black nigger"; and Negroes give Northerners who fought for them "the creeps" (671–72). The only good scalawag was Rhett Butler, who merely acted like one so that he might learn information useful to the defeated South. The manners of Yankees who visit Scarlett are so bad that they use the rugs to spit on "no matter how many spittoons she might put out in plain view" (879).

Yankees are romantic and false because they do not conform to human nature. A novel may legitimately portray a just cause, and most of the good people in fiction can fight on just one side. But whan *all* the good soldiers belong on one side and *all* the bad ones on another, then the novel has become propaganda, even if it was written more than seventy years after the physical conflict ceased. But if Yankees are evil and if some Southerners are guilty of some foibles, perfection on the Southern side does represent the regional perfection of Miss Mitchell's romantic Southland. The most unbelievable character in the book, perhaps the heroine, is Melanie Wilkes. Typically, the chief goodness belongs to a woman; the novel, after all, was written by a woman; and in the plantation tradition the South was a matriarchy, with fumbling but kindly men and competent and altogether loving women. Miss Mitchell explicitly attributes complete goodness to Melanie: "In all her sheltered life she had never seen evil and could scarcely credit its existence, and when gossip whispered things about Rhett and the girl in Charleston, she was shocked and unbelieving" (222). (The narrow puritanism of the novel at times is indicated by things like the equation here of evil and immorality which is only sexual.) Melanie's trivial flaw is that she is physically so "small-hipped" that she has great difficulty bearing a child. Attended only by Scarlett during the birth of her baby while the Battle of Atlanta is raging, she says, " 'Don't bother about talking, dear. I know how worried you are. I'm so sorry I'm so much trouble' " (356). But Melanie, confronted by Yankee evil embodied in a soldier in Tara, can turn to steel. She rises from her bed and gets her dead brother's saber to defend Scarlett. When she speaks after Scarlett shoots him, Scarlett sees "beneath the gentle voice and the dovelike eyes . . . a thin flashing blade of unbreakable steel, [and she] felt too that there were banners and bugles of courage in Melanie's quiet blood" (441). Melanie starves herself to save food for hungry soldiers. She can confront necessity more boldly than Scarlett. After her Ashley has been shot while carrying out a chivalric mission by the Ku Klux Klan, Rhett Butler brings him home. Since hostile soldiers can hear the conversation, Melanie calls in a loud clear voice, "Bring him in, Captain Butler. . . . I suppose you've gotten him intoxicated again. Bring him in" (802). Melanie has too few flaws to be human— and none of any significance. But she is more than an idealization of a perfect woman. Miss Mitchell intended her to be representative of Southern regional goodness to counteract Northern regional badness. She is "the gentle, self-effacing but steel-spined women on whom the South had builded its house in war and to whose proud and loving arms it had returned in defeat" (1026). If Scarlett is all a repressed Atlanta debutante and matron might wish to be in her most fleshly moments, Melanie is what Miss Mitchell knew a woman ought to be. But she is so perfect that she is not a sound basis for good fiction. She contains no evil. She sins too little.

Gone With the Wind is far too prudish to be a good novel. Miss Mitchell flirts with the risque. Four times Scarlett is called one kind of piece or another, and I suggest that Miss Mitchell would have enjoyed protesting her innocence while appreciating the innuendos. Except for offstage trips to Belle Watling's brothel, there is no true piece in *Gone With the Wind*. The point of the love scenes between Rhett and Scarlett even during their marriage is Scarlett's frigidity. The chief sexual characteristic of the women in the novel is an unhealthy curiosity about the life of prostitutes. When Dr. Meade's wife asks him about life upstairs at the whorehouse, the good doctor is "thunderstruck"; and several times women are just this curious. Once Miss Mitchell writes that "most innocent and well-bred young women . . . had a devouring curiosity about prostitutes" (248). But prudishness becomes even more incredible. The devoted Melanie does not wish to have to be so frank in a letter as to tell her husband that she is going to have a baby (282). Scarlett delivers the baby. Later, she kills a soldier who is looting Tara and asks Melanie for her shimmy to "wad it around his head" in order to avoid leaving a bloody trail (444). Melanie's face turns crimson, but all of Scarlett's bluntness and directness do not prove that the "nicey-nice" way is wrong. Girls are auctioned off to dance with men and to make money for the Southern cause, but their reaction is too ridiculous to appear in any believable novel. When Maybelle Merriwether was bid on, she "collapsed with blushes against Fanny's shoulder and the two girls hid their faces in each other's necks and giggled. . . ."

Gone With the Wind is narrowly patriotic, prudish, melodramatic, and sentimental. Belle Watling is as good a whore as ever lived; her patriotic sacrifices, her philanthropy for the Confederate cause, and her protection of good Ku Klux Klansmen make her as fine a woman as Bret Harte's Mother Shipton. It is a pity that Thomas Wolfe never had a chance to turn his parody on *Gone With the Wind*. Rhett is as straight out of melodrama as Wolfe's Faro Bill. Two men are killed during a raid by the Klan. To protect other Klansmen, Rhett gives instructions to "Put them in that lot and put pistols near them—in their hands. . . . Fire one shot from each. It's got to appear like a plain case of shooting. You understand?" "Archie nodded as if he understood perfectly and an unwilling gleam of respect shone in his cold eye" (808). When Wolfe's Faro Jim fixes his "vulturesque eye" on the "little dance girl" with "suave murder in his heart, . . . the cold gray eyes of the Stranger missed nothing. Imperturbably he drank his Scotch, wheeled from the mirror with barking Colt just one-sixth of a second before the gambler could fire. Faro coughed and slid forward slowly upon the floor."[21]

There was no sound now in the crowded room of the Triple Y. . . .

"By God, stranger!" . . . [the sheriff] ejaculated. "I never knew the man lived who could beat Faro to the draw. What's yore name?"

---

[21] Thomas Wolfe, *Look Homeward, Angel* (New York, 1929), p. 273.

"In the fam'ly Bible back home, pardner," the Stranger drawled, "it's Eugene Gant, but folks out here generally calls me The Dixie Ghost."
There was a slow gasp of wonder from the crowd.
"Gawd!" someone whispered. "It's the Ghost!"

In Miss Mitchell's scene Rhett Butler apologizes like a gentleman after he has saved Melanie's husband and almost called her Miss Melly. Then

"I beg your pardon, I mean, Mrs. Wilkes. . . ."
"Oh, Captain Butler, do not ask my pardon. I should feel honored if you called me 'Melly' without the Miss! . . ."

Similarly, *Look Homeward, Angel* parodied this overformal melodrama before it was written. Bruce Glendenning, cast away with the beautiful Veronica on a desert island, has never told the damsel he loves her. When a band of natives charges, at last he feels free to speak. Then a destroyer steams into view.

"Saved! We are saved!" cried Glendenning, and leaping to his feet he signalled the approaching boat. Suddenly he paused.
"Damn!" he muttered bitterly. "Oh, damn!"
"What is it, Bruce?" she asked.
"A destroyer has just entered the harbor. We are saved, Miss Mullins. Saved!" And he laughed bitterly. (107)

Gone With the Wind is much more than a simple story. It also consists of melodrama, sentimentality, perfect characters, evil and good in black and white, anti-Negro racism, discursive essays on history and politics usually at the beginning of a chapter in the manner of Theodore Dreiser, writing in the spirit of a chamber of commerce, artificial dialogue, exaggerated Negro dialect almost at times in the speech of Irwin Russell's Negroes. The flaws of *Gone With the Wind* are not merely those of omission. It is a simple story, almost simple-minded at times. Great literature can occasionally be popular, and certainly popular literature can occasionally be great. But with a few notable exceptions, such as the Bible but not *Gone With the Wind*, greatness and popularity are more likely to be contradictory than congenial.

Reconsideration: Totin' de Weery Load

By James Boatwright

The track record of opposition and disdain toward Gone With the Wind *achieved by* The New Republic *was unmatched.* The Saturday Review of Literature, *the New York* Times, *and the New York* Herald-Tribune *all printed reviews or articles about the book that treated it favorably and some that treated it unfavorably. From the very beginning* The New Republic *has been consistent in damning it.*

John Peale Bishop pounced upon GWTW *in his review in* The New Republic *July 15, 1936. In the issue of September 15, 1936, Malcolm Cowley wrote the criticism that has become the touchstone of later critics attacking the novel: "Gone With the Wind is an encyclopedia of the plantation legend . . . false in part and silly in part and vicious in its general effect on Southern life today."*

A "reconsideration" of the movie Roger Rosenblatt wrote for The New Republic, *January 25, 1975, is an assessment truly "false in part and silly in part and vicious" throughout. Rosenblatt wrote with dazzling cleverness about the film, but he chokes on his own cleverness and on his anti-Irishness, as when he has the near-starving Scarlett find not a radish (as in the novel) but a potato. "She gags on it," he says, "in the obvious discovery of her own roots."*

Before it reconsidered the film, The New Republic *reconsidered the novel September 1, 1973, in the essay reprinted here.*

It seemed like a good idea at first, a piece on *Gone With the Wind,* that most phenomenal of best sellers, not so much a book as a literary Act of God, unexplainable but cataclysmically there. After 37 years, book and movie are still very much with us. Gavin Lambert's long, two-part essay on the making of the film appeared recently in *The Atlantic,* and in the past few years there have been an English musical version of Scarlett's trials and some kind of stupendous Japanese redaction. A thorough and admiring biography of Margaret Mitchell by Finis Farr was published in 1965, by which time *GWTW* had been translated into 25 languages in 29 countries, was being published in 12 countries besides

England and the United States, with the sale of all authorized editions reaching 12 million copies. *GWTW* seems to have a kind of vitality and staying power that the ordinary blockbuster can't come up with. *Everybody* has read it and knows the characters, the famous scenes, the famous lines; *everybody* has seen the movie countless times and can tell you what was left out, what was added, what Scarlett wore when she went to see Rhett in jail.

The novel is folklore now, a part of the culture (of many cultures, of the global village?). Its success has to be evidence of something—of reading habits and tastes, of the topology of fantasy, of the possibilities of promotion and advertising. Nothing with so much aggressive presence can be insignificant, so, as I have said, it seemed like a good idea to write an essay about *GWTW*, now that the world it came from and the world we inhabit might be different planets. That meant, of course, rereading *GWTW*. For a month I doggedly kept at it and must sorrowfully report that reliving those stirring days as described in the 862 pages of the paperback edition is mostly a tedious exercise in totin' a weery load.

Hard words from someone brought up on the book as I was and as my generation in the South was. We were a little young to be aware of its original reception, but Farr's biography documents that with intriguing detail—the front page reviews in the *Times* and the *Herald Tribune,* the praise from Henry Steele Commager and Stephen Vincent Benet, *Publishers' Weekly's* judgment ("*Gone With the Wind* is very possibly the greatest American novel"). Reviewers were fond of comparing *GWTW* to *War and Peace,* and in my late adolescence (1948 or 1949) I must have shared that insight, because I have a clear recollection of reading both of them during the same summer, when I was out of school, didn't have a job and could lie in bed all morning and well into the afternoon. I'm sure they must have seemed the apotheosis of the novel form (a famous poet told me recently that when he was 11 he read *GWTW* four or five times, somehow convinced it was the *only* novel). *War and Peace* was pretty good, but it tended to be somewhat remote and exotic (it was hard even keeping the names straight), but *GWTW* was both a masterpiece and something down home; when I saw the movie it seemed a literal, appropriately reverent transcription of the book, and the two merged in my consciousness never, I assumed, to be broken asunder.

I don't know how *War and Peace* got on my reading list, since I read mostly the books checked out by my mother at the branch library, all of them historical novels and all of them by women (*Forever Amber* sticks in my mind), generally ladies with three names. The only specifically *Southern* writers I knew about were writers from my hometown (Edison Marshall, Berry Fleming and Frank Yerby, the last, *mirabile dictu,* a Negro), the notorious Erskine Caldwell (another local boy) whose works mostly fed my appetite for pornography, and Elizabeth Boatwright Coker, a cousin who had reportedly written a successful novel about the Old Days (*Daughter of Strangers*), but I had never seen it. Faulkner, Welty, Warren, Tate and Katherine Anne Porter were names as yet unknown to me.

Such was the literary landscape that *GWTW* flashed onto, sweeping aside everything in its path. But what are the particulars that impressed me then? Either my memory or the book is at fault, because I can't recall in detail what it was that had me glued to the bed through those sweltering July mornings; I can only attempt my own Reconstruction. Although the ideas and attitudes of the book would have been familiar to me, I'm sure it told me a great deal about the Civil War that I wouldn't have picked up elsewhere. Not from my family—the myth of a Southern childhood has the family gathered on the porch at dusk maintaining the oral tradition, passing on the stories of tragic loss and defeat from generation to generation, but nothing like that was true of my experience. There was plenty of talk about who had married whom, who was her mother before she married (wasn't she one of the Ferguson girls?), but no gossip and I have to conclude not much knowledge about events that my greatgrandparents had suffered through. I didn't see that omission then as *symptomatic* of anything either. Nor do I recall having learned much at school other than opinions and attitudes (I remember a high school history teacher screaming in rage at a boy who was unfortunate enough to have been brought up in Brazil where he had absorbed some very peculiar ideas about race). A book like *GWTW* really was news, and news of a special kind. Here was interesting history, more than interesting because all the places were familiar—Atlanta, Macon, Savannah, Augusta—and the fact that they were the setting for this dramatic action, depicted in this great novel, meant that they were important, significant, which meant, by involved adolescent logic, that I was possibly important and significant (maybe there's nothing unusual here? perhaps this is the purpose of the epic tale anyway?). *GWTW* offered me, and probably many like me, identity, an ordered, dignified, heroic past.

The manners and mores of the novel surely jibed with what I knew, and the sociological passages about nineteenth-century Georgia must have had the clearest implications for my own evolving notions about twentieth-century Georgia. When Margaret Mitchell says of women at a ball (*ladies*, that is), "They were all beautiful with the blinding beauty that transfigures even the plainest woman when she is utterly protected and utterly loved and is given back that love a thousandfold," I could only have reacted with a dumb nod of assent, yes, yes, and more vigorous nods on reading that the Negroes had responded to Gerald O'Hara's gruffness "with unerring African instinct" or on discovering that while the barbecue was served up for the Wilkeses and Fontaines and O'Haras, the house servants and maids "had their own feast of . . . chitterlings, that dish of hog entrails so dear to Negro hearts. . . ." These ripe complacencies would have been easy to deal with, ingested without a moment's hesitation. But what about the *other* part of the story, the shocking part, shocking because here the adolescent sensibility would have encountered something dangerous, attractive and yet *recognizable*? I could only have been enthralled by the "realism" and the rebelliousness of Scarlett and Rhett. Those two "mules," as Mammy calls them, challenge the claustrophobic Southern code of genteel and decorous behavior, of doing what's right. They break out, break loose, are free, and they get away with it—for a while, at least. Rhett leaves Charleston under the pressure of awful scandal, speaks common sense to the hotbloods at the barbecue about the South's unpreparedness for war, gets richer and more handsome as everyone else gets hungrier and shabbier. Scarlett shocks Atlanta by dancing in her widow's weeds with Rhett, fights like a tiger for what she wants, survives Sherman and the Yankees at Tara, thrives as a businesswoman. These two thrilling figures of freedom in a world suffocating under the dead hand of tradition, confinement and duty! Although I must have been aware of the panorama, the generosity of narrative and its peaks of excitement and drama, I'm sure that the chief pull of the story was observing these spectacular exemplars of romantic rebellion.

Where has the old magic gone? Why do I now find myself, like Prissy, wandering distractedly and mournfully complaining of de weery load? The book has undeniable strengths, and Malcolm Cowley, when he reviewed it in these pages in 1936, was moved to admit that it "has a simple-minded courage that suggests the great novelists of the past," this admission pretty much wrenched from him after he presents a catalogue of its defects. (The most interesting of these was that *GWTW* is an "encyclopedia of the plantation legend," a legend "false in part and silly in part and vicious in its general effect on Southern life today.") I don't intend to get involved in *that* question, really a historian's question (it has never been clear to me what the duties to historical "truth" of an historical novel are) except to remark that the recently published collection of letters and journals of a prominent Georgia family in the 1860s, *Children of Pride* (Yale University Press) reflects the social surfaces of Margaret Mitchell's novel in ways that are uncanny. And the symmetries extend: when its editor accepted a shared National Book Award for *Children of Pride,* he quoted without undue modesty, a reviewer's comparison of his book with *War and Peace.*) Cowley's "simple-minded courage" seems to me just right, but I would add *energy* to that praise, an energy of conception and organization that I found really admirable this time around. Mitchell absorbed great quantities of historical and sociological fact from newspapers and various specialized studies, and she worked them into the narrative with wonderful smoothness and assurance. She generalizes with the confidence of a good journalist or sociologist about the blockade, the progress of Sherman's troops, the clothes the ladies wore, what the visiting customs of cousins were, and the generalizations seem to sprout naturally from the narrative, are rooted in the lives of the major characters.

That same energy marks some of the big, heavily plotted climactic scenes. Everybody remembers the last hours in Atlanta, when Melanie is in labor, the doctors are busy with the dying, Prissy dawdles maddeningly on her desperate errands, and Scarlett shows her fierce strength and determination in the face of stifling heat, Prissy's incompetence, Melanie's screams—it all works up to an atmosphere of genuine urgency and terror. Or the scene involving the deception of the Yankee soldiers who have come to arrest Ashley but are thwarted by the superb acting of Melanie. Or Melanie's deathbed scene, where the novel really comes into its own momentarily, as the astringencies of disenchantment and knowledge cleanse Scarlett's perpetually muddied vision. In that same scene the language takes on for once a kind of pithiness hardly in evidence elsewhere in this great pudding of a book, as Scarlett becomes "desolate with the knowledge that she could not face life without the terrible strength of the weak, the gentle, the tenderhearted."

And there are other good things: the faithful attention to place, when it's accompanied by feeling and understanding, moves and convinces (when the feeling and understanding aren't there, the prose slides into what sounds like a Jaycee pamphlet on Growing Atlanta). Despite the book's length and occasional aimless wandering, it has coherence and there are signs of an ordering imagination, seeking for a shape beneath the accidents of experience. Scarlett's nightmare of homelessness and Ashley's comparison of the South's destruction to *Götterdämmerung* both suggest that the center of our desire is a sacred place, implacably threatened by private and public disaster. Scarlett's return to Tara without Rhett, her survival and determination, are an echo of her mother's strength (betrayed only in her deathbed delirium) in surviving the loss of her lover Philippe. Margaret Mitchell said repeatedly that her book was about those who had it and those who didn't: those who had it survived and the others went under. Survival is the obsessive and austere theme of the novel, and there's no denying the power of its insistent dramatization.

And yet, and yet . . . reading the book now *is* a burden, the hopelessly bad outweighing the honestly good. *GWTW* is much too long (Gavin Lambert reports that Selznick was struck by Sidney Howard's comment that Margaret Mitchell "did everything at least twice") and a great many readers of the book and viewers of the film have persistently and legitimately complained about the second half, After the War. The telling of the story, the author's control of point of view, is frequently uncertain: it's disconcerting not to be able to winnow out Margaret Mitchell's opinions from Scarlett's. And where is the famous Southern humor and irony, the broad comic swipes and grotesque exaggeration that have come to be the identifying birthmarks of our literature? It's all deadly earnest, without distancing or wit except when the Nigras shuffle on or Aunt Pitty flutters by (although there is one delicious moment when Margaret Mitchell produces the *ur*-version of the Tom Swiftie: " 'Pride! Pride tastes awfully good, especially when the crust is flaky and you put meringue on it,' said Scarlett tartly.")

The language of the narrative voice is generally functional and sure-footed and Margaret Mitchell was pleased with what she saw as the *stylelessness* of her book ("no fine writing . . . no philosophizing . . . a minimum of description . . . no grandiose thoughts, no hidden meanings, no symbolism, nothing sensational . . . ," quoted in Farr (but it stumbles to its knees when MM forgets her rigorous precepts, when she veers into the metaphoric or poetic: "Scarlett felt the fox of wrath and impotent hate gnaw at her vitals"; "Now he had set his varnished boots upon a bitter road where hunger tramped with tireless stride and wounds and weariness and heartbreak ran like yelping wolves"; "Confronted with the prospect of negro rule, the future seemed dark and hopeless, and the embittered state smarted and writhed helplessly," etc., etc.

These language problems are minor, though: the gaping crater at the center of the book is the sentimentality of vision, the narrowness of perception and sensibility that inevitably affect everything: dialogue, characterization, incident, meaning. Like most of us, I suppose, Margaret Mitchell saw herself as a "realist" and was distressed that a Macon garden club [the Macon Writers Club] had somehow got the notion before publication that *GWTW* "was a sweet lavender and old lace, Thomas Nelson Pagish story of the old South as it never was." MM may have believed with some justice that she had pictured the South more realistically than most earlier *romanciers* (her journalistic training gave her a healthy respect for solid fact, and she is good with *things*—houses, dresses, guns, towns), but the figures in her landscape, their emotions and inner lives, their motives and actions are preposterous and unintentionally comic—the fantasies of a fatally genteel and superficial imagination. The dialogue is a sure sign of this: Ashley and Melanie mouth an unbelievable Victorian pastry, Scarlett and Rhett endlessly repeat their first "witty" repartee, Gerald O'Hara and Rene Picard speak wiz ze foreign accents that Hollywood has instructed us in. The only vigor is found in the speech of the blacks, a minstrel show vigor, usually aimed toward an indulgent chuckle.

The surest evidence of the limitations of MM's sensibility crops up whenever the furthest reaches of the interior life must be exposed. All the stops are pulled out, and it's a strong reader who won't become queasy with embarrassment when he encounters these parodies of ladies' mag prose:

> Her eyes met his, hers naked with pleading, his remote as mountain lakes under gray skies. She saw in them defeat of her wild dream, her mad desires. . . . At his touch, he felt her change within his grip and there was madness and magic in the slim body he held and a hot soft glow in the green eyes which looked up at him. . . . Her body seemed to melt into his and, for a timeless time, they stood fused together as his lips took hers hungrily as if he could never have enough.

The biggest disappointment on coming back to *GWTW* is not discovering that it is a camp classic, with all this ridiculous melting and glowing, the rolling eyes and heaving sighs. One could skip over that if the fine courage and rebellious badness of Scarlett and Rhett that made the adolescent heart jump survived with "My dear, I don't give a damn," with the closing chapter. But twenty-five years have taken their toll, and steadier, soberer eyes regard that pair at the end. When closer attention is paid to what *really* happens, we have to admit the saddest falling off of all, the cruelest fantasy. It turns out that they weren't bad, irresponsible, selfish, free—some grand Promethean figures— they were going through a *phase*. When Scarlett finally comes to realize her roots are at Tara, when Rhett tries to return to society's embraces for dear

Bonnie's sake (by joining the church, patching matters up with Atlanta's *grandes dames*) and has long second thoughts about Charleston and its quieter, more lasting values, what we witness is not transformation through suffering (although both characters have certainly suffered plenty) but a simple victory for the home folks. What was billed as *conflict* ends in mechanical, predictable collapse, a rigged contest, the sheepish return to the fold of a chastened Scarlett and Rhett. What seemed to be a real issue in the book, freedom—of Scarlett and Rhett, of the Negroes—turns out to be no issue. Freedom, as the home folks know, is a *delusion* (Margaret Mitchell on blacks during Reconstruction: "the better class of them [scorned] freedom"). The world of this novel (of the novel of the popular imagination?) is truly deadend and claustrophobic because it flirts with the terrible ambiguities of freedom without ever really believing in its possibility. It sets up the illusion of danger and choice, trots out the dramatic gestures of Scarlett and Rhett, it titillates the audience, but that audience finds out what it has known all along. Once again it is comforted, assured of the rightness of its ideas of safety and propriety, secure in a cozy domestic scene that has blanked out the potentialities of tragedy. Rhett will come to Tara some day, won't he? Readers plagued Margaret Mitchell with this question, but it hardly needs asking.

Gone With the Wind and The Grapes of Wrath as Hollywood Histories of the Depression

By Thomas H. Pauly

The 1970s brought "pop-culture" into the halls of academia. Study of films reached a stature in universities almost everywhere that it had previously achieved in only those few which specialized in such things or which were regularly given to experimentation.

A worthwhile project of research in film history is reported in Thomas H. Pauly's discussion of Gone With the Wind *and* The Grapes of Wrath *as Hollywood histories of the Depression. John Steinbeck's great novel was obviously a book about the Depression. Margaret Mitchell's just as obviously was not. But, as Pauly points out, " 'Gone With the Wind' succeeded as well as it did in large part because it so effectively sublimated the audience's own response to the Depression."*

Miss Mitchell wrote to Rabbi Mordecai M. Thurman of Wilmington, North Carolina, February 6, 1937:

Many people have thought that I wrote "Gone With the Wind" as a parallel to the modern War and depression, but I had almost finished the book before the depression began. When I wrote it everyone thought the boom was here to stay. But I wrote about another world that blew up under the unsuspecting feet of our grandparents, without any idea that the world in which I lived would blow up shortly. Now that I look back on it I feel that the same qualities of courage are needed when, at any period of history, a world turns over. And the same qualities of gentleness and idealism are needed too.

Popular culture of the later Depression years was dominated by *Gone With the Wind* and *The Grapes of Wrath*. As novels, these two creations topped the best seller lists during 1936, 1937 and 1939. Interest in both works was then renewed in early 1940—perhaps even reached its greatest peak—when both opened as movies within weeks of one another *(Gone With the Wind* on December 15, 1939, and *The Grapes of Wrath* on January 24, 1940). Though both were tremendous box office successes, their critics responded to each quite different-ly. While the reviews of *Gone With the Wind* strove to top one another with accounts of all the gossip, glitter and money involved in the making of *Gone With the Wind*, those discussing *The Grapes of Wrath* stressed the outstanding quality of the film itself. "No artificial make-up, no false sentiment, no glamor stars mar the authentic documentary form of this provocative film," asserted Philip Hartung in his review of *The Grapes of Wrath* for *Commonweal*.[1] Similar-ly, Otis Ferguson was confident enough of the dissatisfaction *Gone With the Wind* would bring that he postponed going,[2] but, he opened his review entitled "Show for the People," "The word that comes in most handily for *The Grapes of Wrath* is magnificent . . . this is the best that has no very near comparison to date."[3] Despite the overwhelming critical preference for Ford's movie, however, it won only two Oscars (Best Director and Best Supporting Actress) in the 1940 balloting, whereas Selznick's extravaganza swept all the major awards in 1939 except one (Best Actor). Clearly the latter film was the people's choice. At issue here was an intense, unacknowledged debate over what the age preferred in its movies. In an era fraught with intense sociological upheaval, *Gone With the Wind* seemed consciously intended to project its audience into a realm of sentiment and nostalgia beyond the confines of actual experience. As Lincoln Kirstein complained in the opening paragraph of his scathing review for *Films:*

. . . history has rarely been told with even an approximation of truth in Hollywood, because the few men in control there have no interest in the real forces behind historical movements and the new forces that every new epoch sets into motion. *Gone With the Wind* deserves our attention because it is an over-inflated example of the usual, the false movie approach to history.[4]

Implicit in these remarks is a charge often leveled against the movies produced during this era. Critics and historians of the cinema repeatedly call attention to Hollywood's striking reluctance to address itself to the problems of the Depression. Nothing, they point out, could have been further from the bread lines and the deprivation photographed by Dorothea Lange than the social comedies of Lubitsch, the slapstick of the Marx Brothers, and the polished dance routines of Fred Astaire and Ginger Rogers. Nonetheless, as Andrew Bergman has asserted and then persuasively demonstrated in his book on films

---

1. Philip T. Hartung "Trampling Out the Vintage," *Commonweal* 31 (February 9, 1940), 348.

2. Otis Ferguson, "Out to Lunch," *The Film Criticism of Otis Ferguson,* ed. Robert Wilson (Philadelphia: Temple University Press, 1971), pp. 280–81.

3. Otis Ferguson, "Show for the People," *Film Criticism,* p. 282.

4. Lincoln Kirstein, "History in American Films *(Gone With the Wind)*" in *American Film Criticism From the Beginnings to Citizen Kane,* ed. Stanley Kauffmann (New York: Liveright, 1972), p. 372.

of the Depression, *We're in the Money,* "People do not escape into something they cannot relate to. The movies were meaningful because they depicted things lost or things desired. What is 'fantastic' in fantasy is an extension of something real."[5] In other words, the "dreams" the audience is said to have demanded, those for which they spent the little extra money they had, were not mere illusions or abstractions, but exciting, imaginative articulations of their greatest hopes and fears, their deepest doubts and beliefs. On this score, *Gone With the Wind* possesses a significant measure of both historical validity and importance. The fact that it was far and away the most successful film of the decade probably had less to do with the glittering surface that so annoyed the critics than the common ground it shared with *The Grapes of Wrath.* Though it was less daring and less accomplished than Ford's work as an artistic creation, *Gone With the Wind* was similarly preoccupied with the problem of survival in the face of financial deprivation and social upheaval. Both movies also demonstrate a nostalgic longing for the agrarian way of life which is ruthlessly being replaced by the fearful new economic forces of capitalism and industrialization. By way of extension, both reflect an intense concern for the devastating consequences of these conditions upon self-reliant individualism and family unity, two of America's most cherished beliefs. In each case, however, serious concern for these implications is dissipated into indulgent sentimentalism so that the audience's anxieties are alleviated rather than aggravated.

II

Even if the script had been available, *The Grapes of Wrath* dealt with issues that were too familiar and too painful to have been made during the early thirties. Yet, in deciding to produce a movie of this controversial novel at the time he did, Darryl Zanuck was sufficiently concerned about the specter of the Depression that he decided to mute and even eliminate some of the more charged aspects of Steinbeck's social criticism.[6] As Mel Gussow has explained, "For Zanuck *The Grapes of Wrath* and *How Green Was My Valley* were not really social documents, but family pictures of a very special kind; movies about families in stress."[7] Thus, the movie's emphasis falls upon the sentimental aspect of the conditions confronting the Joads. At the outset this takes the character of the loss of a home which deprives the family of its essential connection with the land. Tom's initial return assumes the character of a search for a place of refuge from the suffering and hostility he has been forced to

---

5. Andrew Bergman, *We're in the Money: Depression America and Its Films* (New York: New York University Press, 1971), p. xii.

6. For a discussion of these deletions, see George Bluestone, *Novels Into Film* (Berkeley: University of California Press, 1971), pp. 156–61. Warren French discusses other important differences between the novel and the film in *Filmguide to The Grapes of Wrath* (Bloomington: University of Indiana Press, 1973), pp. 22–27.

7. Mel Gussow, *Don't Say Yes Until I Finish Talking: A Biography of Darryl F. Zanuck* (Garden City, N.Y.: Doubleday, 1971), p. 95.

endure in prison and on his truck ride. That everything has changed is made clear by his encounter with Casy, but the full impact of this upheaval is registered only when he beholds the vacant, crumbling house in which he was raised and hears Muley's distracted tale of how his reverence for the land has been desecrated. "My pa was born here," he insists, "we was *all* born on it, and some of us got killed on it, and some died on it. And that's what makes it ourn. . . ."[8] Equally striking in this regard is the later scene where Grampa asserts, "I ain't a-goin' to California! This here's my country. I b'long *here*. It ain't no good—but it's mine,"[9] and then underlines his points by distractedly gripping his native soil.

In dramatizing the intense suffering these people experience, these lines serve the more important function of locating its source. The former agrarian way of life predicated upon man's intimate attachment to the land has given way to an economy of industrialization with its efficiency, practicality and inhumanity. For Tom and his fellow farmers, there is no possibility of retaliation. The fury that drives Muley to take up a gun produces only frustration and helpless dejection because there is no enemy to shoot. The man on the caterpillar turns out to be his neighbor who is trapped by the same problem of survival. The machines that level their homes, like the foreclosures which are delivered in dark, sinister automobiles, cannot be associated with particular individuals; they are the weapons of a system devoid of both personality and humanity.

> The Man: Now don't go blaming me. It ain't *my* fault.
> Son: Whose fault is it? . . .
> The Man: It ain't nobody. It's a company. He ain't anything
>   but the manager. . . .
> Muley (bewildered): Then who *do* we shoot?
> The Man: . . . Brother, I don't know.[10]

Deprived of the only home he has known, Tom Joad joins his family in their quest for a new one. However great may be their need for food and money, keeping the family together, Ma Joad makes clear, is the most pressing concern. She sees that nourishment involves the spirit as well and in the face of the increasingly depersonalized world confronting her, the shared concerns of the family offer the only remaining source of humanity. These become the basic issues by which the audience measures the significance of the ensuing trip to California. As Ford dramatizes them, the policemen who harass the Joads, the strawbosses who dictate to them, the thugs who break up the dances and union gatherings are, like the handbills that bring them to California, products of a

---

8. Nunnally Johnson, *The Grapes of Wrath,* in *Twenty Best Film Plays*, ed. John Gassner and Dudley Nichols (New York: Crown Publishers, 1943), p. 338. There may be minor variations between these quotes and the actual movie since this filmscript is not the final version.

9. *Twenty Best Film Plays,* p. 345.

10. *Twenty Best Film Plays,* p. 338.

sinister conspiracy beyond human control. They combine with the inhospitable landscape encountered to create an environment in which the family is unable to survive. Grampa and Gramma die before the destination is reached; Connie cannot stand up to the punishment inflicted upon him and flees; Casy is killed by the growers' hired guns; having avenged Casy's death, Tom is forced to flee for his life.[11]

The Grapes of Wrath, however, is more than a mere drama of defeat. The futility of individualism and the breakdown of the family furnish, in the end, a distinct source of optimism. Having witnessed the miserable living conditions in which the Joads have futilely struggled to endure—the filthy tent in the road camp, the concentration of starving people in Hooverville, the gloomy squalor of the cabin at the Keene ranch—the audience is now introduced to a utopia of cooperative socialism which has been as scrupulously sanitized of communism as it is of filth. In contrast to the derogatory view expressed earlier in the movie, working with the government is shown to offer a more valid prospect of salvation than fighting against the prevailing conditions; at the Wheat Patch camp the spirit of Tom's involvement with Casy is realized without the self-defeating violence and killing. Here, as George Bluestone notes, the Joads find "a kind of miniature planned economy, efficiently run, boasting modern sanitation, self-government, cooperative living and moderate prices."[12] Here people work together with the same automatic efficacy as the flush toilets. Cleanliness nourishes kindness, the caretaker explains with the serene wisdom of his kindly confident manner (does he remind you of FDR?).

Even the language has been changed to accord with this new society; one finds here not a shelter, a house or a home, but a "sanitary unit." Though this community has been conceived to accord with the depersonalized society outside its gates, it has also incorporated a basic respect for human dignity. It is a world characterized by its Saturday dance with its democratic acceptance, its well-controlled exclusion of the forces of anarchy, its ritualistic incorporation of the outdated family into a healthy new society. Above all, the Wheat Patch camp episode affords a bridge to the "new" ending Zanuck was moved to write for his movie.[13] As Tom and the Joad truck return to the outside world and strike out in different directions, they have no idea where they are going, but they all have renewed hope that they can find salvation just by being with "the people."

Rich fellas come up an' they die, an' their kids ain't no good, an' they die out. But we keep a'coming. We're the people that live. Can't nobody wipe us out. Can't nobody lick us. We'll go on forever, Pa. We're the people.[14]

---

11. The movie, for some reason, doesn't include Noah's desertion, though the scene was apparently filmed.

12. *Novels Into Film,* p. 165.

13. Mel Gussow reports that Zanuck wrote Ma's speech which concludes the film, p. 92.

14. *Twenty Best Film Plays,* p. 377.

Such conviction, Zanuck concluded, was not to be thwarted by the "No Help Wanted" originally indicated in Nunnally Johnson's screenplay,[15] so he gave them an open road—which, appropriately enough, leads off to nowhere.

III

The Grapes of Wrath is a fine movie, but it is considerably flawed. Furthermore, for all its "documentary" technique, it is badly distorted history. Its depiction of the plight of the migrant worker contributes considerably less to our understanding of the conditions of the Depression than its suspicion of big business, its manifest agrarianism, and, above all, its sentimental concern for the breakdown of the family. Given the striking commercial success of the movie, one cannot help wondering what it was the public went to see—an artistic masterpiece, a direct confrontation with the reality of the Depression, or its handling of the above concerns. Of the three, the last was perhaps the most important, for this was the one striking point of resemblance between it and the biggest box office movie of the decade. *Gone With the Wind* succeeded as well as it did in large part because it so effectively sublimated the audience's own response to the Depression. For them, the panoramic shot of the Confederate wounded littering the center of Atlanta was not a matter of fact but of feeling. All concern for the scene's historical authenticity simply vanished in the face of its dramatization of the sense of helplessness and devastation they themselves had experienced. Amidst these circumstances, Scarlett's subsequent return to Tara bears a striking resemblance to Tom's homecoming, in her quest for refuge from the adversities she has endured. Yet her expectation is shattered by the same scene of desolation that Tom discovered. For her also there is the same decaying ruin in place of the secure home she formerly knew. Tom's encounter with Muley seems almost a rerun of Scarlett's even more painful confrontation with her father, whose demented condition strikingly illustrates the magnitude of change resulting from the war's upheaval. As in *The Grapes of Wrath,* this breakdown in the integrity of the family is associated with the destruction of an agrarian way of life, which strikes at the very core of Scarlett's emotional being. The radish, encrusted with Tara's red soil, which Scarlett grips in the concluding scene of Part I, reverberates the significance of Grampa's earth clutching gesture in *Grapes of Wrath,* although *Gone With the Wind* makes this point more forceably when Scarlett throws Tara dirt at Wilkerson and, at the conclusion, hears her father's voice reminding her that "the land is the only thing that matters, the only thing that lasts."

Scarlett's response, however, marks an important point of difference. Unlike Tom Joad, who took to the road and sought to survive by working with his family, Scarlett resolves to be master of her destiny. Her moving declaration, "As

---

15. *Twenty Best Film Plays,* p. 377.

God is my witness . . . I'll never be hungry again,"* pits her will against the prevailing conditions. Her determination is such that she not only antagonizes the remnants of her family but she also exploits them; having slapped Suellen, she proceeds to steal her prospective husband, Frank Kennedy. Nonetheless, her actions are prompted by some of the same motives that carried the Joads to California.

In the characterization of Scarlett is to be found most of the complexity that *Gone With the Wind* possesses. As the reviewer of the *New York Times* observed, "Miss Leigh's Scarlett is the pivot of the picture."[16] Were she merely a bitch or strong willed feminist, the appeal of this movie would have been considerably diminished. In order to appreciate the intense response she elicited from the audience, one has to understand the particular way in which Scarlett's return to Tara and her subsequent commitment to rebuilding it qualifies her initial assertion of independence and results in a tragic misunderstanding that brings her downfall. In the opening scenes of the movie Scarlett wins the audience's sympathy for her determined spirit of rebellion. It is she who provides critical perspective on the glittering world of plantation society. Tara and Twelve Oaks, with their surrounding profusion of flowers and lush background sweep of countryside, are as magnificently attired as the people who congregate there and therefore perfect settings for the featured scenes of dressing and undressing, posturing and strutting. The main function of women in this world is providing ornamental beauty. The illusion of grace and elegance they sustain is predicated upon a harsh standard of propriety, a painfully tight corset. Parties become major moments in their lives in helping them to achieve their ordained goal of marriage, but their area of decision is limited to the choice of a dress or hat. Since the threat of a rival is the only war they can be expected to understand, they are all herded off to bedrooms to freshen their appearances and restore their frail energies while the men debate the future of the South. Given the stifling confinement of this role, Scarlett balks. Like the other women, she entertains a vision of marriage and consciously attends to her appearance, but, unlike them, she is determined to act on her wishes. Thus, while her rivals retire according to the convention of the submissive female, she slips downstairs to confront Ashley in the belief that he will not be able to resist her assault.

The war, which preempts Scarlett's fight for Ashley, dramatically affirms these and all the other deficiencies of this society, but as a "lost cause," it also forces Scarlett to determine her highest priorities. At first, she displays only a

---

*Editor's Note: This brief but important passage was carried almost verbatim from book to film. In the film it appears at the end of reel 6, which is also the end of Part I: "As God is my witness. . . As God is my witness. . . They're not going to lick me! . . . I'm going to live through this and when it's over I'll never be hungry again. . . no, nor any of my folks! . . . If I have to lie—or steal—or cheat—or *kill!* As God is my witness, I'll never be hungry again!" Sidney Howard, *GWTW: The Screenplay* (New York: [1980]), p. 243. The comparable passage of the novel occurs at p. 428.

16. Frank Nugent, *"Gone With the Wind," The New York Times Film Reviews: A One Volume Selection* (New York: Arno Press, 1971), p. 185.

selfish interest; its tragedy is for her a source of gain in relieving her of an unwanted husband. However, the flames of Atlanta which occasion a nightmare of emotion as they destroy the Old South, illuminate a new romantic potential in Scarlett's deepening relationship with Rhett. During their flight, their affair of convenience, predicated upon the same spirited, but pragmatic individualism which alienates them both from plantation society, achieves a new level of interdependency in the intense feelings they exchange and share. Having been stripped of her gentility, her vanity and finally her self-confidence, Scarlett is reduced to her greatest moment of need. At this point, Rhett's selfishness, which reveals itself to have been basically an emotional shield, also gives way. For the first time, both reach out for something greater than themselves. The result, however, is not a common understanding. Rhett proposes a marriage and a new future, only to discover that Scarlett prefers to retreat to the past. Survival, she has come to believe, lies in the red earth of Tara. Rejected, Rhett goes off to fight for the cause. Thus the situation which brought Rhett and Scarlett together propels them along separate paths in search of ideals which ironically the war is at that moment destroying. Though they survive to marry one another, the decisions forced by the war constitute an insurmountable breach which the conclusion of the movie simply reaffirms, as Rhett goes off to Charleston in search of "the calm dignity life can have when it's lived by gentle folks, the genial grace of days that are gone," while Scarlett heeds her father's words calling her back to Tara.

In his concerted effort to reproduce the novel as thoroughly as possible, Selznick felt that the increased emphasis he accorded to Tara was one of the few points of departure. "I felt," he explained in one of his memos, "that the one thing that was really open to us was to stress the Tara thought more than Miss Mitchell did."[17] For him, Scarlett's character was grounded in Tara, in agrarianism and the family just as the identity of the Joads was. Yet, in according it much the same meaning, he dramatized its tragic consequence quite differently. Scarlett's vow never to be hungry again as she grips the radish symbolizing Tara's agrarian heritage at the end of Part I moves the audience with its stirring determination, but this vow is severely qualified by the scene's logic. Quite simply, Tara, or "terra," cannot provide the nourishment she requires.[18] Her vomiting up the devoured radish is strikingly emblematic of Tara's true value. In the first place, the fact that the earth is red is an obvious signal that the soil sustains crops with great difficulty. Without the slaves and strongwilled owners, Tara is not even capable of generating enough capital to pay its taxes. The main reason for Scarlett's determination to return to Tara, however, transcends

---

17. David O. Selznick, *Memo From David O. Selznick,* ed. Rudy Behlmer (New York: Viking Press, 1972), p. 212.

18. Despite this meaning which emerges from the dramatized pronunciation of Tara, the plantation was most probably named after the famous hill in County of Meath which for centuries was the seat of the ancient kings of Gerald O'Hara's native Ireland.

all these considerations. Tara is home—its essence is to be found more in the echoing sound of her father's voice and the heart-tugging strains of Max Steiner's music.[19] For her, Tara is the sphere of her father's influence, a refuge where matters were firmly under control and she was treated with tolerance and indulgence.[20] Yet this is equally foolish, for she discovers that her father has been broken by the war and now relies on her for the consolation she has expected him to provide. Nowhere are the disadvantages of Tara revealed more dramatically than in the buckboard visit of Jonas Wilkerson whose association with the new economic forces supplanting agrarianism recalls the nameless men of *The Grapes of Wrath* in their sinister cars. Since money has become the only source of power, Scarlett must seek beyond Tara for survival. Scarlett appears to marry Frank Kennedy to pay the taxes on Tara, but she obviously sees that he is associated with the prospering forces of industrialization. Consequently, in becoming his wife, she really becomes a businesswoman. These conflicting allegiances to Tara and to her lumber mill, place Scarlett in the paradoxical position of shunning the role of wife and mother in order to uphold her passionate commitment to family and the home. Her identification with business and its ruthless practices now loses her the audience's sympathy, yet because she never understands the character and consequences of what she is doing, she proves more tragic than villainous. Her determined quest for the greatest margin of profit is not to be understood as her predominant aim. Much more essential is her desire that Tara be rebuilt. To do so is not only to eliminate the desperate state of poverty to which she had been reduced, but also to restore the spiritual strength of her family home. Only the audience, however, comprehends the hidden cost. Frank becomes her lackey and her marriage no more than a working partnership. She herself becomes a social pariah. Most important, Scarlett begins to die from emotional starvation, as her business absorbs her energies without providing any of the attention and compassion she has always craved. The sorrow she drowns with liquor following Kennedy's death is neither anguish nor a pained sense of confinement—it is a strange lack of feeling.

Once again Rhett comes to offer her salvation. Despite his manifest contempt for propriety, Rhett's invasion of her privacy and his cynical proposal of marriage are joyfully welcomed because they offer Scarlett an opportunity to escape her business and enjoy her own home. Unfortunately, the seeds of her undoing have already been sown. The self-reliant determination of her struggles has rendered her temperamentally incapable of filling the role of the devoted wife she would like to be. Rhett's gifts—the house and even Bonnie—all simply deprive her of the thing she needs most—a challenge. For this she

---

19. The Tara theme song which echoes through the movie subsequently became a popular song entitled, appropriately enough, "My Own True Love."

20. To some extent, Scarlett's failure to find a satisfying husband can be traced to the fact that none was able to measure up to the image she had of her father when she was a young girl.

returns to Ashley whose embodiment of the devoted husband she must destroy in order to win. Her visit with the dying Melanie causes her finally to realize this as well as the fact that Rhett is a much worthier ideal. Sensing her folly, she rushes home to find that he has indeed become unreachable. As a mother without a child, a wife without a husband, Scarlett is left by Selznick at the end of the picture turning to a home she can inhabit only in her dreams. The famous concluding line of the novel "tomorrow is another day" is almost drowned out in the movie by the emotionally charged flashback scene of Tara with Gerald O'Hara's words echoing in the background.[21] Thus Scarlett stands at the end a strong-willed individualist in possession of all the wealth the audience could imagine, yet no better off than they because of her inability to realize her impossible dream of a happy home and a loving family.

IV

At the height of the Depression, thirteen million workers were unemployed. People who had enjoyed marked prosperity during the twenties suddenly found themselves struggling just to stay alive. Equally troubling was their inability to comprehend the reasons for this devastating reversal. As Leo Gurko has observed. "The decade of the 30's was uniquely one in which time outran consciousness . . . the misery of the country was equalled only by its bewilderment."[22] The absence of checks and balances in the market place which was supposed to provide the ordinary citizen with opportunity seemed only to be making the rich richer and the poor poorer. Everywhere big business seemed to be prospering. The general lack of knowledge about those who ran it or how it operated simply added to the pervasive belief that these companies were somehow profiting at the expense of the suffering individual. Similarly frustrating was the helplessness and loss of dignity caused by unemployment. No longer was the working man able to fill his expected role as head of the household. Either he could not support his family or he was forced to strike out on his own in order to do so. Consequently, his traditional source of consolation now only contributed to his distress. In the cities, where these problems were most acute, the idea of "getting back to the land" seemed to offer a ready-made solution. As Broadus Mitchell explains:

In the cities unemployment emphasized crowding, squalor, and cold; the bread lines were visual reproaches. In the country, on the other hand, was ample room. Further, in the cities, workers won bread by an indirect process which for some reason had broken down. But life in the rural setting was held to be synonymous with raising family food. The thing was simple, direct, individually and socially wholesome.[23]

---

21. For its demonstration of the quintessential spirit of the Hollywood ending, the recent four-hour ABC-TV special on "The Movies" concluded with this scene.

22. Leo Gurko, *The Angry Decade* (New York: Dodd Mead & Co., 1947), p. 13.

23. Broadus Mitchell, *Depression Decade: From New Era Through New Deal, 1929–1941* (New York: Rinehart & Co., 1947), p. 107.

This solution, of course, turned out to be most impractical. Yet it reveals the direction in which the people's anxieties were working. Coming at the end of the Depression as they did, *Gone With the Wind* and *The Grapes of Wrath* appealed to viewers who had lived through this ordeal. Both succeeded in large measure because they so effectively tapped the emotional wellsprings of this urban audience who were their chief patrons. Repeatedly the viewer found himself confronting these same troubling issues but they were presented in such a way that he was reassured that everything would work out just as he hoped it would. At the same time neither could have been as compelling had this sentimentality not been treated with a subtlety and understanding notably lacking in similar films like *Our Daily Bread*.

Vivien Leigh, Clark Gable, Margaret Mitchell, David Selznick, and Olivia de Havilland at a party given by the Atlanta Women's Press Club at the Piedmont Driving Club, December 14, 1939.

Margaret Mitchell boarding the Southern Railway's *Crescent Limited* in December 1941 on her way to christen the U.S.S. *Atlanta*.

Miss Mitchell sent this 1944 snapshot of herself with some Army entertainers camped in Piedmont Park to Leodel Coleman of Statesboro, Georgia, a Marine Combat Correspondent in the Pacific.

The last photograph of Margaret Mitchell, a snapshot taken in Piedmont Park in the summer of 1949.

Margaret Mitchell: Gone With the Wind and War and Peace

By Harold K. Schefski

"So many critics," Margaret Mitchell wrote Dr. Mark Allen Patton, July 11, 1936, "have been kind enough, flattering enough to bracket 'Gone With the Wind' with 'War and Peace,' saying of course that it didn't approach it but was the nearest thing to it they could think of. I've read review after review saying the same thing and have realized with a sense of growing horror that eventually I'm going to have to read 'War and Peace.'"

Many reviewers did indeed make quick surface comparisons of Gone With the Wind *and* War and Peace *and James Michener compares Miss Mitchell's novel to Anna Karenina in considerable detail in his introduction to Macmillan's 1975 "anniversary edition" of GWTW. There was no thorough comparison of GWTW and* War and Peace *available until this one by Harold K. Schefski of the University of Georgia faculty was published in* Southern Studies *for fall 1980.*

When *Gone With the Wind* first appeared in 1936 book reviewers and critics everywhere equated it with Tolstoy's *War and Peace.* Edwin Granberry, writing for the *New York Sun,* noted that "in its picture of a vast and complex social system in time of war, *Gone With the Wind* is most closely allied to Tolstoy's *War and Peace.*"[1] Similarly, the editors of the *New York Daily News* asserted that "We've taken *Gone With the Wind* from its regular place in American fiction and parked it alongside Tolstoy's *War and Peace. . . .*"[2]

In view of such frequent commentaries about the general similarities of the two panoramic novels, Margaret Mitchell was obliged to answer her critics. On July 9, 1936, she wrote the following response to Donald Adams, who four days

---

1. Finis Farr, *Margaret Mitchell of Atlanta* (New York, 1965), 129. Granberry's review was published on 30 June 1936. It represents one of the more interesting commentaries on *GWTW.* Subsequently, Granberry became one of Mitchell's closest friends.

2. Farr, p. 178.

earlier had reviewed *GWTW* in the *New York Times Book Review:* "One of my Russian friends has upbraided me frequently, saying that the life in old Russia was more akin to that in the old South than any he had ever known—that the old Russian type of mind was more peculiarly Georgian than a Georgian could realize. But the Russian mind, in fiction, at least, still defies me."[3]

To a large extent this statement typifies Margaret Mitchell's ambivalent attitude toward Tolstoy and the other Russian classics. On the one hand, she realizes that the nineteenth-century Russian writers must serve as the ultimate yardstick for all great class-oriented literature—including her own work. On the other hand, she candidly confesses that though familiar with the Russians, she has never been able to fathom them. The roots of Miss Mitchell's ambivalence can be traced to her formative years, when her parents supplied her with an appropriate reading list and rewarded her accordingly: "Most of my 'classical' reading was done before I was twelve, aided by five, ten and fifteen cents a copy bribes from my father and abetted by the hair brush or mother's number three slipper. She just about beat the hide off me for not reading Tolstoy or Thackeray or Jane Austen but I preferred to be beaten. Since growing up, I've tried again to read 'War and Peace' and couldn't."[4]

Upon attaining adulthood, Miss Mitchell rebelled against these unpleasant childhood associations, rejecting Tolstoy and the other Russian classics, as an adult might refuse to swallow the bitter medicine that parents forced him to take as a child. The nature of Miss Mitchell's rebellion is captured best of all in this statement: "But one of the great joys of growing up, of getting older is being able and unafraid to speak your own mind. And maturity descended upon me in the very moment when I frankly said that I thought Tolstoy and most of the Russian writers were the damned dullest, most muddleheaded, confused thinking bunch I'd ever tried to read."[5]

Mitchell's attitude toward Tolstoy and the other Russians, however, becomes contradictory when leading critics of the 1930s begin to compare *GWTW* favorably with Tolstoy's *War and Peace.* This juxtaposition makes her so proud that she can hardly restrain her enthusiasm. To Granberry she expresses her elation with these remarks: "How much space you gave me! Good heavens, I can never thank you enough for that! And when I read along to the breathtaking remark about being bracketed with Tolstoy, Hardy, Dickens, and Undset—well, I gave out."[6] In a similar vein, Mitchell writes to a reader, Dr. Mark Allen Patton, regarding her joy at being compared with Tolstoy: "I gave a yelp of delight and leaped up and pranced at your remarks about *War and Peace* . . . So many critics have been kind enough, flattering enough to bracket *Gone With*

---

3. Richard Harwell, ed., *Margaret Mitchell's "Gone With the Wind" Letters,* 1936–1949 (New York, 1976), 32.

4. Harwell, p. 32.

5. Harwell, p. 42. This citation comes from a letter dated 11 July 1936 to Dr. Mark Allen Patton.

6. Harwell, p. 28. The letter to Granberry is dated 8 July 1936.

the Wind with *War and Peace,* saying of course that it didn't approach it but was the nearest thing to it they could think of."[7]

In contemporary literary criticism the comparative analysis of *GWTW* and *War and Peace* has not gone beyond the elementary stage represented by Margaret Mitchell's contradictory views on Tolstoy's novel and by the often far too generalized comments about the similarities between the two great works. The latter usually refer to their common broad canvas or their shared theme of individual fate in the midst of social upheaval. It is the aim of this paper to amplify on this comparison through the presentation and discussion of specific comparative aspects that have up to now not been elucidated and deserve to be considered in order to enhance the enjoyment of both novels. Undertaking this assignment, we hope to fill a major gap in comparative criticism.

Before we proceed with our analysis, it is imperative to dispel the notion of some critics (such as Floyd Watkins in his article *"GWTW* as Vulgar Literature") that Mitchell's novel is weak, insipid, and unworthy of a prominent place in American literature.[8] The first reaction to such an unfair condemnation of the work is to cite in refutation H. G. Wells' remark about *GWTW:* "One hardly dares say it, but I believe *GWTW* is better shaped than many of the revered classics."[9] There exists an even more effective endorsement—Leo Tolstoy himself. After all, if anyone is to be offended by the audacity to compare *GWTW* with *War and Peace,* it should be Tolstoy. Yet, there is every reason to believe that Tolstoy would have looked favorably upon *GWTW* and would not have felt insulted by such a comparison.

Support for this conviction comes from Tolstoy's essay *What Is Art* (1896), where he writes: "There is one indubitable indication separating real art from its counterfeit, namely, the infectiousness of art."[10] Who can conceive of a work of art in all world literature (with the possible exception of the Bible) that was as infectious or contagious as *GWTW*? Its popularity cuts across the lines of both nationality (some twenty-nine translations attest to this) and age (Mitchell characterizes its appeal as ranging from "the five year old to the ninety-five year old").[11]

Moreover, Tolstoy would have undoubtedly applauded the author's own justification for her novel's popularity, which she sums up as follows: "Despite its length and many details it is basically just a simple yarn of fairly simple people. There's no fine writing, there's no philosophizing, there is a minimum of description, there are no grandiose thoughts, there are no hidden meanings, no

---

7. Harwell, p. 42. Also taken from the letter to Mark A. Patton.

8. Floyd C. Watkins, *"Gone With the Wind* as Vulgar Literature." *Southern Literary Journal,* 2 (Spring, 1970), 103.

9. Farr, p. 202.

10. Lev Tolstoi, *Sobranie sochinenii v dvadstati tomax.* Vol. 15, (Moscow, 1964), 179. In Russian the title of the article is "Chto takoe Iskusstvo." I have translated this citation into English.

11. Farr, p. 164.

symbolism, nothing sensational."[12] Indeed, it would not even be presumptuous to conclude that the great Russian writer might have included *GWTW* within his second category of true art—that of universal art. To be classified as such, according to Tolstoy, a work of art must "transmit the simplest feelings of common life, but such, always, as are accessible to all men in the entire world."[13]

Since *GWTW* fulfills this description most precisely, one can see Tolstoy and Mitchell as sharing a belief in simplicity and infectiveness as the two most essential criteria of an artistic work. Their definition clashes sharply with Watkins' contention that "greatness and popularity are more likely to be contradictory than congenial."[14] Thus having established Tolstoy's hypothetical position on *GWTW* as favorable, we may now ignore the protests of some effete critics and proceed with a comparative analysis of the two great novels.

The first problem that arises in a comparative study of *GWTW* and *War and Peace* is to determine genre. Confronted by two works which each contain more than one thousand pages, the critic's first response is to try to place them into some kind of framework. Understandably, the two most commonly suggested genre classifications are historical novel and family chronicle. The term "historical novel" refers to the monumental historical event described in each work. Tolstoy's *War and Peace* focuses on Napoleon's invasion of Russia in 1812 and his capture of Moscow—the embodiment of the Russian national spirit. It culminates with a rejuvenated national effort to evict the intruder. On each side of this great event, Tolstoy depicts seven years of Russian public and private life so that the novel comprehensively treats the historical period 1805 to 1820.

In a parallel manner Margaret Mitchell deals with the War Between the States (1861–1865) in *GWTW*. As Tolstoy did, she first prefaces the historical event with a description of private life—the bucolic, elegant existence of the Southern aristocracy prior to the war—and then follows the years of battle with a lengthy discussion of reconstruction (1865–1873), concentrating on the difficulties in the public and private sectors as peace is restored. And so, Mitchell completely adheres to the Tolstoyan model by describing an historical event, its forebodings and repercussions. In this sense both works meet the requirements of an historical novel.

The term "family chronicle" also serves as an appropriate designation for both *War and Peace* and *GWTW*. Each writer delineates the fate of particular families, showing how they fare in the private realm, as the upheaval of a major historical crisis disfigures the public sphere. Tolstoy introduces three families—the Rostovs, the Bolkonskys, and the Kuragins, and traces the rise and fall of their destinies as Russia is vanquished by Napoleon. Similarly, Mitchell also poses three significant families—the O'Haras, the Hamiltons, and the Wilkeses.

---

12. Farr, p. 164.
13. Tolstoi, "What Is Art," p. 192. I have translated this text from the Russian.
14. Watkins, p. 103.

Moreover, both novelists create an additional unattached figure—Tolstoy's Pierre Bezukhov, the illegitimate son of the wealthy Count Bezukhov, and Mitchell's Rhett Butler, the rebellious son of a highly respectable, aristocratic Charlestonian family, who has been disowned by his father for behavior unworthy of a Southern gentleman.

If in the public realm *War and Peace* and *GWTW* present a great historical event and in the private sector they describe families who are exposed to an historical calamity, then the synthesis of the two perspectives is still a third genre—the *Bildungsroman,* where the response of family members to an historical event is plotted and assessed on a positive or negative scale. In his article "A Pattern of Character Development in *War and Peace:* Prince Andrej," John Hagan sums up the traits that define Tolstoy's novel as a *Bildungsroman:*

If we start with the hypothesis that the deepest and most important affinities of this novel are with the nineteenth century *Bildungsroman*—of which it is, perhaps, the supreme example—I think we will come close to discovering the mechanism, the coherent formal principles controlling the entire vast structure. *War and Peace,* I submit, is a gigantic novel of education, centering not on one protagonist but on five, who are divided among three families: Prince Andrej Bolkonskij and his sister Mar'ja; Nikolaj Rostov and his sister Nataša and Pierre Bezuxov. What Tolstoj is principally doing is tracing, against the background of the momentous events of 1805–1820, when the national character of Russia itself was emerging and being tested and its destiny being decided by the events of history, the moral and intellectual development of these five principal men and women, each of whom in his own way is growing toward fuller embodiment of one or more of the values to which Tolstoj gives his allegiance and which, by means of the stories of these five characters, he is progressively defining.[15]

Hagan points out further that all the remaining characters in the novel are static; that is, they exist only to put the five basic characters in perspective and to affect them in some way. For example, Tolstoy's ideal figure Platon Karataev, with his teachings about brotherly love, the simple life, and non-resistance to evil, serves as the beacon for Pierre's ultimate spiritual transformation, leading him to his highest point of development.

In *GWTW* the characteristics of the *Bildungsroman* are also easy to detect. Generally speaking, Mitchell's characters, like Tolstoy's, live, mature, and change under the watchful eye of the reader. However, she gives a significant educational development to only two of the four primary figures—Scarlett

---

15. John Hagan, "A Pattern of Character Development in *War and Peace,* Prince Andrej," *Slavic and East European Journal,* 13 (1969), 165. Hagan has also written two other articles devoted to character development in *War and Peace:* "Patterns of Character Development in Tolstoy's *War and Peace:* Nicholas, Natasha, and Mary," *PMLA,* 84 (1969), 235–44 and "A Pattern of Character Development in Tolstoj's *War and Peace:* P'er Bezuxov," *Texas Studies in Literature and Language,* 11 (1969), 985–1011. It should be noted here that the reason for the varied spellings of character names is that Hagan is using different transliteration system for each article. Thus, Princess Mary sometimes appears as Mar'ja, Nicholas as Nikolaj, Pierre as P'er, and Natasha as Nataša.

O'Hara and Rhett Butler. Ashley and Melanie Wilkes, on the other hand, are equivalent to Tolstoy's static figures, since they influence the destinies of Scarlett and Rhett, while they themselves go unchanged. On her deathbed Melanie still remains the same sweet lady she had been when she accepted Ashley's proposal in the beginning of the work. Similarly, Ashley never evolves beyond the role of a Southern Hamlet, doomed forever to reflect upon a time and a way of life that are "gone with the wind."

Against the background of these two figures, Rhett and especially Scarlett undergo a dramatic development which can be measured in a systematic way. Rhett changes from a suave, sarcastic, aristocratic gentleman who has rejected his past buried deep in Southern tradition, only to return gradually to his roots, first by entering the war during the waning moments (on the Southern side), and subsequently, by seeking to raise his daughter within the parameters of traditional Southern life. Even Bonnie's tragic death toward the novel's end does not halt his return to conformity. He leaves Scarlett ostensibly to renew his familial bonds in Charleston. Thus, Rhett's pattern of education follows to a large degree the archetype of the prodigal son, who rebels, pursues a life of debauchery, and ultimately returns to the original fold.

Since Mitchell obviously devotes more attention to Scarlett's development than to any other character in *GWTW*, her path of education is clearly the more complex. Dawson Gaillard, in her interesting article "*GWTW* as *Bildungsroman*," best describes Scarlett's maturation process, by associating her forms of dress with her steady progression to a higher level of self-knowledge and awareness:

These scenes—Scarlett in a party dress, Scarlett in a new bonnet and a widow's dress, and Scarlett in rags hearing that she is loved because she is courageously ruthless—are significant measuring points in the dramatization of Scarlett's maturation from a petulant girl to a reflective adult. Like the South in which she lives, Scarlett endures a violent disruption of the pattern of life that she has enjoyed. And along with endurance, knowledge of herself comes to Scarlett. Because of the disruption she learns the harsher realities of life and of her own nature.[16]

Although the level of Scarlett's education is less spiritual than that of the Tolstoyan heroes Prince Andrew and Pierre, she, nevertheless, like all of Tolstoy's figures, has embarked on a quest for self-identity, and the results of her passage are ambivalent in character. In one sense Scarlett manages to break away from a life of self-effacement required of all Southern girls of her generation. Such a path is characteristic of the two closest women in her life—Ellen and Melanie. As a consequence of her deviation, Scarlett becomes a successful businesswoman—a position unheard of for females of her generation. In

16. Dawson Gaillard, "*Gone With the Wind* as Bildungsroman," *The Georgia Review*, 28 (Spring 1974), 10.

another sense, Scarlett's aggressive business-like nature drives Rhett away, especially after his renewed acceptance of traditional Southern life which views women as shrinking violets. The price of Scarlett's independence and full development, according to Gaillard is the loss of her man.

To summarize, both *War and Peace* and *GWTW* represent a hybrid of three literary genres—the historical novel, the family chronicle, and the *Bildungsroman*. The latter best of all captures the true essense of the novels—an evaluation of people as they change in response to historical necessity.

The subject of theme in *War and Peace* and *GWTW* provides a second topic deserving of comparison. Farr's definition of *GWTW*'s theme as a story that "glorified a conquered but resisting, never-really surrendering people" not only bears considerable merit for Mitchell's novel, but also can be applied effectively to *War and Peace*.[17] Just as *GWTW* demonstrates the collective determination of an underdog group of Southerners to wage a hopeless battle in defense of their way of life, so *War and Peace* shows the heroic efforts of the Russian people to protect their homeland from an enemy, whose battle preparation and war experience are far superior.

This similarity of themes becomes even more apparent when one realizes that both Tolstoy and Mitchell present them in an anti-historical light. That is, each writer conducts a polemic with the hackneyed textbook view of these two great historical events. Tolstoy takes Napoleon, who, according to historical analysts, was one of the greatest figures of all time, and courageously reverses judgment on him, asserting that such so-called "great men" do not determine history. On the contrary, they serve merely as the pawns of historical necessity, and it is only the height of vanity that causes them to suspect that they as individuals can affect the course of history. In the final analysis, Tolstoy believes that history's flow can be altered only by the swarming behavior of the rank and file soldiers, who unpredictably change the course of battle when they display unexpected acts of bravery.

Mitchell's anti-historical position is also not difficult to elucidate. Directing her attack against historians who have seen the Civil War exclusively from the Union point of view, Mitchell effectively outlines the Confederate position. She supports her argument by emphasizing the crudity and cruelty of the invading Northern troops, who needlessly pilfer Southern cemeteries and terrorize Southern women. How contrary this picture appears to the traditional textbook accounts of the Federal troops as liberators of the oppressed and worthy representatives of the lawful national government! In short, Mitchell and Tolstoy in the broadest perspective both contribute a long awaited dissident voice to the canonical historical interpretation of these vital historical events. Their efforts achieve a necessary balance after decades of bias and slanted viewpoints.

On an individual plane *War and Peace* and *GWTW* offer a second common

17. Farr, p. 214.

theme. This pertains to the discussion of individual survival in the wake of a public trauma and social chaos. Tolstoy's formula for survival is contained in Pierre, who, in his struggle to survive as a prisoner of war, transforms the negative circumstances into a positive experience:

All Pierre's daydreams now turned on the time he would be free. Yet subsequently, and for the rest of his life, he thought and spoke with enthusiasm of that month of captivity, of those irrecoverable, strong, joyful sensations, and chiefly the complete peace of mind and inner freedom he experienced during those weeks.[18]

In Scarlett O'Hara, Mitchell also creates a character who is stimulated by the survival struggle. Writing to Edwin Granberry in 1936, Mitchell reveals her original intentions for the Scarlett figure:

She [Scarlett] just seemed to me to be a normal person thrown into abnormal circumstances and doing the best she could, doing what seemed to her the practical thing. The normal human being in a jam thinks, primarily, of saving his own hide, and she valued her hide in a thoroughly normal way.[19]

In contrast to Pierre and Scarlett, who view their struggle with adversity as a challenge, other characters of Tolstoy and Mitchell cannot meet the survival test with determination. Such figures are doomed to die. For example, Prince Andrew perishes because he is basically cynical about life and does not believe that the effort to survive is worth expending. Melanie and Karataev do not survive because they are too passive and meek to cope with the immoral side of life; adversity is free to trample them because they are too weak to oppose the forces of evil. Although each is imbued with an admirable inner strength, this is not sufficient for survival. It must be transformed into an external strength that confronts life's evil with a powerful will. Perhaps Margaret Mitchell is speaking for Tolstoy as well when she amplifies on the topic of survival in *GWTW*:

If the novel has a theme, the theme is that of survival. What makes some people able to come through catastrophes and others, apparently just as able, strong, and brave, go under? It happens in every upheaval. Some people survive; others don't. What qualities are in those who fight their way through triumphantly that are lacking in those who go under? . . . I only know that the survivors used to call that quality "gumption." So I wrote about the people who had gumption and the people who didn't.[20]

Parallels between *War and Peace* and *GWTW* become more specific than those of genre or thematics, with both Atlanta and Moscow destined to prevail....

---

18. Leo Tolstoy, *War and Peace,* trans. A. Maude, ed. George Gibian (New York, 1966), 1123.

19. Harwell, p. 29. This citation comes from Mitchell's letter to Granberry dated 8 July 1936.

20. Macmillan firm ed., *Margaret Mitchell and Her Novel 'Gone With the Wind,'* (New York, 1936), 16–17.

Apparently, Tolstoy and Mitchell prize their respective cities so highly as symbols of traditional cultures that they both decide to elevate them in stature by equating them with the heroines of their respective works. When Napoleon, perched on Poklonny Hill, gazes down at the vulnerable Moscow below, Tolstoy suggests the image of a woman about to be violated, attributing to the French leader this comment: "A town captured by the enemy is like a maid who has lost her honor."[21] This statement echos, as Hagan astutely points out, the scene two books previously, where the virginal Natasha is compromised by the worthless rake Anatolie Kuragin:

Just as Natasha, who has been virtually identified in the scene at Uncle's with the spirit of the Russian land and people . . . is nearly violated by Anatolie, so the Russian land and people are actually violated by Napoleon, who at one point even thinks of Moscow, spread out before him, as a beautiful woman whom he is about to rape. The personal and national calamities each become metaphors of the other.[22]

The parallel of Scarlett and Atlanta, on the other hand, is more than just a metaphor; it is explicitly stated. As Mitchell explains in a summary of *GWTW* sent to the publisher Macmillan, she wishes to create an obvious juxtaposition which the reader cannot miss: "I thought I would write a story of a girl who was somewhat like Atlanta—part of the old South; part of the new South; [How] she rose with Atlanta and fell with it, and how she rose again. What Atlanta did to her; what she did to Atlanta. . . ."[23]

As the widow Scarlett (Part II, Ch. VIII) goes from Tara to Atlanta to live with Aunt Pittypat, Mitchell specifies that the traits linking Scarlett with Atlanta are character and age:

But Atlanta was of her own generation, crude with the crudities of youth and as head-strong and impetuous as herself. . . .

In a space of time but little longer than Scarlett's seventeen years, Atlanta had grown from a single stake driven in the ground into a thriving small city of ten thousand that was the center of attention for the whole state. . . .

Scarlett had always liked Atlanta for the very same reasons that made Savannah, Augusta and Macon condemn it. Like herself, the town was a mixture of the old and new in Georgia, in which the old often came off second best in its conflicts with the self-willed and vigorous new. Moreover, there was something personal, exciting about a town that was born—or at least christened—the same year she was christened.[24]

---

21. Tolstoy, *War and Peace*, p. 971.

22. J. Hagan, "Patterns of Character Development in Tolstoy's *War and Peace*: Nicholas, Natasha, and Mary," *PMLA*, 84 (1969), 241.

23. Harwell, p. xxxi. Herschel Brickell was the first critic to allude to the juxtaposition between Scarlett and Atlanta. He mentioned it in his review of the novel entitled "Margaret Mitchell's First Novel, 'Gone With the Wind': A Fine Panorama of the Civil War Period," published in the *New York Post* on 30 June 1936.

24. Margaret Mitchell, *Gone With the Wind*, (New York, 1936), 141–43.

Of all the parallels in character development between *War and Peace* and *GWTW*, none correspond more exactly than the comparative traits of Melanie and Princess Mary. Yet, critics up to now have never mentioned this resemblance. Although they are swift to note a similarity between Thackeray's Amelia and Melanie, they do not dream of comparing Mary and Melanie, despite many striking parallels.[25]

First of all, both women are described as physically unattractive, with few potential suitors. However in both cases, this external plainness belies an inward radiance and spiritual integrity that affect all people with whom they come in contact.

Secondly, each woman more than all else dreams about motherhood, though the realization of this desire proves a source of great difficulty. Melanie, a physically weak specimen, has already ruined her health by bearing one child. The second pregnancy, which occurs toward the novel's end, costs her her life.

Princess Mary's desire for a family life is blocked by her obligation to care for her senile father. Thoughts of children which at times pervade her conscious mind, cause Mary considerable guilt, for she believes that they are somehow tied to a subconscious wish for her father's death.

Melanie and Princess Mary are equally comfortable with children. Melanie looks after not just her own son Beau, but also cares for Scarlett's children. Princess Mary, long deprived of the fulfillment of her strong maternal instinct, channels her wish for children into the upbringing of Prince Andrew's motherless son Nicholas, before she ultimately becomes the wife of Nicholas Rostov and mother of his children.

Besides their common traits of physical unattractiveness and heightened maternal instincts, Princess Mary and Melanie share a role as devout Christian women. For example, Princess Mary, before Andrew's departure for Austerlitz, presents him with an icon, saying: "Against your will He will save and have mercy on you and bring you to Himself, for in Him alone is truth and peace."[26] Such a strong religious orientation makes Mary adopt the traits of loyalty and self-effacement, especially where her father is concerned. For example, when Mademoiselle Bourienne criticizes the old man's moodiness, Mary responds as any obedient daughter would be expected to: "Ah, dear friend, I have asked you never to warn me of the humor my father is in. I do not allow myself to judge him and would not have others do so."[27]

Like Princess Mary, Melanie also integrates loyalty and obedience into her Christianity. Her finest manifestation of these virtues comes when she turns the other cheek to the confirmed rumors about Scarlett's attempt to steal Ashley away from her. To squelch these rumors, Melanie at a public dinner party grasps Scarlett's hand in a gesture of solidarity. She can never forget how

25. Farr, p. 125.
26. Tolstoy, *War and Peace,* p. 110.
27. Tolstoy, p. 98.

Scarlett saved her life during the evacuation of Atlanta, and her devotion to Scarlett for this remains in force despite public efforts to draw them apart.

No Christian virtue that Melanie and Mary share is as strong as their love of charity. Princess Mary receives the wandering religious pilgrims at the back entrance to the house, where they are fed and cared for. As Prince Andrew tells Pierre, this is the only form of disobedience before her father that Mary permits herself: "Those are Mary's God's folk, . . . This is the one matter in which she disobeys him. He orders these pilgrims to be run away, but she receives them."[28]

Princess Mary's concern for the religious wanderers strikingly resembles Melanie's habit of receiving Civil War transients, for whom she sets aside a place in the basement:

There were three rooms in the basement of Melanie's house which formerly had been servants' quarters and a wine room. Now Dilcey occupied one, and the other two were in constant use by a stream of miserable and ragged transients. No one but Melanie knew whence they came or where they were going and no one but she knew where she collected them. Perhaps the negroes were right and she did pick them up from the streets. But even as the great and the near great gravitated to her small parlor, so unfortunates found their way to her cellar where they were fed, bedded and sent on their way with packages of food. Usually the occupants of the rooms were former Confederate soldiers of the rougher, illiterate type, homeless men, men without families, beating their way about the country in hope of finding work.[29]

Although both women subscribe to Christian virtues, such as charity, loyalty, obedience, passivity, etc., Melanie proves more resourceful than her counterpart during moments of overt tension. For example, she lends her moral support to Scarlett when the latter kills the Union intruder at Tara; she also possesses the inner strength to console Rhett Butler after he suffers the most grievous of all personal misfortunes—the loss of a child.

Princess Mary, on the other hand, is helpless when her father dies, and she is left to cope with the recalcitrant peasants. Her helplessness turns out to be a blessing in disguise when Nicholas Rostov comes to her aid, initiating their soon to be serious relationship. Thus only in the capacity for coolness under stress does there emerge a noticeable difference between Melanie and Princess Mary. Mary's frailty in this respect lends a greater verisimilitude to her character, while Melanie's too-perfect image cannot be found in flesh and blood.

The last topic for comparison between *War and Peace* and *GWTW* involves structure and stylistics. Here the number of contrasts may be greater than the similarities. For example, while in the structure of his novel Tolstoy interweaves three categories—peace, war, and philosophical commentary, Mitchell creates

---

28. Tolstoy, p. 423.
29. Mitchell, pp. 747–48.

a novel of only a single dimension—the world of Scarlett O'Hara. It evolves in a linear pattern from peace to war to reconstruction, and is free of Tolstoy's complex "linkages."[30] Moreover, unlike Tolstoy, the author of *GWTW* never takes the reader to the war front; it only becomes known through letters, rumors, and eyewitness accounts that are related in Scarlett's presence. Tolstoy, on the other hand, finds the detailed depiction of battle scenes indispensable for the elucidation of his philosophical theories. Consequently, Tolstoy interweaves his topics, bringing them back again and again, while Mitchell moves in a straight line toward reconstruction. The latter, incidentally, assumes a far more integral role in *GWTW* than in *War and Peace,* where Tolstoy devotes only a short epilogue to the reconstruction process.

Upon closer analysis there is one restricted area, in which Mitchell does emulate Tolstoy's penchant for "linkages," though it occurs on a less ambitious scale. This pertains to the interweaving of characters' fates and the exhaustive interaction of the major figures. In *War and Peace* Tolstoy sets up this pattern, by involving each character with all others. For example, Pierre is a childhood friend to Princess Mary and Prince Andrew. He marries Helena and Natasha at various times, and fights a duel with Dolokhov, whose second is Nicholas Rostov. Similarly, Natasha has a puppy love for Boris Drubetskoy, is betrothed to Prince Andrew, falls victim to the seductive machinations of the Kuragins (Helene and Anatolie), acquires the friendship of Princess Mary during the evacuation and eventually marries Pierre. Such an exhaustive pattern of interaction can be established for the other main characters as well.

Mitchell creates similar "linkages" among her four primary figures of *GWTW*. Scarlett is a friend of sorts to Melanie; she carries a torch for Ashley, and she becomes wife to Rhett Butler; Ashley marries Melanie, remains a loyal friend to Scarlett, and serves as an ideological rival to Rhett (except, of course, in the bordello scene at Belle Watling's, where they become conspirators); Rhett is husband to Scarlett, a distant admirer of Melanie (for him she is truly a "great lady"),[31] and a philosophical opposite to Ashley; Melanie is Scarlett's friend, Ashley's wife, and Rhett's understanding sympathizer. By employing this Tolstoyan device of "linkages," Mitchell finds infinite possibilities for exhaustive character interaction, thereby increasing the scope and panorama of her novel.

Also contrastive in the stylistic realm is the difference of the two novels with respect to historical truth. Mitchell, as is well documented, goes to great lengths to recreate the Civil War era authentically in all its details. She pays strict attention to the types of weapons used, researches the weather conditions of certain battles, and studies the medical treatment rendered the sick and

---

30. Boris M. Eikhenbaum, a formalist critic of the 1920s and one of the most brilliant authorities on Tolstoy, discusses the writer's use of "linkages" in detail in his voluminous study of Tolstoy *Lev Tolstoy,* published between 1928 and 1931. An English translation of this work is scheduled to appear in October 1979 under the auspices of Ardis Publishers in Ann Arbor, Michigan.

31. Mitchell, p. 850.

wounded during the war. Summarizing her thoughts on the need for impeccable historical accuracy, Miss Mitchell notes: "However lousy the book may be as far as style, subject, plot, characters, it's as accurate historically as I can get it. I didn't want to get caught out on anything that any Confederate Vet could nail me on, or any historian either."[32]

Tolstoy, by contrast, does not strive for total historical accuracy in his novel. The critic Leontiev, one of the most perspicacious analysts of Tolstoy's style, directs attention to the fact that Pierre and Prince Andrew are given the benefit of philosophical thought that evolved after the age of Napoleon:

> I have said that Tolstoy himself all the same had read in his youth both Turgenev and Dostoevsky; but Pierre Bezukhov and Prince Bolkonsky at the beginning of this century had still not read either "The Superfluous Man" or "Poor Folk" and "The Humiliated and the Wronged"; they still did not know Onegin, Pechorin, Hegel, Schopenhauer, George Sand or Gogol.
>
> Well now I ask you, is it plausible that they, these people from the time of consulates and empires, thought in almost the same style in which we think now, we, overburdened to the extreme by all the speeches and thoughts of our predecessors who have been ill with all their diseases, and who have outlived all their passions?
>
> Somehow it's not believable![33]

In another respect authenticity emerges more as a Tolstoyan trait and less as a Mitchell characteristic. This concerns the topic of fictional characters and their names. Tolstoy prefers to base his fictional figures on people whom he knew; i.e., Princess Mary and Nicholas Rostov are modeled on his own parents, while Natasha is developed from his sister-in-law. Moreover, he often gives his characters the names of real people. The family Bolkonsky, for example, is only a slight distortion of his mother's last name Volkonsky.

Mitchell, on the other hand, tries to avoid the depiction of her family, or for that matter any real people, saying "I wouldn't even think of writing about my own family. . . . True, I did get my background out of what the oldtimers told me. . . . But all the characters and all the incidents came out of my head."[34] On the subject of names, Mitchell at all costs shuns the duplication of existing people's names and is shocked to learn that the name of Gerald O'Hara repeats the name of a living Savannah clergyman.[35] In summary, both Tolstoy and

---

32. Harwell, p. 2. Taken from a letter to Mr. Julian Harris, dated 12 April 1936.

33. Konstantin Leontiev, *Analiz, stil' i veianie, O romanakh Gr. L. N. Tolstogo* (Providence, 1965), 120. Leontiev was an excellent literary critic, who combined various approaches. This article on Tolstoy (the translated title would be *Analysis, Style, and Mood. About the novels of Graf L.N. Tolstoi*) was published in 1911. I have translated this text. Onegin comes from Pushkin's *Eugene Onegin* (1831) and Pechorin belongs to Lermontov's *A Hero of Our Time* (1840). Both figures were manifestations of the social phenomenon of the "Superflous Man," meaning that they were unable to find a niche in society and remained unproductive and useless.

34. Harwell, p. 23. Taken from letter to Gilbert Govan, Dated 23 June 1936.

35. Farr, p. 106.

Mitchell are conscientious about certain aspects of authenticity, but on some separate occasions they stress the fictional element at the expense of real facts.

When we move our focus to the actual writing of the two novels, then under the rubric of style appear two similarities worthy of consideration. First, each author writes the last chapter before any other. In the case of Tolstoy, for example, it is well known that he originally intended to write a novel about the abortive uprising of the Decembrists in 1825. The material he gathered for such a work, especially the information about Pierre's participation in clandestine political meetings in St. Petersburg, ultimately becomes the epilogue of *War and Peace*. From this anchor in the Decembrist period, Tolstoy works back to the Napoleonic era and the battles of Austerlitz (1805) and Borodino (1812).

Similarly, Mitchell often alludes to the fact that her final chapter—the resolution of the relationship between Scarlett and Rhett—is finished first, while the greatest difficulties come with the first chapter, which she writes last of all. Interestingly enough, the latter was not even ready for publication when Mr. Latham, the Macmillan representative, first received the manuscript. One suspects that this curious parallel might be related to the two writers' shared journalistic tendencies. As Farr explains, Mitchell in her role as journalist for the *Atlanta Journal* liked to begin with the punch line and then work back to the story itself.[36] Tolstoy, too, was familiar with journalistic devices, as his first *Sevastopol Tale* ("Sevastopol in December"), written from a reporter's point of view, attests.[37]

Secondly, Tolstoy and Mitchell are both partial to a fast start. In achieving this, they eschew prolonged introductions and give their first sentence an arresting quality. Tolstoy employs such a device in both his large novels, beginning *War and Peace* immediately with the Napoleonic theme ("Well, Prince, so Genoa and Lucca are now just family estates of the Bonapartes"), and starting *Anna Karenina* with an eyecatching thematic statement about family life ("Happy families are all alike; every unhappy family is unhappy in its own way").

These direct plunges into the work without benefit of an exposition correspond to Mitchell's quick entry into *GWTW*: "Scarlett O'Hara was not beautiful, but men seldom realized it when caught by her charm as the Tarleton twins were." Here the author swiftly sets the mood for the entire novel by focusing on Scarlett's ability to captivate—the one trait that stands her in good stead in the subsequent chapters.

In conclusion, this study represents one of the first efforts to ascertain the classical roots of *GWTW*.[38] It suggests several concrete parallels in genre,

---

36. Farr, p. 79.

37. Tolstoy wrote three stories on the Crimean War that became known as *The Sevastopol Tales* ("Sevastopol in December," "Sevastopol in May," and "Sevastopol in August"). These date from his military service in the Crimea in the mid-1850s and anticipate *War and Peace*, written just over a decade later (1865–1869).

38. The only other significant comparative study involving *GWTW* is Edward F. Nolan's short

theme, character, and style between Margaret Mitchell's novel and Tolstoy's *War and Peace*. Their validity is supported by the American writer's frequent references to Tolstoy in her letters. It is hoped that this comparative essay will stimulate comparativists everywhere to engage in further studies of *GWTW* as it relates to other classical literature. Two such comparisons come immediately to mind: 1) The analysis of Scarlett O'Hara within the framework of Dostoevsky's "infernal woman" and 2) The juxtaposition of Ashley Wilkes and Rhett Butler as perceived against the background of Turgenev's *Fathers and Sons*.

Scarlett's role as an "infernal woman" appears to group her with Dostoevsky's Nastas'ia Filipovna (in *The Idiot*) and Katerina Ivanovna (in *The Brothers Karamazov*), both of whom use their beauty and charm to possess men's minds and to overpower their wills. Like Katerina who is torn between Dmitri and Ivan, Scarlett loves both Ashley and Rhett. In her vascillation between the two, she employs her innate charm as a tool of torment. Rhett Butler, echoing the sentiments of Dostoevsky, calls attention to Scarlett's infernal nature when he tells her: "You're so brutal to those who love you, Scarlett. You take their love and hold it over their heads like a whip."[39] In addition, the scene in which Scarlett hopes to sell herself to Rhett for monetary security vividly recalls Katerina's visit to Dmitri to rescue her father from debt by compromising her own honor.

Turgenev's depiction of the "men of the forties" and the "men of the sixties" in *Fathers and Sons* bears a strong resemblance to the opposing world views of Ashley and Rhett in *GWTW*. Ashley truly represents a man from the romantic generation of the 1840s, living by the gentlemanly virtues of love, honor, loyalty, and poetry. Like the family Kirsanov, he removes himself from real life and yearns for the idyllic setting of the old aristocracy. Opposed to him stands Rhett Butler, who makes fun of such old world romanticism and views it as doomed to be swept away by the new accent on progress. To survive in the new world, Rhett adopts a philosophy of pragmatism that is so extreme that he sees nothing wrong with making a fortune off the spoils of war. In many ways Rhett's pragmatism links him with Turgenev's Bazarov, who, believing only in science and progress (symbolized in the work by the dissection of frogs), viciously attacks the previous generation's romanticism. Both Bazarov and Rhett Butler eventually discover that there really can be no decent life without the romantic concepts of love and tradition. Just as Bazarov must confess that his love for the woman Odintsova refutes his belief in pure nihilism, so Butler must admit that his traditional roots are stronger than all else in his life, including even Scarlett.

---

article "The Death of Bryan Lyndon: An Analogue in 'Gone With the Wind,' " *Nineteenth Century Fiction*, 8 (1953), 225–28. Here the author draws a comparison between the death of Bryan Lyndon in Thackeray's *The Memoirs of Barry Lyndon, Esq.* and the death of Bonnie Butler in *GWTW*.

39. Mitchell, p. 1029.

The Anti-Tom Novel and the Great Depression: Margaret Mitchell's Gone With the Wind

By Leslie A. Fiedler

"*I attended a conference a couple of weeks ago at which people were talking about the literature of the Thirties and there were a lot of survivors of the Thirties being very nostalgic about how great it was back in the days of the Depression.*" Leslie Fiedler, the top Guru of pop-culture, was speaking on William F. Buckley, Jr.'s "Firing Line," November 15, 1974. "*And what they were talking about were so-called proletarian novels which were published in 1500 copies and sold 400 of them you know. The rest molded in somebody's basement. . . . These were the books that seemed to them worth memorializing and I said, 'Look, there is one book which was written in the middle of the Thirties images from which, names from which, scenes and situations from which, language from which is in everybody's mind, and that's* Gone With the Wind.'*. . . . It's a book which is really living, both in book form and in the movie form, because the interesting thing about popular literature is its excellences are not tied to the medium in which it appears.*"

A few moments later the listener heard Fiedler saying: "*There's a great series of books in the United States which begins with Harriet Beecher Stowe's* Uncle Tom's Cabin, *is answered by Thomas Dixon's* The Clansman *and* The Leopard's Spots, *which then become D. W. Griffith's* Birth of a Nation, *clearly the best movie an American ever made, and ends with Margaret Mitchell's* Gone With the Wind.*" Fiedler did not develop that conversational tack then but later did so in a five-part radio broadcast for the Canadian Broadcasting Corporation's 1978 Massey Lectures in CBC's IDEAS series. In this series he discussed the novels mentioned and added a fifth, Alex Haley's* Roots. *The Series was printed in Canada by CBC Merchandising and in the United States by Simon and Schuster as* The Inadvertent Epic: From Uncle Tom's Cabin to Roots. *This small book's pages relating to GWTW are reprinted here.*

Dixon, who lived to 1946, recognized his literary kinship to Margaret Mitchell, sending her a letter immediately after the publication of her novel to tell her how much it had moved him, and assuring her that he intended to write a booklength study of her work. In quick response, she acknowledged her indebtedness to *him*, explaining, "I was practically raised on your books and love them very much. . . When I was eleven years old I decided I would dramatize your book 'The Traitor'—and dramatize it I did in six acts. . . ." Unfortunately, Dixon suffered a cerebral hemmorhage shortly thereafter and so never managed to keep his promise. But one can easily imagine how sympathetically he would have responded to her view of Reconstruction as a total disaster and of the Klan as its necessary aftermath; as well as her portrayal of unspoiled Black American slaves as stupid, docile and faithful; since the attitudes which underlay them were indistinguishable from his own. One presumes, also, that he would have tried to make clear how in *Gone With the Wind,* the Southerner's long quarrel with Mrs. Stowe eventuated at last in a fiction as moving and memorable as *Uncle Tom's Cabin* itself.

Though no character in his novels, or any of the anti-Tom books which preceded it, has passed into the mythology of the mass audience, Scarlett, Melanie, Rhett Butler, Ashley Wilkes and Mammy live on in the popular imagination as vividly as Uncle Tom, Eliza, Topsy, Simon Legree and Little Eva. All but one of Miss Mitchell's mythic characters, however, are white. And though the Black Rapist, the archetypal "Bad Nigger," foreshadowed in Dixon and Griffith's Gus, makes a brief appearance in her pages, he has proved less memorable than her "Good Niggers," who serve, protect and, as Faulkner liked to put it, "endure." When all else of the Old South is gone with the wind: the armies of the Confederacy defeated, the great houses pillaged and burned, the courtly lovers—whether impotent cavaliers like Ashley Wilkes or sexy scoundrels like Rhett Butler—departed, her Good Nigger-in-chief, "Mammy" still remains to preside over the book's bittersweet ending.

Like all protagonists of the domestic counter-tradition in American letters, Scarlett O'Hara must be last seen "going home," rather than fleeing to the wilderness, like the anti-domestic Huckleberry Finn. But who is left to welcome her back? Her always shadowy aristocratic mother has long since disappeared, followed by her Irish immigrant father, who has first gone mad; and her children, in whom the childless Margaret Mitchell has never been able to make us quite believe, have died or mysteriously vanished from the scene. Only "Mammy" remains, as she must, since "home" is where she has always been, will always be. "And Mammy will be there," Scarlett re-assures herself.

Certainly she is there in the book's final paragraph, in which Scarlett prepares to return to Tara: "Suddenly she wanted Mammy desperately, as she had wanted her when she was a little girl, wanted the broad bosom, on which to lay her head, the gnarled black hand on her hair. Mammy, the last link with the old days." But "Mammy," we realize at this point, whom no betrayal can alienate, no Emancipation Proclamation force from the eternal bondage of love, is really Uncle Tom, the Great Black Mother of us all.

Even before *Gone With the Wind,* his/her true sex had been revealed: in Faulkner's Dilsey, for instance, whose epitaph (in the androgynous plural) closes *The Sound and the Fury,* "DILSEY. They endured."; and in Aunt Jemima, whose turbaned head has grinned at three generations of Americans from the pancake box that is her final home. But it took Margaret Mitchell, that 1920's flapper and newspaper sob-sister turned laureate to a nation b ʰe Great Depression, to fix her new image for all time. The other women wᵉ remember out of this essentially feminine book, from honey-dripping Melanie to mindless, heartless Scarlett, are projections of the author, when they are not stock-figures, like Belle Watling, the Whore with a Heart of Gold. But Mammy she inherits from the book she thought she despised, the dream of a love transcending the horrors of slavery, first dreamed for the Mothers of America by Harriet Beecher Stowe.

Indeed, almost all of Margaret Mitchell's "darkies," as she preferred to call them, seem latter-day versions of Mrs. Stowe's incredibly faithful and naive hero/heroine; since she perceives them through the same haze of genteel, "female" sensibility as her "abolitionist" predecessor. "Negroes," she instructs us, speaking for herself and Scarlett, "had to be handled gently, as though they were children, directed, praised, petted, scolded. . . ." And, she would have us believe, they *were* so treated in the antebellum South, whatever readers of *Uncle Tom's Cabin* may have been misled into thinking was the case. It is, in fact, with such readers that she is quarreling, rather than with the book itself (which, indeed, she may never have read) in the single passage in which she mentions it by name. "Accepting *Uncle Tom's Cabin* as revelation," she writes, "second only to the Bible, the Yankee women all wanted to know about the bloodhounds which every Southerner kept to track down runaway slaves. . . . They wanted to know about the dreadful branding irons which the planters used to mark the faces of their slaves and the cat-o'-nine-tails with which they beat them to death and they evidenced what Scarlett felt was a very nasty and ill-bred interest in slave concubinage. . . ."

She seems never quite to have realized how much the fate of her own book was to be like that of Mrs. Stowe's, its acceptance by the majority audience as a new, revised secular scripture leading to its rejection by literary critics. From the moment of publication, it was faulted, especially in quarters where a taste for High Literature was combined with leftist politics, for its exploitation of "false sentiment and heady goo," along with its promulgation of the presumably defunct "plantation legend." To such attacks, Miss Mitchell purported to be indifferent, "I'd have to do so much explaining to family and friends," she wrote, "if the aesthetes and radicals of literature liked it"—adding in an apology which seems to echo that of Mrs. Stowe. "I'm not a stylist, God knows, and couldn't be if I tried. . . ." Yet something in her seems to have yearned for critical acclaim, so that she responded immediately and gratefully to the favorable notices in the more popular reviews.

For a little while, in fact, the issue seemed in doubt, but once a best-selling movie had been made of *Gone With the Wind*, she was doomed to critical oblivion, especially since the film proved to be as aesthetically undistinguished as her prose. Though credited to a single director and scriptwriter, it was actually directed by two and written by eleven or twelve, a patchwork job with no controlling intelligence behind it, except her own. The millions who first read, then saw *Gone With the Wind* responded to it not as literature but as myth; remembering not even the original author, much less those responsible for adapting her novel to the screen, but the actors who embodied her *personae:* Clark Gable, already mythic before he was cast as Rhett, and Vivien Leigh, who became mythic from the moment she became Scarlett.

To most of those millions, ignorant or indifferent to history, the Defeat of the Confederacy and the Burning of Atlanta, represented a legend not of the antebellum past but the mid-Depression present. Though she had begun her novel in the 'twenties, Miss Mitchell finished it under the shadow of the great collapse of 1929; and as she revised it for publication, unemployment, strikes and the threat of violence possessed the streets of our desolate cities; while overseas Nazis and Communists goosestepped and chanted, evoking the menace of conquest and war. Small wonder then that it became the most popular work of the age.

Yet no history of our literature in the 'thirties, written then or since, considers it worthy of mention side by side with the novels of James T. Farrell, John Dos Passos, John Steinbeck, Nathanael West or Henry Roth. Dismissed contemptuously to the underworld of best-sellerdom, it is recalled, if at all, as evidence of the decline of taste in an age of Mass Culture. In Gershom Legman's *Love and Death,* for instance, a hysterical attack on comic-books and best-sellers which appeared in 1948, it is condemned, along with such forgotten pot-boilers as *Forever Amber* and *Duchess Hotspur,* as one more debased celebration of the "Bitch Heroine." "The message . . ." Legman cries out in righteous indignation, "is hate. Nothing more. Hate, and the war between the sexes, set, symbolically enough— . . . to the tune of *That's Why the Ku Klux Klan Was Born.*"

In an important sense, Gershom Legman is right. *Gone With the Wind* is as much a sado-masochistic work as *Uncle Tom's Cabin, The Clansman, The Birth of a Nation* and *Roots,* for like them, it is based on a fantasy of inter-ethnic rape as the supreme expression of the violence between sexes and races. In the continuing underground epic of which it is a part, it scarcely matters whether white men are shown sexually exploiting Black Girls or Black men murderously assaulting white ones; only that the male rapist be represented as unmitigatedly evil and the female victim as utterly innocent. This simplistic feminist mythology, Margaret Mitchell qualifies somewhat by making her White female more predatory bitch than passive and helpless sufferer. Nonetheless, it is only the White Woman she is able to imagine threatened; even her passing reference to "slave concubinage," as we have seen, avoiding the mythologically loaded word "rape."

Of the three attempted rapes of Scarlett which dominate the book, however, a Black Man is involved in only one; and even in that instance, he is provided with a rather ineffectual white accomplice. The other two rapists, the first foiled by Scarlett herself, and the second successful because in some sense she collaborates in her violation, are mythological threats to the Southern lady of quite different kinds: the first, a Union Soldier, and the second, a Husband. Both scenes, however, end in the counter-climax of death; the latter stirring in us pity as well as terror; the former terror mitigated only by self-righteous satisfaction, as Scarlett shoots in the face at point-blank range the Union Soldier who dares assault her in her own home. Miss Mitchell takes great pains to make the scene as effective as it is central: "All alone, little lady?" the blue-coated invader asks suggestively, and before she or the reader quite knows what is happening, it is all over. ". . . Scarlett ran down the stairs and stood . . . gazing down into what was left of the face . . . a bloody pit where the nose had been, glazing eyes burned with powder. . . ." That scene was equally well rendered in the movie version, so well rendered, in fact, that the first-night audience in Miss Mitchell's native Atlanta rose to its feet and cheered.

The second White-White rape, however, that of Scarlett by Rhett Butler, elicited more tears than cheers, when it eventuated in an aborted pregnancy on the great staircase which the film made as mythological as those protagonists themselves. First, however, Scarlett achieves in the arms of Rhett, her husband still though long since banned from her bed, what is apparently the only orgasm of her life, unless she had earlier achieved one blowing the head off the Yankee soldier. (Miss Mitchell is so cagy about such matters that it is hard to be sure.) Nonetheless, this time, too, death is the fruit of love, as Rhett forces her to stumble on the same stairs where he began the assault, and she loses the child she has conceived in his brutal but satisfactory embrace.

Only in a third encounter, occurring midway between the other two, is the would-be-rapist what Dixon had taught Miss Mitchell was the proper mythological color. And it remains, therefore, an archetypal scene, however undercut by the author's insistence that Scarlett may have provoked the attempt at rape, deliberately or foolishly. For a moment, Miss Mitchell seems on the verge of suggesting, in fact, that *all* such outrages arise not out of the lustful obsession with white female flesh that presumably afflicts all Black men, but in part at least out of the troubled erotic dreams (cued half by fear, half by wish) of Southern White women. In the end, however, the language and tone Miss Mitchell uses in describing the attack are scarcely distinguishable from those of Dixon, as in a kind of nightmare transformation her faithful Negro retainer, Big Sam, turns into a Black Rapist: "The negro was beside her, so close that she could smell the rank odor of him . . . she felt his big hand at her throat and, with a ripping noise, her basque was torn open from neck to waist. Then the black hand fumbled between her breasts and terror and revulsion . . . came over her and she screamed like an insane woman."* This time, too, Big Sam has been no

---

*Editor's Note: Big Sam does not, as Fiedler says, turn into a rapist. It was he who rescued

more successful in his attempt at righteous murder than was Scarlett; so that the final act of revenge is left, as is proper to the anti-Tom tradition, to the white riders of the Ku Klux Klan.

It is, however, not her penchant for violence which has kept Margaret Mitchell from critical recognition. To many pious opponents of violence in the arts, her sadism remains as invisible as it apparently was to her, camouflaged by what they take to be her "good intentions." They remember not the terror which moves them below the level of full consciousness, but the heroism of Scarlett, and especially the high romance of her troubled relationship with Rhett Butler. The single line, for instance, that most readers and viewers of *Gone With the Wind* can quote is the one Rhett speaks as he leaves her, perhaps forever, "My dear, I don't give a damn." For elite critics, on the other hand, whom the s-m overtones of Hemingway do not trouble at all (as they did, in fact, trouble Miss Mitchell), the low piety and high romance of her novel aggravate rather than mitigate its violence.

What they cannot finally forgive her is her failure to redeem melodrama with high style and pretentious philosophizing, her giving away of the secret they try so desperately to keep: the fact that *all* literature which long endures and pleases many does so largely by providing the vulgar satisfactions of horror, sexual titillation and the release to tears. This is why *The Literary History of the United States,* for example, devotes not a single line of all of its fourteen hundred odd pages to a discussion of *Gone With the Wind* as literature, merely reporting the statistics of its sales at home and abroad, as if it were an event in the market place and not the Republic of Letters.

For similar reasons, I long concealed my own real affection for the novel and the movie, not only from those whom I addressed in my critical books but from myself. A year or two ago, however, a letter arrived on my desk, addressed to "Dr. Lesley Fielder"—spelling both my names wrong and thus setting into operation habits of condescension, which at that point I had learned to be ashamed of but not to repress. "Dear Lesley Fielder," it began, "It is my understanding and that of my A.P. English Class at Sacred Heart Academy [here once more, triggering automatic condescension] that you feel there are no

---

Scarlett from the attack in Shantytown by two unnamed men, "a big ragged white man and a squat black negro with shoulders and chest like a gorilla."

Miss Mitchell describes the incident: "What happened next was like a nightmare to Scarlett. She brought up her pistol swiftly and some instinct told her not to fire at the white man for fear of shooting the horse. As the negro came running to the buggy, his black face twisted in a leering grin, she fired point-blank at him. Whether or not she hit him, she never knew, but the next minute the pistol was wrenched from her hand by a grasp that almost broke her wrist. The negro was beside her, so close that she could smell the rank odor of him as he tried to drag her over the buggyside. With her one free hand she fought madly, clawing at his face, and then she felt his big hand at her throat and, with a ripping noise, her basque was torn open from neck to waist. Then the black hand fumbled between her breasts, and terror and revulsion such as she had never known came over her and she screamed like an insane woman."

It is at this point that Big Sam appears upon the scene and rescues Scarlett. Margaret Mitchell, *Gone With the Wind* (New York: 1936), pp. 787, 788.

great female characters in American Literature. I feel, however, that Scarlett O'Hara of Margaret Mitchell's *Gone With the Wind* should be considered etc. etc." And it concluded, "I am writing to you because of your literary background and I would like to know your opinion of my opinion. . . ."

When I still had proper literary opinions, still thought I knew what "literature" was, I would have written (and, indeed, found myself at the point of writing): "My dear So and So, My generalization about there being no great female characters in American Literature still stands, since *Gone With the Wind* is not really a part of American Literature, but only of sub- or para-literature." And I was on the point of referring my correspondent back to *Love and Death in the American Novel,* in which I had dealt with that novel (nearly twenty years before) in a passage full of phrases like "popular literature . . . fat traditional book . . . stereotypes . . . sentimentality . . . best-seller . . . ready-made masturbatory fantasies . . ."

It occurred to me, however, that not only had I come to believe that the lonely act of reading had always and inevitably something masturbatory about it (and, in any case, who *cared?*) but that citing just those words would not have told the whole truth about my attitudes toward that book even way back in 1960. I had, after all, devoted to it two full pages of the six hundred I had allotted myself to cover the whole span of our fiction. And how could I not, having been haunted then, as—like almost all Americans—I continue to be to this day, by scenes, characters, images, names grown mythological, out of that despised novel. Why, then, I found myself pondering over that still unanswered letter, had I so long resisted really coming to terms with the appeal of *Gone With the Wind,* and, indeed, with all other books like it which constitute Popular Literature, Mass Literature, Majority Literature, as opposed to High Literature, Belles Lettres, the "Classics."

Clearly, I have been exposed for many years in classes in English to a kind of systematic brainwashing, in the course of which I learned first to despise and then to sport my contempt for all fiction the enjoyment of which joins me to rather than separates me from "ordinary readers," which is to say, from those of my family and friends who have not made it all the way to a Ph.D. in Literature, but who have stopped short with an M.A., a B.A. or a high-school diploma.

Moreover, I discover that even now, despite my commitment to a populist aesthetics, I am not completely free of ambivalence on this score: an ambivalence reflected in the vestigial scorn I cannot quite repress for the girl from Sacred Heart Academy who begins with a high regard for *Gone With the Wind* rather than *ends* with it (like me) after having passed through an initiation into the world of elitist standards. Precisely because of that initiation, there persists in me a sneaky inclination to believe that Scarlett O'Hara, despite the mythic dimensions she has achieved over the past forty years, does not deserve to be mentioned in the same breath with other archetypal figures out of our literature, like Natty Bumppo, Captain Ahab, Daisy Miller or Hester Prynne, much less their European prototypes like Odysseus, Aeneas, Hamlet, Don Quixote, Medea, Jocasta or Emma Bovary.

Yet I would be hard-Pressed to defend such hierarchical distinctions, which depend on what I am convinced is a definition of literature no longer viable in a mass society. And I am willing to follow wherever the logic of my anti-elitist position takes me, even if this means the redemption not just of works I have always, however secretly, loved, *Gone With the Wind, The Birth of a Nation, Uncle Tom's Cabin* but even of such a prefabricated piece of commodity literature as Alex Haley's *Roots,* subsidized by *Readers Digest* and blessed by the *P.T.A.* and, therefore evoking in me an initial distrust I find it harder to overcome. . . . Yet much of Haley's *Roots* moves me deeply.

Like *The Clansman* and *The Leopard's Spots*—indeed, like all majority literature—it stirs wonder in us by evoking primordial images, sentimental, violent, prurient, of necessity, *gross.* Works which long endure win our assent not rationally and logically, like history, philosophy or science, but viscerally, passionately, like rituals in primitive societies or dreams in our own. They tend, that is to say, to reinforce our wildest paranoid delusions, along with our most utopian hopes about the relations of races, sexes and generations: self-indulgent reveries, from which we rouse ourselves in embarrassment, or nightmares from which we wake in terror—but which continue to resonate in our waking heads, whether we be racists, chauvinists, fascists and practising sadists, or rightminded liberals, pacifists, feminists and twice-born Christians.

It is, indeed, the function of all art at its most authentic to release us to dionysiac, demonic impulses; and thus to satisfy our shame-faced longing (otherwise repressed or sublimated) to be driven out of control—to permit us, in short, moments of privileged madness, a temporary return to psychic states which we have theoretically abandoned in the name of humanity and sweet reason.

Quite obviously, not only sophisticated artists can produce such works, skilled craftsmen who have lived exemplary lives and worked hard at their trade. They are in the power of anyone—good or evil, energetic or indolent, intelligent or stupid, who is gifted with easy access to his own unconscious and to the collective fantasies of his time and place. Once we have understood this, we will know why the most important, beloved and moving books do not have to pass the traditional tests we pedagogue-critics have imposed on literature in the name of the Aristotelian formula "instruct and delight."

To impart wisdom or to make elegant structures, to console and uplift the heart are optional for song and story—not forbidden, but not required either. What is required is to stir wonder and ecstacy, thus enabling us to be "in dreams awake." Once we have realized this, we will have begun to define a new way of evaluating such long-underesteemed writers as Stowe and Mitchell and Dixon and Haley, inept in form and weak in ideas, but like Shakespeare or Sophocles, Dickens or Mark Twain, endowed—by the grace of God, the muse of their own unconscious—with mythopoeic power.

They are not long, the days of wine and roses:
    Out of a misty dream
Our path emerges for a while, then closes
    Within a dream.

Ernest Dowson, *"Vita summae brevis*
spem nos vetat incohare longam"

A Selected Bibliography

This list includes books and magazine articles relating directly to Margaret Mitchell and to *Gone With the Wind*, book or film. It does not include news stories, with the exceptions of two in *Newsweek* and *Time*. It includes feature articles from Sunday supplements which were published as magazines and one especially significant series of articles which Lamar Q. Ball wrote for the Atlanta *Constitution*.

Abrams, Harvey Dan. *Medora Field Perkerson.* [Atlanta: 196-?] 24 p.

Anderson, Reta Margaret. "Gone With the Wind: An Evaluation. . ." Nashville, Tenn: 1956. 78 p. M. A. thesis, Vanderbilt University.

The Atanta Historical Bulletin. *Margaret Mitchell Memorial Issue,* IX, no. 34 (May 1950), 150 p.
CONTENTS: "Margaret Mitchell and Her People in the Atlanta Area," by Stephens Mitchell, pp. 5–26; "Margaret Mitchell in Public Affairs," pp. 29–30; Margaret Mitchell and the Wide, Wide World," by John R. Marsh, pp. 33–44; "Peggy Mitchell, Newspaperman," by William S. Howland, pp. 47–64; "Georgia Generals for Stone Mountain Memorial," by Peggy Mitchell, pp. 67–99; "Margaret Mitchell in Person and Her Warmth of Friendship," by Blythe McKay, pp. 100–107; "Margaret Mitchell and Her Last Days on Earth," by William Key, pp. 108–128.

The Atlanta Journal Magazine, *Margaret Mitchell Memorial Issue,* December 18, 1949, 40 p.
CONTENTS: "Was Margaret Mitchell Writing Another Book" by Medora Field Perkerson, p. 4–7; "Atlanta's Biggest Week: 'Gone With the Wind' Premiere," by Wylly Folk St. John, p. 8–10; "Her Brother Remembers—Margaret Mitchell's Childhood," by Stephens Mitchell, p. 12; "Margaret Mitchell's Journal Magazine Stories," p. 14–17; "By Peggy Mitchell," p. 18–19; "The Publisher's Story. . . How I Found 'Gone With the Wind,'" by Harold S. Latham, p. 20, 22; "Margaret Mitchell's Last Hours," by Marguerite Steedman, p. 23, 26; "Margaret Mitchell Told in Her Only Radio Broadcast How GWTW Was Written," [by Medora Field Perkerson], p. 24–26; "Peggy in Pictures," p. 29; "What the World Said When Margaret Mitchell Died," p. 32–33.

Atlanta Public Library. *Margaret Mitchell Memorial of the Atlanta Public Library Dedicated December 15, 1954.* Atlanta, Ga., The Atlanta Public Library, 1954. vii, 30 p.
CONTENTS: "Margaret Mitchell—Romantic Realist," by William S. Howland, pp. 1–16; "The Real Story of 'Gone With the Wind,' as told by Margaret Mitchell to Norman S. Berg, pp. 19–25; "Gone With the Wind, the Motion Picture," by Susan Myrick, pp. 27–30.
Reissue *(ca.* 1967?) with a new cover and a two-page Epilogue.

Baker, John F. " 'GWTW' Revisited," by John F. Baker, *Publishers Weekly,* CCX, no. 10 (September 6, 1976), 22–23.

Baldwin, Faith. "The Woman Who Wrote 'Gone With the Wind,' *"Pictorial Review,* March 1937; 5, 69–71.

Ball, Lamar Q. ". . . [A five-part] series of articles based on exclusive interviews with Margaret Mitchell, whose best-selling novel of the South, 'Gone With the Wind,' has made her an international figure. . . . " in Atlanta *Constitution,* November 8–12, 1936.

Ballard, Virginia. "A Guide to the Screen Version of *Gone With the Wind,*" prepared by Virginia Ballard and Adelaide L. Cunningham. *Photoplay Studies,* VI, no. 12, 1940; [8] p.

Barker, Felix. *The Oliviers.* London: Hamish Hamilton [1953]. 313 p.

Baskette, Kirtley. " 'Gone With the Wind' Indeed"; *Photoplay Magazine* (March 1937). (Clippings in Margaret Mitchell Marsh Papers, University of Georgia Libraries)

Baxter, John. *Hollywood in the Thirties.* London: Tantivy Press; New York: A.S. Banes & Co., n.d. 160 p.

Bluestone, George. *Novels into Film.* Berkeley, etc.: University of California Press [c. 1957]. 237 p.

Boatwright, James. "Reconsideration: Totin' de Weery Load" *The New Republic,* CLXIX, no. 9 (September 1, 1973), 29–32.

Boothe, Clare, *Kiss the Boys Good-bye.* New York: Random House [c. 1939]. xx p., 2 ll, 249 p.

Bowers, Ronald. *The Selznick Players.* South Brunswick and New York: A.S. Barnes and Company; London: Thomas Yoseloff Ltd. [c. 1976]. 255 p.

Bridges, Herb. *Favorite Scenes from Gone With the Wind,* compiled by Herb Bridges. [Sharpsburg, Ga.: Herb Bridges 1981]. [54] p.

Burns, Robert W. "Gone With the Wind, a Sermon Preached in Peachtree Christian Church November 8, 1936." *The Peachtree Tower,* unnumbered (June 1937), 3–6.

Caldwell, Erskine. *Call It Experience.* New York: Duell, Sloan and Pearce [1951]. 239 p.

Campbell, Edward D.C. *The Celluloid South: Hollywood and the Southern Myth.* Knoxville: The University of Tennessee Press [1981]. 212 p.

———. "Gone With the Wind: Film as Myth and Message," in Walter J. Fraser, Jr., *From the Old South to the New* (Westport, Conn.: Greenwood Press, 1981), pp. 143–151.

Cantwell, John D. "Private Letters of a Pre-med Dropout," *Scientific Journal* of the Georgia Baptist Medical Center, II, no. 1 (January 1982), 40–42.

Canutt, Yakima. *Stunt Man,* the autobiography of Yakima Canutt, with Oliver Drake. New York: Walker and Company [1979]. 252 p.

Clarens, Carlos. *George Cukor.* London: Secker and Warburg in Association with the British Film Institute [1976]. 192 p. (Cinema One Series, 28)

Clark, George R. " 'G.W.T.W.' " *Harper's Magazine,* CXCVIII, no. 3 (February 1949), 97–98.

Cole, Lois Dwight. "The Story Begins at a Luncheon Bridge in Atlanta." *The New York Times Book Review,* June 25, 1961; 7, 22.

Crickmay, Helen Harrell. " 'I Knew Her When ———' " *Skidmore Alumnae Bulletin,* XV, no. 2 (winter 1937), 9–11.

Dale-Harris, Leslie Ruth. *A Quite Remarkable Father,* by Leslie Ruth Howard. [London:] Longmans [1960]. 280 p.

Daniel, Frank. "Cinderella City: Atlanta Sees 'Gone With the Wind,' " *The Saturday Review of Literature,* XXI, no. 9 (December 23, 1939), 10–12.

Daniels, Jonathan. *A Southerner Discovers the South.* New York: The Macmillan Company, 1938. 346 p.

Darwin, Patsy Evans. "Margaret Mitchell and Her Book *Gone With the Wind*" in her "The Theory of the Creative Personality and Its Application to Three Georgia Women Journalists—Lollie Belle Wyllie, Emily Woodward, and Margaret Mitchell," Athens, Ga., 1965. pp. 95–129. M.A. thesis, University of Georgia.

De Havilland, Olivia. "Olivia de Havilland Seminar," *Dialogue of Film [of] The American Film Institute,* IV, no. 3 (December 1974), 25 p.

DeVoto, Bernard. "Fiction and the Everlasting If: Notes on the Contemporary Historical Novel;" *Harper's Magazine,* LXXVII, [no. 1] (June 1938), 42–49.

———. "Fiction Fights the Civil War," *The Saturday Review of Literature,* XVIII, no. 8 (December 18, 1937), 3–4, 15–16.

Dietz, Howard. *Dancing in the Dark* [New York:] Quadrangle [1974]. 370 p.

[———]. *Gone With the Wind* [New York: Greenstone, 1939]. 20 p. Souvenir program.

Dooley, Roger. *From Scarface to Scarlett, American Films in the 1930's.* New York and London: Harcourt, Brace, Jovanovich, Publishers [1981]. 648 p.

Dyer, Tom. "The Making of G-w-t-W Would Make a Spectacular Movie. . ." *Films in Review,* VIII, no. 5 (May 1957), 205–210.

Edwards, Anne. *Vivien Leigh, a Biography.* New York: Simon and Schuster [c. 1977]. 319 p.

Erlich, Isabel. "Background for Scarlett O'Hara and Co.," *Wilson Library Bulletin,* XIV (1940), 435–37.

Essoe, Gabe. *The Films of Clark Gable.* New York: The Citadel Press, [c. 1970]. 255 p.

———, *Gable,* A Complete Gallery of His Screen Portraits [Los Angeles: Price/Stern/Sloan Publishers, Inc. 1967]. unpaged

Farr, Finis. *Margaret Mitchell of Atlanta, the Author of Gone With the Wind.* New York: William Morrow & Company, 1965. 244 p.

Fetherling, Doug. *The Five Lives of Ben Hecht.* Toronto: Lester and Orpen, Ltd., 1977. 302 p.

Fiedler, Leslie A. *The Inadvertent Epic, From Uncle Tom's Cabin to Roots.* New York: Simon and Schuster [1979]. 85 p.

———. *What Was Literature?* New York: Simon & Schuster, [1982]. 258 p.

Film Score, the view from the podium; edited and introduced by Tony Thomas. South Brunswick and New York: A.S. Barnes and Company; London: Thomas Yoseloff Ltd [1979]. 266 p.

The Film Story of Gone With the Wind; produced by David O. Selznick, released by Metro-Goldwyn Mayer. . .London: Hollywood Publications Ltd. in association with World Film Publications Ltd., 1948. 88 p. (Famous film series)

Flamini, Roland. *Scarlett, Rhett and a Cast of Thousands: The Filming of Gone With the Wind.* New York: Macmillan Publishing Co., Inc.; London: Collier Macmillan Publishers [1975]. 355 p.

The Franklin Library. *Notes from the Editors:* Gone With the Wind [by] *Margaret Mitchell.* . .[Franklin Center, Pa.:] The Franklin Library [1981]. 22 p.

From Quasimodo to Scarlett O'Hara: A National Board of Review anthology: edited by Stanley Hochman. New York: Frederick Ungar Publishing Co. [1982]. 432 p.

Gable, Clark. "Vivien Leigh, Rhett Butler and I," by Clark Gable as told to Ruth Westbury; *Photoplay Magazine* (February 1940), 12–14. (Clippings in Margaret Mitchell Marsh Papers, University of Georgia Libraries)

Gaillard, Dawson. *"Gone With the Wind* as Bildungsroman or Why Did Rhett Butler Really Leave Scarlett O'Hara?" *The Georgia Review,* XXVII 1974), 9–18.

Galphin, Bruce. "The Letters of Margaret Mitchell." *Atlanta,* IV, no. 2 (June/July 1964), 56–58, 86, 87.

Gardner, Gerald. *The Tara Treasury, a Pictorial History of* Gone With the Wind, [by] Gerald Gardner & Harriet Modell Gardner. Westport, Conn.: Arlington House Publishers [c. 1980]. 192 p.

Gelfant, Blanche H. "Gone With the Wind and the Impossibilities of Fiction." *The Southern Literary Journal,* XIII, no. 1 (fall 1980), 3–31.

Gemme, Leila B. *Margaret Mitchell's* Gone With the Wind, a *Critical Commentary.* [New York:] Monarch Press [c. 1974]. 83 p. (Monarch notes)

Goodwyn, Frank. "The Ingenious Gentleman and the Exasperating Lady: Don Quioxte de la Mancha and Scarlett O'Hara." *Journal of Popular Culture,* XVI, no. 1 (summer 1983), 55–71.

Govan, Gilbert E. "Why 'Gone With the Wind'?" *The Library Journal,* XII (1937), 690.

Granberry, Edwin. "The Private Life of Margaret Mitchell." *Collier's,* XCIX, no. 11 (March 13, 1937), 22, 24, 26.

Griffin, H. William. "Margaret Mitchell: 20th Century's Great Catholic Novelist?" *National Catholic Reporter,* December 10, 1976; p. 7.

Griffith, Louis Turner. *Georgia Journalism, 1763–1950,* by Louis Turner Griffith and John Erwin Talmadge. Athens: The University of Georgia Press [1951]. 413 p.

Groover, Robert L. "Margaret Mitchell, the Lady from Atlanta," *The Georgia Historical Quarterly,* LII (1968), 53–69.

Gutwillig, Robert. "In History There's Never Been Anything Like It." *The New York Times Book Review,* June 25, 1961; 6, 22.

Gwin, Yolande. "The Georgia 'Gone With the Wind.' " *Behind the Wheel,* unnumbered (June 1937), 4–5, 9.

Hall, Gladys. "Gone With the Wind: On the Set With Gladys Hall." *Screen Romances*, XVIII, no. 128 (January 1940), 16–18, 68–72.

Hart, James D. *The Popular Book: A History of American Literary Taste*. New York: Oxford University Press, 1950. 351 p.

Harwell, Richard B. "The Continuing War," *Civil War History*, II (1956), 147–152.

———. "Gone With Miss Ravenel's Courage; or Bugles Blow So Red: A Note on the Civil War Novel." *The New England Quarterly*, XXXV (1962), 253–262.

———. "Margaret Mitchell Wrote About Life in World War II." *The Atlanta Journal and Constitution Magazine*, March 17, 1974; p. 12, 14, 44, 46.

———. "Since 1936, a Landmark in American Fiction." Chicago Tribune, *Magazine of Books*, July 2, 1961, p. 8.

———. " A Striking Resemblance to a Masterpiece—*Gone With the Wind* in 1936." *Atlanta Historical Journal*, XXV, no. 2 (summer 1981), 21–37.

Haver, Ronald. *David O. Selznick's Hollywood*. New York: Alfred A. Knopf, 1980. 425 p.

Hecht, Ben. *A Child of the Century*. [New York:] Simon and Schuster, 1954. 654 p.

Howard, Sidney Coe. *GWTW, the Screenplay* . . . edited by Richard Harwell. New York: Macmillan Publishing Co., Inc. [1980]. 416 p.

[———]. . . . "Gone With the Wind," Dialogue cutting continuity; film editor Hal C. Kern, December 9, 1939. [Culver City, Calif.: Loew's Incorporated, 1939]. [208] p. Mimeographed; paged by reel. "Please return to script department, M. G. M., Culver City, Calif."

———. Selznick International Presents "Gone With the Wind" from the novel by Margaret Mitchell, starring Clark Gable, Vivien Leigh, Leslie Howard, Olivia de Havilland. Screen play by Sidney Howard, produced by David O. Selznick, directed by Victor Fleming. Final shooting script, January 24, 1939. [Culver City, Calif.: 1939]. 256 p. Mimeographed.

———. *Sinclair Lewis's* Dodsworth, Dramatized by Sidney Howard, with comments by Sidney Howard and Sinclair Lewis on the art of dramatization. New York: Harcourt, Brace and Company [c. 1934]. 1xxii, 162 p.

Jenkinson, Philip. "Gone With the Wind." *Radio Times*, London, 19 December 1981–1 January 1982; 107–109, 111, 113, 115–116.

Jones, Anne Goodwyn. *Tomorrow Is Another Day, the Woman Writer in the South, 1859–1936*. Baton Rouge: Louisiana State University Press [1981]. 413 p.

Jones, Marian Elder. " 'Me and My Book,' Margaret Mitchell's *Gone With the Wind*," *The Georgia Review*, XVI (1962), 180–187.

Kauffmann, Stanley, *American Film Criticism*, from the beginnings to *Citizen Kane*, . . . edited by Stanley Kauffmann with Bruce Henstell. Westport, Conn.: Greenwood Press [1979, c. 1972]. 443 p.

Kaufmann, Adelheid. "Heartaches in the Search for Scarlett O'Hara"; *Photoplay Magazine* (December 1939). (Clippings in Margaret Mitchell Marsh Papers, University of Georgia Libraries)

Kellam, William Porter. "Margaret Mitchell (1900–1949)" in Louis D. Rubin, *A Bibliographical Guide to the Study of Southern Literature* (Baton Rouge: Louisiana State University Press [c. 1969]), pp. 246–47.

Keyes, Evelyn. *Scarlett O'Hara's Younger Sister*. Secaucus, N. J.: Lyle Stuart Inc. [1977]. 318 p.

Kirby, Jack Temple. *Media-made Dixie, the South in the American Imagination*. Baton Rouge & London: Louisiana State University Press [1978]. 203 p.

Koszarsko, Richard. *Hollywood Directors, 1914–1940*. London, etc.: Oxford University Press, 1976. 364 p.

Kuist, Howard Tillman. "Reflections of Theology from *Gone With the Wind*," [Richmond, Va.: 1939]. 15 p. Reprinted from *The Union Theological Seminary Review*, October, 1939.

Kurtz, Wilbur G. "The Atlanta Campaign and 'Gone With the Wind.' " *The Red Barrel*, XIX, no. 12 (December 1939), 2–9.

———. "Gone With the Wind," by Wilbur G. Kurtz. *Railroad Magazine*, XXVII, no. 2 (January 1940), 58–61.

———. "How Hollywood Built Atlanta," *The Atlanta Journal Sunday Magazine*, December 3, 1939; 1–2.

————. "Technical Adviser: The Making of Gone With the Wind—The Hollywood Journals of Wilbur G. Kurtz," edited by Richard Barksdale Harwell. *The Atlanta Historical Journal*, XXII, no. 2 (summer 1978), 7–131.

Lambert, Gavin. *GWTW: The Making of Gone With the Wind*. Boston; Toronto: Little, Brown and Company [1973], 238 p.

————. *On Cukor*. New York: G. P. Putnam, 1972. viii, 226 p.

————. "Studies in Scarlett." *The* [London] *Sunday Times Magazine*, December 30, 1973; 14–17, 19, 21, 22, 25.

Latham, Aaron. *Crazy Sundays: F. Scott Fitzgerald in Hollywood*. New York: The Viking Press [1971]. 308 p.

Latham, Harold S. *My Life in Publishing*. New York: E. P. Dutton & Co., Inc., 1965. 256 p.

Letters. "War Is Hell" [Letter of Thelma Facchine and answering letter of Margaret Mitchell], *Letters*, III, no. 19 (September 14, 1936), 2.

Lively, Robert A. *Fiction Fights the Civil War* . . . Chapel Hill: The University of North Carolina Press [c. 1957]. vii, 230 p.

McClure, Wallace. . . . *International Law of Copyright*, address . . . before the American Society of International Law, Washington, D.C., April 29, 1938. Washington: U.S. Govt Print. Off., 1938. 24 p.

McGill, Ralph. "Gone With the Wind. The 'Story Behind the Story' of Peggy Mitchell's Famous Novel . . ." *The Red Barrel*, XV, no. 9 (September 1936), 15–20.

————. "Little Woman, Big Book: The Mysterious Margaret Mitchell." *Show*, no. 10 (October 1962), 68–73.

The Macmillan Company, publishers. Gone With the Wind *and Its Author Margaret Mitchell*. [New York:] The Macmillan Company, 1961. 23 p.

————. *Margaret Mitchell and Her Novel* Gone With the Wind. New York: The Macmillan Company, 1936. 22 p.

Martin, Harold H. *William Berry Hartsfield, Mayor of Atlanta*. Athens: The University of Georgia Press [1978]. 230 p.

Mathews, James W. "The Civil War of 1936: *Gone With the Wind* and *Absalom, Absalom!*" *The Georgia Review*, XXI (1967), 462–69.

May, Robert E. "*Gone With the Wind* as Southern History: A Reappraisal," *Southern Quarterly*, XVII (fall 1978), 51–64.

Metro-Goldwyn-Mayer, Inc. . . . *David O. Selznick's Production of Margaret Mitchell's* Gone With the Wind . . . [n.p., 1967]. 20 p. Exhibitors' campaign book. Similar exhibitors' manuals were issued in 1939, 1941, 1954, 1961, and 1968. The principal contents vary little from one of these to another.

Mitchell, Margaret. *Gone With the Wind*. New York: The Macmillan Company, 1936. 1037 p.

————. Gone With the Wind . . . Anniversary edition; with an introduction by James A. Michener. New York: Macmillan Publishing Co., Inc. [1975]. xii, 947 p.

————. *Gone With the Wind* . . . Introduction by Henry Steele Commager; illustrations by John Groth. New York: The Limited Editions Club. 1968. 2 v.

————. "Margaret Mitchell," *The Wilson Bulletin*, XI (1936), 12.

————. *Margaret Mitchell's* Gone With the Wind Letters, *1936–1949;* edited by Richard Harwell. New York: Macmillan Publishing Co., Inc.; London: Collier Macmillan Publishers [1976]. 441 p.

————. "Matrimonial Bonds" [fiction], by Peggy Mitchell. *The Open Door* (Atlanta) March 1926; 5, 16.

Mott, Frank Luther. *Golden Multitudes, the Story of Best Sellers in the United States*. New York: The Macmillan Company, 1947. 357 p.

Myrick, Susan. "40 Years of 'Such Interesting People.'" *The Atlanta Journal and Constitution Magazine*, September 8, 1974; 8, 10, 42–44, 47.

————. "Memoir of GWTW," *Georgia*, XVI, no. 9 (April 1973), 35–37, 47, 49.

————. "My Friends Have Gone With the Wind," *Southern Living*, II, no. 9 (October 1967), 30–33, 46.

————. "Pardon My Un-Southern Accent." *Collier's*, CIV, no. 25 (December 16, 1939), 20, 31–32.

————. "Vivien Leigh IS Scarlett," *The Atlanta Journal Sunday Magazine*, November 19, 1939; 1–2.

————. *White Columns in Hollywood* . . . , edited by Richard Harwell. Macon, Ga.: Mercer University Press [1982]. xii, 334 p.

Newsweek. " 'Gone With the Wind': After 3 Years of Hullabaloo, It Emerges a Great Picture," *Newsweek*, XIV, no. 26 (December 25, 1939), 26–27.

Nolan, Edward F. "The Death of Bryan Lyndon: An Analogue in 'Gone With the Wind,' " *Nineteenth Century Fiction*, VIII (1953), 225–28.

Oliphant, H. N. "People on the Home Front: Margaret Mitchell." *Yank, The Army Weekly*, October 19, 1945. unpaged.

Olivier, Sir Laurence. *Confessions of an Actor*. London: Weidenfeld and Nicolson, [1982]. xxi p., 1 l., 305 p.

Pauly, Thomas H. *"Gone With the Wind and The Grapes of Wrath* As Hollywood Histories of the Depression." *Journal of Popular Film*, III (1974), 202–218.

Pegler, Westbrook. "Our Second Reconstruction," *American Opinion*, XI, no. 4 (April 1963), 21–28.

Perkerson, Medora Field. "Double Life of Margaret Mitchell." *The Atlanta Journal Magazine*, May 16, 1937; 1–2.

———. "How 'Gone With the Wind' Was Written," *The Atlanta Journal Magazine*, May 23, 1937; 1–2.

———. "The Mystery of Margaret Mitchell." *Look*, November 15, 1955; 113–16, 119–120.

———. "Second World Premiere for Gone With the Wind." *The Atlanta Journal and Constitution Magazine*, May 16, 1954; 6–9.

———. "When Margaret Mitchell Was a Girl Reporter," *The Atlanta Journal Magazine*, January 7, 1945; 5–7.

———. "Why Margaret Mitchell Hasn't Written Another Book." *The Atlanta Journal Magazine*, December 14, 1947; 5–7.

Pindell, Richard. "Gone With the Wind: The Making of an American Film Classic." *Southern World*, II, no. 6 (January/February 1981), 32–36, 38.

Platt, Joseph B. " 'Decorating for Scarlett O'Hara,' Joseph B. Platt, House & Garden's Decorating Consultant, describes his designs for the interiors of 'Gone With the Wind.' " *House & Garden*, November 1939, section I, p. 28, 36–40.

Pollard, William C. "Notes on a Best Seller," *The Southeastern Librarian*, IV (1954), 76–83.

Pratt, William. *Scarlett Fever, the Ultimate Pictorial Treasury of* Gone With the Wind. New York: Macmillan Publishing Co., Inc.; London, Collier Macmillan Publishers [1977]. 323 p.

Pringle, Henry F. "Finished at Last," *Ladies Home Journal*, LVIII, no. 1 (January 1940), 25, 58–60.

———. "Hollywood's Selznick: The Man Who Made 'Gone With the Wind' Gambles $4,000,000 on a Smash Success." *Life*, VII, no. 25 (December 18, 1939), 76–80, 82–85.

Reid, Mary. "Southern Personalities: Margaret Mitchell, Pulitzer Prize Novelist," *Holland's*, LVI, no. 9 (September 1937), 11, 41.

Richey, Ronald. "The Other Authors of Gone With the Wind," *American Classic Screen*, V, no. 6 (December 1981), 14–16.

Rose, W. L. *Race and Region in American Historical Fiction: Four Episodes in Popular Culture*. Oxford: Clarendon Press, 1979. 32 p.

Rosembaum, Belle. "Why Do They Read It?" [by] Belle Rosenbaum. *Scribner's Magazine*, CII, no. 2 (August 1937), 23–24, 69–70.

Ruark, Robert C. "The Real Margaret Mitchell," *McCall's*, LXXVI, no. 12 (December 1949), 17, 103–106; LXXVII (January 1950), 17, 64–70.

Rubin, Louis D. "Scarlett O'Hara and the Two Quentin Compsons," in Evans Harrington and Ann J. Abadie, *The South and Faulkner's Yoknapatawpha: The Actual and the Apocryphal* (Jackson: University Press of Mississippi, 1977), pp. 168–194.

Schefski, Harold K. "Margaret Mitchell: *Gone With the Wind* and *War and Peace*." Southern Studies, XIX (1980), 243–260.

Selznick, David O. *Memo from David O. Selznick*, selected and edited by Rudy Behlmer. New York: The Viking Press [1972]. 518 p.

Selznick International Pictures, Inc. "Call Sheets," various dates January–July 1939. Unpaged, single sheets mimeographed, usually on both sides.

Shartar, Martin. "The Winds of Time and Chance: Stephens Mitchell Surveys Seven Decades in Atlanta." *Atlanta*, XIV, no. 3 (July 1974). 42, 43, 90, 92, 94, 96–100.

Shavin, Norman. *The Million Dollar Legends: Margaret Mitchell and "Gone With the Wind,"* by Norman Shavin and Martin Shartar. [Atlanta, Ga.: Capricorn Corporation, c. 1974.] [48] p.

Shipman, David. *The Story of Cinema.* London, etc.: Hodder and Stoughton [1982–   ]. Vol. I: "From the Beginnings to Gone With the Wind."

Southern Educational Communications Association. . . . *Firing Line;* host: William F. Buckley, Jr.; guest: Leslie Fiedler, author, critic; subject: "Democratic culture . . ." [Columbia, S. C.:] Southern Educational Communications Association, 1974. 14 p.

Sparks, Andrew. "Why Margaret Mitchell's Papers Are Now 'Gone With the Wind.' " *The Atlanta Journal and Constitution Magazine,* October 5, 1952; 7–9, 52.

Stern, Jerome. "Gone With the Wind: The South as America." *Southern Humanities Review,* VI (winter 1972), 5–12.

Stevens, John D. "The Black Reaction to *Gone With the Wind." Journal of Popular Film,* II (1973), 366–371.

Swindell, Larry. *The Last Hero,* a biography of Gary Cooper. Garden City, N.Y.: Doubleday & Company, Inc., 1980. 343 p.

Thomas, Robert Joseph. *The Story of Gone With the Wind* [by Bob Thomas]. [New York: National Publishers, Inc., 1967]. [36] p. Souvenir program.

———. *Selznick,* by Bob Thomas. New York: Doubleday & Company, Inc. 1970. 381 p.

Thomas, Tony. *Music for the Movies.* South Brunswick and New York: A.S. Barnes and Company; London: Tantivy Press, [1977, c. 1973]. 270 p.

Time. "G with the W," *Time,* XXXIV, no. 26 (December 25, 1939), 30–32.

Tornabene, Lyn. *Long Live the King, a Biography of Clark Gable.* New York: G. P. Putnam's Sons [1976]. 396 p.

Ussher, Bruno David. *Max Steiner Establishes Another Film Music Record . . .* [Los Angeles: Fox West Coast Theaters, 1940]. [8] p. (Cine-music and Its Meaning)

Vance, Malcolm. *Tara Revisited.* New York: Award Books [1976]. 224 p.

Warfield, Nancy D. "GWTW—1939, the Film and the Year" *(The Little Film Gazette of N. D. W.),* VIII, no. 1 (November 1978), 56 p.

Watkins, Floyd C. *"Gone With the Wind* as Vulgar Literature." *The Southern Literary Journal,* II, no. 2 (spring 1970), 86–103.

Wayne, Palma. "What's Wrong with This Picture?" *The Saturday Evening Post,* CCXI, no. 49 (June 3, 1939), 14, 15, 75–81.

Wells, Charles E. "The Hysterical Personality and the Feminine Character: A Study of Scarlett O'Hara." *Comprehensive Psychiatry,* XVII (1976), 353–359.

White, Sidney Howard. *Sidney Howard.* Boston: Twayne Publishers, 1977. 178 p.

Willet, Julia B. "Margaret Mitchell." *Junior League Magazine,* [unnumbered] November 1936; 16–18.

Index